Education and Social Mobility in the Soviet Union 1921–1934

SOVIET AND EAST EUROPEAN STUDIES

Editorial Board

The National Association for Soviet and East European Studies exists for the purpose of promoting study and research on the social sciences as they relate to the Soviet Union and the countries of Eastern Europe. The Monograph Series is intended to promote the publication of works presenting substantial and original research in the economics, politics, sociology and modern history of the USSR and Eastern Europe.

SOVIET AND EAST EUROPEAN STUDIES

Education and Social Mobility in the Soviet Union

1921–1934

SHEILA FITZPATRICK

Associate Professor of History, Columbia University

STUDIES OF THE RUSSIAN INSTITUTE
COLUMBIA UNIVERSITY

CAMBRIDGE UNIVERSITY PRESS

CAMBRIDGE

LONDON · NEW YORK · MELBOURNE

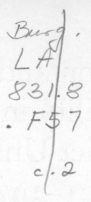

Published by the Syndics of the Cambridge University Press
The Pitt Building, Trumpington Street, Cambridge CB2 1RP
Bentley House, 200 Euston Road, London, NW1 2DB
32 East 57th Street, New York, NY 10022, USA
296 Beaconsfield Parade, Middle Park, Melbourne 3206, Australia

Printed in Great Britain by
Western Printing Services Ltd, Bristol

Library of Congress Cataloguing in Publication Data
Fitzpatrick, Sheila.
Education and social mobility in the Soviet Union,
1921–1934.
(Soviet and East European studies)
Bibliography: p.
Includes index.
1. School management and organization – Russia –
History. 2. Social mobility – Russia. 3. Russia –
Politics and government – 1917–1936. I. Title.
II. Series.
LA831.8.F57   370'.947   78-58788
ISBN 0 521 22325 3

Contents

List of tables

Acknowledgements

A major part of the research for this book was done in Moscow, first as a British Council exchange student at Moscow State University, and later on summer research trips made possible by grants from the Spencer Foundation, awarded by Teachers College, Columbia University, and from the Council for Social Science Research of Columbia University. I would like to express my gratitude to these institutions, and also to the London School of Slavonic and East European Studies, the London School of Economics and Political Science and the Russian Institute of Columbia University, all of which awarded me research fellowships in the period when I was working on the book.

The Chief Archive Administration of the USSR gave me permission to work on the archives of the Russian Commissariat of Education (which are used both in this book and its predecessor, *The Commissariat of Enlightenment*) when I was an exchange student in the late 1960s. In the summer of 1977, I was allowed access to archives of the Central Council of Trade Unions, the Supreme Council for the National Economy and the Commissariat of Heavy Industry of the USSR for the years 1930–33. This deserves special acknowledgement, since I was in Moscow on a tourist visa in 1977 and, moreover, gave the Archive Administration very little advance notice of my wish to work in the archives. I received a great deal of help and cooperation from many workers in the archives, including some expert advice on the contents of the Vesenkha archive, and the provision of a very much larger number of files in a shorter period of time than the archivists thought normal or reasonable. I would like to express not only personal gratitude to the archivists and Archives Administration, but also recognition of the goodwill which they showed a foreign scholar working on the Soviet period and requesting archives not previously used by Western historians.

During the writing of this book, its main reader and critic was my husband, Jerry Hough, who not only made a great intellectual contribution but also passed on many useful pieces of information which he encountered in the course of his own research. He and David Granick were kind enough to let me use their card files, on the political leadership of the 1950s and the industrial enterprises and managers of the 1930s respectively. R. W. Davies, of the University of Birmingham, England, provided me with otherwise unavailable material on Vesenkha in the late 1920s; and I. A. Sats of Moscow, to whom I dedicated my first book, was an unfailing source of information and insight on a wide variety of subjects.

I am greatly indebted to the Russian Institute of Columbia University and its staff, and to my colleagues and students at Columbia, Barnard and Teachers College. Among many scholars who have helped and encouraged me, I would particularly like to mention Loren Graham, David Joravsky, Kendall E. Bailes, S. Frederick Starr, Andrzej Kaminski and my brother, David Fitzpatrick.

August 1978, New York   SHEILA FITZPATRICK

PART I

I

Education and Soviet society

In October 1917, the Bolsheviks had taken power in the name of the proletariat and toiling peasantry, against the almost unanimous opposition of Russian educated society. Education, the Bolsheviks perceived, was one of the traditional prerogatives of the privileged classes. If a small minority of those who had received secondary or higher education under the old regime had embraced the cause of proletarian revolution, the great majority had remained 'class enemies' of the proletariat. It might be necessary for the new regime to employ the 'bourgeois' professionals and 'petty-bourgeois' clerks and office workers trained under Tsarism, but the best that could be expected of them in political terms was passive neutrality.

From these premises, two policy conclusions could be drawn. In the first place, the workers' and peasants' state must provide basic education for the masses of the population. This posed no problem of principle for the Bolsheviks, though there was room for argument on the size of the investment which, in the short term, the state could afford to make in primary education and adult literacy teaching.

The second policy conclusion which seemed to follow naturally from Bolshevik premises was that the new regime must create its own 'proletarian intelligentsia' – an administrative and specialist group drawn from the lower classes of society, trained in Soviet VUZy* and giving whole-hearted allegiance to Soviet power. Such a policy seems to have been instinctively endorsed by Bolsheviks and their working-class and peasant sympathizers from the moment of the revolution, yet at the same time it raised major practical and theoretical problems.

* There are no concise English equivalents for the Soviet acronyms VUZ (higher educational institution) and VTUZ (higher technical educational institution), so, with apologies to the reader, these terms have been used in the text. 'University' is used only for the Russian 'universitet' – a particular type of VUZ including faculties of science and mathematics and the humanities, usually long-established and highly respected.

The practical problems lay in the low educational level of workers and peasants and the regime's immediate need to conciliate the bourgeois specialists. In order to create a proletarian intelligentsia, it was necessary to give working-class and peasant students preferential access to secondary and higher education. But this was likely to mean lowering educational standards; and it was certain to offend the professional and white-collar parents who wanted their own children to receive an education qualifying them for high-status jobs.

In addition, as the regime quickly discovered, there were real difficulties in implementing admissions policies which discriminated on the basis of social class.[1] For the Bolsheviks, social class was defined both by basic occupation and by 'consciousness', which was essentially a political criterion. But it was by no means obvious how these definitions could be applied to children and adolescents, or even how to prevent undesirable applicants from disguising their 'real' class affiliation.

On the theoretical level, Marxist intellectuals found the policy hard to justify. A proletarian intelligentsia meant an elite, created by a process of upward social mobility sponsored and encouraged by the regime. But Marxists did not accept the concept of 'good' – that is, non-exploiting – elites, except in the transitional period of proletarian dictatorship; and the proletarian dictatorship was conceived as the dictatorship of the proletariat *as a class* (however far that might be from Soviet political reality), not by its upwardly mobile representatives.

The concept of social mobility, similarly, scarcely existed in Marxist sociology. In the classless society, with the abolition of the specialization of labour, social mobility would be meaningless. Under capitalism, and during the transitional period of proletarian dictatorship, the working class had an historic mission; and the highest aim of an individual worker should presumably be to raise the level of his 'proletarian consciousness' rather than to improve his social status.

Yet, even with these theoretical reservations, the Bolsheviks had to devise policies for the transitional period. As rulers, they quickly found a term for the kind of upward social mobility which was obviously useful and necessary for the regime – the *vydvizhenie* (promotion) of workers and peasants into administrative and white-collar jobs or into higher education. From the Civil War years, *vydvizhenie* of workers provided a substantial proportion of Soviet industrial managers and party cadres.

Workers were also sent to higher education from as early as 1918, when the first rabfaks (workers' faculties) were established to prepare them for the VUZy. But this was a relatively minor aspect of Soviet education policy until 1928. The Bolshevik educational leaders were sensitive to the possibility that educational opportunities might be monopolized by the bourgeoisie, but their main attention in the early years was focussed on other problems. The revolution, they believed, had given *all* classes and individuals the right to the best possible education. Their first duty, therefore, was to decide what the best possible form of education would be.

Theoretical bases: Marx, Lenin and progressive education

The basic Marxist legacy was the concept of 'polytechnical' education. This concept, unfortunately, provided a most ambiguous guide to Soviet educators, since Marx and Engels were mainly concerned with the education of working-class children who were to remain workers, or, on a more theoretical level, with the education appropriate to a classless socialist society. In the simplest terms, the polytechnical school was one which taught a variety of practical skills – the antithesis of the 'academic' school exemplified by the Tsarist gymnasium. But beyond that there was no agreement on the interpretation of the polytechnical principle and, in particular, on its implications for the relationship of the state and the individual in the period of proletarian dictatorship.

Marx and Engels believed that rigid professional specialization was one of the dehumanizing effects of the capitalist division of labour which would disappear sometime after the proletarian revolution. Under Communism, Engels wrote,

The division of labour...which makes one person a peasant, another a bootmaker, a third a factory worker and a fourth a speculator on the stock exchange will disappear completely. Education will give young people the chance of quickly attaining a practical mastery of the whole system of production. It will allow them to transfer in turn from one branch of production to another, in response to the requirements of society or their own personal inclinations. Education will consequently free them from that one-sidedness which the contemporary division of labour forces on each individual.[2]

For one group of Soviet educators, this meant that the essential purpose of the polytechnical school was liberation of the individual. The Soviet school should therefore offer a broad general education, avoiding narrow specialization and premature limitation of occupational choice. In practice – since the new Soviet secondary school had to build on some existing foundation – it meant preferring the traditional general-educational schools (even the academic gymnasium) over the old trade schools. The schools would become polytechnical by including training in practical skills and study of industrial production in the curriculum; and they would also, of course, open their doors to students from all social classes instead of recruiting them primarily from the privileged groups of society. But they would not be vocational schools; and all students with the desire and aptitude to go on to higher education would have the opportunity to do so.

However, there was another plausible interpretation of the Marxist legacy. Marx, like Engels, had emphasized that polytechnical education should acquaint the students with a variety of technical and practical skills. But, writing specifically about the situation of working-class children under capitalism, Marx had implied that *poly*technicalism had a utilitarian justification: workers with one narrow skill were peculiarly vulnerable because their skill might become obsolete, whereas workers educated in 'the basic principles of all processes of production' and with 'skills to handle the simplest tools of all production' were not in similar danger.[3]

From this, it could be concluded that Marx's emphasis on the acquiring of a *variety* of industrial skills was a response to a particular historical situation. That meant that the universally applicable Marxist principle was not educational breadth, but the technical and industrial orientation of education. It was this orientation which essentially distinguished the ideal industrial trade school described by Marx from the existing 'academic' schools for children of the privileged classes; and Marx claimed that such a school would 'raise the working class significantly above the level of the aristocracy and the bourgeoisie'.[4]

The practical implication for the Soviet school was that it should be *technical* above all, and preferably linked with a factory environment. The Soviet educators who held this view were in effect arguing for a vocational secondary school for children of all social classes; and they usually justified this in terms of the economic interests of the Soviet state as well as faithfulness to Marx's precepts. Engels, in the passage quoted above, had left open the question of whether individual occupation should be determined primarily by 'the requirements of society' or by 'personal inclinations'. The Soviet pro-vocational theorists unhesitatingly subordinated personal inclinations to the requirements of the proletarian state, and considered that those who held the opposite view had succumbed to a 'bourgeois liberal' conception of the relationship of state and individual.

There was, undoubtedly, some reason to accuse Soviet educational theorists of bourgeois liberal tendencies in the early years, since all of them were greatly influenced by the Western progressive education movement of the period. The progressive education theorists saw the primary purpose of education as the realization of individual potential. In practice (though not in principle) they also thought in terms of a socially privileged child – one whose parents were non-utilitarian in their attitude to education, and did not see it exclusively as a preparation for earning a living or as a means of social advancement.

Following progressive principles, Soviet education theorists of the 1920s assumed almost without question that examinations, homework and punishment had no place in the Soviet school, and that rote learning and old-fashioned drilling on the 'three Rs' were equally inappropriate. They also assumed that all children should go to the same kind of school (whether general-educational or vocational); and that a single and comprehensive education system would, in the long run, automatically provide all children with equal educational opportunity, regardless of their social background.

Soviet educators derived the polytechnical principle from Marx; but their exposition of it often seemed to owe less to Marx than to the American education theorist of the 'activity school', John Dewey. Dewey, like Marx, believed that the child should master a variety of practical skills. But these practical studies, Dewey wrote,

shall not be mere...modes of routine employment, the gaining of better technical skill as cooks, seamstresses, or carpenters, but active centers of scientific insight into natural materials and processes, points of departure whence children shall be led into a realization of the historic development of man...[It] is through them that the entire spirit of the school is renewed. It has a chance to affiliate itself with life, to become the child's habitat, where he learns through directed living, instead of being only a place to learn lessons having an abstract and remote reference to some possible living to be done in the future. It gets a chance to be a miniature community, an embryonic society.[5]

The rather vague notion of bringing the school 'closer to life' was central to Soviet progressive educational thought in the 1920s; and it was often combined with an emphasis on the moral and educative value of physical labour which echoed the teaching of Leo Tolstoy. In general, even the most progressively inclined schools had difficulty in finding teachers and equipment to acquaint students with basic industrial trades, as Marx had advocated. But they could certainly teach sewing and woodwork, keep rabbits and plant vegetable gardens, and organize class discussions and neighbourhood excursions for the children. These activities, in fact, were the most conspicuous innovation in Soviet school practice in the first decade after the revolution.

However, the great majority of parents failed to appreciate progressive educational methods. Peasant parents thought that their children ought to be taught reading, writing and arithmetic; working-class parents thought that their children ought to learn a trade. Such criticism saddened the Old Bolshevik intellectuals who were prominent in the first phase of Soviet educational policymaking: for them, progressive educational ideals were part of the mental baggage of any civilized and 'progressive' person, Marxist or otherwise. They believed that the controversy over progressive education in the 1920s was a conflict of ignorance and enlightenment. But less cultured Communists described it as a clash of proletarian and bourgeois values; and sometimes the Old Bolshevik intellectuals feared that they were right.

Lenin appears to have shared the progressive educational views of which his wife, Krupskaya, was a strong advocate; but his main interests in the educational field were elsewhere. Before the revolution, he had written on the question of social mobility through education. In the 1890s, the Russian education system combined traditional 'caste' schools (providing training appropriate to the parents', and therefore the child's, station in life) with schools which, in Lenin's analysis, followed the capitalist principle of opening an upward path to talent. Lenin scornfully rejected a populist proposal to create 'rural gymnasia' offering both agricultural and general-educational training to peasant children. It was a pseudo-progressive reversion to the old 'caste' spirit of Russian education, Lenin considered; and the truly progressive development of recent years was the evolution of the normal academic gymnasia into capitalist-type secondary schools accessible to all children whose parents could pay the fees.[6]

As a revolutionary opponent of the Tsarist regime, Lenin invariably chose the course of political activism rather than that of gradual enlightenment of the people. He showed comparatively little interest in the efforts of Social-Democratic intellectuals to educate the workers in the 1890s, and expressed contempt for the liberal enlighteners of the Committee on Illiteracy who were prepared to settle for gradual change within the existing political framework.[7] He rejected Menshevik arguments that Russia's economic and cultural backwardness stood in the way of a successful proletarian revolution. In the immediate pre-war years, his party gained support from the younger, more rebellious and less educated workers;[8] and, despite a much broader base of working-class support for the Bolsheviks by the time of the October Revolution, Lenin could still threaten to 'go to the sailors' to defeat his own Central Committee during the first months in power.

But, as leader of the new Soviet government, Lenin was second to none in his insistence that popular illiteracy and 'Communist conceit' were major obstacles to the achievement of socialism. He believed, as all the Bolsheviks did, that workers and peasants must be drawn into leadership positions; but he also believed that education was a necessary prerequisite for leadership. *Sansculotte* elements were purged from the party at the end of the Civil War; and Lenin firmly opposed increasing lower-class recruitment into the party until the educational and political quality of potential recruits improved.[9]

Many Communists were very hostile to the idea that they had something to learn from the bourgeoisie; and there was considerable support for various types of proletarian isolationism in culture – Proletkult's attempt to develop a specifically proletarian literature and art, for example, and the creation of proletarian 'caste' schools like the rabfak which were supposed to exclude students from other social classes.

Lenin had little sympathy with the idea of 'caste' schools, though he tolerated the rabfak. But he was really annoyed by the theorists of proletarian culture because – apart from his political objections to Proletkult[10] – he thought they were providing an intellectual justification for ignorance and 'Communist conceit'. Unlike many of his fellow Bolshevik intellectuals, Lenin never felt the need to apologize for his intelligentsia background or subordinate his own judgement to the truer class instincts of the workers. His judgement was that people with education were more cultured than people without it. Workers and Communists who pretended that 'bourgeois' culture was inferior to 'proletarian' were simply confusing the issue: the basic cultural task of the Soviet state was to raise the educational level of the masses, and the basic task for Communists was to raise their own cultural level by learning the skills of the bourgeoisie.[11]

Lenin's sense of the autonomous value of education and culture meant that, in the short term, he was more interested in preserving the old universities and higher technical schools than in proletarian-izing them. In the technical field, he had a high regard for the 'bourgeois specialists' and saw little need to force the pace of training proletarian and Communist replacements.[12] His position on the social sciences was more complex. In the first place, the old universities needed Marxist (and, if possible, Bolshevik) professors of social science, though they would also have to keep most of the old, non-Marxist professors. In the second place, social science was the basic training which Lenin recommended for the *smena* – the new generation of Communist intellectuals, largely recruited from the working class, which would ultimately replace the Old Bolshevik leadership.

But even in his attitude to the training of the *smena* Lenin was cautious. There was, no doubt, an immediate need to bring working-class and Communist students into the VUZy via the rabfaks; but one should also be mindful of the need to maintain academic standards in higher education. In the future, the *smena* would come to higher education through the secondary schools, which Lenin continued to see as the main educational channel for upward social mobility. Pending the consolidation of the Soviet secondary school, the training of the *smena* would have to be a small-scale undertaking, and social class would only be one of the criteria for recruitment.

The formation of education policy: institutional conflicts

In the first decade of Soviet power, there were many different opinions on education policy, and none of them – not even Lenin's – had absolute priority. A number of different government and party institutions contributed to the formation of policy, and their positions were often directly related to the particular needs and interests of the institutions concerned. The institutional dimension of Soviet politics, which has often been overlooked in Western and Soviet scholarship, is essential to our understanding of the process of educational policy-making: in this sphere, institutions played a far greater role than party factions, and some of the institutional battles assumed almost epic proportions.

The government agency directly responsible for education and culture in the RSFSR was the Commissariat of Enlightenment, known by the acronym Narkompros. From 1918 to 1929, Narkompros was led by a triumvirate of Old Bolshevik intellectuals – Lunacharsky (the Commissar), Pokrovsky and Krupskaya. Both Lunacharsky and Pokrovsky had been estranged from the Bolsheviks between 1909 and the summer of 1917, following a philosophical and political disagreement with Lenin which, like most emigré quarrels, was conducted with great bitterness (especially on Lenin's side) and to no real purpose. Lunacharsky, an erudite, tolerant and kind-hearted man, was widely known for his literary and oratorical skills. Pokrov-

sky, whose temperament was combative and sarcastic, was probably
the best Marxist historian of his generation and the Bolsheviks'
most visible scholar.

Krupskaya, Lenin's wife, was Narkompros' expert on educational
theory, having written a short book on the subject in emigration[13]
and earlier contributed to the progressive Tolstoyan educational
journal *Svobodne vospitanie*. During Lenin's lifetime, her relationship with him was a political asset for the commissariat. Later, as
Lenin's widow and the object of Stalin's dislike, she became a
political liability.

But, even under Lenin, Narkompros was a political lightweight.
Neither Lunacharsky nor Pokrovsky was ever a Central Committee
member; and Krupskaya was elected to the Central Committee only
in 1927, after her break with the Zinovievite Opposition, when her
feud with Stalin was already common knowledge in the party elite.
Two criticisms were frequently made of Narkompros. The first,
dating back to the Civil War, was that the commissariat was disorganized, impractical and excessively sympathetic with the old
intelligentsia. The second, which became common in the latter years
of NEP,* charged Lunacharsky and his colleagues with excessive zeal
in their defence of Narkompros' *vedomstvennyi* (bureaucratic)
interest.

However, Narkompros' behaviour in this respect was certainly not
unusual. If it stood out, it was probably because many Communists
thought it was defending the wrong kind of interest. In the first
place, Narkompros supported the principle of general as against
vocational and specialized education. This brought it into conflict
with the Supreme Council for the National Economy of the USSR
(Vesenkha), as well as with the Ukrainian Narkompros, the trade
union leadership and the Komsomol Central Committee. In the
second place, it attempted to minimize social discrimination in
education, objecting particularly to the social purging of schools.
This provoked public attacks by the Komsomol leaders, and was a
cause of constant low-level tension between Narkompros and the
Central Committee secretariat.

In the 1920s, the Komsomol aspired – on the whole, quite
successfully – to play an independent role in national politics as
representative of the young workers. Its belligerence was not only
directed at Narkompros: in fact, Narkompros was sometimes a
Komsomol ally in battles with management (Vesenkha) and

* The New Economic Policy, 1921–27.

organized labour (VTsSPS, the Central Council of Trade Unions) on questions of youth employment and training. But on general educational and cultural questions, the Komsomol persistently labelled Narkompros as a defender of the 'intelligentsia' and 'bourgeois' interest; and by the end of NEP the Komsomol had formulated a comprehensive educational platform, differing from that of Narkompros on virtually every controversial issue, and was energetically lobbying for its acceptance by the party in an organized, nation-wide campaign.

The party leadership did not always take the Komsomol's political activity very seriously. 'The Komsomol should help Narkompros in all aspects of its work', Zinoviev said in 1924, adding unkindly 'it is time to stop this war of mice and frogs which is going on between Narkompros and the Komsomol'.[14] However, Narkompros could not take the Komsomol challenge so lightly. In the first place, the Komsomol Central Committee learned to speak as if it were the party organ responsible for supervising Narkompros' work. This was in fact the responsibility of the agitprop department of the party Central Committee; but since that body took only intermittent interest in education, Narkompros often had difficulty getting authoritative support against the Komsomol even when, on principle, it should have been forthcoming.

In the second place, the Komsomol's constant criticism of Narkompros probably had an impact on party opinion. Many Communists, especially those who joined the party after Lenin's death, would no doubt have been extremely surprised to learn that on basic questions of education policy Narkompros' position was almost identical with the position Lenin had taken in the early 1920s. The conventional wisdom, frequently expressed at party conferences and in the daily press, was that Narkompros was the special protector of bourgeois students and the non-Communist intelligentsia – a 'liberal' commissariat, lacking Bolshevik toughmindedness and drive.

Narkompros recognized that many of its policies were unpopular with the Communist rank-and-file and the working class; and of course it had to find ways of explaining this to its own satisfaction. V. N. Yakovleva, one of Lunacharsky's deputies in the latter years of NEP, sometimes adopted a tone of cultural and even moral superiority which made a very poor impression on Communist listeners. On one occasion, she justified Narkompros' opposition to social purging in the following terms:

If we educational leaders are going to say yes to all the decisions which the [proletarian and Communist] masses demand, and are not going to stand up for our own point of view energetically,...then the masses are never going to learn from their mistakes...[Our problem of] leadership is probably more complicated than that of any other Soviet organization. Why? Because it is a question of cultural leadership, and our country is uncultured.[15]

Lunacharsky himself was more tactful, but some of his arguments also took him into rather dangerous ground. In 1924 (in the course of the debate on literature) he differentiated between a 'party' interest, which would legitimately press for greater discrimination in favour of working-class and Communist groups, and a 'government' interest, which would with equal legitimacy defend the rights of those who were not proletarian or Communist.[16] This was, in fact, quite an accurate description of one of the processes of educational policy-making during NEP; and it was as good an explanation as any of the observable fact that Narkompros had much better working relations with its government superiors (the Russian and All-Union Sovnarkoms) than with the party Central Committee and its apparat. But it was presumably not a description of what most members of the leadership thought *ought* to be the interaction of party and government organs.

If it can be said, with many reservations on specific questions, that Russian and to a large extent Soviet education policy followed the educational principles formulated in Narkompros RSFSR until the end of NEP, there was no reason to suppose that this situation would continue indefinitely. In the latter part of the 1920s, the mood of the Narkompros leadership became increasingly pessimistic and beleaguered, and with good cause.

In the first place, Narkompros was unable to resolve its differences with Vesenkha (in effect, the all-Union commissariat of industry). These had begun during Dzerzhinsky's tenure at Vesenkha, but became worse under his successor, Kuibyshev. By 1927, Vesenkha was pressing strongly for a transfer of all technical education (including the VTUZy) out of Narkompros' jurisdiction and into that of Vesenkha. On the eve of the First Five-Year Plan for rapid industrialization, Vesenkha's political weight was increasing, and so was its budget. It was hard to imagine that Narkompros could resist such pressure for long, even though the transfer was seen by Narkompros as an unmitigated disaster, both for the technical schools and Narkompros itself.

In the second place, party opinion was hardening on the question of proletarian discrimination. There was concern in the Central

Committee secretariat at the low educational level of party cadres, many of them former workers, holding responsible administrative and managerial positions. Since 1924, the party had absorbed an enormous influx of workers, and every year more of them moved into full-time work in one of the apparats. As administrators, their instincts were anti-bourgeois and often anti-intellectual, and they tended to support discriminatory policies in education. But above all, from the standpoint of the party leadership, these working-class Communists themselves were in need of some kind of training in order to cope with their administrative responsibilities.

These problems and conflicts were to be resolved in the last years of the 1920s, as Stalin consolidated his power and pushed forward with the policy of rapid industrialization. During the First Five-Year Plan, the party adopted a programme of 'affirmative action' comparable to that undertaken in the United States in the 1960s on behalf of blacks and other minority groups. Like American affirmative action, it was based on the assumption that the position of educationally disadvantaged groups could be radically changed only by changing the basis of recruitment to *higher* education, not by gradually improving and extending the secondary schools. As in the US, it involved a temporary lowering of academic standards; and it was accomplished by a series of government actions which were resisted by the educational institutions involved and resented by middle-class parents.

The Soviet affirmative action, however, was remarkable in that it was undertaken by the 'proletarian dictatorship' on behalf of the proletariat. Workers and working-class Communists were the main beneficiaries of *vydvizhenie* to higher education during the First Five-Year Plan. They were sent, according to official statements, because the regime needed reliable 'proletarian cadres', and these cadres needed technical education. The function of affirmative action, in short, was to use working-class upward mobility to create a loyal elite capable of leading an industrializing state.

The purpose of this book is to explore the decision for affirmative action and its antecedents and consequences within the context of education policy. But the significance of this decision goes far beyond the educational realm. The Soviet mode of economic and political development adopted during the First Five-Year Plan was unique; but its socio-political dimension, in contrast to the economic, has received very little attention from scholars. Yet clearly the decision for affirmative action is of the greatest importance for understanding the social support of the Soviet regime, both before and after the First Five-Year Plan period.

From the October Revolution of 1917 to the Stalin Constitution of 1936, the regime styled itself a 'dictatorship of the proletariat', implying that the industrial working class constituted its main body of support within the society. But Western scholars have tended to reject any such idea. The Bolsheviks, no doubt, had substantial working-class support at the time of the October Revolution, although most of their leaders came from the intelligentsia. But during the Civil War the working class was dispersed as a result of hunger in the towns and the closing of industrial plants, while many workers who were active Bolshevik supporters volunteered for the Red Army or were promoted into administrative jobs. There were signs of estrangement between the ruling party and the proletariat – among them, the Bolsheviks' repudiation of radical interpretations of 'workers' control' in industry, the subordination of trade unions to the state, the suppression of the Workers' Opposition within the party, and the revolt of the Kronstadt sailors in 1921. By the end of the Civil War, most Western historians agree, the Bolsheviks' 'dictatorship of the proletariat' had become, in effect, a dictatorship of the party; and the party's policies did not necessarily represent the desires and interests of the industrial working class.

Yet the party leaders did not lose their sense of commitment to the working class, as any reader of their debates in the 1920s will be aware. This sense of commitment was surely a factor in the large-scale recruitment of workers into the party after Lenin's death (though Trotsky considered it simply a factional ploy to ensure his defeat,[17] and some historians seem to have overlooked the large element of special pleading in his argument), as it was in the affirmative action programme of 1928–32. The commitment was an emotional one, but it was also a matter of practical politics. The Bolsheviks could not rely on the peasantry for support; and, during NEP, they had doubts of the loyalty of the professionals and salaried employees inherited from the old regime which cannot have been wholly without foundation.

The hypothesis that during the 1920s the Bolsheviks not only looked to the working class for support but did so with some success seems to be confirmed by the statistics of party membership. Even in January 1927, with a large recruitment of workers still to come, 56.1% of Communists had been workers by occupation when they entered the party and 39.4% were currently workers by occupation.[18] At the same time, more than 10% of *all* workers were Communists;[19]

and this proportion also continued to rise through the First Five-Year Plan, despite the great expansion of working-class numbers. Among the young, skilled, male workers whose allegiance was most important to the regime, the Communist percentage was much higher: in Leningrad, for example, 41% of all metalworkers in the 23–29 age group in 1929 were Communists.[20]

Perhaps one of the problems in understanding the Bolsheviks' relationship to the working class in the 1920s has been the assumption that, for Russian workers, anything less than a dictatorship of the proletariat *as a class* represented a Bolshevik betrayal of the revolution. Yet we really have very little evidence to indicate that a class dictatorship (whatever that might mean) was what workers actually wanted or expected from the revolution.

The commonsense assumption would be that, as individuals, workers and peasants desired to improve their own position in society and that of their children. But during NEP, opportunities for upward mobility were limited. Most of the old professionals and salaried employees kept their jobs and privileges under the new regime; there were practical restrictions on access to secondary and higher education; and peasant movement into towns was inhibited by urban unemployment. These were all causes of popular grievance. Workers expressed strong resentment of the perpetuation of 'bourgeois' privilege, both in the society as a whole and in education in particular. Workers and peasants frequently complained that the regime was depriving them of 'rights' which they had won through the October Revolution. These rights, it appears, were the rights to education and, above all, to upward mobility *out* of the working class and peasantry.

The Bolshevik decision to undertake rapid industrialization was bound to promote upward mobility in the long term, because it meant expansion of the industrial labour force and simultaneous increase in the number of white-collar, administrative and professional jobs. But this, of course, in no way committed the regime to a programme of affirmative action, indeed it could be argued that it removed the necessity for such a programme. There was no consensus in the leadership in 1928 on the need for affirmative action: Stalin supported it, but it was opposed by members of the subsequent 'Right Opposition' and by the education commissariats, and received only lukewarm support from the industrial authorities.

However, Stalin's policy prevailed, and in retrospect it must surely be seen as a very bold and imaginative policy which did in fact serve to consolidate and legitimize the regime. At the very beginning of the industrialization drive, before there was any natural expansion of opportunity for upward social mobility, the regime demonstratively repudiated the 'bourgeois' professionals and began to promote very large numbers of workers and peasants into the administrative and specialist elite. This meant that, despite the relatively short duration of the affirmative action policy, the regime gained lasting credit as a sponsor of upward social mobility. The Bolsheviks never tried to fulfil the Marxist promise that the workers would rule. But they did fulfil a simpler and more comprehensible promise of the revolution – that workers and peasants would have the opportunity to *rise* into the new ruling elite of the Soviet state.

2

The new Soviet school

From the viewpoint of Soviet Marxists, an apolitical school was neither desirable nor possible. Education was, by definition, ideological; and only hypocrites would deny this. The Soviet school must train Soviet citizens, freed from the prejudices of religion and understanding the meaning of class war, the legitimacy of the revolution and the goals of the Soviet state. There were no 'neutral' facts to be learned in the social sciences; and there was no 'pure' literature to be appreciated solely on its own terms. Marxism was not one of a number of possible modes of interpretation: it was an all-encompassing world-view which Soviet students should assimilate and put to practical use.

These, however, were statements of principle, not descriptions of the educational realities of NEP. In the 1920s, the great majority of teachers were non-Marxists and religious believers. Among their most immediate problems were dealing with an unruly body of pupils and attempting to maintain their authority in the schools against competition from the organs of student 'self-government' and the Komsomol. The 'revolutionary liberation' which probably most affected the schools was a liberation from discipline and an absence of clear instructions from the centre on questions of methodology and curriculum. Until 1927, there were no compulsory school programmes in the RSFSR: local education departments and individual schools were given considerable freedom of choice by Narkompros (which in principle valued local initiative, and in practice did not effectively control its local departments), and consequently there was enormous variation between schools and regions in the kind of education that emerged.

Remembering their own revulsion against the teaching of 'official ideology' in the Tsarist school, the Narkompros leaders found it impossible to recommend any similar inculcation of regime values in the Soviet school. Thus the schools were forbidden to teach Christian doctrine, but not required to teach atheism; and the old course in

Russian patriotic history was abolished, but replaced only by a vaguely defined course in social studies which, until 1927, was not necessarily taught from a Marxist point of view.

The Narkompros methodologists looked for a way of instilling the Marxist method of intellectual enquiry which would not, in practice, create 'catechism' classes on orthodox Marxist and Soviet doctrine. The solution, they believed, was to be found in the adoption of progressive methods of teaching. Once the teachers had grasped the principles of the 'activity' school and learnt the habit of intellectual synthesis required by the complex method (*kompleksnyi metod*) of teaching which Narkompros recommended, it was hoped that they would automatically develop a Marxist world-view and pass it on to their pupils.

For Narkompros, therefore, the first priority was to introduce teachers to progressive methods of education, and political confrontation or ideological coercion of the teachers was to be avoided at all costs. But this approach was too subtle for many local soviets and education departments, which often put much cruder political pressure on the schools than Narkompros desired; and it offended militant Communist organizations like the Komsomol – which constantly provoked political confrontations with the teachers – and the League of the Militant Godless. Narkompros' progressive methods were frequently criticized during NEP, both by 'ideologists' and advocates of a more traditional academic school. But they survived, nevertheless, to flourish in particularly radical form during the First Five-Year Plan. In the 1920s, Soviet educators and many foreign observers believed the Soviet education system to be the most advanced in the world.

Progressive methods

In the early 1920s, Narkompros' Academic Council (GUS) set about devising programmes which would embody the polytechnical activity principle. Krupskaya directed the work, but she drew heavily on the advice of non-party progressive theorists of education as well as young Marxists: Blonsky, Shatsky, Pistrak, Pinkevich, Shulgin and Krupenina were all members of GUS' pedagogical section; and Blonsky, neither a Marxist nor a party member, headed the subcommission responsible for the primary-school programmes published in 1923.[1]

The 'complex method' which GUS adopted was an attempt to get away from teaching by subject, and involved the linking of separate school disciplines by a general 'complex' theme. These themes were to be socially oriented and related directly to the child's environment and experience of the world. From studying the familiar and domestic in his first school years, the child would progress to a study of the world beyond his own immediate horizons. Each theme was studied under three basic headings: Nature, Society and Labour. Thus in Blonsky's primary-school programmes, the main theme in grade I was The Child, incorporating seasons of the year (Nature), work in the house (Labour) and elementary social skills (Society). In grade II, the village or urban district in which the child lived was the basic theme, incorporating cultivated plants and domestic animals (Nature), labouring life in the area (Labour) and social institutions (Society).[2] In higher grades, the children studied their own province, then the USSR – its geography, social institutions, government and so on – and, finally, the world.

GUS did not give detailed instructions on how these themes were to be taught. But, as a note appended to the programmes for lower-level secondary school stated, 'it is assumed that pupils will master this material by way of observations and independent working over material; that excursions and laboratory and labour methods will be used to a large degree...[It] is assumed that Russian language, mathematics, art and labour are only means of studying particular material.'[3] In primary school, the basic skills (*navyki*) of reading, writing and arithmetic were no longer to be taught as separate subjects: according to a 1924 instruction, 'mastery of the skills of speaking, writing, reading, counting and measurement must be closely linked with the study of the real world; and arithmetic and Russian language must not exist in the school as separate subjects'.[4]

For grades I to V, the GUS programmes came into effect in the 1923/24 school year. Teachers were, for the most part, completely bewildered. The primary-school teachers knew how to teach reading, writing and arithmetic, but they had never heard of Dewey, never read Marx, and had absolutely no idea of what the GUS methodologists were talking about. Narkompros had provided them with three headings (Nature, Labour, Society), and a number of suggested themes ('Man', 'The Steamboat as a Form of Transportation', 'Sheep', 'Successes of Agriculture', 'Day of the Female Worker', 'First of May', etc.) which were extremely difficult to fit into any logical sequence. The teachers had also been told that the school should abandon academic for activity methods, but they did not really know what these were – not surprisingly, since it was a question hotly debated in Narkompros itself.[5]

The sociologist Bolshakov reported that in Goritskaya volost the teachers met to discuss new methods in 1922 and concluded that 'it is necessary that mental and physical labour should be bound together in school studies. That is the essence of the labour (*trudovoi*) method which must be accepted and introduced into the schools.'[6] Bolshakov regarded this as an extremely simplistic interpretation, but it seems something of an achievement for the teachers to have penetrated even so far into the mysteries of polytechnicalism, GUS' instructions were exceptionally difficult to understand, relying heavily on jargon and undefined abstract concepts. The teachers normally got these instructions in the paraphrase of the local education department. But, as Bolshakov writes:

In the provinces there was nobody from whom one could have obtained information on all the innovations in the school field. But, since it was embarrassing to the leaders of the district education department to admit ignorance on questions of school reform, new methods and so on, they gave the kind of explanations on questions which they didn't understand that simply compounded the confusion. Twice, summer courses were arranged for the teachers in the district centre. It's true that the authorities even invited a few representatives of the Moscow higher school as lecturers for these courses. The invited visitors pronounced many witty words and elegantly turned phrases, but...the teachers still left the courses without any idea of what actually was the essence of the new method which had to be introduced into the school.[7]

When they received the new programmes, the teachers' approach to the 'complex' was often purely formal. Shatsky reported after a tour of the provinces that

everyone is busy arranging material under headings...I asked the teachers how they followed these schemes in their work. They replied frankly: 'We don't work by them. We work as we used to work, and when the inspector comes and asks for the scheme we show it to him. He looks into the distance and says: "This is in the wrong place; you ought to put it there".' This produces an academic, scholastic, medieval approach to the problem.[8]

Investigators reported that the 'complex' was often taught as a separate subject ('One hour for writing, one hour for arithmetic and one hour for Sheep', Lunacharsky remarked of this finding).[9]

In the secondary school, the 'complex' method was recommended more cautiously by Narkompros; and Blonsky, for one, claimed later that he had never regarded it as appropriate.[10] The programmes for grades v–vii, published in 1925, introduced 'complex' themes and the three headings of Nature, Labour and Society, but did not formally abolish the traditional school subjects. Physics, chemistry and biology were grouped together under Nature. Social studies – using history and literature as illustrative material – was put under the heading of Society. 'Labour' became a subject in its own right, but it was theoretical rather than practical, containing 'information from various branches of production, technology, organization of production and the history of labour'.[11] In this scheme, the subjects which suffered most were Russian, foreign languages and mathematics, which were to be treated as tools, to be used when the occasion arose. In the words of the programme, 'mathematics in itself does not have educational value in the school; mathematics is important only to the extent that it helps solve practical problems'.[12]

Narkompros' approach to secondary education tended to put the social sciences at the centre of the programme, emphasize interdisciplinary 'synthesis' and discourage the traditional systematic teaching of the physical sciences. 'The secondary school does not exist...in order to give systematic knowledge', Lunacharsky told a conference on Marxism and the natural sciences in 1929. 'The secondary school exists to initiate the student in the basic labour and cognitive methods and the basic approaches to labour and knowledge of all kinds which he will use later in life.'[13]

The problem of ideology

In the mid-1920s, the major ideological controversy was whether the schools should be required to teach atheism. Narkompros required only that instruction should be 'non-religious' (*bezreligioznoe*),[14] although there was a strong lobby from the Komsomol and the League of Militant Godless to change the formulation to 'anti-religious'. Narkompros' position was not (as was sometimes suggested) a product of Lunacharsky's personal wavering on the religious question.[15] Narkompros' reasoning, supported by the government, was that it would be harmful and premature to enforce the teaching of atheism in the schools while not only a majority of parents but also a majority of teachers remained religious believers. However, a distinction was made between the basic school curriculum and informal study circles which might be organized in the school, often in association with the Pioneer group. Such circles might teach atheism and subscribe to the Militant Godless publications, but they did not have the status of regular school classes.[16]

At the same time, Narkompros had clear ideas about the teaching of a 'materialist' world-view, and these were reflected in the GUS programmes for secondary schools. In Russia, as elsewhere, the scientific proofs of the origin of man and the evolution of the species were regarded as basic arguments against religion and the teaching of the Church. The theme of 'Darwinism and Marxism' was present in all the GUS programmes of the 1920s; and, in the words of a Soviet historian, this theme 'gave the progressive secondary-school teacher the chance to work on the formation of a materialist world-view in his pupils, to inculcate scientific–atheistic views of the world, and to make them active transformers of nature'.[17]

Clearly literature could also be used to develop the child's world-view; and for intellectuals of Lunacharsky's and Krupskaya's generation, strongly influenced by Tolstoy's view of the 'infective power' of art, it was axiomatic that literature would play a major role in the emotional formation of the Soviet citizen. Literature, Krupskaya said,

is a mighty means for the creation of a new man, a means for the strengthening of particular emotional feelings, a means for influencing human conduct...One must consider what should be given priority, which 'good' feelings one wants to arouse, what one wants to make hated and what loved. One must choose writers who live not by the old way of life but who reflect the new that is being born.[18]

Yet, paradoxically, this view of literature was considered hopelessly old-fashioned by the younger generation of Marxist intellectuals in the 1920s; and the ideological uses of literature were largely neglected in the school programmes of the period. In practice, the teaching of literature was usually reduced to what was later called 'vulgar sociologism'. Writers were identified in terms of their class affiliation, and their works were taken as illustrations of a particular socio-historical situation. Thus the themes for study in grade VIII in the 1927 programmes included 'The literary style of the feudal aristocracy in the epoch of developing merchant capitalism of the XVI century (Shakespeare, *Hamlet*; Cervantes, *Don Quixote*)'; and in grade IX, students were introduced to 'The literary style of the Russian petty bourgeoisie in the middle of the XIX century (Dostoevsky, *Crime and Punishment*)' and 'Literature of the rising trading and industrial bourgeoisie (Goncharov, *Oblomov*)'.[19]

This emphasis reflected both the current intellectual fashion for sociology and the 'scientific' approach, and the extraordinary importance attached to class affiliation in Soviet political and social life of the 1920s. Pereverzev, who was the chief Marxist theorist of the sociological approach to literature, admitted the 'enormous infective strength' of literature, but considered that the task of literary scholarship was to develop immunity through scientific analysis, to 'conquer literature' so as not to be enslaved by it.[20] In the secondary school, Pereverzev argued, 'the task of literary studies consists in giving a completely clear understanding of the class character of the literary works which are being studied';[21] and, to Lunacharsky's chagrin, this view won majority support in the GUS debates of 1926/27 on the composition of new literature programmes.

When I asked in bewilderment [Lunacharsky wrote], 'What happens to the significance of literature as a force acting on the consciousness of children? Is there really no way we can use literature to educate people, as an enormous force of emotional–cultural action?', he retorted: 'You have to ignore that. It is absolutely non-scientific, and anyway nobody was ever educated by literature, it is impossible; and if the school tries to make any book a literary–educative force, it will only make that book hateful for the pupil, [and he] will hurl your books under the table and read something like [Conan Doyle's] *Black Prince*.[22]

A somewhat similar kind of Marxist iconoclasm dominated the approach to history teaching in the 1920s. In this case, the iconoclastic view was put by Pokrovsky, a professional historian as well as one of the original Narkompros *troika*, who argued that, since history was not a science but ideology, there was no need to teach it systematically in the secondary school at all.[23] Pokrovsky believed that all the historical knowledge necessary to the Soviet schoolchild was a handful of sociological generalizations which were of relevance to his understanding of the vital contemporary issues presented in the school programme of *obshchestvovedenie* (social studies). In fact, during the 1920s history was not taught as a separate subject in secondary school; and a move to have it reinstated in the GUS programmes of 1927 was defeated.[24]

As in the case of literature, both Lunacharsky and Krupskaya had some old-fashioned, non-scientific reservations about this policy. Lunacharsky, while instinctively repudiating the thought that school history courses might be used to inculcate orthodox ideas, argued that history, properly taught, could develop the appropriate *feelings* in the students – a sense of human solidarity, 'a new civic self-consciousness' and an awareness of personal responsibility for the continuation of man's upward progress.[25]

Krupskaya offered the commonsense objection that it was futile to teach children sociological generalizations about history when they had no historical context in which to understand them. They should be given at least an outline of the sequence of historical events and a few basic names and dates.[26] (But Pokrovsky found this view naive: 'Nadezhda Konstantinovna', he interjected, 'History *tout court* does not exist! It is always the history of something. Not just history.'[27])

But neither Lunacharsky nor Krupskaya wished to push their objections too far. This was partly because they deferred to Pokrovsky's professional expertise on the question. But it was probably also because Pokrovsky had forced them to regard history as ideology; and, as he reminded them, 'there are no completely fantastic ideologies, but nevertheless all ideology is a distorting mirror which gives a quite unfaithful representation of real life'.[28]

For Old Bolshevik intellectuals, as well as for younger Marxists who wished above all to be scientific, there were deep objections to teaching 'ideology' as part of the school curriculum. Although, as we shall see later in this chapter, social studies in practice tended to become the ideological part of the school programme, it was not so conceived by the Narkompros methodologists. To them, social studies was progressive, because it had not been taught in Tsarist schools; scientific, because it was associated with sociology and political economy; relevant, because it dealt with the contemporary world; and peculiarly suitable for teaching by 'activity' methods, including discussions, excursions and research projects.

Social studies was the centre of the 'complex' approach to education. As long as the 'complex' survived in the secondary schools, the Narkompros methodologists were able to reassure themselves that Soviet social studies was not a means of teaching pupils officially approved dogma, but part of an intellectual framework which would lead the student to think in Marxist terms as he learned to understand the world he lived in.

Political consciousness in the school: Pioneers and Komsomols

Whatever they were formally taught in school, Soviet children developed political consciousness mainly by observing and imitating the adult world. In the adult world, an individual Soviet citizen was identified by occupation and social class, party membership, attitude to the revolution and activity during the revolutionary years. He was also identified, in an unofficial and more traditional way, by income, living standard and degree of culture and education. For children, the parents' social classification – worker, employee, artisan, *intelligent*, Nepman, and so on – was extremely important. Parents in the wrong social categories, like Nepmen, priests, kulaks and former nobles were *lishentsy* (deprived of the right to vote).[29] The children of such parents were likely to be unable to enter secondary and higher education, ineligible for Pioneer and Komsomol membership, and the object of discrimination when they sought employment. Workers' children, conversely, had preferential access to higher education, although they might have less desire or financial opportunity to take advantage of it. The child might or might not accept the values of his parents, but his prospects in Soviet society were to a large extent defined by their social background and political affiliation.

Urban children seem to have had a high degree of political consciousness in the 1920s, although, of course, it was not always the right kind of consciousness from the regime's standpoint. There was, nevertheless, a belligerent nucleus of pro-Soviet children in the schools, strongly influenced by the images of revolutionary liberation and class war. Their cops-and-robbers games were Reds against Whites, 'workers' against 'the bourgeoisie'. Their organizations, both official and unofficial, followed Soviet models, with great stress on correct procedure and the cultivation of oratorical rhetoric. They strongly resented discipline, because the revolution had liberated them from the oppression of adults.

In the school, the politically conscious Soviet child tended to be an enemy of authority and a vigilant defender of the pupils' democratic rights. 'A lot comes from the old school', remarked a character in Ognev's *Diary of Kostya Ryabtsev*.[30] 'For example, compulsory greeting. Each pupil has to greet the teacher [the word used is the derogatory *shkrab*, short for *shkol'nyi rabotnik*] when he meets him for the first time in the day. That's not right – what if the pupil doesn't feel like greeting anyone?'

The young 'Communist by conviction', as Kostya Ryabtsev described himself, fought the class war against *intelligentshchina* in the school, regarded pure knowledge and pure science with suspicion, and was troubled by doubts about whether true proletarian status was compatible with attendance at secondary school. He made free use of the insulting terms *burzhui* and *intelligent*, described the more offensive of his schoolmates as Fascists, and cultivated an image of proletarian toughness by swearing, smoking, despising girls and refusing to dance. His life style was modelled on the literary type of iron-willed revolutionary, crossed with the daring Chapaev-type partisan of Civil War legend. There were influences, too, from the glamorous, anarchic and criminal life of the *besprizornye* (children lost or abandoned during the Civil War), who haunted the towns and the railroads during NEP, developing their own outcast and anti-authoritarian culture.[31]

In organizational terms, political consciousness was developed within the school by the institution of pupils' 'self-government' (*detskoe samoupravlenie*). This was not a form of administration, since the schools were actually run by a headmaster appointed by the local education department, acting in consultation with a School Soviet in which pupils had only minority representation.[32] But the pupils themselves elected class committees and held general meetings to discuss important issues; and Narkompros intended this to be a practising ground for democratic political participation.

In practice, 'self-government' provided a forum for pupils' complaints against teachers, or for the disciplining of individual students by the collective. Sometimes, according to Narkompros reports, 'children set up their own courts and police, applying quite harsh penalties such as expulsion from school. They arrange trials in the classroom – exactly copying the whole ritual of the peoples' courts.'[33] In other cases, the pupils decided that 'the class committee must lodge information [*donosit'*] on the conduct of undisciplined children'.[34] This was not at all what Narkompros intended by 'self-government'; and in 1928 Krupskaya warned that 'forms [of self-government] which can in no way educate Communists but, on the contrary, are instilling a completely alien psychology, have developed spontaneously in our education'.[35]

For many children and adolescents, however, it was not the school but the Communist youth organizations which provided the basic political and ideological training. The Pioneer organization – established by the Fifth Komsomol Congress in 1922 for the age group 10 to 14 – was in many respects modelled on the 'bourgeois' Scout movement which it replaced. Like the Scouts, the Pioneers had their own codes of behaviour[36] and their own rituals ('Pioneers, be prepared!' Answer: 'Always prepared!'); and they were instructed to be disciplined, hard-working and pure in thought and deed. Their activities included a good deal of marching and singing: what the Pioneers liked most of all, according to one survey, were 'the banner, the flags, the drum, the [red Pioneer] scarf, marching in formation, going to Red Square and so on'.[37]

But the Pioneers, like the Komsomol, took a serious view of their political responsibilities. Bukharin, who reported on the youth movements to the XIII Party Congress in 1924, thought that the Pioneers showed not only initiative and enthusiasm but also unnecessary belligerence.[38] To the best of their ability, they both participated in and imitated adult political life (sometimes, Bukharin noted with disapproval, keeping formal minutes of meetings and carrying brief-cases). The burden of public responsibility on the Pioneers was said to be so great that it not only interfered with their school work but affected their health. In 1925, it was found necessary to forbid 'the frequent appearances of Pioneers at party, Komsomol and workers' meetings, where children usually sit until midnight or two in the morning';[39] but the prohibition seems to have had little effect.

Politically, both the Komsomol and Pioneer organizations suffered from 'avantgardism' – the fear that adult Communists might lose the revolutionary impulse if not kept up to the mark by the younger generation.[40] In the Komsomol, this took the form of assertion of political independence, demands for equal rights with the Communist Party, and considerable support for the left oppositions of the 1920s. But some Pioneers, according to Bukharin, suspected that even the Komsomol might be drifting into complacency: 'In Leningrad, for example, one proclamation calling for the formation of "new life" groups was distributed in the schools. . .It said, more or less, that the party had already degenerated, youth and the Komsomol are beginning to degenerate, and the only hope now are the Pioneers, who must stand in the vanguard.'[41]

During NEP, neither the Pioneers nor the Komsomols were mass organizations in the schools. About 15% of primary-school pupils and 23% of those in secondary schools (excluding the School of Peasant Youth (ShKM) and factory-apprenticeship (FZU) schools) were Pioneers at the end of 1925.[42] The Komsomol, which had principled objections to the 'bourgeois' secondary school, did not even allow secondary schools to form Komsomol cells of their own until 1924.[43] Recruitment into the Komsomol, as into the Communist Party, was socially discriminatory, with preference being given to adolescent workers. Until 1926, all secondary-school applicants regardless of social origin had to go through a special candidate stage for 'intelligentsia'.[44] If, despite these obstacles, a quarter of all pupils in grades VIII and IX in Russian secondary schools had managed to become Komsomol members or candidates,[45] this was an indication not of the Komsomol desire to recruit them but of the pupils' own enthusiasm[46] and, no doubt, their desire to improve their quali-fications for entering higher education.

The Komsomol, nevertheless, had a lively interest in the schools. This was expressed both in its policy conflicts with Narkompros and its direction of the Pioneer organization, which was directly sub-ordinate to the Komsomol. Unlike Narkompros, the Komsomol took a radical and aggressive position on all questions relating to the transformation of school life. Its instructions to the Pioneers were to participate in school self-government, celebrate revolutionary festivals and join with 'progressive teachers in the reorganization of the school on new foundations and in struggle with the old method of teaching'.[47] These were, in effect, instructions to the Pioneers to display aggressive leadership over the 'non-party' majority of pupils and challenge the authority of the great majority of teachers who were both non-aggressive and non-party. (The Central Committee of the party, in contrast, directed that 'the chief duty of a Pioneer is to be an exemplary pupil'.[48])

The basic issue, which was never fully resolved during NEP, was whether final authority over school disputes involving Pioneers lay with the Komsomol or the teachers. The Komsomol should refrain from ordering the teachers around, Bukharin told the Teachers' Congress in 1925. But, on the other hand, teachers must avoid all 'cultural superciliousness' towards Komsomols and recognize their superior qualifications in the political realm. 'In school, the teacher is in charge and the Komsomol cooperates. In the Pioneer movement, the Komsomol is in charge and the teacher cooperates.'[49]

As the teachers and Narkompros perceived it, Bukharin's apparent even-handedness was actually almost an encouragement to the Komsomol, who were notoriously prone to bully the non-party teachers.[50] According to Narkompros reports, 'the Pioneers and their leaders isolate themselves from school life as a whole, and the teacher is afraid to meddle in their affairs – "Bukharin did not authorize it." But there are also teachers who are not afraid of Bukharin and make trouble for the [Pioneer] leaders because they disorganize school life.' Teachers refrained from offering help to young and ill-equipped Pioneer leaders 'because Bukharin did not allow it'; and Pioneer leaders would not have accepted such help if it had been offered.[51]

However, even in terms of Narkompros' own instructions (as co-signatory with the Komsomol Central Committee in 1927), the Komsomol seems to have been given the upper hand. Conflicts arising in the course of Pioneer work in the school were to be adjudicated by the Komsomol cell responsible for the local Pioneer detachment, with the local education department having only a consultative role.[52]

Teachers

In harassing the teachers – the great majority of whom were non-party[53] – the Komsomol was following a pattern which became very well established in Soviet provincial life during NEP. Teachers were 'intelligentsia'; and, if they did not share the material advantages of engineers and professors, they also lacked the social status and patronage which partly protected those groups from local persecution. Rural teachers, who were particularly vulnerable to harassment, had another black mark against them: not only were they 'intelligentsia', but they were also assumed to be offspring of prosperous peasants and priests.[54]

✗ The view of teachers as class enemies had been implanted during the Civil War, when the pre-revolutionary teachers' union had opposed the Bolsheviks and, in the words of one delegate to the 1924 Party Congress, 'the teachers were in league with the kulaks'.[55] In 1921, the Central Committee had directed that 'local party organizations must give up the attitude that they have so far commonly held that educational workers are saboteurs, for they have long ceased to be if they ever were'.[56] But in 1926, Narkompros reported that local party organizations still treated the teachers as class enemies and used 'command methods' in dealing with them. Local authorities had wrongly deprived teachers of voting rights in Novgorod; and in Astrakhan, 'they extract payment for accommodation, water supply and so on from teachers as they do from Nepmen'.[57]

Political harassment was, however, only one aspect of the teachers' problems. One of the main problems was that their salaries were very low. In an emotional speech to the XIII Party Congress in 1924, Krupskaya claimed that rural teachers were completely unable to survive on the salaries they were getting from local soviets.[58] In the same year, the central government introduced a subvention to local soviets which was specifically to be used for the payment of teachers' salaries, but it was less than the average of 30 roubles a month which was taken as the pre-war norm and the required minimum.[59] Even in 1928, the salaries of primary-school teachers were estimated at 66% of pre-war in the countryside and 76% in the towns. Secondary-school teachers, who had held a relatively respectable place in Tsarist society, were receiving under a third of their pre-war salaries.[60] Throughout the 1920s, there were repeated reports that local soviets were behindhand in salary payments to the teachers, or were transferring the subvention funds to other purposes.

By the end of NEP, virtually all teachers belonged to the Teachers' Union (Rabpros).[61] But it was often remarked that the union – whose members included non-teaching employees in the school, scientific workers and (between 1922 and 1927) journalists[62] as well as schoolteachers – did little to defend the teachers' interests. The president of the union, Korostelev, apparently had no connection with the teaching profession: he was concurrently a member of the party Central Control Commission and its state counterpart, Rabkrin, and before the revolution had been a metalworker by occupation.[63] At local level, a similar situation prevailed, for branch secretaries were often not teachers but 'candidate members of the party or experienced administrators'.[64]

Elections to union positions, Narkompros reported in 1926, 'are still conducted according to a recommended list which ordinary voters are not accustomed to challenge openly, confining themselves to indignant whispers and ironical smiles'; and the union officials thus elected 'immediately begin to find jobs for their wives and other protégés' and 'often act with the administrative organs (the local education department, the village soviet, the volost executive committee) against the teachers, instead of defending them'.[65]

However, in formal terms the union had no power over appointment, transfer and dismissal of teachers, for this was a prerogative of the education department of the local soviet.[66] The teachers were continually complaining of 'unfounded and arbitrary dismissals' by local authorities. When the Teachers' Union and Narkompros agreed in 1927 to an annual review of the teachers' professional competence, even the union journal expressed outrage at what it interpreted as legal sanction for persecution and abitrary action against individuals. 'Such annual purges on the grounds of professional fitness', the author claimed, 'do not exist in a single other institution.'[67]

Yet, for all this, the party leadership had made a real effort in 1924–25 to improve the situation of teachers and change the attitude of local authorities to them. This campaign seems to have been initiated by Zinoviev, strongly supported by Rykov, Kalinin and Krupskaya. In the spring of 1924, Zinoviev published a long and passionate article in *Pravda* arguing that the rural teacher shared the Bolsheviks' mission of enlightenment in the countryside:

The task of our generation [of Social Democrats] and your generation of teachers consists of loving the muzhik as he is – benighted, calloused, illiterate, superstitious, believing in spirits and the devil – and going to him, being able to work not just for a year or two to cure him of his backwardness and help him to raise himself up.

The rural teachers, Zinoviev wrote, had no class interest in pulling the school in a 'bourgeois direction'. Unlike the old university professors, they had not belonged to the privileged stratum of society under Tsarism. There were no longer, he concluded, any real obstacles to cooperation between the teachers and the Communist Party:

The way we look at it, in the coming years the rapprochement of our party with the teaching profession will be so firm and strong that the teachers as a group will become a real agitprop organ of all Soviet power, and not in the narrow sense of the word. Perhaps not every teacher will be a Communist – probably that will not even happen very soon – but we will be working in a common cause; we will be teaching literacy and political literacy together, propagating the real brotherhood of the working class with the toilers as a whole. That is the foundation of all Communism.[68]

At the XIII Party Congress, held the next month, 'tens of thousands' of teachers gathered in Red Square, to be greeted by an assortment of party dignitaries including Zinoviev, Kamenev, Kalinin, Kirov and Lunacharsky.[69] 'One gets a feeling of 1918', Rykov said 'hastily adding, in case anyone remembered the teachers' strike of that year against the Bolsheviks, 'that is, the teachers now have the enthusiasm for cooperation with us which workers and peasants had in 1918...There is a revolutionary rebirth going on among the teachers.'[70]

The Congress resolved that, since the teachers' attitude to Soviet power was now one of sympathy, it had become possible to 'draw the teachers further into Soviet society' and even to use them 'as a conductor (*provodnik*)' and disseminator of party and soviet policies in the countryside. The teachers' material situation should be improved. Party and Komsomol organizations should support the teachers in the 'very great positive role' which they were now called on to play.[71] The 'most progressive' rural teachers should be allowed to join the party.[72]

The immediate outcome of the policy of rapprochement was the First All-Union Teachers' Congress, held in Moscow in January 1925. Considerable efforts were made to ensure that the congress was genuinely representative of the non-party teacher. Party committees were instructed that a majority of delegates should be rural teachers from the provinces (that is, not local union officials or party representatives);[73] and, in the event, 73% of the 1,559 delegates were non-party and 44% were visiting Moscow for the first time.[74]

Rykov, the main government spokesman, promised the teachers protection from arbitrary actions of local authorities, pensions and salary increases.[75] Zinoviev rejected any idea that teachers should be subjected to social discrimination: 'Without fear of sinning against the tenets of Marxism, we must now boldly say...that the majority of teachers are part of the toiling masses led by the proletariat, and must be accepted into our milieu as toilers having equal rights'. Noting that some people were sceptical that local party committees would change their attitudes to the teachers, Zinoviev added: 'I dare to say in the name of the Central Committee of our party – and you know the authority of the Central Committee in the country – that undoubtedly, as far as this depends on us, the situation will certainly not remain as before.'[76]

The campaign, however, had very little visible effect on the teachers' situation in the last years of NEP. Salaries remained low, and local authorities continued to harass the teachers. Reports from the provinces indicated that 'the teachers' mood, which was observed to rise at the end of 1924 and the beginning of 1925 – that is, in the period preceding the All-Union Teachers' Congress and for some time after it – has been slowly sinking, starting from 1926'. By the beginning of 1928, 'depression of spirits' was noted among teachers in the North Caucasus, and 'dissatisfaction, a feeling of burden, apathy, apprehensions, fears and hopelessness' in the Volga region.[77]

The regime's failure to carry out its promises to the teachers may partly be explained in terms of Zinoviev's defeat and the abandonment of the 'Face to the countryside' policy with which the promises were associated. But, in a more basic sense, it may be seen as the almost inevitable failure of a campaign initiated, on a secondary political issue, by the leadership against the habits and instincts of the Communist rank-and-file.

Not everything, as even Zinoviev had hinted, depended on the Central Committee. For the old Bolsheviks in the leadership, the rural teachers might belong to a noble tradition of enlightenment, like 'those members of the revolutionary intelligentsia who "went to the people" in the '60s and '70s of the last century'.[78] But this vision had little appeal for Communists who had joined the party during or after the Civil War, and saw the countryside almost as occupied territory which inadequate Communist forces had to keep under control. Zinoviev, Kalinin and Krupskaya were surely less representative of party opinion on this question than S. A. Bergavinov, the one delegate to the XIII Party Congress who openly dissented from the official party line in 1924.

Teachers were allies of the class enemy, Bergavinov told the Congress; and they were all the more dangerous for holding a position in the village which was (at least potentially) one of respect. Their links were with the kulaks and the priests, and it was hard to believe that any pledges of loyalty they might make to the

Soviet regime could be genuine. 'Our rural party forces...will be threatened if we open the door of party membership widely to the teachers...The teachers will get more authority in the village than our Communists; and, comrades, you know what that means.'[79]

Reaction against progressive methods

If the teachers suffered a political disappointment in the latter years of NEP, they at least received partial satisfaction of their grievances in another sphere – that of methodology. Very few teachers either liked or understood Narkompros' progressive ideas. At the 1925 All-Union Congress of Teachers, delegates not only complained but 'literally wept' at the inadequacy of Narkompros' instructions on the new methods.[80] According to the school inspectors, teachers were doing their best to undermine the 'complex':

You go into a school, take up the teacher's diary, and see that for the first term the school appeared to be working on the 'complex' system according to the GUS programmes. From the second half of the second term there is usually a break: they are 'coaching' the pupils on the old subject system. Why? Because they have got terribly behind with formal skills.[81]

Schoolchildren and their parents were also unhappy with the progressive school. Peasants complained that the school was not carrying out its basic function of teaching children to read, write and count: growing vegetables and breeding rabbits, the peasants reasoned, was something they could teach their children themselves and was not the business of the school.[82] A letter in the teachers' newspaper noted that 'children, under the influence of their elders, are demanding that we do more work with them on arithmetic, writing, reading and so on. They work willingly on these subjects, and grumble when we work with them through any of the GUS themes. We are boring the pupil with monotonous material.'[83]

Often the school's progressive intentions were incomprehensible and offensive to the local population. Peasants, traditionally distrustful of state agents asking questions, objected when teachers introduced the 'complex' with discussion of the child's immediate environment:

[In the first grade] they ask [the children] what their families do. We parents did not like that. A boy or girl goes to school; they ask him about his family; but, as it seemed to us, they don't teach him arithmetic. Second grade: here in our school they come to what happens in the district. Why are you so interested in the district?[84]

Local soviet officials thought that their money was being put to frivolous uses: as one teacher sadly reported, 'the president of the. . . local soviet executive committee ordered the nature corner, the first collective undertaking of the school pupils, to be destroyed; and with his own hands, before the children's eyes, took a rabbit by the ear and threw it out the window'.[85]

There were some genuinely progressive teachers in the urban secondary schools (though many of them were non-Marxists);[86] but the majority of former gymnasium teachers held strongly to the formal and academic approach. Science and mathematics teachers, in particular, were almost automatically hostile to the 'complex', which not only interfered with systematic teaching but also put social studies at the centre of the school curriculum.[87]

Grass-roots hostility to the 'complex' began to be reflected at a higher level. Bukharin, the Politburo spokesman on youth questions, expressed concern about the anarchic effects of educational experimentation.[88] Even a staunch friend of Narkompros such as Rykov, head of Sovnarkom, was disturbed by the large numbers of complaints about the 'complex' which he received. Perhaps, he suggested, too great demands were being made on the teachers. Perhaps, too, in the eighth year of Soviet rule, 'one might have expected more stability and certainty in questions of methodology, structure of programmes and the organization and life of our school from Narkompros'.[89]

Scepticism about Narkompros' approach extended to the State Publishing House, Gosizdat, which preferred to update pre-revolutionary textbooks designed for the old curriculum rather than publish large editions of the new textbooks proposed by Narkompros.[90] 'The sober men of Gosizdat', Pokrovsky complained, 'understand perfectly that our new textbooks, written and compiled on the new method, are, of course, a fantasy of Krupskaya and Pokrovsky and perhaps a few other learned old fools – [they know] that it is not these textbooks that are needed, but "real" textbooks.'[91]

The image of Narkompros as a home for 'fantasists and theoreticians'[92] gained wider currency. Narkompros had certainly failed to convince Communists that 'progressive' methods were necessarily progressive in a political sense. Their reputation, like that of the 'futurist' trends in art and literature, was at a low ebb in Communist circles in the mid-1920s. In Ognev's *Diary of Kostya Ryabtsev*, published at this time, the school activists heard that the progressive methods had been invented by 'some Lord Dalton, a bourgeois',[93] and they burned him in effigy.[94]

By 1925, Lunacharsky himself was having second thoughts about the practical viability of the GUS programmes, which he had earlier enthusiastically endorsed.[95] But the decision to change course was taken out of Narkompros' hands. On top of the wave of criticism from teachers and parents came a loud and authoritative protest: Vesenkha, the chief industrial authority, claimed that the quality of Soviet-trained engineers was so low that it was necessary to send students abroad for their education.[96] Vesenkha's protest led to a thorough examination of the defects of Soviet education at secondary and higher level. The basic defect, the government concluded, was that teachers did not know what to teach and pupils were failing to acquire elementary knowledge and skills.

In July 1926, Sovnarkom RSFSR issued a resolution deploring 'the absence of firmly established programmes. . .and textbooks' in the secondary school, and instructing Narkompros to prepare new teaching plans, programmes and textbooks for the 1927/28 school year which 'should be guaranteed to continue for a period of not less than three or four years'.[97]

In the autumn of 1926 – when, for the first time, a large number of VUZ places were open to free competitive enrolment – the performance of secondary-school graduates was closely scrutinized. Professor Kancheev, of the scientific workers' section of the Teachers' Union, reported extremely unfavourably in an article published in *Izvestiya*. Secondary-school graduates were academically weaker than almost any other group of applicants, and graduates of the class of 1926 were even worse than those who had graduated in previous years. Many of them were unable to cope with the simplest mathematical problem, and were totally ignorant of literature. Kancheev concluded:

If you take into account that in the last months before graduation this year many schools gave [pre-examination] coaching to pupils and, in addition, that those wanting to enter the VUZ were also studying at home, you can't help wondering what they learned in nine years of schooling. And if the secondary-school graduates who applied for VUZ entrance (who, after all, are the best pupils) were markedly weaker not only in the field of formal knowledge but also in general development, you can't help wondering what kind of development and what kind of training for practical life the rest of the pupils, who did not risk taking the examination, can have.[98]

Narkompros was required to revise both its primary[99] and secondary programmes; and in 1927 it came out with the first *compulsory* teaching plans and the first timetable it had ever issued. The compulsory subject timetable for secondary school gave mathematics, chemistry, physics and natural science pride of place, with eight hours a week in grades VI–IX, compared with an average four hours a week given to social studies throughout the secondary school. Russian language and literature were given four to five hours a week. Geography was to be taught as a separate subject, though only in grades V–VII. History was not to be taught separately, but remained an aspect of the social studies course. The remaining hours were devoted to art, music, physical culture, foreign languages and labour – the last consisting of workshop and craft occupations in grades V–VII and the *profuklon* (vocational bias) in grades VIII–IX.[100]

In reinstating formal subjects in secondary school, the new programmes in effect abolished the 'complex' method of teaching, moving social studies out of the centre of the curriculum in favour of more traditional disciplines. This had one, probably unpredicted, consequence which was particularly distressing for Narkompros. For the first time, it was necessary to write a detailed and compulsory social studies programme – and thus for Narkompros to overcome its natural squeamishness on the question of teaching ideology.

With the camouflage of the 'complex' removed, Narkompros was indeed faced with a major problem, since its own theoretical requirements for a social studies programme were almost impossible to meet. The programme must be non-dogmatic, scientifically rigorous and ideologically sound. At the same time, it had to be so clear and simple that even a non-Marxist teacher (usually, in fact, the history teacher from the old school) would be able to teach it and unable to distort it.

Understandably, Narkompros' initial reaction was to procrastinate, putting the social studies programme aside while compiling the new compulsory programmes in other disciplines. Then, after some prodding from above, the social studies programme was thrown together with great speed. As Epshtein, head of the Narkompros schools administration, reported: 'One must say that here…"ideology" in the form of a Central Committee resolution served as a kind of organizing basis for Narkompros; it pushed Narkompros, so to speak, into a more active approach to the tasks of social studies in the schools.'[101]

The new programmes were remarkable, in the first place, for the sheer volume of information which pupils were required to ingest. They included, for grades V–IX, detailed studies of the Soviet economy and Soviet political institutions; a point-by-point comparison of town and countryside before and after the revolution; the history of capitalism before and after the revolution; the history of capitalism in Europe; the history of the populist and Marxist revolutionary movements in Russia; political theory (including Lenin on the dictatorship of the proletariat); and political economy (including such topics as 'The distribution of surplus value among various categories of owners of the means of production').[102]

The second striking feature of the programmes was that they allowed no scope at all for intellectual enquiry or discussion, since not only the relevant questions but also their answers were given under each heading. Thus in studying the bases of the Soviet economy in grades VIII and IX, the teacher dealt with the essence of NEP and its dangers, and then moved on to 'The means possessed by the proletariat for overcoming the dangers of NEP', which were listed as follows: 'Nationalization of the land, heavy industry, the banks and the railways; the monopoly over external trade; state power in the hands of the working class; and united leadership from the party of the proletariat – the Communist Party (Bolsheviks)'.[103] There were no alternative views presented, no recommended reading and no textbooks (Narkompros had not yet, in 1927, finished preparing them). Everything was in the programme, and teachers were urged not to deviate from it at any point.[104]

Narkompros had always feared the introduction of 'catechism' methods in Soviet schools. But this was the obvious and only way to teach the 1927 social studies programme, and naturally the schools used it, as they had done in the old school. The following example, which might be taken for a parody, was apparently in fact recorded in a provincial school and comes from the archives of Narkompros' school administration:[105]

Q.   When was the First International organized?
A.   In 1864.
Q.   Where was the Paris Commune?
A.   In France.
Q.   What was the First International?
A.   An international organization.
Q.   With whom does exploitation begin?
A.   With the dog.
Q.   And then?
A.   With man.

Narkompros was extremely unhappy with the new social studies programmes – so openly unhappy, in fact, that it seems possible that they were basically the work of the Central Committee agitprop department rather than of the commissariat itself. One Narkompros commentator noted that schoolchildren called the social studies teacher 'the Soviet priest' and regarded his subject as 'the most boring and dreary' in the school.[106] Epshtein, in an article accompanying the programmes, scarcely tried to conceal his embarrassment and chagrin. Recalling his own revolutionary past, and the contribution that literature and the natural sciences had made to his formation as a Marxist, he warned that social studies courses might turn out to be a form of 'canonization' of Marxism, teaching 'a Soviet "Law of God"' which people understand only as 'the Red lie':

It is not only dangerous and harmful because canonization repels the adolescent from social studies. It is awful, above all, because this kind of canonization opens the broadest paths for the most genuine kind of opportunism, emasculating the revolutionary essence of Marxism and Leninism...

Through canonization we are training opportunists, that is, people who have no spiritual convictions, who believe in nothing, who mechanically and endlessly repeat the dogmas they have learnt...

For illustration, I will give an example of the particular kind of canonization in the form of the 'Red lie' that I am talking about...

A class is going on in the fourth grade of primary school. It is a discussion about the life and customs of the peasantry...before the revolution and now. You ought to hear how the teacher described the unreal life of the Soviet countryside to the peasant children in the fourth grade, where there are grown lads with a lot of experience of life, who know what the contemporary village and its life and standard of living can be. Before, said the teacher, there were no creches, no veterinary or medical centres and so on. Now they exist in abundance. With the coming of Soviet power, everything changed, as if with the waving of a magic wand. No drunkenness, religious superstitions, raping of women and so on. In short, a Communist idyll. What is the point of this? It can do nothing but harm. The children learn, in the first place, to be passive (everything is fine already); and, in the second place, they stop believing us.[107]

The 1927 reforms look, at first glance, like the beginning of a return to the old school; and undoubtedly many people at the time thought that this was what was happening. Yet within less than two years, the pendulum was swinging in the opposite direction. During the First Five-Year Plan, as we shall see in a later chapter, progressive methodologists with even more radical ideas than those current in the NEP period became dominant in Narkompros. They moved social studies back to the centre of the curriculum, dropped the formal programmes, and recommended that it be taught solely by 'activity' methods. Epshtein, whose mournful remarks on the 1927 social studies programme have just been quoted, found himself labelled as a tradition-bound conservative by the younger generation.

We do not know what was 'typical' in the Soviet school of the 1920s and early 1930s: the system was in flux, and there must always have been schools and teachers following the 'catechism' method in social studies, just as there were other schools and teachers engaging in the most radical experimentation. There can be little doubt, however, that traditional methods in the secondary school became more popular in the years when the VUZy were open to free, competitive enrolment by examination, as was the case in 1926 and 1927. But if the students were *not* to be examined on the 'Soviet catechism' – as in the First Five-Year Plan years, when social selection became the main criterion for admission to higher education – then presumably only a small number of teachers were anxious to teach it.

Parents' views on school methods were presumably also affected by the current trends in higher-education admissions. The 'traditionalist' parent, who wanted his child prepared for the examinations in 1926, was probably more interested in getting the child into the industrial apprenticeship school (FZU) in 1930, because that had become the best route for advancement. The attitudes of Communists were similarly changeable: in 1926, many of them clearly perceived progressive methods as essentially 'bourgeois'; but in 1930 – when the same methods were being actively fostered by Communist youth as part of the campaign against 'rightism' – most Communists seem to have believed that these methods were bold and revolutionary.

Moreover, if Narkompros had not converted parents and teachers to the progressive cause, it may have had more success with local education departments. During NEP, a number of local departments regarded themselves as *more* progressive than Narkompros. This was the case with the Leningrad department, headed by Zinoviev's wife Lilina,[108] and also with the Siberian and Saratov departments, headed by radicals who appear to have been discontented both with Narkompros and their own provincial exile.[109]

The Komsomol, too, had embraced the progressive cause in education: and this was a factor to be reckoned with both at central and local level. In short, both the 'new school' and the old one had their supporters in 1927, and the ultimate form of the Soviet school had yet to be determined.

3

The education system: problems of mobility and specialization

In its first policy statements in 1918, the Russian Narkompros envisaged a single 'polytechnical' school, secular and co-educational, which would be attended by all children between the ages of eight and seventeen. The whole school system, from kindergarten to university, was to be 'a single unbroken ladder...All children must enter the same type of school and begin their education on the same footing, and all have the right to go up the ladder to its highest rung.'[1]

This declaration was approved without discussion by the Soviet government because of its 'completely uncontroversial nature'.[2] To the Bolsheviks in 1918, the ideal Soviet school system was one appropriate to a future socialist society, in which classes and the capitalist division of labour would have disappeared. But they were thinking not only in terms of the distant future but of the immediate past. The Tsarist education system had not offered an 'unbroken ladder', but had been full of discontinuities. Parish-school graduates were not educationally prepared to enter the lowest grade of secondary school; trade schools gave no qualification for further education; graduates of the 'urban' or extended primary school – basically a school for peasants and lower-class urban children – could not proceed directly to gymnasia or *Realschulen*; pupils from the girls' gymnasia had the educational prerequisities for higher education but were not admitted to the universities as regular students. In the last years of the old regime, efforts were made to eliminate some of these discontinuities and weld the system into an *école unique*.[3] But it remained in many respects an irrational system in which, to use Lenin's terminology, 'capitalist' elements had not yet triumphed over 'caste' ones. It was clear that, whatever other plans might develop for the education system, the first action of a revolutionary government must be to repudiate the remnants of a caste system which restricted the mobility of lower-class children.

Yet, as it turned out, the principles on which the Russian Narkompros proposed to build the new education system were far from uncontroversial. They were very quickly challenged by a number of institutions with specific interests in education, hotly debated throughout the 1920s, and so much modified in implementation that they could scarcely be recognized in the actual education that emerged during NEP. The two most controversial issues raised policy questions which ultimately had to be decided at a higher level than that of a republican education commissariat. The first was the degree to which the education system should discriminate on grounds of social class, and what steps should be taken to further proletarian upward mobility through education. The second was the question of vocational specialization in education, involving the short-term requirements of economic reconstruction and the long-term imperatives of the commitment to industrial development.

Alternative models: the Russian, Ukrainian and Komsomol systems

Clearly in a socialist society all children would have equal opportunity. However, this was not socialism but the transitional period of proletarian dictatorship. The educational disadvantages of working-class and peasant children inherited from the old regime had still to be overcome; and the Bolsheviks also recognized special obligations to the industrial working class in whose name they ruled. Were 'bourgeois' children to enter the schools on equal footing with the working class, and thus effectively keep their present educational advantages? Were priests' sons to have the same access to higher education as Communist workers, when the higher schools were training the future Soviet elite?

The Russian Narkompros took a firm stand on egalitarian principle: all children should have equal access to a single type of school which qualified them for higher education. This excluded the possibility of social discrimination in admission to primary or secondary education, except in a situation where the number of applicants exceeded the number of places available. Working-class and peasant children should be encouraged to remain in school by all possible means including the provision of stipends (though stipends, in fact, were never available for secondary-school pupils during NEP). But 'bourgeois' students also had a right to education, and the Soviet state should not deny them this right.

In the first decade after the revolution, Narkompros modified this principle only in one respect, though this was a very important one. It recognized the necessity of social discrimination in admissions to higher education and, as a transitional measure, of actively encouraging proletarian recruitment through the preparatory rabfaks. At the same time, it pressed for a broad channel of access to higher education from the normal secondary schools, for without this the ladder principle on which its educational system was based became meaningless.

On paper, Narkompros' single school system was quite quickly created. It was divided into four grades of primary school (grades I–IV), three grades of junior secondary school (grades V–VII) and two grades of senior secondary school (grades VIII–IX), on completion of which the student was ready to enter higher education. In theory, all 4th-graders could move smoothly into grade V and all 7th-graders into grade VIII. In practice, however, smooth transitions were not so easily accomplished. Behind the new Soviet names were old Russian schools with established notions of their educational functions and social clientele. A great many rural primary schools had only three grades, and therefore gave no real access to the junior secondary school. The old extended primary schools – even if renamed urban '7-year schools' – tended to remain terminal for most students and to attract a predominantly lower-class group. The senior secondary schools – formerly gymnasia, commercial schools and *Realschulen* – remained 'bourgeois' in social composition, and both teachers and pupils often showed hostility to the new regime.

The incorporation of the old gymnasium in Narkompros' single school system was widely criticized by Communists. The first criticism was directed at its social composition, which disqualified it for its traditional function of preparing students for higher education. The second criticism was a logical consequence of the first: if secondary-school graduates could have only restricted access to higher education, the school should be teaching them a trade or preparing them for specific forms of employment after graduation. It should, in other words, become a specialized vocational school serving a useful function in the Soviet economy.

However, this was another issue on which the Russian Narkompros had taken a firm stand on principle. All schools should be 'polytechnical', but that did not mean training pupils for any single trade or profession. Premature occupational choice limited the freedom of the individual; and an education which was specialized rather than broad limited his potential intellectual and cultural development. All children had a right to a general (though 'polytechnical') education up to the age of 17. The right which they should *not* have, in Narkompros' view, was the right to impose limitations on themselves by opting at the age of 12 or 13 for purely vocational training.

This position proved impossible to defend, though rhetorically the Russian Narkompros never wholly abandoned it. Narkompros' original idea was apparently to abolish the whole network of junior and senior vocational schools taking pupils under 17. It denounced the junior trade schools as 'a circle of hell for the children of the poor [which] must be destroyed once and for all'.[4] But this immediately provoked hostile reactions from a number of different quarters.

The industrial and economic authorities protested for practical reasons, but their objections were also stimulated by traditional institutional jealousies which were considerably older than the Soviet regime. In Tsarist Russia, technical education had developed largely as a result of the initiative of the Ministry of Finance under Vyshnegradsky and Witte and the subsequent support of the Ministry of Trade and Industry.[5] The Ministry of Education had almost no jurisdiction over technical education at any level, and this situation was regarded by industrialists and engineers as a very desirable one.

After the October Revolution, the Russian Narkompros succeeded, not without difficulty, in gathering all educational institutions except military schools under its own control. Many of those directly concerned with technical education regarded this as a retrogressive step; and this attitude was soon communicated to Vesenkha, the leading Soviet institution in the industrial sphere, which began to take on the role of the old Ministries of Finance and Trade and Industry as protector of the interests of technical and trade schools against the amateurish interference of educational officials.

At the same time, Narkompros' attempts to eliminate vocational schools aroused another kind of opposition. The trade schools, in particular, were traditionally working-class schools; and many working-class and peasant parents regarded them not as 'circles of hell' but as useful and valuable institutions in which children might learn a trade and become qualified for skilled employment. In general, the lower-class preference was clearly for vocational schools which taught a trade, just as the middle-class and professional preference was for general-educational schools which gave access to higher education. Narkompros was accused of taking the 'bourgeois' side in this argument, ignoring proletarian opinion, and trying to deprive working-class children of a type of school that they both wanted and needed.

The result was that Narkompros failed either to abolish trade and technical schools or to incorporate them in its supposedly single and comprehensive polytechnical school system. Two parallel education systems emerged, one vocational (consisting of a variety of trade and apprenticeship schools at lower level, and vocational 'technicums',[6] recruiting graduates of the 7-year general school, at higher level) and the other general. Both were under Narkompros' administrative control; but, with the exception of a few technicums and the rabfaks, the primary and secondary schools were financed on the local budget and not that of the central commissariat from the beginning of NEP, so Narkompros had little real leverage in a situation where its views ran counter to those of the local soviets.

As a republican commissariat, the Russian Narkompros also lacked jurisdiction over the non-Russian republics. While most of them followed the Russian lead in educational matters, the Ukraine (and, to a lesser extent, Belorussia) demonstratively dissented. In the Ukraine, a quite different education system was established after the end of the Civil War. All senior secondary education was vocational: the 7-year general school was followed by a 2–3 year *profshkola*, which gave both a professional qualification and eligibility for entrance to higher education. Ukrainian higher educational institutions, or VUZy, were of two types: the technicum (a secondary school in the RSFSR), which trained 'narrow specialists'; and the former universities and polytechnics, renamed 'institutes', which had a broader curriculum and longer course of study than the technicums.[7]

The Ukrainian system, as advocated by the education commissar G. F. Grinko and his deputy Ryappo at the Party Meeting on Education of 1920/21,[8] was the basis for the Meeting's instructions to the Russian Narkompros; and the Ukrainian example was subsequently to be held up as a model both by Vesenkha and the Komsomol in their disputes with the Russian Narkompros. This was partly a rhetorical device, since it was well known that the Ukrainians' radicalism was related to the near collapse of the secondary-education system during the Civil War in the Ukraine. The theoretical appeal of the Ukrainian system lay in its 'practical' orientation and emphasis on state economic needs. But, if the Russians had devised a system to fit a yet unrealized classless and prosperous socialist society, the Ukrainians were really equally impractical in their own way: their system was predicated on the similarly distant ideal of a smoothly functioning socialist economy, in which all resources including human ones were rationally supplied and distributed according to a central plan. Thus the Ukrainian technicums were supposed to supply 'narrow engineers' to the exact specifications of industry, while the *profshkoly* were to supply skilled workers for immediate absorption into the labour force.

In fact, neither industry nor any other branch of the economy was able to supply exact specifications; and, according to one observer at the end of the 1920s, the industrial technicums were graduating 'third-rate engineers' without any particular speciality.[9] Since the Ukrainian technicum degree was not recognized outside the Ukraine, many students 'find that the best way out of the situation is to transfer to an Institute'.[10] The *profshkola* – advertised as a high-minded rejection of that 'creation of a bourgeois government',[11] the academic secondary school – was neglected and under-financed by the Ukrainian Soviet government.[12] The vocational qualifications of its graduates were not accepted; they had difficulty finding employment; and, like their Russian counterparts in the general secondary school, their aspirations were towards higher education. As a final insult, the central statistical organs invariably – and probably correctly – classified them as general secondary schools, along with those of Russia and the other republics.

To solve the contradictions between the Russian and Ukrainian systems, a second Party Meeting on Education was frequently mooted but (until 1930) never held.[13] A good deal of the pressure for a Party Meeting came from the Komsomol Central Committee, which had its own disagreements with the Russian Narkompros and considered that a party decision was more likely to endorse its position than a government one.

Among the many government and party institutions with which the Russian Narkompros argued policy in the 1920s, the Komsomol falls into a special category. To Lunacharsky and Krupskaya, the Komsomol leaders were 'our boys': they could be aggressive, abusive, even dubious in their political machinations, but still they deserved parental indulgence and were the objects of parental hope. The Komsomol boys, for their part, treated Krupskaya with affection and Lunacharsky with comradely, though sometimes truculent, familiarity: there was none of the hostility and apparent personal dislike characteristic of their dealings with Bukharin, the Politburo's specialist on youth, or Tomsky, the trade union leader. This did not mean, however, that the Komsomol refrained from causing Narkompros political embarrassment. On the contrary, it was the Komsomol leaders' earnest desire to force Narkompros to change its policy on almost every important educational issue.

Komsomol thinking on education was strongly biased against the general secondary school – or, more exactly, its upper grades VIII–X – and in favour of a 'workers' school' for adolescents already in employment. This reflected the interests of the Komsomol's main constituency of working adolescents, reinforced by the leader's idealization of the working class (they themselves came mainly from white-collar and professional families) and an understandable revulsion against the gymnasia which many of them had quite recently attended. The Komsomol regarded Narkompros' secondary school simply as the old gymnasium under a new name. The school remained bourgeois, Oskar Ryvkin told the Komsomol Congress of 1919, 'and cannot be used for the purposes of educating worker youth...It is in no way desirable to send worker youth into the present...school in order to reform it. The school is cut off from life, and bourgeois traditions in it are too strong: it lacks the prerequisites for rebirth.'[14]

The outlines of the Komsomol system were presented by Andrei Shokhin in 1922 (Shokhin, who was then 21 years old, was emerging as the Komsomol's principal educational theorist, and held that position until the end of the 1920s). The Komsomol rejected not only the general secondary school but the whole ladder principle of Narkompros' system. Students should not go straight from school to higher education. 'We think that it is not just middle school or any other school that gives the right to enter higher school, but also some sort of labour experience. We consider that each school should have a clear purpose [*tselevaya ustanovka*], so that it prepares workers not for a higher [educational] stage, but for life...'[15] Instead of going on to grades VIII and IX, 15-year-olds should enter industry or vocational 'schools of worker youth'. 'After finishing the schools of worker youth and working for a time at the factory, the best of the pupils – about 10–15% – can enter the workers' technicum...or go straight to VUZ through a one- or two-year preparatory course at the rabfak.'[16]

The Komsomol philosophy of vocational schools, in contrast to the Ukrainian, was distinctly non-utilitarian, justified with reference not to state economic needs but to the inherent value to the individual of contact with the industrial environment. For this purpose, the old trade schools were not adequate. The workers' school which the Komsomol promoted and helped to create[17] – the factory-apprenticeship or FZU school – had the paradoxical distinction in the mid-1920s of being an industrial training school which industry did not want. The apprenticeship schools combined general post-primary education with basic training in industrial skills; and, although under Narkompros jurisdiction from 1924, they were housed and maintained at the factories' expense.[18] The factories, however, preferred traditional and less expensive methods of on-the-job apprenticeship. This negative attitude was reinforced by industrial resentment of the adolescent quota (*bronya*), by which industry was legally obliged not only to employ a certain quota of adolescents (usually around 5% of the total work force) but also to give them a reduced working day and pay them an adult wage.[19]

The trade unions, which were early supporters of the apprenticeship school, came to share industry's objections to it, because the adolescents were in competition with unemployed union members. Narkompros supported the school, since it did provide general education for a group which would otherwise have dropped out of school altogether, but did so with reservations: the apprenticeship school violated the ladder and polytechnical principles, and provided a proletarian alternative to Narkompros' own, ideally classless, school. 'There is no point in spending 20,000 [roubles] on the FZU school when we don't need any more skilled workers', Krupskaya remarked grumpily in 1924.[20] But a school which was impeccably proletarian and apparently practical had great appeal to party as well as Komsomol members. In 1923, the Tenth Congress of Soviets declared itself for 'decisive expansion of the [apprenticeship school] network until it reaches a size capable of accommodating the whole adolescent worker generation'.[21]

Access to higher education

For Soviet policy-makers, the peculiar importance of higher education lay in its function of training at least a part of the future Soviet elite. This led them to prefer other sources of recruitment over the 'bourgeois' and probably anti-Soviet senior secondary school. But their recruitment policies corresponded with an apparently widespread ambition among Soviet youth to acquire higher education without completing secondary school. 'Everyone thinks it necessary to get a taste of VUZ learning', Krupskaya wrote.

And especially in the autumn, when you see all these young people – completely unprepared young people who want to study, and think that learning, the real authentic learning, is only available at the VUZ – then you sometimes begin to think that we are jumping over one step [in the educational ladder]. . .I am struck by how little developed in our country is the concept of secondary education.[22]

Local authorities showed the same preference for higher as against senior secondary schools: the possession of a VUZ, not a technicum or 9-year school, was the symbol of culture and revolutionary liberation in the provinces. As Pokrovsky reported in 1920, 'the local working masses revealed an enormous and touching naivete on the VUZ question. Each big workers' centre wanted its VUZ.'[23] One obvious solution was to give that title to the local agricultural school or teachers' training college, and this is exactly what many provincial towns did. The central authorities resisted, and a number of provincial higher schools were in fact downgraded to technicums in the early 1920s.[24] But the result was not entirely satisfactory on either side. There remained great variations of quality in the education offered by different Soviet higher schools, which was a source of concern not only to Narkompros but also to Vesenkha and the planning authorities. On the other hand, the number of places available in higher education dropped sharply in the first half of NEP and continued to decline, though at a slower rate, until the beginning of the First Five-Year Plan. Provincial centres were deprived of their symbols of prestige and revolutionary achievement, while only a small proportion of those young workers and peasants who aspired to higher education were actually able to achieve their desire.

In the first years, the Soviet government had done a great deal to kindle such ambition. In 1918, higher educational institutions had been declared open to all who wished to enter, and the requirement of a secondary-school diploma had been abolished. Preparatory rabfaks were created to give workers and Communists privileged access to higher education.[25]

The rabfaks shared in the glamour associated with the VUZ, although they were essentially secondary schools for adults. Entrance requirements were low: according to the 1924 rules of enrolment, entrants should 'have a firm command of the four arithmetical functions, using whole numbers; be able to express their thoughts adequately in written and spoken form; and possess general political education to the level of elementary programmes of *politgramota* [political literacy]';[26] and Narkompros found it necessary to point out that 'the rabfaks are not schools for the liquidation of illiteracy'.[27]

The Russian Narkompros had very mixed feelings about the rabfak. It supported democratization of the higher schools, and recognized the real popularity of the rabfaks, not only in party circles but among workers and peasants. On the other hand, the rabfak was a direct competitor of Narkompros' secondary schools; its academic standards were low; and its existence as a 'proletarian' school undermined both the egalitarian principle and any claims that Narkompros might make for the socially representative nature of the general secondary school. For most of the 1920s, secondary-school graduates had to compete for a small number of 'free enrolment' places in the VUZy, after the automatic admission of rabfak graduates, and the distribution of a majority of the remaining places to nominees of party, soviet and trade union organizations. In the enrolment of 1924 – admittedly an unusually bad year for the secondary school – only 650 out of a graduating class of 30,000 went directly from grade IX to VUZ, with the remaining 12,850 VUZ places going to nominees of organizations and rabfak graduates.[28]

Narkompros took the position that in the long term it was the democratic general secondary school which must supply candidates for higher education, not the rabfak. 'The rabfaks', Krupskaya said, 'are only temporary schools which have been set up because a whole generation of worker youth grew up outside any kind of school and must get an education somewhere.'[29] Narkompros was anxious to avoid a full-scale confrontation on the rabfak issue; but in the mid-1920s, nevertheless, it was clearly conducting a cautious campaign for the phasing out of the rabfaks. Lunacharsky commented in 1924 that the rabfaks had put the secondary schools in a difficult position and threatened their identity. 'Do we really think that even in the future we will be recruiting for higher education through the rabfaks and social selection? No, we do not think so.'[30] However, meetings held by regional party committees took a more positive view of the rabfak's prospects;[31] and in the summer of 1925 the Narkompros collegium formally resolved that 'in the general system of education, the rabfak is not a temporary but a normal type of school'[32] – acting, Lunacharsky later suggested, under pressure, after a congress of rabfak delegates which was 'unusually stormy, because its leaders. . . suspected the Narkompros collegium of an inclination to give in to the [anti-rabfak] lobby'.[33]

It was almost impossible for Narkompros to make a convincing case against the rabfaks because they had such strong popular and party support. With almost 50,000 students in 1927/28 (see below, Table 1, p. 62), the rabfak was seen by party leaders as an agent of Soviet and party influence in the VUZy and a basic channel of recruitment for the new 'proletarian intelligentsia'. The rabfak students were adults (in 1926/27, less than 3% of students in the Russian rabfaks were under 18, and almost 70% were aged 20–29), and the majority were members of the Communist Party or the Komsomol (there were more than 10,000 Communists alone in Russian rabfaks in 1926/27 – almost a third of all students).[34] In no other type of school did the students have so clear a sense of 'Soviet' identity and of their own responsibilities in the building of socialism.

To young workers and peasants, the rabfak was a symbol of the regime's commitment to opening a path for upward social mobility through education. In 1926/27, 84% of students in Russian rabfaks had an educational background of four years primary schooling or less, and 93% had previously been workers or peasants.[35] To have abolished the rabfak during NEP would have been interpreted as a repudiation of the promises of the revolution and capitulation to the class enemy.

The 'bourgeois' secondary school and the working class

In objective terms, the main threat or competitor to the general secondary school might seem to have been the vocational technicum – a school which was expanding, with the support of the economic commissariats, and whose graduates competed with those of the general secondary school for places on the 'free enrolment' of the VUZy. But this was not the focus of the main NEP debate on secondary education. The technicum required seven years general schooling and had a high percentage of white-collar students, so it could not be seen as a 'proletarian' alternative, accessible to the masses and peculiarly deserving of Communist support. To Communists, the 'proletarian' schools were the apprenticeship (FZU) school and the rabfak, while the general secondary school and technicum were essentially 'bourgeois'. To justify the general secondary school, Narkompros had to prove that this school, too, was proletarian.

The general secondary school was not, of course, traditionally a working-class school; and this was particularly true of its upper level, grades viii–x, and of the old gymnasia which had been turned into Soviet secondary schools. In the 1920s, most urban children went through the four grades of primary school, and in the urban schools working-class children were the largest social group.[36] But in grades v–vii they were overtaken by children of employees (white-collar workers),[37] and this increased with every year of secondary school. Thus for every 100 white-collar children in grade i of the urban school, there were 93 in grade v and 23 in grade ix; but for working-class children there was a drop from 100 in grade i to 49 in grade v and 3 in grade ix (and in the Urals, where the situation was particularly bad, numbers of working-class children dropped from 100 in grade i to 25 in grade v and 1 in grade ix).[38]

Despite this, general secondary school was still quantitatively one of the major educational institutions for working-class children in the RSFSR, and *the* major institution if we exclude the old terminal trade schools. In round figures for the school year 1926/27, we find 155,000 working-class children in grades v–vii, as against 38,000 currently in apprenticeship schools; and in grades viii–ix, working-class numbers were around 23,000, which more or less equalled the number of working-class students in all grades of technicums and exceeded those of young adult workers in rabfaks.[39]

Further, in demonstrating the 'proletarian' nature of general secondary school, Narkompros could argue that workers' *children* who reached higher education normally did so via the general schools and not the rabfaks;[40] and that there were more Komsomols (in absolute terms) in grades viii–ix alone than in the entire rabfak system.[41]

These arguments, however, missed the major thrust of the Communist preference for the rabfak and the apprenticeship school. The apprenticeship school was preferred just because it was, in Narkompros' terms, a 'caste' school for the working class – a school which workers wanted for their children and regarded as a specifically Soviet creation. The rabfak was preferred because it brought adults, who had themselves formerly been workers, into higher education. A child of working-class parents who had gone through secondary school might have absorbed the 'bourgeois' world-view of his fellow pupils; and a secondary-school Komsomol member might have joined for purely opportunist motives. For the party leadership, in particular, democratization of the school system was a less immediate goal than 'sovietization' of the elite, and working-class adolescents were less desirable recruits to higher education than adults who had previously been workers.

Because the task was seen as relatively unimportant, Narkompros' efforts to increase the numbers of lower-class children in secondary school received verbal encouragement but little tangible support from the government. In 1921/22, local soviets found themselves unable to support the schools and reintroduced school fees.[42] This was an enormous disappointment to Narkompros, but it was powerless to change the situation since it could not support the schools on its own budget. In 1922, the Congress of Soviets gave *de jure* recognition to the charging of fees in urban primary, secondary and higher schools, with adjustment according to parents' income and exemption only for 'the poorer strata of workers and war invalids'.[43] In fact, though not in law, fees were also sometimes charged by rural schools.[44]

By the second half of the 1920s, the local soviet budget had become stronger, and the question of school fees was re-examined. Problems were arising in connection with regional plans for the introduction of universal primary education.[45] Fees were resented by the population, especially by workers; and, according to Narkompros data for 1926, income from school fees was only providing an average of 6% of the budget of local education departments.[46] At the beginning of 1927, therefore, the government of the RSFSR decided to abolish fees in primary schools. They were to be retained, however, in secondary schools, technicums (except pedagogical) and VUZy (except the Communst VUZy).[47]

But this put the general secondary school in a uniquely disadvantaged position since, unlike technicums and higher schools, it had no stipends at its disposal for the support of lower-class students. Workers, except in the lowest wage brackets, were not exempt from secondary-school fees;[48] their liability – at 1–3% of wages, not exceeding 100 roubles a year – was equal to that of white-collar employees and artisans, and higher than that of peasants, who had a 60-rouble maximum.[49] If a working-class child did not go to secondary school, he might get a job or get into the apprenticeship school and earn a wage, and at the very least he would be available to stand in queues for the family food and clothing. Explaining the high rate of drop-out of working-class children, the head of the Moscow education department said that 'after finishing primary school or grade v, they go to apprenticeship school...or simply live at home if they don't find employment, because...it costs more to keep a boy or girl at school than if he just hangs round at home'.[50]

Where local soviets exempted working-class children from payment of fees (as in Moscow from the autumn of 1927[51]), they attended secondary school in larger numbers. But many of them seem only to have been filling in time until they could get a job or enter the apprenticeship school. Secondary-school teachers complained that their September enrolments melted away in the course of the year.

At the beginning there is enthusiasm for the 7-year [general secondary] school. The 7-year school fills up, and they open extra classes. But in December, the apprenticeship schools announce their enrolment, and a mass drop-out begins. In Orekhovo-Zuevo, 300–400 students leave to go to the apprenticeship school, having somehow managed to register at the labour exchange.[52]

An investigation of one Moscow secondary school reportedly showed that three-quarters of the pupils were registered at the local labour exchange waiting for work.[53]

The employment problem and the schools

The phenomenon of adolescents who were neither working nor in school existed throughout the NEP period, though it became a topic of government and party concern only in 1926/27. Adolescent unemployment was part of a general urban problem: there were about one million registered unemployed in the last year of NEP, with an employed work force of only nine million.[54] But it was exacerbated by the fact that a rather large cohort (the generation born in the immediate pre-war years) was entering or about to enter the labour market, possessing few skills and a generally low level of education.[55] White-collar jobs were scarce, especially with the government cut-back in the 1927 'regime of economy'; and in any case most of the young who were employed had manual jobs.[56]

In industry, the level of adolescent employment fluctuated. A large increase in 1925 was followed by a decline, both in absolute terms and as a percentage of the total industrial labour force, after 1927.[57] The number of adolescents registered as unemployed at the labour exchanges was increasing every year.[58] Even for those adolescents who obtained a place in the apprenticeship school, and thus on the factory quota, there were problems. FZU entrants normally had three or four years of primary education, which meant that they left school at about 12. But factories, and hence the factory-apprentice-ship schools, normally took adolescents only from the age of 16. 'Life created the apprenticeship school', Shokhin said in 1929, 'but an accursed gap developed between elementary school and the apprenticeship schools – a gap in which workers' children had to hang around the streets and chase stray dogs, waiting until they could get into the factory and get an education. (Interjection from the floor: 'What difference is there from what happens in capitalist countries?'[59])

The Komsomol distributed blame for the high level of adolescent unemployment liberally and loudly. Vesenkha was to blame for not enforcing the full adolescent quota in industry. The trade unions were to blame for closed-shop practices. Narkompros was to blame for its failure to extend the primary education system and enforce a requirement of 7 years schooling for apprenticeship school entrants; for half-heartedness in supporting the apprenticeship school against its enemies in management and organized labour; and for its inability to produce employable graduates from the general secondary schools.

On the last point, Narkompros could scarcely argue: secondary-school graduates differed from the mass of their contemporaries by being educated, not by being employable. Lunacharsky himself referred to the school as 'an institution preparing semi-theoreticians, whom at the present time nobody needs';[60] and said that its gradu-ates, after a 'bookish, scholastic' education, 'were very often left with no alternative than to become unqualified manual labourers'.[61]

After the sharp controversy of 1920/21 on the issue of general *versus* vocational secondary education, there was a temporary respite, since after all it appeared that the economy had no urgent need of technicians. In 1924, the issue was revived, but with a different emphasis. The secondary school was still described as bourgeois, and it was still argued that it should provide training for specific occupations. But by 1924 the Komsomol, which was the prime mover in the debate, had identified the apprenticeship school as the workers' school, and was planning the new complementary School for Peasant Youth (ShKM). Logically, then, it remained to incorporate a white-collar school for employees' children into the Komsomol scheme – and the existing secondary school was obviously ideal for the purpose. The justifications for turning the general secondary school into a vocational school specializing in clerical and teaching skills were that the school was already 'bourgeois' and its graduates were unable to find employment or get into higher educa-tion.

It was completely against Narkompros' principles to create schools training children of one social class to follow the occupations of their fathers, but this was a difficult principle to argue since it had already accepted the apprenticeship school and would shortly endorse the School for Peasant Youth. It was also, of course, highly offensive to Narkompros to suggest that its potentially democratic secondary school should be formally labelled a school for employees' chil-dren, training future bookkeepers, accountants, sales personnel and primary-school teachers.

It was unfortunate for Narkompros that at the height of Kom-somol pressure on the secondary school, its own standing with the party leadership should have been peculiarly low, as a result of its very reluctant cooperation in the current purge of politically and socially undesirable VUZ students.[62] The Komsomol chose the XIII Party Congress (held while the VUZ purge was still in progress) to press for vocationalization of the general secondary school. Komsomol representatives 'took the most active part' in the work of the committee formulating a resolution on Bukharin's paper 'On work among youth'; and, although Bukharin had concentrated on the deficiencies of higher education and hardly mentioned the secondary school, 'the Komsomol wanted to put point-blank not only the question of the higher school. . .but of the secondary school and the vocational schools'.[63]

The Congress' resolution was indecisive;[64] but sometime in the next month (June 1924), the situation changed and the Komsomol, in the words of its secretary, scored a victory.[65] The victory consisted in the introduction of a *profuklon* (vocational bias) in the general secondary school. Narkompros' resolution on the introduction of the *profuklon* was taken at an unscheduled meeting of the collegium on 7 July 1924; and Narkompros spokesmen later made it clear that the decision was made unwillingly and under duress.[66]

Three years earlier, Narkompros had been forced to 'professionalize' grades VIII and IX, but had managed to circumvent the directives and retain the school's general-educational character. This process was in essence repeated in 1924. Again, Narkompros dragged its feet: it was not until 1927 that it managed to get out the first programmes (for teacher training, Soviet administration and cooperative biases) and teaching plans.[67] There was resistance from the schools, which Narkompros did not try very hard to overcome. 'Only two hours a week are being given to the *profuklon*', Epshtein reported after a provincial tour in 1926, 'and that purely as a formality.'[68] An emigré journal commented that

a tendency to reduce the number of hours given over to the special subjects is clearly visible. The schools prefer the vocational bias which includes the most general-educational material, that is, the pedagogical and cooperative. It is easy to guess that the schools are trying in this way to get round the reform which has been foisted on them from above.[69]

Pressure to consolidate the school as a white-collar vocational training school diminished as it became clear that the graduates were scarcely more employable than before. Of 3,500 Moscow graduates in 1926, only 400 had found employment by the beginning of 1927,[70] and 'a good half' were still unemployed in the summer of 1928 – a failure explained by the choice of white-collar professions, 'at the very moment when there is a harsh contraction and rationalization of the state apparat, and members of the union of Soviet employees are being retrained in industrial specialities'.[71] The Commissariat of Labour and the labour exchanges did not recognize the *profuklon* as a professional qualification; and Narkompros could hardly complain since, as an employer, it did not really recognize it either.[72]

Most *profuklon* graduates had a quasi-qualification in clerical work, accounting or retail trading; but it was reported that 'the labour exchanges already have accountants, book-keepers, clerks and so on who are more experienced, and our graduates cannot compete with them'.[73] The 37% who had specialized in teaching[74] were in no better situation. In spite of the apparent need for more teachers to implement the policy of universal primary education, there was no money to create more jobs or build schools; and in fact Narkompros was even thinking of reducing the output of its pedagogical technicums because of the growing number of teachers registered as unemployed at the Moscow and Leningrad labour exchanges.[75]

Moreover, as was often the case with Soviet policy-making, the secondary-school *profuklon* was being drastically undermined by another policy, simultaneously implemented in response to different pressures and circumstances. In 1925, Vesenkha raised an outcry about the poor quality of Soviet VUZ graduates.[76] The result was that Narkompros was instructed at all costs to raise academic standards in secondary and higher schools. A new system of VUZ recruitment was introduced in 1926 and 1927, involving compulsory entrance examinations and relaxation of social and political criteria in enrolment.[77] This changed the whole situation for the secondary schools, since their graduates now – for the first time in the Soviet period – had a real chance to get into higher education.

Among entrants to higher education in the RSFSR in 1927, 46.4% were secondary-school graduates.[78] Not all the graduates, of course, went directly from grade ix to higher education: since social criteria were still applied, though less rigorously than before, an intermediate period of employment might be desirable to improve the student's chance of a 'proletarian' classification; and in any case there was a large reserve of earlier graduates who had previously been denied admission. In Moscow Higher Technical School – a high-prestige school – only a quarter of the secondary-school entrants in the autumn of 1927 had graduated from school that summer.[79] But it was undoubtedly easier to get into schools like Smolensk University, in whose 1927 enrolment secondary-school graduates constituted 62%.[80]

With these possibilities opening before them, the schools lost all interest in the *profuklon*. Secondary-school teachers – mainly trained before the revolution, and used to the gymnasium routine – needed little encouragement to concentrate on preparation for university entrance in grades VIII and IX. Parents and pupils had similar priorities. 'Vocationalization of the school satisfies nobody', Epshtein reported. 'The children, even peasants, are all trying to get into the VUZ...'[81]

Schools for peasants

Peasants, unlike urban white-collar employees, were officially part of the social base of Soviet 'worker–peasant' power. But this did not mean that they had the same privileges as the working class in access to education. When social criteria were applied, peasants as a group had some advantages over white-collar workers, and poor peasants and agricultural labourers were supposed to be treated as an agricultural proletariat.[82] On the other hand, when academic criteria were applied, these advantages were wiped out by the much inferior quality of rural education. In addition, the peasant's social status was ambiguous: from the Soviet viewpoint, it depended on his class position within the peasantry, but the schools normally operated with the single broad category of 'peasant'. It was well known that the peasants who had traditionally sought higher education for their children were the more prosperous – at best, middle peasants, in Soviet terminology, but more likely prosperous peasants or even kulaks. Sometimes enrolment boards and educational statisticians chose to ignore this, but it was remembered whenever there was a campaign for social 'cleansing' of the schools. Both on social and academic grounds, the peasants' position in secondary and higher schools was vulnerable.

From the peasant viewpoint, the Soviet education system discriminated in favour of the urban population and against the rural. It was relatively unimportant whether current policy leaned towards 'proletarianization' or towards raising of academic standards, since either emphasis was effectively anti-peasant. Communists, industrial workers, government employees and Nepmen all belonged to the educationally privileged group. The university 'used to be inaccessible to the poor, and now it's no different', said one peasant speaker in 1927. 'The son of a party man or someone with an official position can get into the VUZ, but if I don't have money or an official position, then my child will stay uneducated. And I have no money to pay. It's unjust.'[83] Another speaker emphasized the discriminatory effect of competitive examinations: 'Now only the rich, those whose papa or mama can hire a teacher to coach them for the competition, can get into the rabfak. We don't need competitions; they're no good and they ought to be done away with.'[84]

There was obviously ground for complaint. The traditional form of post-primary education for peasant children was the 'urban' or extended primary school, now part of the Soviet general secondary school. But the 60-rouble maximum fee which the schools were entitled to ask of peasant parents was extremely high – much higher, in comparative income terms, than the fee which could be taken from urban businessmen and professionals. It implied that prosperous 'kulak' parents were expected to use the schools, and may well have ensured that they were the only ones to do so.

Although the rabfaks admitted peasants, this by no means removed the peasants' consciousness of discrimination. In the mid-1920s, when the leadership was at its most conciliatory towards the peasantry, this provoked concern. 'I remember', Lunachasky said in 1929, 'how Kalinin called me in – it was four years ago – and said: "The peasants are up in arms because there are rabfaks but no 'krestfaks' (peasant faculties). I said: "May I point out that we have more than 50% peasants in the rabfaks." "Oh well", he said, "that's quite sufficient." '[85] But obviously it was nowhere near sufficient to equalize educational opportunity in a country whose population was still three-quarters peasant. According to a recent calculation, the probability that a peasant child would get into higher education was about one twenty-eighth that of an urban child from a white-collar family.[86]

Peasant frustration at the lack of educational opportunities was no doubt linked with dissatisfaction with the employment situation in the towns. The revolution had given the peasants land, but at the same time their chances of outside earnings in the towns had diminished. At the end of the nineteenth century, 80 out of 1,000 rural inhabitants had been *otkhodniki*, that is, peasants working some months of the year in non-agricultural employment. But in 1923/24 the number had dropped to 15 out of 1,000, and it had not risen beyond 28 by the end of NEP.[87] This meant not only a loss of earnings but a limitation on the possibility of upward mobility into the industrial working class.

The trade unions, concerned about unemployment of their own members, did their best to limit peasant employment in the towns and to enforce closed-shop rules on Soviet employers of labour. The industrial apprenticeship schools followed a similar policy: their apprentices had first claim on the relatively small numbers of industrial jobs reserved for adolescents by law, and the schools accepted extremely few peasant applicants during NEP. At some big enterprises, apprenticeship schools were restricted entirely to children of workers employed at those enterprises. In 1926/27, 77% of all apprentices in Leningrad apprenticeship schools were the children of workers.[88]

Young peasants did, however, have access to one school which offered the possibility of upward mobility. This was the School of Peasant Youth, or ShKM, officially designated as a general educational school with an agricultural bias.[89] The educational level was equivalent to urban grades v–vii, though the students tended to be older than those in the corresponding grades of urban schools. In addition to general subjects, the schools taught the skills appropriate for small-scale farming.[90]

The School of Peasant Youth was a product of Komsomol initiative,[91] and, like the industrial apprenticeship school, it was supported by the Russian Narkompros with rather mixed feelings. Lunacharsky was particularly uneasy about the principle of a specifically peasant school, perhaps remembering Lenin's strong objections to the idea of 'peasant gymnasia' in the 1890s.[92] In the early years of the ShKM, Lunacharsky said, 'some people objected: "Why peasant schools in particular? Do you want to restrict the peasantry within caste boundaries? Why should the peasant not study in the general school?"'[93] Although this was obviously Lunacharsky's own objection, he was able to find an answer which was satisfactory at least in terms of progressive educational theory: a school with an agricultural bias was appropriate in rural areas because all schools should be linked with the local environment and local forms of production.

The problem was, however, that for Marxists the urban industrial environment was innately superior to the rural agricultural one. As Lunacharsky went on to say, 'it is only possible to realize the complete and genuine Marxist school in an educational institution which is located near the factory or industrial plant and participates in its life'.[94] The School of Peasant Youth, in other words, might be the best school peasants could have, but it would still be inferior to other types of school.

In practice, the agricultural bias was probably not a very important aspect of the school from the peasant standpoint. Had the Commissariat of Agriculture succeeded in wresting control from Narkompros,[95] the School of Peasant Youth might have become a school teaching scientific agriculture to the sons of prosperous peasants. But in fact Narkompros and the Komsomol put greater emphasis on the school's function of general and political education. Half the students were Komsomol members in 1926/27;[96] and the percentage of Communist teachers was markedly higher than in other types of secondary school.[97] Despite a curriculum designed to give useful knowledge to small individual farmers, 'the majority of pupils (62% of all those who have a farm) are poor peasants' with no incentive to remain on the land.[98]

A survey of seven Schools of Peasant Youth in Siberia showed that more than half the pupils were from batrak or poor peasant families, and only about a third of the graduates returned to work on the farm. The rest were more or less equally divided between those who departed for further study (School of Peasant Youth graduates were eligible to enter the second year of rabfak,[99] but most of them probably went on to agricultural or pedagogical technicums) and those who took white-collar jobs in the countryside.[100] This pattern seems to have been characteristic of the Schools of Peasant Youth as a whole – and perhaps of all graduates of rural 7-year schools,[101] though the School of Peasant Youth graduates had the advantage of the school's strong 'Soviet' reputation in gaining admission to higher education or finding jobs in the apparat. In effect, the School of Peasant Youth was a small but effective channel for the promotion of peasant youth into white-collar and professional employment.

Educational achievements and perspectives of NEP

During NEP, as may be seen in Table 1, two types of education expanded dramatically. The first was general education at junior secondary level (grades v–vii), where the numbers were up 248% on those of 1914/15. The second was trade and vocational education, up 234%. In addition, the Soviet education system possessed two types of school unknown in Tsarist Russia: the apprenticeship school (FZU), for the general and vocational education of workers' children, and the rabfak, preparing young adult workers and peasants for entry to higher education.

Clearly the expansion of junior secondary education was to a large extent the result of pre-war expansion of the primary schools; and it was accompanied by a worrying phenomenon of continuing illiteracy among a substantial proportion of older adolescents and young adults.* But it constituted a three-fold increase in the number of junior secondary places available in the towns, and a five-fold increase in rural areas.[102] This suggested that in the near future a large

* Questions of literacy and primary education are discussed in detail in Chapter 7.

number of young people with seven years general schooling would be seeking some type of further education.

But the question of what type of further education would be offered remained controversial. The Russian Narkompros had done its utmost to support the development of grades VIII–IX of the general secondary school. But at this level the general school had two strong competitors – the vocational technicum and the proletarian rabfak. The technicum, which in 1914/15 had less than a third the number of students in senior general secondary school, now had half as many students again as the general school (see Table 1). Since 1924/25, moreover, enrolments in grades VIII and IX of the general school had actually been declining: in urban schools they were down 8% by 1927/28, and the drop in rural schools was 42%.[103]

TABLE I

Numbers of students in primary, secondary and higher education, 1914/15 and 1927/28 (for the territory of the USSR in the pre-September 1939 boundaries)

	1914/15	1927/28
Primary schools (grades I–IV)	7,390,144	9,910,407
General schools (grades V–VII)	382,618	1,331,646
General schools (grades VIII–X)	123,490	126,625
Trade schools, including FZU	93,200	243,400
FZU schools alone	—	86,000
Upper vocational schools (technicums)	35,800	189,400
Rabfaks	—	49,243
Higher educational institutions	112,000	159,800

Sources:

Kul'turnoe stroitel'stvo SSSR (Moscow, 1956), pp. 122–3 (primary and general secondary schools);

Kul'turnoe stroitel'stvo SSSR (Moscow, 1940), pp. 105 and 107; *Sotsialisticheskoe stroitel'stvo SSSR* (Moscow, 1934), p. 406 (higher and upper vocational schools);

Podgotovka kadrov v SSSR 1927–1931 gg. (Moscow–Leningrad, 1933), p. 55 (trade schools);

Planovoe khozyaistvo, 1927, no. 12, p. 139 (FZU schools) (a higher estimate of 99,000 pupils in FZU schools in 1927/28 was published in *Pravda*, 26 October 1928, p. 6).

The rabfaks and apprenticeship schools remained comparatively small, but the importance which Communists attached to them was out of proportion to their numbers. The original Bolshevik objection to 'caste' schools had quickly given way to enthusiasm for schools with a specific proletarian and Soviet orientation. The rabfaks were now in a position to supply about a third of the intake of the higher school, supposing that both VUZ and rabfak numbers remained constant. The apprenticeship school, which formally served a quite different purpose, in fact also tended to further upward working-class mobility. Like the School of Peasant Youth, it was a school in which Komsomol influence was very strong; and many of the Komsomol activists among its students were clearly destined for white-collar administrative careers, beginning in the Komsomol or trade union apparats.

The three basic principles of the Russian Narkompros were equal educational opportunity for children of all social classes, universal general education at secondary level, and the continuous educational ladder. None of these principles had been implemented, and there appeared no practical or political possibility of implementing them in the near future.

The Komsomol, on the other hand, had suggested a 'proletarian' alternative which had so far been implemented only on a small scale. The proletarian alternative combined vocational specialization and active discrimination on behalf of working-class students. Secondary schools should teach a trade, since this was what workers required of a school. But, after a few years work in industry, the brightest young workers should be brought back to study in higher education. One of the main tasks of the education system was to promote upward working-class mobility and deprive the bourgeoisie of its previous privileges, since this was the meaning and promise of the proletarian revolution.

The Komsomol seems to have successfully identified what many Communists and workers saw as the basic proletarian interest in education: trade training and opportunity for upward mobility. But it still had the problem of expanding the 'proletarian' sector of the education system. During the latter part of NEP, growth of the apprenticeship schools was restricted by the adolescent quota in industry, while rabfak growth was limited by the official policy of reducing numbers in higher education to the pre-war norm. A major re-orientation of Soviet economic policy was required before the Komsomol alternative could be implemented on a large scale or become anything but a peripheral part of the total educational system.

4

Professors and Soviet power

In the Civil War years, almost all professors* regarded the new regime with deep hostility. In the provinces reached by the White Armies, the professors simply voted with their feet. Virtually the entire faculty of Perm University fled east as the Red Army approached Perm in 1919.[1] Of the faculty of Tomsk University, 3 out of 39 full professors were actually ministers in Kolchak's Siberian government.[2] Eighty professors left Kazan with the Czechs in the autumn of 1918; and both the Kazan and Perm faculties established short-lived universities-in-exile in Tomsk under Kolchak.[3] In southern Russia, most of the faculty of the former Imperial University of Warsaw (evacuated to Rostov on Don in 1915) retreated with the White Armies in 1920 and took the boat to Constantinople.[4]

This hostility is explained by Soviet historians in terms of the bourgeois political affiliations of the professors, and by emigré writers in terms of the hostile and provocative actions of the Soviet government. There is much to be said for both views. Many of the professors were Cadets, a number of them had been active in politics before October, and some undoubtedly continued covert political activity against the new regime. Yet 'bourgeois' political affiliations were not necessarily a barrier to cooperation with the Bolsheviks: S. F. Oldenburg, a former Provisional Government member and secretary of the Academy of Sciences, quickly established a working relationship with the new government; and M. M. Novikov, Rector of Moscow University during the Civil War years, seems to have been prevented from doing so mainly by the recalcitrance of his colleagues.

Within the government and Bolshevik party, the official policy towards the professors was relatively conciliatory, but the rhetoric was often belligerent.[5] In particular Pokrovsky, the deputy com-

---

* Unless otherwise specified, the term 'professor' is used for the two senior categories of faculty, *professor* and *dotsent*.

missar of education, went out of his way to offend the sensibilities of the professors. Unlike Lunacharsky, he had no instinctive feeling that the vicious polemical tone which he had always used to his liberal academic colleagues was now inappropriate. Lunacharsky tried to ignore the fact that the Cheka quite frequently arrested Cadet professors (though usually releasing them shortly afterwards); but Pokrovsky, and no doubt many other Communist officials, tended to use this as a rhetorical means of frightening and humiliating the professors.

There were many causes of annoyance within the universities as well. The professors resented the creation of the rabfaks. They were harassed by *ad hoc* administrative bodies set up (essentially without Narkompros approval) by Communist students. In Petrograd University, as Pitirim Sorokin later recalled with disgust, a first-year student bearing the title of 'commissar' briefly headed the university administration.[6] Revolutionary *troiki*, including students, usurped administrative functions in the Moscow Higher Technical School and the Petrovskaya (later Timiryazev) Agricultural Academy at the same period.[7]

The most important conflict between the professoriate and the new regime occurred in Moscow University on the issue of autonomy of higher educational institutions. Until the autumn of 1920, both Narkompros and Novikov, the elected Rector of the university, were trying to reach an accommodation.[8] This was prevented, essentially, by the persistence of the Cadet professors in dabbling in anti-Soviet conspiracy (or perhaps simply engaging in anti-Soviet conversation), and the persistence of the Cheka in arresting them. The final hardening of Narkompros' attitude on university autonomy directly followed the trial of the Cadet 'Tactical Centre', in which those accused and convicted of anti-Soviet conspiracy included Professors Struve and Novgorodtsev (*in absentia*) and Professors G. V. Sergievsky, S. P. Melgunov, S. A. Kotlyarevsky, M. S. Feldshtein and N. K. Koltsov.[9]

The issue of autonomy was formally settled by the new VUZ constitution of 1921. The higher schools were to be directly under Narkompros control, with Narkompros appointing the rector, who was president of a 3–5 man governing body, and also approving professorial appointments, while the governing body appointed deans and junior faculty.[10] This was seen as an infringement of democracy not only by the professors but also (from a quite different point of view) by the Communist students, whose participation in the running of the higher school was now theoretically limited to electing representatives to departmental committees, curriculum commissions, soviets advising the dean, and so on. Both professors and revolutionary students sincerely believed that democracy required an electoral system which they could monopolize; and Narkompros found itself in the unenviable position of violating 'bourgeois' and 'revolutionary' democracy at a single stroke.

The formal constitution, however, tells us little about how the higher schools actually operated in the 1920s. Narkompros appointed rectors, but their functions were often taken over by Communist students, either on the initiative of the students (who suspected that administration 'bureaucrats' might collaborate with the old professors) or because the rectors were too busy to do their jobs. In the Moscow Mining Academy, for example, A. P. Zavenyagin (later a major industrial administrator) served as deputy rector from his freshman year: the Rector, I. M. Gubkin, was simultaneously a member of Vesenkha in charge of the oil industry and had little time for the routine administrative tasks in the Academy.[11] Communist students often served as school or departmental secretaries, which, among other things, meant that they were too busy to study.[12] All through the 1920s, party spokesmen complained about this situation; and there were dozens of fruitless instructions from the agitprop department and elsewhere telling students to keep out of VUZ administration. Bukharin made the point with characteristic sharpness (and some exaggeration) in 1924: 'In the VUZy our Komsomols often appoint professors and purge students – but look at their academic performance: 80% fail. A lot of independence and not the slightest real knowledge...'[13]

It is, in fact, extremely doubtful that students were ever able (after 1921) to 'appoint professors'. Narkompros had the formal power, but it made appointments on the basis of departmental recommendations. There is no record of conflict on appointments in the archives of the Narkompros collegium or in the quite extensive coverage of VUZ affairs in the professors' journal *Nauchnyi rabotnik*. Provincial VUZy were vulnerable to pressure from local party committees and soviets. Marxists, especially in the early period, might be appointed to social science chairs against the opposition of the old professors. But in the prestige VUZy of the capitals, it seems that professorial appointments (with the possible exception of some appointments in the social sciences) were effectively made by the departments and schools concerned and more or less automatically ratified by Narkompros.

From a Soviet standpoint, the old university faculty was as socially and politically alien as the old student body. But it was more difficult to replace, and during NEP the regime made little attempt to replace or even rejuvenate it. In spite of the belligerence of rabfak students and some Communist officials,[14] the official policy was to employ and conciliate 'bourgeois specialists', including professors. When the professors of Moscow Higher Technical School (now the Bauman Institute) went on strike in the spring of 1921, after the appointment of an unacceptable governing body, Narkompros and the Politburo jointly revoked the appointment and instructed Communist students at the school to behave less aggressively towards the professors.[15] The next year – when professors of Moscow Higher Technical School went on strike again, together with those of the physics and mathematics school of Moscow University and some from Petrograd and Kazan Universities – two high-level commissions investigated the circumstances and offered concessions to the professors.[16]

The professors, Stratonov implies,[17] were not fooled by the Bolsheviks: they knew what promises of 'almost autonomy' meant. But really nobody, including the Bolsheviks, knew what those promises meant or would mean. To the scholars deported in 1922, the situation of 'old' professors in Soviet universities understandably looked very gloomy. The crucial event, from their point of view, was that in 1920/21 the higher schools lost the autonomy which had been conferred on them by the Provisional Government. For different reasons, Soviet historians have tended to give similar emphasis to the 'consolidation of Soviet power' in higher education, implying that the old professors' sphere of internal political influence was reduced virtually to nothing.

But it is clear, if only from the events of 1928/29 when the higher schools lost their autonomy for the second time, that this is simply not so. The pattern that emerged in the NEP period was a division of spheres of influence in the VUZy between 'new' Communist students and 'old' professors, with Narkompros and the appointed rectors playing a mediating role. Between the deportations of 1922 (which will be discussed later in this chapter) and the campaign against 'bourgeois specialists' which began in 1928, the old professors lived increasingly comfortable and relatively independent lives in their own sphere, dealt with the Soviet government as negotiators rather than petitioners, and enjoyed privileges which, *mutatis mutandis*, put them in much the same position vis-à-vis the society as a whole as they had had before the revolution.

Marxism and the social sciences

Social science was the area of greatest conflict, repression and violation of scholarly autonomy. From 1918 to 1923, relations between the Soviet government and 'bourgeois' professors in the social sciences, humanities and law were extremely strained. Both sides perceived it as a conflict of ideology. The party leadership, whose intervention in other spheres of university life was infrequent, exerted the greatest efforts to introduce Marxism and create social science schools capable of training a new Soviet elite. The old professors resisted; and, as we shall see, the outcome was by no means a clear victory for Marxism and Soviet power.

During the Civil War, Narkompros began to reorganize the existing schools of history, philology and law as social science schools (*fakul'tety obshchestvennykh nauk*), to which Communist professors were appointed.[18] The Socialist (later Communist) Academy, then little more than a Marxist debating club with a library, was invited by Narkompros to work out the bases of a new social science programme,[19] introducing Marxist methodology and developing the concepts of scientific socialism.

The old faculty reacted with indignation, non-cooperation and demonstrative contempt for the Marxist professors. In Moscow University, Narkompros' first initiative foundered when a 'bourgeois' professor (A. M. Vinaver) was elected dean of the new social science school.[20] In Petrograd, leadership was assumed by the flamboyant 'leftist' but non-Communist academician N. Ya. Marr,[21] who gave the school an unusual bias towards ethnology and linguistics but not much in the way of orthodox Marxism.

The situation changed, however, when Narkompros' initiative was taken up by Lenin and the party leadership in 1920. At this time the system of party schools and Communist Universities (specifically for the training of Communists, and outside the Narkompros education system) was still in its infancy.[22] In the early 1920s, the Central Committee and Narkompros treated the new Communist Universities and the social science schools of the old universities as institutions of a similar type, issuing instructions to them jointly and sending the same small group of Communist intellectuals to lecture at both. But the social science schools, unlike the new Communist Universities, had a hard core of committed anti-Communists and non-Marxists on the existing faculty. Of all 'bourgeois' professors, these had the strongest objection to Communists and their beliefs, included the largest proportion of former Cadet politicians, and had the least ground for ideologically neutral cooperation with the new regime.

Lenin, who was extremely interested in university teaching of Marxist social science, was not discouraged by this, and even devised a cunning scheme for making the old professors teach Marxism in spite of themselves. 'Bind them to firm programmes', he told Pokrovsky.

Give them themes which will objectively force them to take our point of view. For example, make them teach the history of the colonial world: there, after all, even bourgeois writers can only 'expose' each other in all kinds of dastardly behaviour: the English expose the French, the French the English, and the Germans both at once. 'The literature of the subject' will oblige your professors to recount the atrocities of capitalism in general. As well, require from each of them a basic knowledge of Marxist literature; announce that anyone who does not pass a special Marxist exam will be deprived of the right to teach. I assure you that even if they still do not become orthodox Marxists, they will nevertheless assimilate things which were completely excluded from the programme of their courses before; and then it will be the business of the students, under our political guidance, to use that material as it ought to be used.[23]

Clearly Lenin was still thinking in terms of a pre-revolutionary situation, in which Marxism as an intellectual system tended to influence even non-Marxists, and non-political intellectuals had a general sympathy with the revolutionary cause. But all that had changed, even by 1920. For non-Marxists, Marxism had become the ideology of the ruling group; and in the universities there were already signs that religious philosophy was acquiring the seductive anti-regime appeal which before the October revolution had belonged to Marxism.

The non-Marxist professors were never in fact required to pass an exam in Marxism. But in the early 1920s a rich variety of covertly anti-Soviet courses were being taught, both by old professors and new. In the Moscow University social science school, the old professors managed to include no less than nine courses on the history of religion and Church law in the programme.[24] Of the new Marxist professors, those who taught full-time were almost all Mensheviks[25] or political deviants of some kind: that was the reason they were teaching full-time instead of carrying out more important government and party work. The anarchist Grossman-Roshchin lectured on ethical sociology.[26] Lenin's old rival Bogdanov lectured on political economy and 'some sort of cloudy idealist "organizational science"'.[27] Of the Mensheviks, Gorev 'replaced the concept of dictatorship of the proletariat with that of dictatorship of the party in his lectures', and Sukhanov 'tried to "disprove" the Leninist theory of the possibility of the victory of socialism in one country, propagating his own opportunist "theory of productive forces", which led to the conclusion that there were no objective economic preconditions for socialism in Russia'.[28]

Under these circumstances, it seemed hopeless to rely on the university social science schools to teach Marxism; and, even before the first appearance of significant numbers of Communist students in 1921, the concept was changed. The social science schools, it was decided, should be training institutions for Soviet government personnel, with departments of economics, Soviet law and 'social pedagogics'.[29] This meant, in effect, that the instruction they would offer would be technical rather than ideological.

Following the new conception, government agencies began to send students and offer special stipends for training specialized personnel. The Moscow University social science schools, which had the special function of serving the central commissariats, added departments of statistics and international relations: in the early 1920s it received 40 stipends from the Central Cooperative Union for the training of future specialists for the cooperative network, 30 from the Finance Commissariat for future financial experts and 25 from Vesenkha for future economists.[30] To some extent, this pattern seems to have been duplicated in the provinces. In 1924, for example, 88 out of 300 students in the Saratov University social science school were 'in directing work in the *guberniya* (regional) and city organizations, including workers from the regional party committee, the courts, the regional economic council, and so on'.[31]

The social science schools remained acutely short of Communist teachers. This was so even in Moscow, where they were able to use the services of Old Bolshevik intellectuals in government work – Pokrovsky, Lunacharsky, Skvortsov-Stepanov, Krylenko, Kursky, Stuchka, V. N. Meshcheryakov, F. Rotshtein and others[32] – for occasional lecture courses in their areas of expertise. The same Bolshevik names are repeated in the lists of the Communist Academy, the Institute of Red Professors, the Sverdlov Communist University in Moscow, the Moscow University social science school and the Plekhanov Economics Institute. Not surprisingly, the amount of time which any of these men could give to any individual institution was extremely limited. There were constant complaints that Communists ordered to teach in one of the higher schools by the Central Committee were not in fact doing so.[33]

The old professors still provided the basic faculty of the social science schools and were responsible for most of the teaching. In 1923, Moscow University reported that 21% of the teachers in its social science school were Communists, but almost certainly they were doing less than 21% of the teaching.[34] In the provinces, the situation was worse. Kazan University opened a social science school with departments of law and politics, economics and history in April 1919, but 'the teaching personnel transferred almost without change from the [old] law school and in part from the history school'.[35] On Lenin's suggestion, the Marxist scholar V. V. Adoratsky – like Lenin, a pre-revolutionary graduate of the Kazan law school – was sent to teach in the Kazan social science school.[36] But by 1921 he was back in Moscow; and subsequently the Central Committee did not even try to get leading Communists to go to provincial VUZy on a longterm basis, but simply sent them out to give a few lectures and organizational advice.[37] In some cases, the provincial school's problems were more basic than a lack of Marxists. The Tomsk social science school, for example, collapsed after a year as a result of 'the departure from the city of Tomsk of a large number of professors'.[38]

In 1922 the Central Committee decided that there were just not enough Marxists to go round, and abolished all the university social science schools except those in Moscow, Petrograd, Saratov and Rostov.[39] Most of the provincial universities re-established the law schools and teachers' colleges which the social science schools had briefly replaced.[40] The four remaining social science schools continued to struggle with the problem of assembling an acceptably Marxist, or at least pro-Soviet, faculty. In Rostov, an investigation ordered by Mikoyan's South-Eastern Bureau of the Central Committee found a total of 13 Communists (including instructors and other junior teaching personnel) on the faculty. Of the full professors, 48 out of 56 were classified as the 'old reactionary' type, and the remainder apparently belonged to the intermediate group of non-Communists prepared to cooperate with the Soviet regime. According to a Soviet historian, 'there were Cadets among the reactionary professors. Some of them had completely mastered Soviet phraseology and even acted as delegates to the city soviet, but at the same time worked with the reactionary groups linked with the reactionary professoriate of Novocherkassk and Moscow.'[41]

As the Communist University system developed, the presence of 'reactionary professors' put the old universities at an increasing disadvantage as centres of Marxist social science training.[42] The deportations of 1922 demoralized the social science schools of the old universities, with which many of the deportees had been associated.

The commissariats turned out to be too disorganized to predict their own need for personnel and make effective use of the schools as a service training facility. In 1924, accordingly, a commission of the Orgburo of the Central Committee recommended dissolution of the university social science schools over a two-year period, and cessation of enrolment from 1924/25.[43]

This did not mean that the universities, or even the schools and departments which had been incorporated in the social science schools, lost their function as elite training institutions. They continued, after the 1925 break for reorganization, to enrol high-quality 'Soviet' students. But these students were taught by 'old' professors, more or less in the traditional disciplines of law, history, philology and so on. They were ideological training institutions only in the most marginal sense – and in fact, given the predominance of 'bourgeois' students preparing for academic careers in the graduate schools, they probably functioned more effectively as transmitters of the professors' ideology than of that of the regime. They were service training facilities only in the very general sense that the old universities had been for the old regime.

The Orgburo's decision of 1924 allowed the university social science schools to break up into their traditional constituent parts and the old professors to resume their traditional role of leadership. In Moscow University the reorganization, which took place in 1925, created schools of ethnology (the *etnofak*) and law. There was no problem re-establishing the law school, since it already existed as a department of the social science school. The *etnofak*, in spite of its name, was a revival of the old historical–philological school. The main subject taught was not ethnography (which was in fact taught in the geography department of the school of physics and mathematics) but history.[44] Economics, statistics and sociology seem to have vanished as separate academic disciplines in Moscow University at this time, no doubt because they had not been taught before the revolution and the social science teachers had been borrowed from the old Moscow Commercial Institute (now the Plekhanov Economics Institute).

In Leningrad, similarly, the old historical–philological school re-emerged under the attractive title of *yamfak* (a contraction of *yazykoznanie*, i.e. linguistics, and *material'naya kul'tura*, the term favoured by Professor Marr for the disciplines of history, archeology and anthropology). The law department was officially dissolved, presumably because its faculty, unlike Moscow's, had not acquired an energetic Marxist or Soviet-oriented group. But it continued to function normally under the title of 'the former law department' until re-established as a law school in the autumn of 1926.[45] The economics department of the social science school was transferred to the Leningrad Polytechnical Institute, and the social–pedagogical department to the Herzen Pedagogical Institute.

The teaching of ideology

It was Lenin's belief that all VUZ students should take a basic social science–civics course called the 'general scientific minimum'. This was to be primarily informational, covering Marxist sociology, elements of natural science and the government and economy of the USSR.[46] Sovnarkom subsequently pruned Lenin's very long list of compulsory subjects in the scientific minimum to three (dropping, among others, 'the electrification plan'). These were historical materialism, capitalism and proletarian revolution, and the political structure and social tasks of the RSFSR.[47]

Although the scientific minimum was officially introduced for all students, there is very little indication that it was actually taught in the higher schools in 1922/23. The people who were supposed to teach it in the Moscow VUZy were those same Old Bolshevik intellectuals to whom the Central Committee delegated all Marxist theoretical work, and they simply did not have the time. At the Timiryazev Agricultural Academy, Bukharin said in 1924, 'I have been told that ten Communist lecturers have been appointed – Stuchka, Milyutin, Teodorovich and others – but not one of them gives lectures. They are there on paper but not in fact.[48] (But Bukharin, also a member of the Marxist theoretical pool, was in the same position as those he criticized: he was too busy to teach Marxism in the VUZy.)

The situation changed, however, after the discussion with the Trotskyites in the winter of 1923/24, when a distressingly large proportion of Communist cells in the VUZy voted for Trotsky. At that point, it became clear to the Central Committee majority that the younger generation of Communists, including those in higher education, were ill informed about the history of the party before the October Revolution and Civil War, and unaware of important and damaging facts in Trotsky's biography. Trotsky, after all, had been first a Menshevik and then a conciliator, who had joined the Bolsheviks only in the summer of 1917. He and Lenin had engaged in acrimonious polemical exchanges in emigration, from which very useful quotations could be culled. Accordingly, the resolution of the XIII Party Conference early in 1924 'On the results of the discussion and on petty-bourgeois deviation in the party' stated:

One of the most important tasks is raising to the necessary level the study of the history of the Russian Communist Party, and above all the basic facts of the struggle of Bolshevism and Menshevism, the role of separate factions and trends during the course of that struggle, in particular the role of those eclectic factions which tried to 'reconcile' Bolsheviks with Mensheviks. The party Central Committee must take a series of steps to facilitate the publication of the appropriate textbooks on the history of the All-Russian Communist Party, and also make the teaching of its history obligatory in all party schools, VUZy, political study circles and so on.[49]

An explanatory circular sent out by the agitprop department of the Central Committee and the political-education administration of Narkompros spelled out the political implications by recommending that 'special attention be paid to the illumination of Trotskyism in the past and present', and that Lenin's writings and other literature be used 'with the purpose of exposing the intellectual essence of Trotskyism'.[50]

Stalin took a leading part in introducing the study of 'Leninism'. Two months after Lenin's death he was lecturing to students of the Sverdlov Communist University in Moscow on 'The Foundations of Leninism';[51] and a month later he published a 'Plan for seminars on Leninism' in a new journal for Communist students edited by Molotov.[52] Seminars on Leninism were being held in Moscow University as early as the 1924/25 academic year.[53] In January 1925, the Central Committee secretariat instructed all 'big pedagogical and socio-economic VUZy' to establish chairs of History of the RKP(b) and Leninism. Other higher schools were to create departments teaching what was now called the 'social minimum'. Local party committees were to be responsible for directing the work of these departments. The new subjects were to be compulsory, and students would be examined on them.[54]

Some effort was made in the elite VUZy to keep the new courses at a reasonable intellectual level. The Moscow University seminars, for example, made relatively little use of textbooks – which in Pokrovsky's view led to blind and dogmatic memorization of material[55] – and studied the newly published collections of Lenin's works.[56] A similar approach was taken in Sverdlov Communist University; and one can see from Astrov's fictionalized memoirs that the discovery of old controversies involving current political figures was genuinely exciting (even scandalous) for the young Communists preparing themselves for future leadership.[57] Excitement, perhaps, was less of a factor in Leningrad. It took Leningrad University two years to put together a course in party history and Leninism, though when it finally came out it included a special seminar for physics and mathematics students on 'Darwinism and Marxism' which was apparently not taught in Moscow.[58]

But for most higher schools and most students the new courses were dreary in the extreme. Both the content of the courses and the students' approach to them resembled that of the secondary-school programme in social studies: the difference was that the VUZ courses included attacks on Trotsky, but these were only interesting for those students who cared about Trotsky in the first place. The 'social minimum' subjects were learned by rote, and often reduced to an almost meaningless catechism. 'To the question "What is a trade union?" one gets the laconic reply that "It is a school of communism"; imperialism is "the best path to socialism." '[59] In 1926, Kalinin told a meeting of rectors that 'our teaching of social sciences has become something like the teaching of the Law of God in the old gymnasia';[60] and when this remark was quoted by the Trotskyite Sosnovsky in a Communist Academy debate in 1927 it produced cries of approval and prolonged applause.[61]

Professorial organizations and attitudes

For the old professors, the teaching of Marxism and party history was not really important so long as they themselves did not have to teach it in their own courses. What was important to them was their own teaching and research – in which they achieved relative independence in the very years when party history was being effectively introduced into the VUZ curriculum – and the conditions of life within the profession.

The question of professional organization was a very lively political issue at the beginning of the 1920s. The professors wanted an 'autonomous' form of professional organization; and the regime assumed that they wanted it for primarily political purposes. There seem to be some grounds for this assumption. The group of Moscow liberals with which Stratonov was associated strongly resisted Soviet pressure to join the Union of Workers in Education and Socialist Culture (Rabpros, hereafter referred to as the Teachers' Union).[62] They tried to organize concerted action against the Soviet proposals on a national scale. They attempted to use organizations like the Commission for Improving the Life of Scholars (TsEKUBU), established during the Civil War on Gorky's initiative, and the All-Russian Committee of Aid to the Starving[63] as fronts for non- and probably anti-Soviet professional organization.[64]

Soviet authorities, and the Cheka in particular, interpreted these activities as counter-revolutionary. However, emigré memoirists do not actually admit to conspiracy, although they clearly indicate deep hostility to the Soviet regime, and one can only make guesses on the question. Stratonov's memoirs, for example, deny conspiracy while presenting attitudes which would make absence of political resistance apparently dishonorable and cowardly:[65] they were written in 1930, and it is possible that he was afraid of compromising colleagues who had remained in the Soviet Union.

The confusion is compounded by the fact that the major Soviet reprisals against the liberal professors – the Tactical Centre trial of 1920 and the deportations of 1922 – were apparently exemplary actions designed to intimidate the group rather than responses to specific offences.

In the autumn of 1922, a group of 'anti-Soviet lawyers, *literati* and professors'[66] numbering 100–150 persons was deported from the Soviet Union. Its members seem to have been randomly chosen from among the leaders of the liberal intelligentsia. A number of them were historians and philosophers who were either teaching in the university social science schools of Moscow and Petrograd or had earlier taught there – A. A. Kizevetter, S. L. Frank, I. A. Ilyin, N. A. Berdyaev, F. A. Stepun, L. P. Karsavin, N. O. Lossky, S. P. Melgunov and Pitirim Sorokin among them.[67] Others in the group of deportees were the biologist Novikov, former Rector of Moscow University; V. V. Stratonov, dean of the Moscow University school of physics and mathematics and later memoirist; Ovchinnikov, the former Rector of Petrograd University; Professors Troshin and I. A. Stratonov from Kazan University; and Professor V. Yasinsky of Moscow Higher Technical School, who had been effectively in charge of the Commission for Improving the Life of Scholars.

The Central Committee report for 1922 justified the expulsions in terms of the ideological competition which the old intelligentsia was offering the Marxists.

The growing influence of a revitalized bourgeois ideology in the young Soviet Republic made it necessary for us to apply decisive measures of struggle against this evil...The Soviet government took measures for the administrative deportation beyond the borders of the Soviet Republic of a considerable group of ideologists of the 'new' bourgeoisie. In the contemporary situation, the expulsion of some dozens of old bourgeois activists and ideologues of the petty bourgeoisie from the largest cities was a necessity.[68]

The deportations no doubt intimidated the scholars who remained, and facilitated their acceptance of the new university constitution and the new Soviet Teachers' Union. But it did not put them in a permanently outcast position, and during NEP there were no further punitive actions against the liberal intelligentsia as a group. At the end of 1923, in fact, Zinoviev announced that a breakthrough had been achieved: both intelligentsia and party understood the need for working together, and 'we will not remember the past any more'.[69] The assembled intellectuals must have felt reasonably secure at this point, since they drew Zinoviev's attention to 'the pitiful position of Russian scholars living in emigration and prepared to return to Russia to work in the service of Soviet power'. Zinoviev's response was quite sympathetic. 'There are no obstacles from the side of the Soviet government', he replied, 'to the return from abroad of those scholars who are sincerely prepared to break with the White emigration. They will meet the same kind of careful treatment on the part of Soviet power as the scholars in Russia receive...'[70]

Apparently with this encouragement some members of the Berlin emigration, like the writer Viktor Shklovsky,[71] did return, and were in fact treated in the same way as other members of the literary intelligentsia. Within a year, the professors received permission to publish a thick monthly journal, in which they published *inter alia* a long list of scholars who had perished in the post-revolutionary years.[72] Scholars who had been deported or emigrated remained members of the Academy of Sciences and other scholarly organizations without protest from the regime.[73]

The professors had bitterly objected to their inclusion in the Teachers' Union, since the expressed purpose of bringing them in was to democratize the professorial aristocracy through contact with the cultural proletariat of rural primary-school teachers and, for that matter, school cleaners and watchmen who were also included in the union. As a 'transitional measure' before full absorption, they were allowed to form a separate section within the union[74] – the Section of Scientific Workers (SNR).

The Section in fact turned into a permanent institution whose links with the Teachers' Union were minimal. It became possible to enrol in the Section without becoming a member of the Teachers' Union: of the Section's 9,000 members in the Russian Republic in 1926, more than 60% were *not* registered members of the Teachers'

Union but belonged only to the Section.[75] The Section had its own independent local branches; and by 1927 its secretary, N. I. Loboda, was writing of the Section's nominal subordination to the Teachers' Union as a pure formality. In the past, he said,

> many people looked on the Section as a temporary organization, whose basic function was to unite scientific workers (a category of worker which submits itself to professional organization only with the greatest difficulty) within its ranks, so that this mass could be poured into a single Union of Education Workers...This is a completely incorrect view. Life has shown that the Section of Scientific Workers is the only possible union for scientific workers and the most flexible way of meeting their needs.[76]

The working definition of a 'scientific worker' was a member of a higher educational or scholarly research institution. But membership of the Section was on an individual and not an institutional basis, and scholars without institutional affiliation could join if the Section considered that their work merited it. VUZ administrators could not join, unless they happened also to be scholars. Rabfak professors were included at the discretion of the Section, which required evidence that they possessed the appropriate scholarly qualifications and publication.[77]

The Section was as exclusive an institution as could be desired; and it seems to have elected its own officers and represented its members' interests with a success which is in striking contrast to the situation in the Teachers' Union as a whole.[78] But the 'caste' spirit of the professoriate and old intelligentsia was manifested even more strongly in another institution – the Commission for Improving the Life of Scholars.

The Commission, originally established during the Civil War for the purpose of distributing the special 'academic ration' issued to scholars and prominent members of the intelligentsia, provided salary supplements and a variety of rest and recreational facilities, to scholars during NEP. Financed from the mid-1920s by Sovnarkom RSFSR,[79] the Commission ran the Scholars' Club in Moscow, where local and visiting scholars crowded to hear scholarly lectures and concerts by the finest Russian artists. At its disposal were, appropriately, a number of monuments of aristocratic culture which were used as resorts and sanatoria for the scholars – among them, the 'Uzkoe' estate near Moscow, the 'Gaspra' estate in the Crimea, and sanatoria in Detskoe Selo, near Leningrad, and Kislovodsk.[80]

Before 1929, Communist or Soviet influence on the internal

workings of the Commission seems to have been minimal. At 'Uzkoe', whose facilities included a working church, Easter was celebrated but not Mayday.[81] The Commission's register of scholars – divided into status categories ranging from 'young scholars at the beginning of their careers' to 'outstanding scholars whose work has international significance'[82] – included not only scholars who had emigrated or been deported but also (in 1930) eighteen scholars who had been sent to Solovki or otherwise exiled within the Soviet Union.[83] 'Among middle and lower scientific workers', one member of the Section of Scientific Workers said, 'The Commission is regarded as an aristocratic institution because it is the milieu of certain circles of old scientific workers – old not in the sense of years, but as a characterization of attitude.'[84]

Professorial salaries and privileges

When professorial salaries were low in the early 1920s (in the range of 28–33 roubles a month in 1924,[85] which was not much higher than a schoolteacher's salary), the Commission for Improving the Life of Scholars provided additional salary supplements. In 1923/24, 9,000 scholars received salary supplements and these ranged from 7.5 roubles a month for young scholars to 40 roubles for the highest category of established scholars.[86] From 1924/25, the Commission paid salary supplements only to the two highest categories on the professorial scale. But professorial salaries had already begun a sharp rise: in January 1925, the average professorial salary was given as 80 roubles, and an estimate at the end of the year put the average at 120–150 roubles.[87]

Given the instability of the currency and the different types of rouble being quoted,[88] there is not much that can usefully be said about pre-1925 salaries in comparative terms. But it should be pointed out that throughout the 1920s virtually all VUZ faculty in the capitals and big cities held down two or even three jobs, either working simultaneously in several higher schools[89] or employed in various government agencies. Since professors had a six-hour teaching load in Russian VUZy, even three appointments were quite feasible,[90] and because of the shortage of teaching personnel there was little difficulty finding the jobs. In real terms by 1925 we are dealing with professorial incomes in the bracket of 200–350 roubles a month.[91] This compares rather favourably with the 30 roubles which Narkompros was currently trying to secure for the rural teacher,[92] with the average of 55 roubles received by workers in census industry in 1925/26, or even with the average 141 roubles received by employees in the central government apparat (the most highly paid category of state employee) in the same year.[93]

This, however, does not mean that the professors were happy with what they earned. The non-scientists, in particular, resented the fact the 'government specialists' earned more than they did. As Professor Sergievsky said, the income of those who worked only in the higher schools remained lower than that of the engineers, chemists, agronomists, financial experts and so on who worked for the central commissariats on a full- or part-time basis. The financial incentive was such that

the majority of professors who have even the smallest opportunity to apply their knowledge in some field of production prefer not to load themselves with teaching work in the higher school but, taking care to keep their connection with the VUZ, construct their material well-being on the salary from enterprises of Vesenkha, the Commissariat of Agriculture or the Commissariat of External Trade.[94]

The professorial organizations were vigilant in defending and extending the rights of their members, especially in the material realm. In Moscow, where a good proportion of the academic population was concentrated, one of the main social problems of the 1920s was an acute housing shortage. The formal housing privileges of scientific workers – secured through the activity of their organizations and the cooperation of Sovnarkom and the Moscow Soviet – included the right to extra space for study purposes and the right to *samouplotnenie*,[95] that is, to choose extra occupants for the family apartment when it exceeded the permitted norm of square metres per inhabitant.

Their actual privileges went further, since the old Muscovites were still living in their bourgeois pre-revolutionary apartments, and most of them managed to satisfy the space norms by bringing in relatives or domestic servants. (Employment of a servant remained the norm in the professorial milieu throughout NEP, and indeed beyond it.) There was, however, the constant fear of arbitrary eviction, or illegal orders to share the apartment with unknown lower-class families, since local authorities desperate for housing space were less sensitive to professorial privilege than Sovnarkom. The Commission for Improving the Life of Scholars had a special office of legal consultants handling housing problems at the rate of 30 a day.[96]

But for all their efforts, disasters occurred. 'The people's judges showed a tendency towards restricted interpretation of the housing rights of scientific workers',[97] and the professors themselves found violation of their domestic privacy the most difficult of all Soviet impositions to bear.[98] Housing problems, according to the Old Bolshevik Mitskevich (deputy head of the housing section of the Commission) had led to the premature death of many scholars, including Mikhail Gershenzon, the last surviving *Vekhi* contributor in Russia. The linguist D. S. Shor, returning from a trip abroad in the summer of 1926, found his room already inhabited by new occupants and his possessions thrown out of the apartment. Professor D. S. Krein of the Moscow Conservatorium shot himself two hours before the court hearing which was to decide whether local authorities had violated his rights by settling strangers in his apartment.[99]

Job security was not an important issue for scholars during NEP, despite the fact that in formal terms professors did not have indefinite tenure but were supposed to come up for reappointment at the end of terms which ranged from 5 to 10 years.[100] There are no reports that this procedure was followed in practice, or that professors were dismissed by this means, between 1922 and 1928. Evidently the shortage of qualified teachers and the delicacy with which they were normally handled by Narkompros in this period made the law a dead letter (as is confirmed by the outrage of the professoriate in 1928/29, when the law was actually and punitively applied).

Children of faculty were exempt from payment of VUZ fees, whatever their parents' income.[101] But, since the social selection process put some obstacles in their way, the Scientific Workers' Section was given a reserved quota of places.[102] Apparently the number of places kept for scholars' children was more than adequate in the provinces, but less than the demand for places in the Moscow and Leningrad VUZy. This was not only because two-thirds of the professors were concentrated in the capitals, but because provincial scholars also wanted their children to go to the prestige institutions.

The Section was naturally concerned about the training of new scholars; and on this question it would seem that the professorial interest in self-perpetuation must have come into conflict with the party interest in bringing in Communists. Local party committees were instructed to be alert for vacancies at junior faculty level and to select candidates from the graduating Communist students.[103] But there is no evidence of Communist success in this realm. In 1926, senior and junior faculty were alike in having a high proportion from intelligentsia families (53% of senior faculty, 48% of junior). But the senior faculty had proportionately *more* Communists than the junior

(6%, as against 4%), and the only real differential was by sex – 32% of junior faculty members were women, but only 4% of senior.[104]

From 1925, there was a formal system of *aspirantura* (graduate studies), replacing the old system of informal apprenticeship with a professor. Stipends were available for about 60% of the graduate students.[105] But the stipends were small, and Communist students were neither attracted nor energetically recruited into graduate studies.[106] The professors effectively had control of the system of graduate studies in the latter years of NEP, and the only really controversial issue was whether the (presumably non-Communist) graduate students should have to study Marxism.[107]

Accommodation with the Soviet regime

There were Communists who thought that the old professors were being altogether too successful in upholding 'bourgeois' academic tradition in higher education. Communist students resented the informal alliance of 'bourgeois' students and professors. In 1927 a speaker at the All-Russian Congress of Soviets warned against the local dominance of 'lords of the kafedra'. 'There are separate individuals', he said, 'quite important ones, who have pretensions to monopolize the leadership of all scientific fields. We must struggle with these individuals, who do after all have influence...We must take the most energetic measures to bring new young forces into the ranks of scientific workers.'[108]

But during NEP the party leadership did very little to encourage this point of view. The professors were untouched by the 1924 purge of students. Communist students were repeatedly instructed not to harass the professors. In response to the critical comment at the Congress of Soviets quoted above, Lezhava, the deputy president of Sovnarkom RSFSR, produced a sharp rebuttal: while such criticism might conceivably apply to the extreme right wing of the professoriate, 'we already have a large body of scholars and teachers who are completely devoted to the construction of the worker-peasant state'.[109]

No doubt the technical specialists were more willing to make peace with the Soviet regime than professors in the humanities and the social sciences, for whom opportunities and potential rewards were less. There was, nevertheless, a general accommodation in the mid-1920s. As Professor Sakulin pointed out, 'attaining victory, the party could neither expect nor demand a lightning change of attitude in the intelligentsia. It seems to me that the intelligentsia would even have lowered its dignity if it had at once run after the victor's chariot...The intelligentsia. . .waited to see what political circumstances would be established for its creative work.'[110] But this, perhaps, was too high-minded a view even for the majority of professors. If the professorial organizations accurately reflected the concerns of their members, what was crucial was improvement of material circumstances from the low point of the Civil War, and confirmation of the social status and privileges of the group. In this direction, a great deal was achieved during NEP, and more was promised and expected.

As for the political circumstances, there were both pluses and minuses. The Soviet government exercised censorship, but permitted the re-establishment of private publishing in the early 1920s. Scholars appear to have been comparatively little affected by the censorship, in contrast to writers of fiction and drama. The regime required the teaching of Marxism in the higher schools, but did not require that the old professors should teach or study it. (Those who did teach Marxism complained bitterly of the contemptuous attitude of their scholarly colleagues.) Preference in admissions was given to Communist students, and the professors sometimes said that they felt obliged to pass such students even if they were academically below standard. But the professors' children also had preference in admissions from 1924, and the reintroduction of entrance examinations suggested that the regime was beginning to listen to the voice of the experts.

During NEP, the leadership behaved in a conciliatory manner towards 'bourgeois specialists', but lower-level officials usually did not. But a situation in which prominent members of the intelligentsia were conventionally allowed to appeal over the heads of underlings to the top political leadership was, in its own way, flattering. In personal terms, the party leaders treated intelligentsia leaders with respect. Professors were not simply offered conciliation by second-level Communists like Lunacharsky and Semashko (who, as the professors obviously appreciated, had goodwill but no political clout). They were publicly approached by such real leaders as Zinoviev, Rykov and Bukharin.

The high intelligentsia, indeed, was a part of Soviet high society, and its members had relatively free access to the holders of power. They might be invited to Olga Kameneva's salon, rub shoulders with the military and GPU leadership at the Meyerholds, breakfast with Kirov or Kuibyshev for a discussion of scientific research prospects. This did not necessarily imply political influence or security. But for the intelligentsia leaders there were personal and status advantages in the situation which, except perhaps during Count Witte's ascendancy in the 1890s, had never been equalled under the old regime.

Of all party leaders, Bukharin was probably closest to the intelligentsia. This was not because he was the most conciliatory (Rykov was far more so), but because he was the most involved in the spiritual and psychological problems which members of the old Russian intelligentsia discussed among themselves. In 1924, he devoted two long articles to dissection of Pavlov's views on society and politics.[111] His own views were sharply at variance with Pavlov's, but the result of the argument was to establish a relationship of respectful friendship between the two men.[112] The next year Bukharin took part in a public debate on the fate of the intelligentsia. It was on this occasion that Professor Sakulin, defending the principles of intellectual and creative freedom, mentioned the lack of dignity that would have been involved if the intelligentsia had immediately 'run after the victor's chariot' – a remark, directed at Bukharin, that suggests the peculiar mixture of intimacy and role-playing which sometimes characterized the intellectuals' exchanges with the politicians in the latter years of NEP.

In the debate on the intelligentsia, Bukharin played the role of Bolshevik commissar to the full. 'We will not repudiate our Communist aims', he thundered. 'It is necessary for us that cadres of the intelligentsia should be ideologically conditioned [*natrenirovany*] in a definite way. Yes, we will put our stamp on intellectuals, we will work them over [*vyrabatyvat'*] as in a factory. . .'[113]

Of course, a serious advocate of such a policy would not have engaged in debate with intellectuals on 'the fate of the intelligentsia' in the first place; and one might also remark that Bukharin was using the language of the artistic avantgarde[114] rather than the language of Soviet politicians. But it is particularly interesting to discover that this debate was used to substantiate the claim (which in general terms was almost certainly correct) that Bukharin was a supporter of the intelligentsia's aspirations. According to Sakulin's later recollection of the debate, Bukharin 'promised in the name of the party' that at some future time the regime would relax ideological controls and allow greater intellectual freedom.[115]

It would be a mistake, however, to regard the issue of intellectual freedom as the central concern either of the regime in its dealings with the intelligentsia or of the intelligentsia leaders themselves. In political terms, the intelligentsia leadership came from the Academy of Sciences and the high-salaried specialists and consultants associated with the government commissariats; and for these men the issue of intellectual freedom was secondary to the issue of political influence and specialist input in government policy-making. It was impossible for the scholars to refuse all contact with politics, wrote S. F. Oldenburg,[116] chief negotiator with the regime for both the Academy of Sciences and the Section of Scientific Workers. To do so, in Oldenburg's view, was not only impossible but short-sighted. How else but through contact with politics was a working partnership of intelligence and power to be established?[117]

At the Second Congress of Scientific Workers, held in 1927, the mood of the leading scholars appeared not only confident but demanding. Their demands were for money, but the terms in which they were put both emphasized a special relationship with the political leadership and made claims on it. This marked a change in the conventions of public discourse: 'bourgeois specialists' had previously spoken aggressively only from an anti-Soviet position. But Academicians Oldenburg and Marr, who led an attack on Narkompros for its failure to obtain adequate finance for higher education and scholarly research, not only appeared to speak from a Soviet position but from a position of special access to the highest authorities. Their treatment of Lunacharsky, in fact, had the mixture of condescension and intimidation which, in the old days, 'com-missars' had used in their dealings with politically inferior 'bourgeois specialists'.

In his speech to the Congress, Lunacharsky rather plaintively defended Narkompros' record of asking for money: 'Narkompros almost every year warns of the danger [that industrialization would be held up for lack of specialists]. These warnings are quite sensi-tively received, and the government will not miss the moment when it will be necessary...to make a basic investment to raise the stan-dard of all our academic work.'[118]

But this struck Oldenburg as completely unsatisfactory. For ten years, he said, the specialists had witnessed Narkompros' 'misfor-tunes' and tolerated its failure to get adequate finance for scholarly institutions. He had expected Lunacharsky to make it clear to the leadership that the situation, on the eve of the industrialization drive, was now critical. He had expected self-criticism from Narkompros.

I am deeply disappointed...and it seems to me that we are left to do in an amateur way what our Commissar could and should have done with the skilled hand of an expert. *We cannot be silent*, because I think that the Commissar will *only thank* us if we point out to him those very large failings which we see in the work of Narkompros.[119]

Marr reinforced this criticism. Narkompros leaders seemed to have no concept of the urgency of the situation, he said. Khodorovsky seemed to be speaking from 'a place in the moon', and Lunacharsky was still worse. 'To speak in a serious way about the state of our professional affairs in a situation where responsible Narkompros workers are distributed around points in the galaxy is absolutely impossible.'[120]

The Academicians were conveying two messages: first, that they expected to get what they wanted because it was in the national interest; and second, that if Narkompros could not look after the interests of higher education and science, the scholarly community could find itself other patrons.[121] But Lunacharsky was afraid that the specialists had misread the political situation. This may have been because he already had intimations of the forthcoming Shakhty trial;[122] or it may have been simply on the general grounds that the specialists were in touch with the party leadership but not with the mood of the party rank-and-file or, for that matter, with the worsening situation of some sections of the intelligentsia.[123]

In an article written shortly after the Congress, Lunacharsky warned that

at the present time we have entered, if not a major crisis in our relations with the intelligentsia, at least a period in which there are some complicating circumstances...The issue is not that the intelligentsia is demanding certain civil rights – they already have them and can use them. No, the point is that the intelligentsia has become the representative of a general political formation sympathetic to democracy and to a distinctly watered-down version of proletarian dictatorship; *the intelligentsia is waiting for an invitation from Soviet power for the most valuable elements of the aristocracy of the mind to enter the highest organs of government* [my emphasis].

This kind of talk is dangerous, and these tendencies cannot but be nipped in the bud...There is not the slightest doubt that rightist elements... would like to blow a flame out of this spark, would like to create something like a conflict on the question of participation of 'chosen intellectuals' in power. It is impossible to refrain from warning our intelligentsia away from this path.[124]

The intelligentsia leaders (*verkhushechnaya intelligentsiya*)

may, of course, hope that organs like Narkompros which care for the interests of science will obliquely defend them, and even go out of their way to do so, in order to keep them, as major theoreticians, for the country. But they must not be surprised if the revolution, which has to defend itself from its enemies meticulously and ruthlessly, has also produced organs which look on such things from a completely different point of view.[125]

5

Recruitment to higher education

At the time of the October Revolution, Bolshevik support in the universities was almost non-existent. Among the professors, the dominant political orientation was liberal, the Cadet party having the strongest following. Among the students, patriotic feelings were strong in the first years of the war, and the small Bolshevik organizations were almost annihilated by police action. By 1917, patriotism had given way to a more revolutionary mood, and the students came out on the streets in February. But there was only a handful of active Bolsheviks in the universities of Petrograd and Moscow,[1] with most of the politically active students supporting the Cadets, the SRs or the Mensheviks. 'In the period of the October battles [in Moscow]', one Bolshevik recalled, 'class contradictions attained an extreme sharpness and were expressed with a clarity which was almost sculptural. On the side of the revolution were workers and soldiers; on the side of the counter-revolution, Junkers, officers and the overwhelming mass of students.'[2] So firmly were students associated with the Whites that during the street-fighting they were able to cross White lines simply by showing their student cards.[3]

The first action of the Soviet government in regard to higher education was to declare open admissions,[4] with the intention of thus democratizing the student body. When this produced only an influx of white-collar students without secondary-school diplomas, the new regime looked for other ways of bringing in working-class and peasant students. The rabfaks, created for this purpose in 1918 and 1919, were regarded as Communist impositions on the old higher schools, and resented by students and faculty alike. The rabfaks, initially set up in the premises of the old higher schools, competed with the traditional departments for classrooms, blackboards, desks and even chalk.[5] As Pokrovsky put it, 'the workers had to take the higher school more or less as the legendary siege of Saragossa was conducted: corridor by corridor and room by room'.[6]

In most higher schools, student organizations remained dominated by non-Bolshevik students for several years. In Kazan University, for example, Cadets still had control of the *starostat* (the student representative council) in mid-1919; and the small number of student Bolsheviks preferred to conduct their political activity outside the university, since 'it was not worth spending their small resources on work among the bourgeoisie and philistine intelligentsia which still filled the universities'.[7] In Petrograd University, 'bourgeois' and Communist students clashed at elections to the student council: during the election meeting, there were 'shouts, insults' and 'chairs began to be used' by the opposing groups; 'passions were so inflamed that one of the leaders of the council challenged a representative of the Communist students to a duel'.[8]

At the Moscow Commercial Institute (later the Plekhanov Economics Institute), there were 8 Communists out of a total of 16,000 students. But the local party committee contained one of the Institute's former Communist students, the fiery Ter-Vaganyan, who found it intolerable that the student council should remain under the control of his old political opponents. He urged the Institute Communists to action:

Shame on you, comrades. All around you are hundreds of factories and plants – or have you forgotten? You have forgotten that in October the worker actually conquered the higher school for himself, and you want to accept the Cadet suggestion that you should get one place in the *starostat*? Call in the workers from the Mikhelson [factory],...Tsindel... Brokhar.[9]

This was done, with the party committee's help; and 985 workers, mainly from metalworking and electrical plants, enrolled at the Institute, voted at the elections for the student council and ensured a Communist victory.

Like Ter-Vaganyan, most Communists who were students in 1917 quickly left higher education for full-time political work or the Red Army. There was a general outflow of students in 1918 and 1919, as a result of Civil War, mobilization and dispersion of the urban population; but in 1920/21, when the higher schools began to fill up again, 'bourgeois' and non-Communist students still predominated. According to Narkompros' very unreliable figures, the rabfaks in that year had 30,000 students and the VUZy 166,000.[10] Opposition parties still had a considerable following among the students. Mensheviks, SRs and Christian Socialists debated with Communists in the medical students' club of the Second Moscow University (combining the old Shanyavsky People's University and the former

Moscow Higher Women's Courses) in the autumn of 1920. In Moscow University itself, where the Mensheviks and SRs were particularly strong, 'counter-revolutionary leaflets' were distributed, and 'any academic question was translated [by the non-Communist students] into political terms: it is impossible to study freely, they said, under the pressure of a dictatorship.[11]

It was a time of rapprochement between the old students and the old professoriate. As one professor, later an emigré, recollected, 'friendly relations unheard of earlier, as it seems, were established between the professoriate and the mass of students. Not a hint of friction! The students came to us to consult with us and about their own affairs, and very often followed our advice. We also managed to restrain them from risky undertakings.' This state of affairs lasted until the autumn of 1922, when finally 'the Bolshevik blow was directed against that fine student youth. They swept them away to Solovki, to the Arkhangelsk raion, to Siberia.'[12] The blow, however, fell largely on the Cadet students. Menshevik groups were still active in Moscow and Petrograd VUZy in mid-1924, when the 'so-called student bureau of the Central Committee of the Russian Social-Democratic Workers' Party distributed leaflets against Communist party policy in the higher school, with an appeal to struggle against the party 'for a free democratic republic" '.[13]

The selection process

It was clearly difficult, if not impossible, to win over the mass of the old student body; and Communist hopes were centred on the recruitment of new working-class and Communist students. The procedure of recruitment was first worked out for the rabfaks, which, according to the resolution of the First Party Meeting on Education, should take 'only proletarians, and Communists as first priority'.[14] The system of *komandirovanie* (nomination of candidates by organizations) was introduced for rabfaks in the autumn of 1920.[15] Priority in entrance was given to workers and peasants (16 years and over, with three years working experience in manual jobs) sent by party and trade union organizations, factory committees and the soviets. The remaining places should go to individual applicants, providing they had recommendations from a government commissariat or local authority. Of more than 700 students enrolled in the Moscow University rabfak in 1920/21, 122 were sent by the metalworkers' union, 72 by the builders' union, 102 by the railways workers' and transport unions, 69 by the textile-workers' unions, 159 by leather-workers, printers etc., 127 by the Moscow Party Committee and 74 by the Narkompros department of rabfaks.[16]

The system of nomination was extended to all higher schools in 1921 and 1922. In the case of the VUZy, the main concern was the recruitment of Communists; and in the early years most of them went to the university social science schools. Some of the Communists were sent directly to the local VUZ by regional party committees; but in 1922 the majority went through the registration and allocation department of the Central Committee, which in that year sent 1,280 Communists to VUZ.[17] The Central Committee, however, does not seem to have initiated the system of nominations: its apparat simply responded to an unplanned and uncontrolled flood of individual applications and local committee nominations of Communists who wished to enter higher education.[18] Most of the Communists wished to study in Moscow, and that is where the majority of them were sent.

There were no hard and fast rules on nomination and selection of students in the early 1920s, although clearly Communists and rabfak graduates had absolute priority. In 1921, Narkompros informed the VUZy that the social science schools, in particular, should follow a 'class principle' in enrolment, recognizing 'the pre-eminent right of toilers and their children to register as students'.[19] It was apparently up to the individual VUZy to allocate places among party, soviet, Komsomol, military and trade union organizations; and to decide how many places should be left open to free individual enrolment. In 1922, the Moscow University social science school distributed all of its 1,200 places between the Central Committee, the government commissariats and the Red Army – but then enrolled an additional 600 students, most of whom were probably individual 'bourgeois' applicants.[20] In the same year, Petrograd University took in an enrolment of which one third were categorized as intelligentsia, *meshchane* (excluding government employees and their children), nobility, former officers of the Tsarist Army, merchants and priests.[21]

It was only in 1923 that the new enrolment procedures were more or less coherently formulated by Narkompros. Rabfak students had priority in entrance to VUZ; and, of the remaining places, 20% went to party organizations for distribution, 45% to the trade unions, 15% to the Komsomol, 3% to the Army (reserved for those who had fought in the Civil War), 2% to local education departments for secondary-school and technicum graduates, 10% to peasants demobilized or invalided out of the Red Army and Navy, and 10% for the free enrolment of fee-paying students.[22] It will be noted that coherence was not completely achieved, since the percentages add up to 105. The achievements in social and political terms were also mixed, since the nominating organizations tended not so much to recruit desirable students as to accept applications from people who wanted to go to VUZ. One gets some sense of the system in practice from Narkompros' instructions to the nominating organizations not to send people 'who are not needed in local work' but rather 'those who by their capacities and training can study in higher school with reasonable success. The trade union organizations must send only trade union members to VUZy, and not members of their families or clerical workers from the apparats.'[23]

Once nominated, candidates were required to go through a social selection process conducted by the local education departments with party cooperation.[24] There were, however, no official quotas for different social categories; and this filter was evidently not very effective, and may often have been purely formal. Narkompros rules required that VUZ entrants should either have completed secondary school or rabfak, or have passed an entrance examination establishing an equivalent level of competence. But this, too, seems often to have been disregarded: one candidate for the Leningrad University social science school is quoted as saying 'I want to study at the university, but I will not be able to pass the exam, since for four years I have been engaged in defence of the socialist motherland' – at which he was immediately admitted without examination.[25]

Recruitment to the rabfak had an equally haphazard quality, despite the official system of nomination. The rabfaks were less subject to 'bourgeois' infiltration than the VUZy; but they attracted a steady flow of would-be students from the countryside who had heard that there was a Soviet school for the poor and simply set off to enrol in it. Krupskaya told the story of one boy from a poor peasant family 'who didn't even know that anything called Narkompros existed in the world, but made his way to Moscow, sought out the monument to Lomonosov and sat down at its base, hoping that someone would see him there and take him where he ought to go' – that is, to the rabfak.[26] We have another account, from the early 1920s, of no less than 98 peasants who were inspired by a demobilized soldier to go to rabfak. They got documents from the local soviet for Saratov rabfak, but it turned out to be full. More than 30 of them then went on to Krasnodar, again without success. A handful then set out for Moscow without documents. They were outraged that Narkompros should refuse them placement just because they had not been formally nominated. One (who later recounted the story) asked: 'Why don't they accept me? I served in the Red Army as a volunteer; I am worthy; I have deserved the rabfak.' Finding Kalinin out of town ('a good *muzhik* – they say he satisfies all requests'), he considered other possibilities. 'What a pity Lenin is dead, otherwise I would have gone to him for help. I found that Rykov had been chosen in his place. I found Rykov's office and went directly to him.' The result was an authorization – one of the notorious *zapiski* by which official regulations were constantly evaded in the 1920s – and, finally, placement at an evening rabfak.[27]

Communist students

By the beginning of 1924, there were about 20,000 Communist students in the normal higher schools and Communist Universities of the USSR;[28] and in the higher schools of the RSFSR (excluding Communist Universities) Communists made up 7% of the total student body.[29] These students were seen as the party's future elite, and were referred to as the *smena* (those who would one day take over from the present leadership). This was a position of great responsibility and, at the same time, some political danger. The party leadership was sensitive to the mood of the *smena*, but it was also alert for possible deviation, or 'avantgardist' challenges to its own authority. 'These young people are our hope', wrote *Pravda* editorially of the Communist students. 'These young people will be the replacement of our old guard. But at the same time it is just these young people who...can much more easily than any other group (partly because of greater receptivity, but mainly because of *specialization*) be subjected to ideological influences alien to Marxism.'[30]

The higher school was alien territory, still dominated by the old professors, 'bourgeois' concepts of pure scholarship, and the apolitical or anti-Soviet mass of 'bourgeois' students. The Communist student had both to acquire an education and retain his proletarian Communist identity – to learn from the 'bourgeois' professors without being influenced by them. The Communist students were to become a 'proletarian intelligentsia'. But in the meantime they were neither intellectuals nor proletarians. Those who came from the intelligentsia had renounced their background by embracing the proletarian cause. Those who came from working-class or peasant families were separated from them by education.

To compound the psychological problem, the majority of Communists and Komsomols who were sent to higher education in the early 1920s were proletarian by conviction, but white-collar or professional in terms of origin. More than half of the 5,000 Komsomols sent to VUZ in 1924 came from white-collar or professional families, and the group contained only 450 workers and 480 children of workers.[31] In the same year a survey of Communist students in Moscow VUZy revealed that three-quarters were of white-collar origin.[32]

The dilemma was clearly set out in a letter written by a group of Communist students to Zinoviev in 1924. 'Yes, we will be a proletarian intelligentsia, we are not ashamed of that', the students wrote. But in the meantime, before the 'proletarian intelligentsia' came into being, what were they to consider themselves?

The majority of students are very young, 20–25 years old, with work experience appropriate to their age, perhaps four to six years. The majority took part in the Civil War...Of course there are only a few real workers here. You don't become a worker by serving from the age of 17 in the Army or the party. But, on the other hand, we're not intelligentsia (as people make us out to be). The devil knows what we are!

Communist students were accused of succumbing to alien bourgeois influences. But

Where would we have got a petty-bourgeois coating? Where do we run into the bourgeoisie? We live in dormitories, among other Communists. Our young people have long forgotten not only acquaintances but family, even working-class parents.[33]

Apart from the general danger of succumbing to bourgeois influences in the VUZ, there were specific ideological dangers which caused the party leadership concern. Mensheviks lectured to Communist students in the social science schools; and, according to the (Bolshevik) Central Committee in 1923, there was some recruitment of students into Menshevik organizations.[34] The former Bolshevik Bogdanov also taught in the Moscow University social science school, and Bogdanovite Marxism and 'organizational science' evidently had some appeal to the Communist students at this period.[35] Although Lenin, in particular, was peculiarly sensitive to any influence emanating from Bogdanov, the Communist students up to 1924 had not fully absorbed the nuances of Bolshevik party history, and were more likely to read Bogdanov's work out of an interest in Marxism than for any other reason. But there were exceptions: the 'Rabochaya pravda' group, described as a conspiratorial opposition faction within the party, was thought by the Central Committee to be Bogdanovite, and most of its members were students.[36]

Another identified danger – not organizational, in this case, but purely ideological – was 'Enchmenism'. Enchmen's 'Theses'[37] dealt with the new biological study of physiological reflexes, which he interpreted as discrediting all abstract thought and philosophical systems, including that of dialectical materialism. What Enchmenism meant in practice was physiological reductionism; and it is certainly true that reductionism (both physiological and sociological) was extremely attractive to young Communists in the 1920s. This was particularly evident in the realm of sexual ideology,[38] where it meant theoretical rejection of all 'psychology' and acceptance of the pure physiological imperative.

The party leadership was somewhat concerned about the sex lives of Communist students, but much more about their political attitudes. The really offensive aspect of 'Enchmenism' – and the one which caused Bukharin, on Central Committee instructions, to refute Enchmen's ideas[39] – was the implication that the Old Bolsheviks were becoming physiologically unfit to lead a revolutionary government. 'One cannot make too much of a fetish of the "old ones" ', wrote a group of Communist students to *Pravda* and the agitprop department of the Central Committee in 1924. 'Too many are already invalids'; and, as well, a high proportion of the Old Bolsheviks came from the intelligentsia, and therefore tended towards liberalism, *metsenatstvo* (condescending patronage) and dualism of theory and practice. By virtue of age and position, the Communist students concluded, the present leadership was bound to offer conservative resistance to new revolutionary initiatives.[40]

Bukharin, who was the youngest of the 'old' leadership, was particularly upset by this attack. From this time on, he regularly warned of the dangers of youthful 'avantgardism', lack of respect for experience, and undue realiance on the pure revolutionary instincts of youth; and he also disavowed much of his own earlier radicalism. Resentment was clearly evident in a *Pravda* editorial, presumably written by Bukharin, commenting on the Communist students' letter:[41]

We have already had examples of how intellectual tendencies among youth, tearing it from the Marxist umbilical cord, declared the old guard not only old but *old-fashioned*, and refused to issue it with Enchmenite 'physiological passports'. They say that the 'old ones' are not necessary for new undertakings. Sometimes voices are heard which refer contemptuously to the 'underground men' [*podpol'shchiki*], in the same way some comrades talk about '*apparatchiki*'. . .

The Old Bolsheviks' anxiety reached its height during the battle with Trotsky in the winter of 1923/24. Trotsky, because of his Civil War role, was something of a hero to Communist youth; and it was to youth that he appealed in his letter on 'The New Course'. Trotsky wrote:[42]

Only continual interaction of the older generation with the younger, within the framework of party democracy, can preserve the old guard as a revolutionary factor. Otherwise the old ones may ossify and, without noticing, become the most complete manifestation of *apparat* bureaucratism...It is absolutely not enough that the young should repeat our formulas. Youth must acquire revolutionary formulas in battle, translating them into flesh and blood, working out their own opinions and their own image, being capable of fighting for their own opinion with that bravery which is given by sincere conviction and independence of character.

For the Communist students, the call to a revolutionary struggle against bureaucratization had powerful appeal. As Preobrazhensky told the Sverdlov Communist University students, they now had the chance to apply some of the learning that they had acquired at the VUZ;[43] and Trotsky's image of Communist youth was obviously a flattering and reassuring one. Communist students took an active part in the 'discussions' between Trotsky and the Central Committee majority in 1923/24; and in the first round a large majority of the students were for Trotsky. Students at the Institute of Red Professors criticized the 'persecution' of the opposition and defended Trotsky against the attacks of the 'old men' (*stariki*) in the party leadership.[44] At the Plekhanov Institute (currently known as the Karl Marx Institute of Economics), the students resolved that 'in the field of internal party policies the Central Committee took its stand on the party apparat and the good party bureaucrat'.[45] Sverdlov Communist University students attacked Stalin for his accusations against Trotsky, and *Pravda* for partisan coverage of the debate; and agreed with Trotsky that youth was indeed 'a barometer which reacts most sensitively to party bureaucratism'.[46]

Apart from its feelings about the *smena*, the party leadership had good reason for concern about the attitude of Communist students. In 1924, about 10% of all party members were students of some sort (half of them in VUZy and Communist Universities); and students made up 25% of the entire Moscow party organization.[47] 'It was rather hurtful', as Zinoviev said, 'for the founding generation of worker–Bolsheviks to see the kind of situation there was in Khamovniki', the main student centre in Moscow; but it was also threatening, since in Khamovniki not only the student cells but the local party committee supported Trotsky.[48]

According to the early unedited reports of voting in the party in the winter of 1923/24, 32 VUZ cells with 2,790 members voted for the Central Committee line and 40 cells with 6,594 members voted for Trotsky.[49] 'It was a golden time for the Trotskyite Opposition', recalled one student observer. 'They reaped laurels at practically all VUZ meetings of Communists. The students greeted their speakers with prolonged applause. Often, in fact almost always, they won a majority in the VUZ cells.'[50] Speakers for the Central Committee line (Kalinin, Yaroslavsky, Kuibyshev and others) had to go through unpleasant moments at the VUZy: at the Moscow Mining Academy, for example, Kalinin was at first not even given the floor on the grounds that he was not a student.[51] During the students' winter vacation, which occurred in the middle of the discussion, there were reports that students were returning home and organizing local support for Trotsky.[52]

Trotsky's support, however, was largely confined to cells in the higher schools, the Red Army and the central government apparat; apparently even the first votes in factories and the provinces went against him. Even without arm-twisting from the Central Committee majority, this put the students in a difficult position, and by February 1924 the VUZ cells had begun reversing their original resolutions.[53] *Pravda* published an open letter from Communist students of the city of Moscow attacking Trotsky. This was periodically updated with lists of 'additional signatures' – among them those of Mekhlis and Poskrebyshev, later closely associated with Stalin, and Inessa Armand's son Alexander, who became head of the Communist students' union (*Proletstud*).[54]

At the same time, the Central Committee launched a counter-attack focussed on the Communist students' doubtful proletarian credentials. The Trotskyites, the XIII Party Conference resolved in January 1924, had 'made youth rather than the working class the barometer of the party...There is no doubt that this "opposition" objectively reflects the pressure of the petty-bourgeoisie on the proletarian party.'[55] 'Is not the "hurly-burly" of the temptations of NEP, ideological "envelopment" and so on *especially* dangerous [for the students]?' asked *Pravda*. 'Have they not less "force of resistance" to those negative influences which surround us on all sides?'[56] Zinoviev put the point most bluntly. The VUZ students of Khamovniki may have voted for Trotsky, he said, but look at their social composition: '15% former workers, 7.7% former peasants and

72.5% employees and others!!' Naturally non-proletarian student–
intellectual types had been more adept at getting into the party than
the slow but honest worker: the worker would not know to make out
his application or get recommendations, but in no time the would-be
student would have gathered his five recommendations, gone before
the committee and secured both his party membership and – as a
Communist – his ticket to higher education.[57]

In the aftermath of the leadership struggle, there was a massive
recruitment (the 'Lenin levy') of 200,000 workers into the party and
400,000 into the Komsomol. There were also purges of party cells in
government offices and higher schools. The purpose may well have
been to remove Trotsky's active supporters, but support for Trotsky
was obviously not cited as a reason for expulsion. In a number of
cases, the reason given for the expulsion of students from the party
was their social origin: a merchant's son, for example, was characterized as 'an offspring of a petty-bourgeois environment who had not
mastered the Communist line', and a social science student at
Moscow University described as an *'intelligentka'* was expelled
simply as an 'alien element'.[58]

According to one source, a quarter of all Communists in the
VUZy were purged in 1923/24.[59] It is not clear whether this includes
students in the Communist VUZy as well as the normal ones; but
the main Communist school – Sverdlov Communist University in
Moscow – suffered enormous losses. Only 290 students remained in
1924/25, as against 444 in the previous year, and even the numbers
in the working-class group had dropped by a third.[60]

The 1924 student purge

Communists were not the only students to suffer as a result of the
party discussions of 1923/24. Having drawn attention to the non-
proletarian nature of the Communist cells in the VUZy, the party
leadership turned to the student body as a whole. According to
official figures, in 1923/24, 15.3% of the students in Russian VUZy
were workers or workers' children, 23.5% peasants, 24.4% employees
and 36.8% 'others' or social aliens.[61] Such figures, of course, would
not give us a complete picture of the degree of 'Sovietization' of the
student body, even if they were more accurate than they probably
are. But it was the perception of the leadership – and of most contemporary observers – that the higher schools remained dominated
by 'old' students; and the leadership evidently felt that this 'bour-

geois' or 'philistine' influence on the Communists had been partly responsible for their supporting Trotsky.

On 26 March 1924, a special meeting of the Narkompros collegium was called at Zinoviev's request to discuss the question of a general purge of the higher schools.[62] Zinoviev attended the meeting; and it is an indication of the importance attached to the question that this appears to be the only Narkompros collegium meeting ever attended by a Politburo member in the 1920s. The meeting resolved to reduce the number of students to pre-war level by a general purge, in which each individual student would be assessed on the basis of 'academic success, social position and, for the socio-economic VUZy, political suitability'.[63]

There were clearly different opinions about the extent to which students would be purged on social and political grounds rather than academic. In the previous year (1922/23), Narkompros had already effected a considerable reduction in the numbers of students by downgrading, amalgamating or closing many small VUZy;[64] and Narkompros' and Sovnarkom's public statements on the 1924 purge implied that it was essentially a continuation of this policy, necessitated by overcrowding and low academic standards.[65]

But party organs usually emphasized the social and political purposes of the purge. For example, an early *Pravda* report described the state of affairs in one VUZ in terms of the political threat represented by socially-alien students: 'only 30% [of students] satisfied the conditions of class enrolment, and the rest were the sons of former (and now prospering) merchants and former landowners', who had got into the school either 'by using connections' or by producing forged documents and giving false information about their origins.[66] It was obvious that the task of the purge commission in this case was to remove students who were politically and socially undesirable.

Although Khodorovsky of Narkompros headed the Central Purge Commission,[67] Narkompros actually had very little control over the conduct of local purge commissions. In Smolensk, the university was purged by the local agitprop department;[68] and this may have been a general pattern. In any case, the only first-hand report of the activities of a local purge commission (in Perm) shows that the investigators were mainly preoccupied with establishing the real social position and political sympathies of the students' families and – if the family was socially or politically undesirable – the degree to which the student had repudiated his origins. The report describes the exchanges between students and investigators as follows:[69]

After introductory questions about educational background, time of entry
to VUZ and actual length of stay, and examination results, they turn to
more intimate conversation. . .

'What did your parents do before [the revolution]?'

'My father is a worker – here is proof.'. . .

'And what was he doing in 1918?'. . .

Nearby a student is remonstrating with another investigator.

'You must understand, colleague, that although my father is a merchant,
I have no kind of political ties with him. . .'

One student, the daughter of a peasant (she has the documents) studied
in Moscow in 1916–17.

'Our farm, you know, is, well, smaller than average.'

'But all the same you obviously had the means to study earlier in
Moscow. Perhaps your father has some little business, workshops?'

The purge began in May 1924 and continued, despite Narkompros' efforts to end it in August,[70] well into the autumn. Throughout
this period, a running battle was going on, as Narkompros and
Khodorovsky's Central Purge Commission tried to adjudicate the
appeals of expelled students and the counter-appeals of the commissions which had expelled them. Students besieged Narkompros
with 'fainting fits, attacks, threats and so on'.[71] Leningrad professors
petitioned successfully for the reinstatement of 50 students[72] (though
in Moscow, according to a Menshevik report, the professors had been
bought off by the promise that their own children would have equal
status with 'proletarians' in the purge[73]). The Holy Synod petitioned
for the re-admission of expelled children of priests.[74]

From local purge commissions and agitprop departments came
accusations that Narkompros was showing excessive liberalism in its
handling of the appeals. The Smolensk authorities, for example,
wrote in high indignation to the Central Committee agitprop department, 'categorically protest[ing] against the reinstatement of citizens
Senkovskaya, Yudenich and Fridman as students by the Central
Purge Commission. . .and insist[ing] that the agitprop department of
the Central Committee put pressure on the commission to change its
decision'.[75]

It was clear, indeed, that Narkompros was trying to minimize the
impact of the purge. In September, the collegium resolved

to publish a clarification in the name of Narkompros indicating that owing
to oversights on the part of some commissions reviewing the student body,
the comment 'alien element' was written on the documents of some of
those expelled. It is obvious that what was meant in these cases by the
description 'alien elements' was that these persons under the present

straitened circumstances of higher educational institutions, are the least appropriate to go through the VUZ; but the persons expelled from the VUZ are not in disgrace, and their expulsion from the VUZ does not carry with it any limitation of their rights.[76]

Not surprisingly, the collegium was unable to get this clarification endorsed by other authorities or published in the newspapers, and it appeared only in the Narkompros house journal.[77]

According to Narkompros' summary of the purge results, 18,000 students were purged in the RSFSR; and three-quarters of these were purged on academic grounds, although most expulsions occurred in 'the more sullied [*zasorennye*] and overcrowded artistic, socio-economic and pedagogical VUZy'.[78] This summary, however, scarcely told the full story. Out of over 150,000 students officially registered in Russian VUZy at the beginning of 1923/24, only 135,000 presented themselves to the purge commissions; and between May and September a further 7,000 students dropped out of school in addition to those formally purged or graduating.[79] The net result was that in 1924/25 the total student enrolment in Russian VUZy dropped to 117,485 (of whom 15,280 were new admissions);[80] while the proportion of students classified as 'others' (social aliens) dropped from 36.8% in 1923/24 to 19% in 1924/25[81] – a decline in absolute terms of 33,000.

This surely confirms the hypothesis that the 1924 purge was in practice a purge of social aliens, though it probably also had side effects which were at least partly unintentional. The purge almost certainly contributed to the leadership's disillusionment with the social science schools,[82] and the subsequent tendency for enrolment (including Communist enrolment) in engineering schools to rise. It may also have been responsible for removing a great many of the women who had entered higher education after the revolution, since most of the women were of 'bourgeois' origin. In 1923/24, 38% of all students in higher education were women; but in 1928, with a smaller total number of students, women made up only 28%.[83]

If both the purpose and the result of the purge had been to weed out socially-alien students, the party leadership should have viewed the whole undertaking in a very positive light. But this was apparently not the case: no party leader susbequently spoke favourably of the purge, Bukharin and Rykov both referred to it as something which should on no account be repeated,[84] and Narkompros spokesmen repeatedly implied that it had been an unmitigated disaster.

The reason was probably that the process of purging had demonstrated the enormous problems of classifying adolescents and young adults in terms of social class, especially when this classification was also intended to discriminate between those who were sympathetic to the Soviet regime and those who were hostile. In general, the Bolsheviks distrusted class classifications based on social origin, preferring to use the criterion of 'basic occupation'.[85] But most of the students had no basic occupation, and employment before entering higher education often bore little or no relationship to any plausible class identification. Many students worked in government offices in order to support themselves during their studies: were they to be classified as 'employees', even if they came from working-class or peasant families? Secondary-school graduates from white-collar families frequently worked for two or three years as manual labourers before applying to higher education: should they be considered 'proletarian'?

The reports of the Perm purge give many examples of the almost insoluble problems confronting the investigators. If the son of a merchant or priest claimed to have broken with his father on political grounds, what proofs (or what length of experience in another occupation) were required to accept him as a politically or socially-desirable student? But perhaps the most perplexing problem of all arose from the massive occupational mobility produced by the war, revolution and Civil War. Communist workers had become white-collar administrators; other workers had returned to the villages; peasants conscripted into the Tsarist or Red Army had drifted into casual work in the towns; some former nobles were no doubt working as nightwatchmen and their wives as cleaning-women. The case of one Perm student epitomized the problem: her father had been a metalworker before the war; then a baker; then a white-collar employee, first of the White government in Siberia and then of the Communist government; then an employee of the American Relief Association; then unemployed for a year; and finally the business manager of a private entrepreneur.[86] Was she, as she claimed, proletarian? Or white-collar? Or – since her father had worked for the Whites and for foreigners, and was currently employed in a responsible position by a Nepman – was she really a social alien?

Everyone involved in the work of the purge commissions must have become aware of these problems. But there was a further reason for disenchantment with the purge: in statistical terms, its results seemed literally too good to be true. During 1923/24, Russian VUZy lost almost 49,000 students through drop-out, graduation and the purge. Yet on the basis of the official figures it can be calculated that *no* employee students, and only a small number of working-class students, dropped out, graduated or were purged in the course of the year.[87] Assuming that both groups must have had a substantial drop-out (as they did in all other years), as well as losing some students through graduation and the purge, two conclusions could be drawn. Either the data was totally worthless (which in itself would be disappointing, after individual interviewing of 135,000 students to determine their social origin); or, more probably, the ranks of working-class and employee students in 1924/25 included large numbers of students formerly classified as 'others', social aliens, who had transferred, bribed or forged their way to a better social status.

Communist and Komsomol students after the purge

The Trotskyite discussions and subsequent purge left Communist students a prey to confusion and self-doubt. 'We can't show ourselves anywhere', a group of students wrote to Zinoviev.[88]

> Those lads who once, when they were very young, gave out leaflets or did some small thing in other parties are feeling particularly bad...This letter is not written by such people, but we can't bear to look at their bewildered faces. It's a shame – they are good Communists. The main thing is that the lads are extraordinarily upset. Everyone has stopped studying, at least one notices a great slackening off. *Many* people are now giving up serious study. Many are distraught, thinking that they, who have linked their whole life with the revolution and the party, are being discarded.

Despite an intensified effort to recruit Communists to higher education from 1924, the cloud hanging over Communist and Komsomol students was not entirely dissipated during the following three years. Zinoviev had suggested that these students had been corrupted by the 'petty-bourgeois environment' of the VUZ, and this theme was taken up in the campaign against '*Eseninshchina*' of 1926 and 1927. The label of *Eseninshchina* was attached to manifestations of youthful moral degeneracy after the suicide of the poet Esenin at the end of 1925. It covered sexual promiscuity, drunkenness, hooliganism and suicide based on romantic disillusionment with the revolution.[89] As a group, students in higher education were thought to be particularly vulnerable to *Eseninshchina*, but the criticism was primarily directed towards Communist and Komsomol students.

At one level, the official campaign was simply intended to correct the belief, common among revolutionary youth, that the revolution meant not only liberation but license in the sphere of sex and morals. But, at another level, moral degeneracy of young Communists was clearly being linked with Trotskyite influence. The link was made most explicit in a sensational and widely discussed novel by Sergei Malashkin, *Luna s pravoi storony*, published in 1926.[90] Malashkin's novel showed the corruption of a young Komsomol girl under the influence of a group of Communist students of non-proletarian origin, whose leader was both a Trotskyite (clearly identified as Jewish) and an advocate of free love. Communist students, of course, protested that no such 'Athenian nights' of drug-taking and promiscuous sex as were described by Malashkin went on in their dormitories. Radek – one of the Opposition leaders – protested at the implication that Trotskyites, and specifically *Jewish* Trotskyites, were responsible for the moral degeneracy of Russian working-class student youth.[91] But if anything the Opposition protests tended to reinforce the officially projected image of Communist student degeneracy. The Opposition did not deny that students were degenerate, but explained it as a product of justified political disillusionment with a degenerating party leadership: in Radek's words, 'it is not the thermometer which is to blame'.[92]

Leaving aside the question of sexual morals, there is in fact some indication of political disillusionment among Communist students. Radek was probably right when he said that young Communists looked back to the Civil War as a period of heroic endeavour, and tended to regard NEP as a somewhat shameful retreat from revolutionary ideals.[93] Komsomol students, according to one apparently non-partisan observer,

sometimes see the difference between the students' standard of living and that of an employee, especially one in a responsible position, as a social injustice which the revolution could not correct. On that soil grows scepticism, lack of belief in the success of our work of construction – in a word, a mood which really comes wholly under the rubric of 'What did we fight for?'[94]

Those who suffered most acutely from this kind of disillusionment, according to the writer, were working-class students who felt that they had become déclassés by going into higher education.

The New Opposition of 1926/27 apparently directed its appeal mainly to young workers rather than students.[95] But the Opposition's condemnation of NEP, particularly on the grounds of growing social inequality and continuing adolescent unemployment, probably did arouse a response among the students, especially when it was coupled with recommendations for improving the material conditions of student life and diminishing the ideological spoonfeeding of Komsomols and students.[96] As in the earlier Trotskyite discussions, the Komsomol Central Committee showed clear Oppositionist tendencies.[97]

Among Communist students, overt support for the Opposition was below 10% in all reported cases,[98] but the VUZ performance was still considered sub-standard. 'Neither wild underground work, which the oppositionists carried on in lecture-rooms and dormitories, nor "appearances" by the "leaders" helped', reported the student journal. 'All their techniques proved ineffective. Not one student cell went Trotskyite. . .' But even in this report there was a note of doubt:

Of course a hundred oppositionists among 1,800 Communists of the cell (as there were in, say, the First Moscow University or the Plekhanov Institute) do not present any threat to the party. But if we compare these big VUZ cells with the factory giants, where at best the opposition picked up pitiful ones and twos, we will see that the opposition found a certain response in the VUZy, although an insignificant one.[99]

The party leadership of 1926/27 clearly continued to hold the suspicion (expressed by Zinoviev in 1924) that student Communists and Komsomols were not truly proletarian – even though at the same time it was following a policy of 'Sovietizing' higher education by admission of 4–5,000 Communists per year.[100] The suspicion was probably justified. While the 1927 Party Census showed that 54% of Communists currently studying in all types of educational institution had entered the party as workers and only 24% as employees, the 8,396 Communists who had completed higher education as of January 1927 seem to have been an overwhelmingly white-collar group: 7,669 (91%) had entered the party as employees.[101]

The leadership's suspicion is most clearly evident in the policy of restricting admission of Komsomol students to the party. For purposes of party admission, students were classified as white-collar ('employees') regardless of social origin.[102] The student journal, which disapproved of this policy, published a short story in which a fictional working-class Komsomol student protested in the following terms:

What kind of strange line is this? They keep jabbering and talking about worker promotion [*vydvizhenie*], but once they've promoted a worker that puts the lid on him! What kind of stupidity is this? Does the party really need only workers from the bench? And if I am also a worker, who went cold and hungry and have now studied to become an engineer or a teacher, am I no longer needed?...What is this? Does it mean that to get into the party I have to ask to be sent back to the factory? Work at a lathe? What the hell did we sit in the rabfak for, why the devil did we waste all our youth on books?! What am I meant to do, go back to the factory?[103]

The answer, as given in the same issue of the journal by a spokes-man for the Central Committee agitprop department (and attacked by a Komsomol in the following issue[104]) seemed to be yes. The higher schools trained specialists, the students were told, but they were not a suitable environment for the training of Communists. The VUZ Komsomol organizations 'cannot be called a reserve or future *smena* for the party'.[105]

At the same time, Communist and Komsomol students had problems within the higher schools. Their extra-curricular responsi-bilities were much greater than those of non-party students, and their average academic performance seems to have been worse. 'The lads feel themselves to be the salt, if not of the earth, at least of the VUZ', wrote one observer. 'They are more preoccupied with affairs of "state importance" than with academic matters and, regarding swotting with contempt, miss seminars and lectures without trying to make up the work.' When they did attend seminars, the non-party students had their revenge: 'the more literate students, having more time and to some extent getting material support from their families, "make mincemeat" of the weaker and less prepared students who have not yet learned to study, and very often these turn out to be former rabfak students, Komsomols and sometimes party mem-bers'.[106]

Party leaders often referred to the academic deficiencies of the Communist/Komsomol group, and Bukharin's comments were particularly scathing. 'We have the same picture in all our VUZy', he said in 1927, 'that our dear Communists and Komsomols do worse work...than the non-party people...Twenty thousand times we have raised this question at party meetings, and still have not made any real impact.'[107]

Recruitment to higher education after the purge

The system of nomination and social selection remained in force in 1924 and 1925, with rabfak graduates and Communists taking an increased share of the places, and the total number of admissions beings sharply reduced.[108] But in 1925 the leadership's attention shifted to the quantity and quality of Soviet VUZ graduates. In

1923/24 – with a total of more than 150,000 students in higher education in the RSFSR at the beginning of the academic year – only 7,611 students graduated. The next year the number rose to 15,085.[109] But this was still a very small output; and, in the opinion of Vesenkha – the main employer of engineering graduates – it was also of very low quality.

In 1925, Vesenkha provoked a major reassessment of the question of higher education by requesting permission to send students abroad for engineering training. Vesenkha's position was that Soviet VTUZy under Narkompros direction were incapable of supplying graduates of the appropriate quality. A government commission, set up under Rykov's chairmanship to investigate the whole question of specialist training, was less critical of Narkompros but agreed on the need to raise academic standards in higher education.[110] The result was an important change in Soviet priorities: from 1926, academic criteria had equal or greater weight in admissions to higher education than the established socio-political criteria.

In VUZ recruitment, this meant abandonment of the system of nomination and the introduction of entrance examinations. From the autumn of 1926, the majority of new entrants came on the 'free enrolment', that is, as individual applicants who had not been nominated by any organization. Entrance privileges were reserved only for a few groups: national minorities, Red Army and Navy nominees, children of specialists (reflecting the concern for academic performance) and rabfak graduates.[111] But the rabfak graduates, who had hitherto been admitted automatically, were now required to pass a final examination at the rabfak before being admitted to the VUZ.[112] Other applicants were selected on the basis of competitive written and oral examinations conducted by the higher schools, although they still needed the approval of the social selection commissions.

The new procedure was highly praised by the professors, while some party spokesmen expressed the fear that it would tend to exclude working-class applicants from higher education.[113] In fact, the working-class percentage in admissions did drop slightly in 1926; and Russian VUZy admitted 9,000 white-collar and intelligentsia students out of a total of 20,000.[114] But in the 1927 admissions the working-class percentage rose again, exceeding the level of 1925.[115]

Taking the 1924/25 to 1927/28 period as a whole, the tendency was for working-class, Communist *and* white-collar percentages to rise, while total enrolment dropped from 117,000 in the RSFSR in

1924/25 to 107,000 in 1927/28.[116] The annual intake into higher education was around 20,000, of which 5–6,000 entrants per year were working-class and 4–5,000 Communist.[117] The working-class percentage of all students rose from 20.7 in 1924/25 to 26.5 in 1927/28. Over the same period, white-collar students rose from 35.8% to 39.4%, Communists from 10.1% to 17.1%, and Komsomols from 9.5% to 20.1%. The group of 'others' dropped from 19% to 9.7%. Peasants, at a more or less constant 24% of the student body, declined in absolute numbers.[118]

In the latter years of NEP, discrimination in admissions to higher education cut two ways. The examination process presumably favoured white-collar applicants and put lower-class applicants at a disadvantage. But the social selection process continued to discriminate against white-collar applicants, especially if they were secondary-school graduates applying to the VUZy of Moscow and Leningrad. In 1927, for example, working-class and peasant applicants to higher education, both in the capitals and the provinces, had a 1 in 2 or 1 in 3 chance of being admitted. But white-collar applicants – a much larger group – had a 1 in 5 chance of success in the provinces and a 1 in 10 chance in the capitals, while applicants classified as 'other' had zero chance in Moscow and a 1 in 16 chance elsewhere.[119] In 1927, the Timiryazev Agricultural Academy in Moscow accepted almost all *non*-secondary-school applicants who passed the examination, as well as a number of workers and peasants (including working-class and peasant secondary-school graduates) who failed; but only half of the white-collar secondary-school graduates who passed the examination were successful in gaining admission.[120]

There was a further dimension of economic discrimination. Tuition fees, which were in practice required of white-collar and 'bourgeois' students from high-income families, were paid by 14% of students in Russian VUZy in 1926/27; and the percentage was higher in the prestige schools of the capitals.[121] Stipends were theoretically available to all working-class and peasant students, as well as to others of outstanding academic merit.[122] But in practice it was a great advantage, and sometimes a necessity, for students to have an additional source of support. In the first half of the 1920s, many students had outside jobs.[123] But in the later period this seems to have been less common, and a large number of students seemed to have received some support from their families.

The low budgetary allocation for student stipends was a source of constant complaint: according to Narkompros spokesmen, this was responsible not only for working-class drop-out but also for the high incidence of physical illness and nervous breakdown and possibly even for manifestations of political disillusionment and moral degeneracy. Lunacharsky claimed that 'nowhere in the world is there such a poverty-stricken student' as in the Soviet Union (though on second thoughts he added that perhaps 'Chinese students are still poorer').[124] A speaker at the Communist Academy debate on youth reinforced the point with a story of a 'comrade [who] was on all the fronts [in the Civil War], and now...dies of existence on a state stipend and infects his other room-mates with tuberculosis'.[125] The Old Bolshevik economist Larin asserted that because of low stipends and poor living conditions 'a person from the working class has in fact been almost deprived of the possibility of becoming a real specialist, a VUZ graduate. A person from the working class can in fact only enter a VUZ – and leave it a semi-invalid, without graduating'.[126]

These were polemical speeches intended to make a political point. But there is no doubt that the stipends were small, and there were not enough of them to cover all working-class, peasant and Communist students in higher education. According to figures for the RSFSR, 33,000 students (29%) were receiving state stipends at the beginning of the 1926/27 academic year, and a further 6,800 received stipends from industrial and other organizations, which were usually higher.[127] The value of the state stipends ranged from 17–20 roubles a month in the provinces to 21–25 roubles in the capitals,[128] with the minimum budget of a Moscow student variously estimated from 21–35 roubles a month.[129]

The conflicting restraints and encouragements to recruitment from different social groups did not, as one might expect, cancel each other out. Instead, they produced two distinct patterns of social recruitment, the first characteristic of the elite VUZy – the socio-economic and engineering schools of the capitals – and the second of the rest.

Pedagogical, agricultural and medical schools belonged to the non-elite category. They had comparatively large numbers of peasant and white-collar students (though few of the latter were 'bourgeois' enough to pay fees), and comparatively few Communists or rabfak graduates.[130] The percentage of students in the under-23 age group in pedagogical and medical schools was well above the norm;[131] and in these schools, more than half the students were women.[132] As a group, women students were unlikely to be Communists,[133] and likely to have completed secondary education and come from a working-class home[134] (as one observer commented, 'there is a great deal of the "ladylike deportment" [*baryshenstvo*] which the female gymnasium often strongly inculcates' in the female group[135]).

The elite socio-economic and engineering schools, which had few women students, were distinguished by high percentages of Communists, rabfak graduates, former workers and students aged 25 years or over.[136] The working-class category in these schools contained relatively few youngsters with working-class background but 'bourgeois' secondary education: it was predominantly composed of adults who came to higher education directly from industry or, if they were Communist party members, from administrative jobs. In 1927, adult workers constituted 46.7% of all admissions to engineering VTUZy and 29.7% to socio-economic VUZy.[137]

But the elite schools did not simply follow the rabfak patterns of enrolment, as the above characteristic might suggest. They also recruited fairly heavily from the 'Soviet bourgeoisie', whose children did not and could not go to rabfaks. In 1926, 20.7% of all students in socio-economic VUZy paid tuition fees, and the figure for the Moscow and Leningrad engineering schools was 18%. In contrast, the fee-paying group in pedagogical and medical schools was only 11–12%, and in agricultural VUZy as low as 7.5%.[138]

The percentage of Jewish students in socio-economic and engineering schools was also high, respectively 19.5% and 18.4% of all students.[139] Almost certainly, Jewish over-representation in higher education created resentment, especially if, as seems probable, many of the Jewish students belonged either to the Communist or the fee-paying categories.[140] Lunacharsky reported (with a mixture of indignation and embarrassment) that there were many complaints about the numbers of Jewish students in higher education. He quoted a letter from one Leningrad student suggesting that Jewish entrance to higher education should be restricted, since Jews were 'representatives of a bourgeois nation, representatives of a people hostile to us in a class sense'.[141]

In the latter years of NEP, the regime in some respects moderated the policy of social discrimination in admissions because of its concern to raise academic standards in higher education. But, as the statistics indicate, the 'elite' institutions – socio-economic and engineering schools – were already establishing a pattern of heavy recruitment of *adults* who were Communists and/or former workers. In this type of recruitment, the engineering VTUZy were overtaking the socio-economic VUZy. Since there is no clear evidence that the regime actively encouraged adult applicants to choose engineering schools, we may tentatively conclude that the trend simply reflected the inclinations and interests of the majority of former workers who decided to enter higher education.

Since working-class and Communist adult males dominated the elite institutions of higher education by the end of NEP, the regime could be reasonably satisfied with the results of the admissions policies of these schools, if not of the VUZ system as a whole. But there was little cause for satisfaction in the current output of the elite schools.

In 1925, 9.8% of all students in higher education in the RSFSR graduated. This was a low graduation rate, but what was particularly disturbing was that the graduation rate for the elite schools alone was considerably lower; 6.3% of all students in engineering VTUZy and 7.6% of all students in socio-economic VUZy graduated in 1925. In Moscow, in the same categories, graduation rates were respectively 5.1% and 3.4%.[142] For the USSR as a whole in the years 1918–28, well under 10,000 Communists graduated from higher education.[143]

Even for the *vydvizhentsy* – perhaps, particularly for this group – higher education was a leisurely process during NEP. The traditional five-year courses were rarely completed in the appointed time, and students who went through the preparatory rabfaks spent a minimum of eight years getting a degree. It was recognized that there was a problem not only in getting Communist and working-class students into higher education but also in getting them out of it. But the problem did not seem urgent until the beginning of the First Five-Year Plan, when the regime realized that, in addition to wanting 'proletarian cadres' in principle, it actually needed them in practice.

PART II

6

The 'great turning point' of 1928–1929

In March 1928, the State Prosecutor announced the discovery of a 'counter-revolutionary economic conspiracy' in the Shakhty region of the Donbass, in which engineers and other persons associated with the coal-mining industry had engaged in systematic disorganization of production at the behest of former mine owners and agents of foreign intelligence.[1] This marked the 'great turning-point' (*velikii perelom*) in Soviet policy towards education and the intelligentsia. The Shakhty engineers were essentially on trial not as individuals but as representatives of a class: in the words of one of the accused, 'all technical personnel brought up in the spirit of the old regime, with a very few exceptions, are tarred with the same brush and are equally unreliable for Soviet construction'.[2]

The trial came at a time when the regime was launching the great industrialization drive of the First Five-Year Plan, and when engineers and technical personnel were therefore of increasing importance. The clear implication of the Shakhty trial was that Soviet construction required new technical personnel – a great many new technical personnel, whose loyalty could be relied on. The class on which the Soviet regime believed it could rely was the proletariat; and the campaign against the 'bourgeois intelligentsia' initiated by the Shakhty trial was to be accompanied by a massive recruitment of workers and Communists to higher education.

Class vigilance and the Shakhty trial

The leadership's policies during NEP were on the whole designed to impose stability and social cohesion on an extremely volatile society, in which the political and social tensions of the revolution and Civil War period were barely submerged. But these policies were constantly breaking down under pressure of spontaneous and unpredictable outbursts against the 'class enemies' – kulaks, priests, speculators, intellectuals, Jews.

Cooperation with bourgeois specialists was party policy during NEP. But workers and rank-and-file Communists did not see it as 'natural' Communist policy, and even the leadership usually justified it on grounds of expediency rather than principle. At factory level, it seemed more natural to regard the chief engineer – often the sole remaining representative of the pre-revolutionary bosses after the flight of the owner and the expulsion of unpopular foremen – as a class enemy rather than an ally. *Spetseedstvo* (specialist-baiting) was endemic in the NEP factories, although it was often rebuked by higher authorities: in 1926, for example, the Vesenkha newspaper ran a series of articles criticizing the Communist director of the Vakhitov soap factory in Kazan – a factory with a proud Civil War tradition of worker self-management and armed resistance to the Whites – for driving out a number of engineers by his contemptuous attitude to 'bourgeois', degree-holding specialists.[3]

Working-class resentment of the specialists was often associated with resentment of their material privileges and higher standard of living. This attitude was particularly clearly expressed in 1931 by a working-class speaker who can scarcely be accused of political opportunism, since her comments on the specialists immediately followed a denunciation of the regime for starving the workers. Lunacharsky, she noted, was trying to rehabilitate the bourgeois scientific workers.

But apparently Ramzin [chief defendant in the Industrial Party trial] said that he lived in the best possible material conditions, yet at the same time he was a wrecker anyway. It doesn't matter what privileges you give them, it's just like the proverb: 'No matter how well you feed the wolf, he still looks to the forest.' If our scientific workers do not have the proletarian sensitivity, the working-class feelings of our workers on production,...then no matter how we feed our scientific workers, they will not help us if they do not want to help our socialist construction. Those who are with us are with us, but those who are alien will not come with us, no matter what privileges you give them.[4]

In the 1920s, many specialists experienced a mixture of local harassment and high-level support,[5] and this lends an element of ambiguity to the interpretation of Soviet policy which is illustrated in the case of V. V. Oldenberger, chief engineer of the Moscow water authority in the early 1920s. Oldenberger committed suicide under harassment from Soviet officials; but, after his death, the state brought criminal charges against the officials concerned. A Soviet historian tells this story as an example of Communist commitment to cooperation with non-party specialists, while Solzhenitsyn uses it to illustrate the ingrained hostility of Communists towards the intelligentsia.[6] Both versions are surely correct: Communist policy was conciliatory, but Communist emotions were often hostile.

The leadership, moreover, was not totally consistent in its defence of the bourgeois specialists. The campaign against Trotsky in 1923/24 hovered on the brink of appealing to working-class anti-intellectualism; and at its height we find *Pravda* reporting the trial of a Professor Kler, accused of giving information on the platinum industry to French capitalists.[7] There were a number of other such cases in the 1920s, both at central and local level;[8] and at least some of them seem to have been organized as 'show trials' – that is, trials which were primarily intended to convey a political message rather than bring specific offenders to justice.

The Shakhty trial, however, was a show trial on a grand scale. Discussion of its political implications began well before the trial actually opened in Moscow, late in May 1928. Party cells passed resolutions on the need for vigilance against the bourgeois wrecker. Professional organizations condemned the Shakhty wreckers and reaffirmed their own absolute loyalty to the Soviet state. In April, the practical implications of the Shakhty trial were even discussed at the joint plenum of the Central Committee and Central Control Commission.

The trial itself was held in a blaze of publicity, and with confessions from the accused. Engineers immediately understood it as an incitement to *spetseedstvo*, and they were surely right.[9] In the Vakhitov soap factory in Kazan, local officials were wary because of the recent rebuke from the Vesenkha newspaper, but this earned them another rebuke for their slowness to react to the Shakhty trial. However, when the local GPU finally got the new 'conspiracy' off the ground, it was an enormous success. Letters written by engineers to the former factory owner, Krestnikov (now an emigré) were discovered; workers in the soap factory sent Krestnikov a mocking letter commiserating with him on the failure of his revanchist plans; and Krestnikov was even mentioned *in absentia* as a co-conspirator in the second major Moscow show trial, that of the 'Industrial Party' wreckers in 1930.[10]

Thus the Shakhty trial not only unleashed and legitimized *spetseedstvo*, it also put local officials under pressure to discover comparable cases of wrecking and sabotage in their own backyard. If no wrecking was found, the local officials themselves were liable to be accused of inertia and rightist deviation.

But the impact of the Shakhty trial was not restricted to engineers.

In May 1928, Krinitsky, the head of the Central Committee's agitprop department, spelled out the implications for professionals in all spheres of education, science and culture. It was necessary to expropriate the cultural bourgeoisie – that is, the old intelligentsia – and establish proletarian hegemony in all aspects of cultural life. Communists could not be passive in the struggle:

The most dangerous distortion of the party line in cultural work, and that which most seriously disarms a Communist, comes from an opportunist, anti-revolutionary conception of cultural revolution as 'peaceful' cultural development, a process of raising the general cultural level irrespective of class war and class contradictions. This conception...does not see the fierce struggle of the proletariat against the class enemy in daily life, in the school, in art and science.[11]

This 'opportunist' conception was, in fact, almost indistinguishable from the conception of cultural revolution set forth by Lenin in some of his late writings.[12] But in some ways Krinitsky's usage was more appropriate, since he really did have a revolutionary upheaval in mind. In this book, the term Cultural Revolution will be used, as it was during the First Five-Year Plan period, to describe the process of class warfare, Communist assertiveness and challenge to established 'bourgeois' or 'bureaucratic' authorities in culture legitimized by the Shakhty trial.[13]

Leadership conflicts on education: Stalin's call for a proletarian intelligentsia

The old Left Opposition had been routed before the xv Party Congress in December 1927, but its criticisms still rankled, and to some extent the Shakhty trial and the crisis atmosphere it produced were a response to them.

In 1926/27, the Left Opposition had repeatedly accused the party leadership of bureaucratic degeneration and loss of revolutionary conviction. In foreign policy, the Opposition claimed, the leadership had brought the Chinese Communists to disaster by encouraging them to cooperate with the 'bourgeois nationalist' Kuomintang, and had put the Soviet Union itself in danger of a military intervention by the Western capitalist powers. In culture, similarly, the leadership's lack of faith in Communist strength had blinded it to the fact that 'the bourgeois attack on the cultural front is being mounted with full force, and moreover is often hidden under Soviet and even party guise'.[14]

In the summer of 1927, Stalin responded by suddenly conceding the danger of intervention, and making the counter-accusation that the Opposition was prepared to attack the government even if the nation should be in mortal danger.[15] However real the fears of intervention, the 1927 war scare certainly became a political weapon which Stalin used to advantage; and the Shakhty trial may be seen as a continuation of the same policy of rallying the party around the leadership by emphasizing the threat from internal and external enemies.

But the leadership also adopted many of the Opposition positions which it had earlier condemned. Krinitsky essentially took over the idea that the bourgeoisie had mounted an attack on the cultural front, and the proletariat must assert its primacy. The Comintern began to denounce Communist cooperation with bourgeois nationalists and Social Democrats even under Bukharin's leadership.[16] The policy of 'class against class' which was adopted in 1928 by the Comintern closely paralleled the domestic policy of Cultural Revolution.

Although the victorious leadership appeared united in the early months of 1928, there were already strains and unpublicized disagreements on basic policy issues. The two central policy questions were the speed of industrialization in the Five-Year Plan and the solution of the grain procurements crisis following the 1927 harvest. Stalin advocated high industrialization targets and coercion of the peasant 'hoarders' who were holding back grain in the hope that the state would raise its prices. He spoke of hoarding as an act of conscious political sabotage, and was soon to claim that the survival of the regime – even of the nation – in the face of foreign capitalist hostility depended on the speed with which the country could industrialize. He assumed the necessity of a radical break with past traditions and habits, aggressive party leadership, and a period of high political and social tension as the regime confronted and overcame its class enemies.

The future Right Oppositionists, Rykov and Bukharin, warned against unrealistically high industrialization targets and the alienation of the peasantry by policies reminiscent of the grain requisitioning of the Civil War period. They believed that the industrialization drive would fail if the political and social framework of NEP were destroyed; and probably, even in the early months of 1928, they feared the further consolidation of Stalin's power over the party.

By the spring of 1928, the Shakhty affair and its implications had become one of the areas of leadership disagreement. The initiative was Stalin's, not only because of his reported sponsorship of the Shakhty trial[17] but because he was the only member of the leadership with a clearly formed concept of the policy which the trial represented.

In all his speeches, Stalin took the disloyalty of the Shakhty wreckers and others like them for granted, using it simply as a basis on which to rest his practical conclusions. In the first place, he said, it showed that the capitalist powers had not abandoned their hope of overthrowing the Soviet regime. Having failed to do so by military means, they had summoned their class allies within the Soviet Union to sabotage the industrialization drive. Therefore there could be no illusions about the security of the Soviet Union: constant vigilance was necessary against the ploys of the internal and external enemies.[18]

In the second place, the Shakhty affair had demonstrated the weakness of Communist industrial managers.[19] They needed more authority and more knowledge:

In order to build, you need knowledge, you need to master science. And to get knowledge, you need to study. To study patiently and stubbornly. To learn from everybody – from enemies and friends, especially from enemies. To learn with clenched teeth, not fearing that our enemies will laugh at us, at our ignorance and our backwardness. . .[20]

Bolsheviks must master technology. It is time for Bolsheviks themselves to become specialists. In the reconstruction period, technology decides everything. And the industrial manager who doesn't want to study technology, who doesn't want to master technology, is a joke and not a manager.[21]

In the third place, it was necessary to train a large number of new specialists 'from people of the working class, from Communists and Komsomols'.[22] This was not just an industrialization imperative, but a political imperative. Since 'not a single ruling class has managed without its own intelligentsia', the Soviet working class must also create its own intelligentsia:

We don't need just any kind of commanding and engineering–technical personnel. We need commanding and engineering–technical personnel capable of understanding the policies of the working class of our country, capable of mastering those policies and prepared to carry them out conscientiously. What does that mean? It means that our country has entered the phase of development when *the working class must create its own productive–technical intelligentsia*, capable of standing up for its own interests in production, as the interests of the ruling class.[23]

Finally, the Shakhty affair had demonstrated that the VTUZy

were not doing their job properly. This point was 'sharply raised' by
Stalin during the April plenum,[24] and he developed it in his subsec-
quent report on the work of the plenum. The VTUZy were turning
out specialists who were useless on the job because 'they have studied
by the book, they are book specialists without practical experience,
they have been cut off from production'. Soviet industry needed
engineers who 'are not only strong theoretically but strong in practical experience and in their link with production'.[25]

One of the reasons, no doubt, that Stalin expressed himself with
such clarity in his commentary on the work of the April plenum was
that the plenum's own resolution was both diffuse and confused.
The inadequacy of the VTUZ training was not mentioned, although
in fact the plenum had set up a commission headed by Molotov,
Stalin's supporter, to investigate the conditions of higher technical
education.[26] But the resolution indicated that *vydvizhenie* (promotion) of workers to managerial and technical positions should be increased, and that a predominance of workers' must be assured in the
engineering VTUZy and technicums. 'Now, more than ever before',
the resolution stated, 'the party must bring forward Red proletarian
specialists to replace elements from the milieu of bourgeois specialists
which are alien to socialist construction. That is one of the basic
tasks of economic construction, and, unless it is successfully accomplished, socialist industrialization cannot be carried out.'[27]

Stalin's colleagues had reason to be startled by his new, comprehensive policy; and many of them also had reasons for dissent.
The first reason was that the campaign against the old intelligentsia
carried a threat, even to members of the party and government
leadership. In the real world, most Communist leaders were friends
and patrons of a number of 'bourgeois' intellectuals, writers and
artists. But attempts to intervene on their behalf, as Krinitsky indicated in May, would show that Communists had been 'disarmed' by
'opportunist, anti-revolutionary conceptions' of the possibility of
peaceful coexistence between the proletariat and the bourgeoisie.
Furthermore, all commissariats employed 'bourgeois' experts. These
might turn out to be wreckers (the Shakhty group had included a
member of Vesenkha's central apparat and the head of its expert
council on the coal industry, somewhat improbably linked with the
fifty rank-and-file Donbass engineers and the handful of Germans
who were also accused[28]), and their employers in turn would be
charged with insufficient vigilance. As the previous year's campaign
against the Trotskyites had shown, even former party leaders were
not immune from GPU action.

If the Menshevik emigré journal *Sotsialisticheskii vestnik* swiftly concluded that the Shakhty trial was a ploy to discredit 'Rykov and his group',[29] we may assume that the same thought occurred to members of the leadership (who were, in any case, among the journal's readers). But Molotov – who appeared obsessed with intelligentsia wrecking, and must have spent a good hour giving details from current GPU files to the First Moscow Oblast Party Conference in 1929 – drove the point home:

It is impossible to overlook yet another curious manifestation in the intelligentsia milieu. Among various [intelligentsia] representatives, especially those working on agricultural questions, you can now find open attacks on the policy of the party and the Soviet government under the guise of statements of solidarity with. . .[*sic*] 'the right deviation'.[30]

However, many of the party leaders had more specific reasons for concern about the Shakhty policy. The industrialists could scarcely be happy about the arrests of some thousands of engineers which followed the trial.[31] Both the present head of Vesenkha (Kuibyshev) and his future successor (Ordzhonikidze) warned about the dangers of encouraging *spetseedstvo*.[32] Rykov cited Lenin's view that good relations with the non-party specialists were essential, and produced documentation to show that the specialists were currently irreplaceable.[33]

There was additional cause for anxiety in the new emphasis on class selection for higher education. Over the past years, Vesenkha's concern had been the low educational level of VTUZ graduates rather than their social origins; and this still seemed to be Kuibyshev's concern in his first statement on the Shakhty affair.[34] None of the leaders, presumably, had any quarrel with the recruitment of workers to higher education – as long as they could pass the examinations. But a greatly increased recruitment of workers was likely to mean lowering admissions standards to an extent which many of the leaders found unacceptable. There was no reason to bring 'the class issue' into the discussion of specialist training, Rykov told the April plenum.[35]

The most articulate critic of the policy of worker promotion – whether through higher education or directly at enterprise level – came from Uglanov, who headed the Moscow Party Committee until his removal as a Rightist in the autumn of 1928. Uglanov's views, which provoked a number of interjections at the Moscow party plenum in January 1928, were that promotion should largely be based on educational and political qualifications rather than social

class, and that indiscriminate promotion of workers was just a way
of swelling the bureaucracy. Too many promotions meant a rate of
turnover in responsible jobs which could 'slow down the tempo of
our construction effort by thirty percent'.

The best engineering graduates should be quickly promoted into
responsible jobs, Uglanov said. But, objected one of the delegates,
'We need to take those graduates who come from the shop floor,
from the factory bench!' 'No', Uglanov answered,

That is not always the case. There are comrades graduating from VUZy
who were division commissars in the Red Army, who were presidents of
regional soviets in the first years of the revolution, and then went to
finish their studies...For us, the greatest happiness is that we have finally,
in the eleventh year of the proletarian revolution, begun to build some
elements of culture into our construction. That is also a process of promotion [*vydvizhenchestvo*], a process of cultural promotion tempered in the
proletarian revolution.[36]

The Narkompros leaders had particular reason to be disturbed by
the Shakhty policy, since their effort had always been to keep peace
with the old intelligentsia, maintain educational standards and minimize the impact of social selection on educational admissions. The
new policy, moreover, involved a direct attack on the commissariat
itself. Narkompros was severely criticized by Krinitsky at the agitprop meeting in May 1928.[37] Two months later, it was singled out
for criticism by Stalin for its handling of higher technical education.[38]

Of all authoritative spokesmen, Lunacharsky came closest to dis-
sociating himself entirely from the campaign against the old intelligentsia. After the announcement of the Shakhty conspiracy, Lunacharsky said:

I am not one of those people who willingly follow a line of suspicion,
wariness or lack of goodwill. It would now be very easy to come to the
conclusion that the Shakhty affair teaches us to intensify an attitude of
suspicion, but that would be incorrect...A general policy of this kind could
only lead us to cast off our friends and semi-friends, withdraw our sympathy from them, make them lose heart. Any change of that sort by the
regime would be disastrous for socialist construction.[39]

Not surprisingly, Lunacharsky and Narkompros quickly became
victims of a strident campaign, organized by young Communist and
Komsomol militants, against their protection and patronage of
'bourgeois specialists' in the arts.[40] But, despite Lunacharsky's

personal interest in the arts, he was really much more deeply agitated about what was happening in the schools. VUZ students were being purged;[41] and, as in 1924, secondary and even primary schools followed suit. By the autumn of 1928, expulsion or non-admission of 'socially-alien' children was a widespread phenomenon.[42] Schools felt themselves under pressure to show improved social composition (even the enlightened Moscow education department was offering free passes on the tramways to working-class children in an effort to improve the composition of some of its 'bourgeois' schools[43]); and, worst of all, purging had been encouraged by the agitprop department of the Central Committee[44] and, later, by *Pravda*.[45]

But the official endorsement of purging of schools (in contrast to VUZy) was somewhat ambiguous; and Narkompros felt able to oppose the practice in a categorical instruction that 'the expulsion of children from general-educational schools on grounds of their social origin or their parents' deprivation of voting rights...cannot be allowed under any circumstances'.[46] Krupskaya published an article in *Pravda* protesting that Communists had no right to deprive anyone of 'the right to education and development'.[47] Lunacharsky pointed out that 'nobody chooses his parents', and asked whether those 'sons of Tsarist generals holding high positions in the Communist Party' should also be expelled.[48] Skrypnik, head of the Ukrainian Narkompros, took an equally firm position: working-class quotas, he said, were 'not a class approach but a closed-shop [*tsekhovoi*] or pseudo-proletarian approach'.[49]

In defending the Narkompros position, Lunacharsky raised a question that must have been troubling many other government and party leaders: the question of legality. The current grain procurements campaign, the elimination of the NEP entrepreneurs and the post-Shakhty arrests of engineers on dubious or fraudulent charges all involved violation – or, at the very least, abuse – of Soviet laws by the regime itself. It is reported that Lunacharsky had protested against the arrest of private businessmen who had not broken previously existing Soviet laws;[50] and he was surely taking a general stand rather than a parochial one when he argued that it was against Soviet law to deprive children of the right to education. This right, he said, belonged to all children, including those whose parents had lost the right to vote. Deprivation of voting rights did not take away the right 'to drink, eat bread, sleep, educate oneself...It does not mean that the [person] must be immediately seized and sent to Narym, or subjected to the highest measure of punishment.' During the grain procurement drive in the Urals, local authorities had instructed that the children of peasant 'hoarders' should be expelled from the schools; and Lunacharsky was asked if he thought this policy correct. 'Of course it is not correct', Lunacharsky answered. 'The thing is that the basic premises of revolutionary legality are so unclear to many of our functionaries that they think they can introduce whole laws locally on their own initiative.'[51]

Training for industry: Narkompros against Vesenkha

The leaders of Soviet industry may not have shared Stalin's concern for proletarian recruitment to higher education. But on a number of other issues Stalin raised the industrialists were in basic agreement with him. They too thought that engineering education should be the first priority. They were critical of the performance of new engineering graduates in industry, and blamed Narkompros for its poor management of technical education. Indeed, when Stalin made his criticism of Narkompros in 1928, he was implicitly taking Vesenkha's side in a longstanding institutional conflict.

For a number of years, Vesenkha had been arguing that the VTUZy should come under its control and not that of Narkompros. The issue was first raised in 1925, when Dzerzhinsky, then head of Vesenkha, claimed that the low quality of engineering graduates demonstrated Narkompros' incompetence in the technical field. He argued, moreover, that the education commissariats, as republican institutions, could not provide the national leadership and coordination necessary.[52] Vesenkha had the all-Union status, political authority and financial resources to provide such leadership.

Dzerzhinsky's proposals for transfer were defeated, which Lunacharsky attributed primarily to opposition from Rykov, head of Sovnarkom and himself a former member of the Vesenkha collegium.[53] But Dzerzhinsky may also have been unwilling to push the issue too far because the industrialists as a group were not very eager to take on these new responsibilities: one of the enthusiasts for technical education whom Dzerzhinsky brought into Vesenkha reported that it was necessary to wage 'desperate struggle with the leaders of the industrial organs to make them realize the importance of supporting the VUZy and linking their work with production'.[54]

Nevertheless, the issue was raised early in 1927 once more, this time by the Russian Vesenkha.[55] Then, in the summer of 1927, Vesenkha USSR prepared a draft resolution for the all-Union Sovnarkom by which a number of higher technical schools would be declared 'all-Union institutions' (by analogy with industrial enter-prises, which were classified as of 'all-Union significance' if sub-ordinated directly to Vesenkha USSR rather than its republican or regional organs).[56] This meant that they could not, by definition, remain in the jurisdiction of republican education commissariats. The proposal seems to have made no headway in Sovnarkom, which was still headed by Rykov. But in the autumn of 1927 Vesenkha con-tinued the offensive by organizing an all-Union meeting on technical education.

The meeting was dominated by representatives of industry and pervaded by criticism of the policies and administrative practices of the Russian Narkompros. Lunacharsky and Khodorovsky spoke for Narkompros, but their tone was defensive and they got virtually no outside support. The main issues discussed were higher technical education and the training of skilled workers (worker training and the apprenticeship schools were also under Narkompros jurisdic-tion, but apparently Vesenkha took Lunacharsky by surprise on this issue, since he had come prepared to answer criticism on the non-vocational secondary school, not on the FZU[57]).

By implication, Vesenkha was challenging Narkompros' control both of the engineering VTUZy and technicums and the industrial apprenticeship schools. But evidently public discussion of these questions had been vetoed, since they were not on the agenda and Kuibyshev, in an interview with *Izvestiya*, denied that he was for 'complete takeover' of technical education by Vesenkha.[58] In fact, the meeting did pass a resolution calling for the transfer of appren-ticeship schools to Vesenkha – a proposal that (unlike transfer of VTUZy) had not been considered and rejected by Sovnarkom. But only the Vesenkha newspaper *Torgovo-promyshlennaya gazeta* reported it. Other newspapers, evidently regarding it as controversial or improper, either ignored the resolution or reported the demand for transfer as a minority opinion.[59]

The VTUZ issue was not a simple question of institutional control, but was associated with a dispute on the kind of engineers that ought to be trained. Narkompros and the engineering professors were for the 'broad' engineer on the German model, which meant in effect that they were for the type of training currently offered in the engineering schools. Vesenkha took the position that industry needed only a small number of 'broad' engineers for planning and senior supervisory positions. The majority of engineers should be trained on the 'narrow' profile to be 'specialists in a definite concrete and limited branch of industry'.[60]

Vesenkha's position could be justified in a number of different ways, and it is by no means clear that the Vesenkha leaders were thinking realistically on the issue. There was, however, a quite realistic justification, which at least some of the industrialists offered. Among the existing VTUZy, they argued, there were many upgraded technicums with low academic standards. In spite of the fact that Soviet schools were producing proportionally too many engineers and too few technicians in the 1920s, it had proved impossible to convert the low-quality VTUZy into technicums. Thus the only solution was to allow them to produce 'narrow engineers' who were in fact technicians with a fancy title, leaving the old high-quality VTUZy to turn out real engineers under a broader curriculum and a longer course of study.[61]

Stalin, evidently, was thinking on somewhat the same lines, although for him the two basic categories were VTUZ-trained engineers and *praktiki*, promoted and trained on the job. In the 1920s, almost 40% of persons holding engineers' and technicians' jobs in Soviet factories were *praktiki*, and most of these were promoted workers and foremen.[62] Stalin seems to have believed – perhaps correctly – that it was the *praktiki* who were keeping production running,[63] not the 'bourgeois' senior engineers with degrees who were rarely seen on the shop floor. When he said that VTUZ graduates should have more practical competence and acquaintance with production, he was really recommending that the engineering schools should lower their standards (which, in terms of the current debate, meant opting for the 'narrow engineer' profile) and offer the kind of training which was most accessible to worker *vydvizhentsy*.

However, Vesenkha, did not share this particular interest of Stalin's, and its advocacy of the 'narrow' profile often seemed to have quite different motivations. In the first place, Vesenkha clearly wished to embarrass the Russian Narkompros by any available means. Thus the 'narrow engineers' produced by Ukrainian technicums were highly praised at the 1927 meeting, although it was common knowledge that the graduates had not been very successful in production.[64] Similarly, Vesenkha took up the cause of Kagan-Shabshai, director of a private Electro-technical Technicum which the Russian Narkompros refused to upgrade to a VTUZ. Shabshai's technicum offered a two-year course in which students worked more than half time on production for the whole two years; and his system looked attractive to many Communists not only because of its speed and low costs but also because of Shabshai's expressed contempt for

intelligentnost'. But to the Narkompros leaders Shabshai was something of a charlatan, as well as a slightly shady NEP entrepreneur;
and, if he graduated competent engineers, it was only because he got
the bright students from the wrong social background who could not
get into the state VTUZy and technicums.[65]

Another Vesenkha argument appealed to an optimistic but un-
realistic image of the 'Soviet America' which would emerge in the
transformation of the First Five-Year Plan. The conventional wisdom of the period was that narrow specialization was appropriate
for highly developed economies and large-scale industry. Hence, the
argument went, it would shortly also become appropriate for the
Soviet Union, and the engineering schools should be reorganized
accordingly. Similar assumptions were made about Soviet labour
needs. Industrial modernization would soon eliminate the need for
workers with a medium level of skill, it was argued, despite the fact
that such workers (described as *kvalifitsirovannye*) were still the
backbone of the Soviet labour force in the late 1920s. The future
requirement would be for a few highly skilled workers to set up and
service the machines, and a mass of workers with minimal skills to
man the assembly lines in giant industrial plants.[66] The implication
was that the apprenticeship schools, graduating turners and fitters,
would become obsolete within a very few years.

In 1927/28, some apprenticeship schools were in fact being closed
down, since enterprises were feeling the financial pinch of the
'regime of economy'; and both Narkompros and the Komsomol
interpreted this in a most sinister light.[67] Their fear was that
Vesenkha would turn to the low-cost training methods offered by
the trade unions' Central Institute of Labour (TsIT); and this
fear was reinforced by the appearance of A. K. Gastev, TsIT's
director, at Vesenkha's 1927 meeting on technical education, and
the favourable response of delegates to an organized tour of Gastev's
Institute.[68]

Gastev's method of training was a short course, held outside the
factory, familiarizing novice workers with the basic physical movements involved in operating a machine or performing manual jobs
like bricklaying. Gastev's real interest was the scientific organization
of labour; and in his opinion Narkompros had not progressed from
an 'artisan' conception of labour training to a modern, scientific
one.[69] The Narkompros leaders in turn thought Gastev – originally
a metalworker, but more recently a leading proletarian poet of the
'cosmic' school – was a fantasist,[70] unable to comprehend that the
apprenticeship school gave many workers their basic general educa-

tion, and that his method of training was essentially degrading to the working class.

In 1928, Narkompros published a manifesto on labour training attacking Gastev's methods and their supporters in the trade unions and Vesenkha. Under these methods, Narkompros argued, workers were simply conditioned (*trenirovany*) to become efficient cogs in the industrial machine. If the Soviet regime abandoned the apprenticeship school and adopted Gastev's methods on a large scale, the factories would soon 'be filled with conditioned "executants", like the peasants who filled the [pre-revolutionary] Morozov and Prokhorov factories'.[71] Certainly the Soviet Union must adopt modern industrial methods, including the conveyor belt and the assembly line. But this did not mean that workers could be treated as automata. Soviet workers were members of the dictator class, and they had a right to education no matter what kind of industrial functions they performed. Adoption of Gastev's methods would mean 'the degradation of the working class into a mere labour force', that the Soviet Union was involuntarily following the example of capitalism.[72]

As one critic pointed out, Narkompros had a somewhat undifferentiated approach to the working class, and showed little sensitivity to the possibility of working-class upward mobility into white-collar occupations[73] or, for that matter, to the fact that peasants entering the industrial labour force had already achieved some upward mobility. But Narkompros' conclusions on the importance of maintaining the industrial apprenticeship school with its general-educational functions had some powerful support. Stalin, Lunacharsky reported, was inclined to favour the apprenticeship schools – not for the same reasons as Narkompros, but on the grounds that, given the inadequacies of the general-education system, they were useful as channels for upward mobility.[74]

The political resolution of the education conflicts

Throughout the first six months of 1928, Vesenkha and Narkompros lobbied energetically for the support of other Soviet institutions on the issues of control of the VTUZy and the 'narrow' engineer, and sought the widest possible publicity for their views. *Pravda*, among other publications, solicited the opinion of interested persons (students, professors, engineers, workers, industrial managers) and published a broad and apparently non-partisan selection. The issues were argued in terms of industrialization imperatives, and there was almost no mention of the Shakhty trial or the question of social discrimination in admissions. Khodorovsky likened the atmosphere to that of a 'bourgeois election campaign'.[75]

It became clear during the discussion that very few outsiders (and by no means all industrialists) supported the Vesenkha leadership on the question of control of the VTUZy. The engineers' union resolved in May that transfer of VTUZy to Vesenkha was 'lacking adequate justification in principle'.[76] The Section of Scientific Workers voted against transfer, emphasizing that 'the view which is gaining ground in various economic organs that study plans need radical revision might lead to a complete disorganization of the scholarly life of the higher school'.[77] The Komsomol concluded that transfer was a 'bureaucratic' solution.[78] Even the radical students' union (Proletstud) decided against Vesenkha, though the students were also extremely critical of Narkompros. At meetings held in 'an extremely tense atmosphere' at the end of April, Vesenkha and Narkompros spokesmen put their cases to the students; and 'the overwhelming majority of [student] speakers...categorically objected to transfer of VTUZy to Vesenkha. The speakers emphasized that so far the economic organs (and Vesenkha in particular) had paid very little attention to the higher technical schools'.[79]

However, control of the VTUZy was also one of the questions to be discussed at the July plenum of the Central Committee, when Molotov's commission presented its report on the state of higher technical education. Molotov himself obviously supported Vesenkha's claims: he pointed out that the problem was to train specialists for the national economy, and asked: 'After all, who understands the economy better, Narkompros or Vesenkha?'[80] Stalin evidently took the same view, since he wrote after the plenum that, 'We are training cadres badly in our higher schools...The facts showed that Narkompros was not coping with this important task. We have no grounds for thinking that Narkompros, left to its own devices, will be able to cope with this task in the near future.'[81]

The opposing position was, of course, argued by the Narkompros representatives invited to the plenum, Lunacharsky and V. N. Yakovleva, with Yakovleva asserting in her usual blunt manner that transfer of control was 'a notion dreamed up in offices by idle people from Vesenkha'.[82] The Ukrainian Commissar of Education, Skrypnik, who was a Central Committee member, supported the Russian Narkompros:[83] his commissariat's interests were also at stake and, in addition, the Ukrainians were worried that Russian might become the language of instruction in any Ukrainian engineering school transferred to the control of the All-Union Vesenkha.[84]

The Narkompros position was also supported by the emerging Right Opposition, led by Rykov, Bukharin and Tomsky. According to Stalin's later account, the Rightists offered 'desperate resistance' to the idea of transfer.[85] In the long run, this was definitely an association which the Narkompros leaders would have done well to avoid; and Lunacharsky (although not Krupskaya[86]) seems to have realized this. But its immediate effect was to produce a compromise resolution. According to a report in the Trotsky Archives, the first vote produced a two-thirds majority *against* transferring all VTUZy to Vesenkha, with Rykov leading the majority and Stalin voting with the minority.[87] A subsequent vote produced the compromise decision (this time with the Right voting in a minority against it[88]) to transfer six VTUZy and five technicums to Vesenkha USSR on an experimental basis.[89]

It is highly unlikely that most members of the Central Committee saw themselves as casting a factional vote on the issue of transfer, for Narkompros' two-thirds majority on the original vote must have included many regional party secretaries or even industrialists who were never otherwise linked with the Right.[90] It is probable, for example, that Kirov, the Leningrad party secretary, voted against Vesenkha, since the plenum's final decision left the prize Leningrad VTUZ (the former Imperial Polytechnical Institute) in Narkompros' hands; but this would scarcely have been a vote for the Right and against Stalin.

For Stalin, the question of transfer must have been secondary. What was important to him was that workers and Communists should be sent to engineering schools, and that the curriculum should be adapted to their experience and needs. On these issues, the July plenum produced the desired results, apparently without effective interference from the Right or open objections from Narkompros. The autumn admissions to VTUZy were to include 65% workers, and special preparatory courses were to be established to facilitate their entry. A thousand experienced Communists were to be mobilized for study in the VTUZy; and the rabfaks were to take in three thousand workers over and above their normal admissions. New VTUZy were to be set up (under Vesenkha's control) for the training of 'narrow' engineers; and all VTUZy were to increase the amount and seriousness of practical work on production required of the students.[91]

With the great *vydvizhenie* (which is discussed in detail in Chapter 9) set in motion by the decisions of the July plenum, some of the most important policy conflicts were decided. But other questions remained negotiable; and, for Narkompros, the immediate problem was to discover how much negotiating room remained.

It was clear from the summer of 1928 that Narkompros' political fortunes would henceforth be linked to some degree with those of the Politburo Right. Lunacharsky himself did not belong to the Right Opposition:[92] but his attitude to the Shakhty trial, and indeed the commissariat's whole orientation on social issues, were said to show 'rightist tendencies'. In addition, the Right Opposition had given its support to part of the Narkompros platform, while Stalin had supported the opposing position of Vesenkha. In the autumn of 1928, the Right Opposition lost a crucial political base when Uglanov was removed from the leadership of the Moscow party organization. The renovation of the Moscow organization was supervised by Molotov, one of Narkompros' most consistent opponents.

But Narkompros was not the only institution weakened by association with the Right. The trade union leadership, under Tomsky, was in an even more vulnerable position. Narkompros had a long-standing disagreement with the union leaders on the value of Gastev's methods and the industrial apprenticeship school (FZU). This was exacerbated in June when, administering 'an exceptionally severe rebuff' to Lunacharsky, the union leaders agreed to support Vesenkha's demand for control of labour training.[93] The issue of control may, as Gastev claimed, have been already decided at this time,[94] although it was many months before such a decision was formally ratified or implemented. But in any case, Narkompros and the Komsomol regarded Gastev's challenge to the FZU form of training as a still greater threat than Vesenkha control. Their strategy in the autumn of 1928 was to attack the trade unions, as the main advocates of Gastev's methods and protectors of his Institute of Labour.[95]

Narkompros based its attack on very basic principles of trade unionism, perhaps hoping to convince a future trade union leadership to reverse Tomsky's policies. The trade unions represented workers, Lunacharsky argued; and if they really had the workers' interests at heart they would allow them to be educated in the apprenticeship schools instead of subjecting them to 'conditioning' by Gastev's methods. Moreover, they would not make deals with management at the expense of ordinary workers, even if the management leaders were also Communists. The unions 'must stand up for the interests of the working class, as a complex of living individuals, while the managers must look on the working class as a source of labour power'. Conflict was inevitable and appropriate. If the unions were not able to fulfil their function 'as a counterweight to the industrialists', they might as well be abolished.[96]

The present union leadership was understandably offended. 'We ask', wrote a commentator in *Trud*, the trade union newspaper, 'how these accusations differ from the talk from the Trotskyite Opposition of blessed memory on the degeneration of the trade unions, the refusal of unions to defend the workers' interests, and so on.'[97] Yet Narkompros' attacks were probably less politically damaging than those of the Komsomol, whose campaign against the trade unions had some encouragement from Stalin.[98]

The Komsomols' main accusation was that the trade unions were 'bureaucratic'. But this covered some very specific grievances relating to adolescent employment as well as to the apprenticeship school and Gastev's methods. When the attack reached its climax at the Eighth Congress of Trade Unions in December 1928, labour training was one of the central issues, and the Komsomol mood was extremely belligerent. The unionists were also angry: one delegate interrupted I. P. Zhdanov, a Komsomol specialist on labour and education, with the cry: 'Who gave you the right to cast absolutely unjustified aspersions on the trade union movement?'[99] Tomsky insulted the 'lousy FZU school' and suggested that the Komsomols were trying to destroy him politically.[100]

The Congress was Tomsky's last appearance as trade union leader, and it was also the end of the public battle on labour training. In March, the apprenticeship schools were quietly transferred to Vesenkha's control.[101] This, however, did not entirely determine the outcome of the battle, since Vesenkha had not yet indicated what its policy on labour training would be. Nor, rather surprisingly, did it mark Vesenkha's total victory over Narkompros, since the issue of control of the VTUZy remained unresolved.

The July plenum of 1928 had transferred only a small number of VTUZy to Vesenkha, but they were of the highest quality. This gave Vesenkha an edge in the competition with Narkompros which the July plenum had recommended; and Vesenkha also expected that its VTUZy would be substantially better funded. At first these expectations were disappointed. As one Vesenkha official indignantly reported:

All the Akaky Akakieviches of the Finance Commissariat had acquired copies of the [July 1928] plenum resolution, and had found in it an instruction that Vesenkha was not to go beyond the limit of the Narkompros budget. They kept harping on this, and trying to bring us down to the level Narkompros had been on. We had to make a lot of fuss and appeal to some of our most high placed and responsible men.[102]

The appeals were ultimately successful, and Vesenkha's VTUZy received a larger budgetary allocation than those of Narkompros in 1929.[103] But the Vesenkha department administering the VTUZy (Glavtuz) performed very poorly. It was no more successful than Narkompros in dealing with the industrial enterprises which had to arrange students' practical work, and it fought with other departments of Vesenkha.[104] The Rector of Moscow Higher Technical School, which was Vesenkha's prize VTUZ, spoke of the Vesenkha administration with contempt;[105] and it received a lot of criticism in the student press.

VTUZ administrators and professors, judging the issue of control still open in the early months of 1929, tried to keep a foot in both camps by attending meetings of both Vesenkha and Narkompros departments, regardless of their formal affiliation.[106] As late as the summer of 1929, Narkompros was still staunchly insisting that it was winning the competition for best VTUZ administration, and that the Vesenkha engineering schools should therefore be returned to it.[107]

It was perhaps a measure of the incompetence of Vesenkha's department that the issue of VTUZ control remained undecided even after the Narkompros leadership lost all political credit. In the winter of 1928/29, Narkompros' standing plummeted as Stalin finally moved against the leaders of the Right Opposition. The Right's defeat in the Politburo in February was made public at the April (1929) plenum of the Central Committee.[108] Lunacharsky became the target of slanderous rumours and petty harassment.[109] In March, his erstwhile friend Maxim Gorky attacked him in the pages of *Pravda*, suggesting that on questions of 'science and labour' Lunacharsky's views were not in accord with Stalin's.[110]

Anticipating an early departure from their posts, the Narkompros leaders became, if anything, more belligerent in defence of the educational causes they espoused. They launched a campaign to raise the educational budget, with Lunacharsky promising to 'use all methods, the most extreme loyal and legal methods possible' to achieve this end.[111] They pressed their attack on the question of social discrimination in schools, challenging the ambiguous stand of the Central Electoral Commission on the educational rights of children whose parents had been deprived of the vote in the forthcoming soviet elections.[112]

In February 1929, Lunacharsky wrote a formal letter of protest to Stalin on social discrimination in the schools. Among the 'sorest points' of the education system, he said, were

the various 'purges' which are now being conducted on every possible pretext in various educational institutions. Sometimes they expel the children of *lishentsy* straight after some commission has deprived the parent of voting rights; sometimes they get rid of them for, as they say, hiding their parents and social origins, in cases where somebody has not stated in his official documents that he is related to a priest or that he is an aristocrat by birth...Do we suddenly have to throw out these young people who are already studying, when they have done nothing at all, just because of the problematical guilt of their parents? Personally, I have grave doubts.[113]

Stalin did not respond to this letter; and sometime in the spring of 1929 Lunacharsky and a number of members of the Narkompros collegium handed in their resignations.[114] It is reported that the resignations were motivated not only by the leadership's failure to act against social purging but also by the loss of the six VTUZy and the apprenticeship schools to Vesenkha: the collegium members 'consider[ed] that Narkompros was an inferior organism after such an amputation and evaluat[ed] it as lack of trust'.[115] The old collegium remained on the job until the summer, when most of them departed on vacation. In September 1929, the resignations of Lunacharsky, Yakovleva and Svidersky (head of the Narkompros arts administration) were formally announced, together with the appointment of A. S. Bubnov as the new commissar.[116]

This was the end of a chapter in Soviet cultural history. With Lunacharsky's departure, the Russian Narkompros lost its special character as a 'commissariat of enlightenment', dedicated to high ideals, a bridge between the old intelligentsia and the regime, a stalwart defender of its own principles and institutional interest. Yet the 'great turning-point' in educational policy had really come earlier, with the decision of the July plenum of 1928 to embark on large-scale recruitment of workers and Communists to higher technical education. The implications of that decision were still being worked out at the time of Lunacharsky's resignation; and it was not until the next year that it was possible to draw up a balance sheet of gains and losses for the old Narkompros policies.

Narkompros lost the battle for the VTUZy at the end of 1929; and this meant an absolute, though relatively short-lived, victory for the principle of narrow specialization which Narkompros had opposed.[117] But its central labour-training principle – general education for young workers in the factory apprenticeship school – was accepted completely by Vesenkha in the middle of 1929.[118] On the issue of social purging in the schools, to quote Lunacharsky's own words early in 1930, 'I won my point – true, it was after my transfer to other work, but I won my point.'[119] In January 1930, the Russian Sovnarkom ruled that no child should be expelled from school because of his social origin or parents' deprivation of voting rights and directed that all purges of primary and secondary schools should immediately be halted; and shortly afterwards the Central Executive Committee of the All-Union Congress of Soviets outlawed a number of punitive measures commonly taken against the families of those who were deprived of voting rights, including expulsion of their children from school.[120]

This last victory was perhaps some compensation for the fact that the reputation of the former Narkompros leadership was steadily sinking. Bubnov, the new commissar, invariably characterized the old leadership as 'rightist'; and the militants of Cultural Revolution were beginning to speak not only of Lunacharsky's 'rightism' but of his 'rotten liberalism'. The nadir was reached late in 1930 – appropriately enough, in the context of the Industrial Party trial, which reiterated the themes of the earlier Shakhty trial.

The prosecutor in the Industrial Party trial, A. Ya. Vyshinsky, was also the head of Narkompros' administration of technical education. Appointed to this position in the summer of 1928,[121] he had superintended the reorganization of VUZy and VTUZy according to the directives of the July plenum. This gave him good reason to dislike both the 'bourgeois' professors and his Narkompros colleagues, who had actively or passively resisted the reorganization. At the end of 1930, in a commentary on the Industrial Party trial, he pointed to a link in the conspiratorial chain which had hitherto been overlooked – the old leadership of Narkompros.

The wreckers had opposed the reorganization of the VTUZy, Vyshinsky wrote, and they had argued against the 'narrow engineer' profile and increased emphasis on practical work. They had published their opinions in a book called *What Kind of Engineer Should Our VTUZy Prepare?*[122] (This book, though Vyshinsky did not go further than giving its title and date, had been a programmatic statement of the Narkompros position in its debate with Vesenkha, published by Narkompros in 1928 and edited by Khodorovsky, Vyshinsky's predecessor as head of the administration of technical education.) The book was one of 'those historic documents on which the investigative process and judicial prosecution of the Shakhty wreckers was based', and it demonstrated

that the voices raised two or three years ago against our general line in the matter of reorganization of VUZy and VTUZy. . .were voices arising from a single centre, which was trying in an organized and systematic manner to influence public opinion with the aim of sabotaging the reorganization of the higher school, just as they sabotaged – or, more exactly, tried. . .to sabotage – the whole of our socialist construction.[123]

Objectively, therefore, Narkompros had been the centre of bourgeois intelligentsia wrecking and the chief impediment to educational reform. Vyshinsky's innuendo was unusually pointed, but the impression that Lunacharsky and the old Narkompros leadership had been not only wrong but somehow tainted with disloyalty persisted throughout the Stalin period. This kind of taint could have very serious consequences during the purges. Lunacharsky, who died at the end of 1933, escaped with only a damaged posthumous reputation and a funeral oration by Vyshinsky almost ignoring his services to Soviet education and culture.[124] Khodorovsky seemed briefly to have re-established his educational reputation in 1932, when he became deputy head of the committee in charge of a new radical reorganization of the higher technical schools.[125] But in 1938, Vyshinsky named Khodorovsky as a conspirator in the Bukharin trial, in which V. N. Yakovleva was also indicted,[126] solidifying the image of the old Narkompros as a locus of political deviation. It was only in the 1960s that Lunacharsky and his commissariat achieved a complete posthumous rehabilitation by Soviet historians.

7

Cultural Revolution and the schools

The new Commissar of Education for the RSFSR, Andrei Sergee-vich Bubnov, was appointed on 12 September 1929.[1] In terms of status within the party, Bubnov was a relatively high-level appointee for Narkompros. He was a member of both the Party Central Committee and the Orgburo, and had previously served as head of the Central Committee agitprop department and, for the past five years, the political administration (PUR) of the Red Army.[2] He was regarded – in contrast to Lunacharsky – as a stern, no-nonsense administrator, and he was expected to introduce order and discipline into the commissariat.

This, however, was not Bubnov's only task in Narkompros. The old Narkompros leadership had been accused of 'rightist' and 'bureaucratic' tendencies, demonstrated above all by its lack of response to the new slogans of class warfare and Cultural Revolution. Bubnov had to show himself to be a true militant revolutionary on the cultural front, and this meant allying himself with the various radical groups which had been criticizing Lunacharsky's 'bureau-cratic conservatism' over the past two years. But the radicals, un-fortunately for Bubnov, had no interest at all in orderly and disciplined procedures.

The call for class-war Cultural Revolution came from above, but it aroused a genuinely enthusiastic response not only among young Communists but among all those with grievances against the 'bour-geois' cultural establishment. The response was iconoclastic, and often led to organizational chaos. The radicals produced a real revolution in educational methodology, and they came close to over-turning the whole bureaucratic structure of educational administra-tion. Bubnov – hard-nosed, practical and unimaginative – found himself presiding over a brief period of wild experimentation with educational methods and organization in which almost all semblance of order and discipline disappeared.

Reorganization of the educational administration

The atmosphere within Narkompros during Bubnov's first months was described by one observer as 'self-flagellation in a collective of intellectuals'.[3] This was a period in which the whole government bureaucracy was under fire for its alienation from the working class and the new spirit of socialist construction; and a purge of all the commissariats was scheduled for the winter of 1929/30.[4] Over the previous six months, Narkompros had been criticized for its un-willingness to take worker-*vydvizhentsy* into the apparat, and deputations of workers (organized by the Komsomol) had come in with complaints about its 'bourgeois' policy orientation.[5]

To counter this criticism, the collegium under Lunacharsky had already begun a public relations campaign involving greater recruit-ment of worker-*vydvizhentsy* and visits to factories, in which col-legium members and *vydvizhentsy* discussed Narkompros' policies with the workers.[6] Bubnov continued this campaign, announcing at the beginning of October that an *aktiv* of fifty workers from major industries and the railways would be set up to supervise Narkompros' work and ensure its responsiveness to working-class opinion.[7] Workers' brigades were also mobilized to help the Commissariat of Workers' and Peasants' Inspection (Rabkrin) to conduct the purge of commissariat personnel which began on 1 January 1930.[8]

Bubnov had already dismissed about 10% of the staff of the central commissariat;[9] and the Rabkrin purge removed an additional 14%, mainly on grounds of social and political background.[10] But the purges had less impact on the running of the' commissariat than Bubnov's new high-level appointments, which included radical education theorists like V. N. Shulgin, and Komsomol activists who had been campaigning against the 'bourgeois' secondary school. Shulgin and the Komsomol leader Andrei Shokhin were appointed members of the Narkompros collegium.[11] Other Komsomols were drafted[12] (not always willingly) to work under Shokhin in the Nar-kompros schools administration, or under Krupskaya in the sphere of political education[13] which included the campaign against illiteracy.

The Komsomol Central Committee had already demonstrated its interest in the campaign against illiteracy by declaring a *kul'tpokhod*,[14] mobilizing Komsomols and other volunteers to the task of teaching illiterates to read and write. Like many Komsomol undertakings in education, this one implied a criticism of Narkom-pros' 'bureaucratic' methods and failure to achieve results. By the time of Bubnov's appointment, the *kul'tpokhod* was firmly linked with the campaign against bureaucracy, and specifically the educational bureaucracy of Narkompros' local departments. But in this aspect of the campaign the initiative had passed from the Komsomol leaders to one of Narkompros' own bureaucrats – G. I. Broido, head of the education department of the Lower Volga and Rector of the Saratov Communist University.[15]

Broido was an ambitious man who had suffered a political setback when he was sent to Saratov and was evidently looking for a chance to recover his previous position. With the help of the local party committee, he made Saratov the centre of a dramatic drive against illiteracy which, in October 1929, won a special commendation from the Central Committee of the party for its successful mobilization of local resources and volunteer labour.[16] The drive was led by an *ad hoc* General Staff (*kul'tshtab*) assembled by Broido, which co-ordinated the campaign work of the Komsomol, the education department, the voluntary society 'Down with Illiteracy' (ODN), the trade unions and the cooperatives.

Broido was quite explicit about his opposition to the Narkompros leadership, and he attacked it particularly strongly in the spring of 1929, when Lunacharsky's collegium had already suffered a series of political defeats. 'We began [our] work outside the education system', Broido said, '. . .and that work was in fact an attack on the education authorities and an attempt to reorganize the system on new bases.'[17]

The summer of 1929 was a period of interregnum in Narkompros, between Lunacharsky's departure and Bubnov's arrival.[18] In this period, it seems that Narkompros' own radical forces gained a dominant position, for in July the commissariat circularized the education departments with an urgent appeal for revolutionary rebirth and the repudiation of old bureaucratic habits. A Cultural Revolution, it proclaimed, had already been initiated by the masses and was being carried forward by such movements as the *kul'tpokhod*. Educational administrators must hurry to join it or risk becoming entirely superfluous. 'To work, comrades!' the document concluded. 'We can procrastinate no longer.'[19]

Shortly afterwards, *Pravda* called on the education departments to transform themselves from 'bureaucratic institutions' into 'militant General Staffs of cultural revolution'.[20] The Orgburo of the Central Committee, of which Bubnov was a member, authorized the creation of educational soviets, drawing on the initiative of 'workers, teacher–activists and Komsomol personnel' and intended to revitalize the work of the education departments to which they were attached.[21]

At local level, however, the militants of Cultural Revolution wanted to go further. They were not content to call their campaign organizations 'educational soviets' and subordinate them to the control of the education departments. They wanted the departments to be abolished altogether, and replaced by permanent campaign-type organizations based on voluntary popular participation and guided by the local party committees. In some areas, including Saratov, the education departments had in fact been virtually abolished by the spring of 1930; and the All-Union Party Meeting on education, held in April 1930, disclosed considerable local pressure for a really radical administrative reorganization.[22]

Under this pressure, Narkompros itself seemed uncertain whether its education departments remained viable.[23] But, if the education departments were to be dissolved as 'bureaucratic institutions', that had serious implications for the whole structure of local soviet administration. The *kul'tpokhod* enthusiasts were really demanding that the entire administrative burden at local level should be transferred to the party committees, supported by voluntary campaign organizations, and this was a far more radical step than the party leadership was prepared to countenance.

In the aftermath of the Party Meeting on Education, the Central Committee issued a resolution making it clear that education departments (under the new title of 'education organs') would remain in existence. But the principle of voluntary participation and campaign organization would be supported by the creation of 'soviets of cultural construction' mobilizing the initiative of the population.[24] The *kul'tpokhod*, Bubnov told the XVI Party Congress a few months later, had demonstrated that it was possible to achieve a breakthrough in mass education, using local resources and the enthusiasm of young volunteers. 'The lever for the development of cultural revolution has been found', Bubnov concluded.[25] 'The *kul'tpokhod* is the organizational method of cultural revolution.'

The call for Cultural Revolution in educational theory and methods

In the realm of pedagogical theory, a radical group had been defining its position and issuing challenges to the 'conservative' Narkompros establishment with increasing vehemence during the last eighteen months of Lunacharsky's tenure at the commissariat. The leading radical theorist was Viktor Nikolaevich Shulgin, a young Communist intellectual who had entered Narkompros early in the 1920s on Krupskaya's invitation.[26] In the latter part of the 1920s, he headed a pedagogical research institute (the Institute of Methods of School Work, renamed the Institute of Marxist–Leninist Pedagogy in 1929), belonged to the pedagogical section of Narkompros' Academic Council, and contributed frequently to Krupskaya's journal *Na putyakh k novoi shkole* and occasionally to the agitprop department's journal *Kommunisticheskaya revolyutsiya.*

Epshtein, the sober head of Narkompros' school administration under Lunacharsky, once credited Shulgin with bringing 'the Mayakovsky style' into educational theory.[27] During NEP, Shulgin was one of Narkompros' house radicals – a 'leftist', or iconoclastic innovator, of the type of Mayakovsky, Meyerhold, Averbakh, Zalkind or Gastev in their various cultural fields. He was a prolific writer, whose style was closer to that of *Komsomol'skaya pravda* or the RAPP journal *Na literaturnom postu* than to that of the scholarly journals. Apart from Krupskaya, Shulgin had no admirers in the old leadership of Narkompros; and his senior professional colleagues – sober and learned Marxist professors like Kalashnikov and Pinkevich of the Moscow Institute of Scientific Pedagogy – saw him as both a lightweight and a troublemaker.

As an innovator, and to some extent a professional outsider, Shulgin was keenly interested in new scientific developments outside his own discipline, in particular those in the fashionable fields of sociology and psychology. He was sympathetic to the new science of pedology, and supported the pedologists in their attempt to legitimate their discipline on the borders of pedagogy and social psychology.

Pedology – literally the study of children – arose in Russia as an offshoot of medical research, and in particular of the 'reflexological' studies of Bekhterev's Psychoneurological Institute.[28] Unlike the Pavlovians, the Bekhterev school was interested less in individual psychological reflexes than in the complex reflex reaction of man to his social environment. The pedologists, accordingly, were especially concerned with the child's social environment and its relation to learning capacity, behaviour and ideology.[29] These were also the main concerns of Shulgin's Institute (which had a department of pedology), although Shulgin himself had no background in psychology and never described himself as a pedologist.[30]

There was a peculiar excitement attached to environmental and behavioural studies in the Soviet Union of the 1920s. It was not just that (as in the West) psychology and sociology were new and exciting disciplines, and those involved in them had the sense of being on the frontiers of knowledge; nor just that, as Marxists, many Soviet scholars were particularly interested in changes in the social environment. The point was that they were studying an environment in the process of *revolutionary* change, which in turn was expected to produce a revolutionary transformation of man. Shulgin, the pedologist Zalkind and other Communist enthusiasts were poised to record and celebrate a great turning point in human history.

However, even the enthusiasts were not totally confident. They were aware that conclusions from another new branch of science – genetics – cast doubt on the possibilities of transformation, and they respected science. In the 1920s, the Soviet press, both popular and scholarly, reported in detail on the contemporary debate on environment versus heredity and, as Zalkind put it, 'the public was avidly interested in an optimistic solution'.[31] The 'optimistic solution' was that acquired characteristics could be passed on to succeeding generations (as Kammerer's experiments, for example, sought to prove[32]): and that a radical environmental change such as that produced by social revolution could produce behavioural change that would subsequently become permanently characteristic of the species. If not, Bukharin wrote, 'if we took the view that racial or national peculiarities are so persistent that it would take thousands of years to change them, then of course our whole work would be absurd because it would be built upon sand'.[33]

Despite this interest in environmental and behavioural change, Communists of the 1920s – as the history of the Soviet eugenics movement indicates[34] – tended to stop short of the idea of direct 'human engineering' or behaviour-conditioning. Shulgin was quite typical in this respect: in his educational writings, he almost invariably took the stance of a passionate observer of change rather than an interventionist. He believed that environmental change would produce the desired transformation of man, but limited his own role to analysis and the identification of environments as either favourable or unfavourable for the education of Soviet citizens.

The existing Soviet school, in Shulgin's view, was a largely unfavourable environment. Early in 1928 he noted that the process of socialist construction was forming a new man – that is, a new adult – but not a new child, because children were not directly involved in the construction effort. The child remained in the pre-revolutionary environment of the classroom.

You go into the classroom. Everyone stands up. Why do they need to do that?...It doesn't happen when you go into a library reading-room for adults or children. There everyone is occupied with their own business, everyone stays sitting, and nobody pays any attention to someone coming in...The same thing in a children's laboratory, a room where they are working on the Dalton Plan. Not in the classroom. Why? Well, it is the old residual past; the old dying order; the old type of relationship between adults and children, 'bosses' and 'subordinates', the 'teacher' and the 'pupil'. An awful fart, a fart of the past...It must be driven out of the school, driven out.[35]

Shulgin's doubts about the existing Soviet school were expressed in more moderate terms by a number of other educationists in 1927 and 1928. Progressives suspected an educational Thermidor in the revived emphasis on academic standards and preparation for VUZ entrance examinations. 'It was just at that time', one of Shulgin's colleagues later wrote,

that the dead started to suffocate the living through the introduction of monitors, grades and examinations; through the liquidation of [student] self-government, the abandonment of the complex system of teaching in order to retain the subject system, renunciation of moral-educational [*vospitatel'naya*] work on the pretext that it was necessary to instill knowledge and skills, and refusal to review the educational system.[36]

Communists were disturbed by reports of the anti-Soviet mood of secondary-school students.[37] They saw the Soviet school losing the battle with a non-Soviet environment. 'At every step we feel how cruelly this...environment is lashing out at us', said the pedologist Rives.

We see that to a significant extent it is not we who are doing the moulding, but the environment which is moulding us. We see that the spirit of the environment from which our children come is manifested in their social conceptions, their behaviour and their relations with each other both in school and out. And naturally the question arises: 'Well, are we conquering the environment or not? What, in the last analysis, is forming the child's conduct? Are we in control of those elemental factors which, as everyone acknowledges, mould the child, or are we not?'[38]

Shulgin's hopes were not in the 'pedagogy of the school' but in the 'pedagogy of the environment', by which he meant the specifically Soviet environment of Pioneer and Komsomol organizations, factories and socialist construction.

We must accustom our child to construction and struggle, and that does not mean refined, artificial struggle, but very real struggle and very real social construction. That is the centre of *social* [*obshchestvennaya*] work.

Thus achievement is measured not only by the sum of knowledge and skills but by the *result* of the work, by what is done that not only the school but society needs.[39]

Critics (including some pedologists) felt that Shulgin took no account of the particular needs and capabilities of different age groups; and that he was trying to 'turn the child into an adult', part of an exploitable labour force.[40] Critics also felt that Shulgin rejected the school as an educative force. This was a reasonable supposition, given some of his early remarks on the subject and despite later disavowals.[41] He wrote in 1925 that 'in my opinion there will be no school at all in the future Communist society; the children will go straight into work in society [*obshchestvennaya rabota*]'; and in 1927 that

the school is ceasing to be a school, is withering away as a school...The teacher is withering away...A specialist in a given branch of labour will work [with the children in the factory or in other production situations]. True, he will at the same time be an educator. But that is a completely different thing. He will not be a teacher [*uchitel'*] at all. And there will be nothing for him to do in the school.[42]

It was only in 1928 that Shulgin's ideas became the subject of serious discussion within Narkompros, and this appears to have been a direct result of the agitprop department meeting on Cultural Revolution organized by Krinitsky in May.[43] Like Krinitsky, Shulgin and his supporters were disturbed by signs of increasing 'bourgeois' influence in the schools. They also possessed the spirit of aggressive Communist vigilance which Krinitsky recommended. As Lunacharsky put it: 'When I read the works of comrade Shulgin, I kept feeling some sort of dance tempo running through them. I have a picture of comrade Shulgin doing an Iroquois war dance. He wants to scalp someone, and since nobody knows whom, everyone involuntarily clutches his own head.'[44] After Krinitsky's criticisms of Narkompros, the collegium found it expedient to give at least a formal hearing to Narkompros' own militant cultural revolutionary. For, as one of Shulgin's supporters pointed out, those who denied the necessity for basic reformulation of Marxist pedagogical premises in the light of Cultural Revolution put themselves in 'a really philistine, reformist, Menshevist position'.[45]

In December 1928, the collegium of Narkompros held a special meeting of educational theorists to consider Shulgin's call for a revolutionary reappraisal of the foundations of Marxist pedagogy.[46] The question formally under debate was the definition of pedagogy itself. Was it, as Kalashnikov and Pinkevich argued, the study of formal educational processes in the context of the school? Or was it, as Shulgin suggested, the study of *all* formative and educative influences on the child, including the crucial conditioning factor of the social environment?

But the real issues, of course, were not those of definition. The theorists were arguing, in the first place, about the future of the Soviet school: Shulgin's broad definition of pedagogy, in the opinion of his opponents, arose from his belief that the school was an essentially bourgeois institution which was destined to wither away under socialism. In the second place, the established leaders of the Marxist pedagogical profession had received a political challenge. Shulgin and his supporters were not only declaring the imminence of Cultural Revolution but also announcing their intention of leading it.

The opportunity to lead came with Bubnov's arrival at Narkompros. He made Shulgin both a collegium member and the head of the department of teacher training within the new Methodological Sector.[47] This was not, as Bubnov later explained, because he really agreed with what Shulgin and his supporters wrote in 'their little books', but because of their political orientation and enthusiastic response to the slogan of Cultural Revolution. 'I felt a militant political spirit emanating from them; I felt that they were trying to pose the question in accordance with the requirements of our epoch.'[48]

The Komsomol campaign against the secondary school

In the period in which Shulgin was developing his critique of the pedagogical theory of the school, the actual Soviet secondary school was under heavy attack from another quarter. The Komsomol had long considered that the secondary school was bourgeois, and that its upper level (grades VIII–IX) should be transformed into a vocational school. In 1928, when the Shakhty trial highlighted the bourgeois threat and the First Five-Year Plan underscored the need for technically-trained personnel, the Komsomol position gained credibility, and the Komsomol activists prepared for an all-out attack.

In October 1928, a plenary meeting of the Komsomol Central Committee resolved that the upper level of general secondary school should be abolished and reorganized into trade schools and technicums. Local Komsomol organizations were instructed 'to conduct the broadest propaganda for the Komsomol's proposals on the reform of the secondary school in local party, economic, trade union and social organizations, in the education departments, among teachers and pupils and in the press, so as to secure support for the [Komsomol] Central Committee proposal'.[49] The locus of battle was to be the forthcoming Party Meeting on Education, imminently expected throughout 1928 and 1929 and finally held in April 1930.

The proposal for abolition of grades VIII and IX was only one part of a Komsomol plan for reorganizing the whole educational system. As Shokhin described the plan to a Teachers' Union meeting in the summer of 1929, it required a basic 7-year general school for children aged 8 to 14, followed by vocational schools of various types (FZU, ShKM, trade school, technicum) for the 15-plus age group. Graduates of the 7-year school would, of course, have no direct access to higher education. The VUZy should recruit from young workers who had graduated from the vocational schools and spent at least two or three years in full-time employment.[50]

The Russian Narkompros opposed the Komsomol scheme (though Krupskaya seems to have wavered[51]) and stood for retention of the general secondary school. The school should retain its existing vocational biases to serve those who were not going on to higher education, but its graduates should have direct and increased access to VUZ.[52] Early in 1929, the Russian and Ukrainian commissariats reached agreement on a common platform against Komsomol attack[53] – a *volte-face* on the Ukrainian part, since it meant admitting that the much-touted Ukrainian *profshkola*[54] was essentially similar to the Russian general secondary school.

In the first rounds of the battle, the education commissariats held their own. By mobilizing young workers to the engineering schools in the autumn of 1928, the party Central Committee had in practice limited secondary school access to higher education (at least for the year 1928/29) and might implicitly seem to have endorsed the Komsomol proposal for VUZ recruitment. Nevertheless, the Central Committee stated in July 1928 and again in November 1929[55] that the secondary school was a necessary source of student recruitment for the expanding network of higher schools. Although the Komsomol put its case against the secondary school to the party leadership, this 'did not at first receive support in the Central Committee of the Party'.[56]

Both the All-Union and the Russian Sovnarkoms supported Narkompros on the secondary school. In 1929, the Russian Narkompros campaigned successfully for the addition of a 10th grade to the general secondary school, and for VUZ admission of secondary-school graduates, like those of the rabfak, without examination.[57].

A. P. Smirnov, deputy chairman of Sovnarkom RSFSR, strongly defended Narkompros against trade union criticism.[58] Vesenkha, Narkompros' chief opponent on the issue of technical education, apparently did not intervene in the secondary-school debate.

But the Komsomol continued to conduct an energetic campaign, both in the centre and in the provinces. This irked Lunacharsky considerably since, as he claimed, it was only the Komsomol that was keeping the secondary-school issue alive.[59] In June 1929, Lunacharsky and Shokhin enlivened the Teachers' Union Congress with mutual heckling. Lunacharsky, who had a paternal fondness for Shokhin and his colleagues, was nevertheless convinced that their youthful stubbornness was on the point of wrecking one of the few policies he had successfully maintained through the last difficult year. Shokhin, for his part, became increasingly offended by the suggestion that the Komsomol's adroit and persistent campaigning was not taken totally seriously by the older generation.

It appeared that both sides had put their cases to the agitprop department of the Central Committee and reached an impasse: the department agreed with the Komsomol's criticisms of Narkompros, but also approved Narkompros' theses on the education system.[60] The campaign had then gone to the oblast party committees, some of which were holding local meetings preparatory to the projected All-Union Party Meeting on Education. In general, as of June 1929, the Narkompros viewpoint had prevailed:

Lunacharsky: So far there have been a whole series of [local] meetings, and the Komsomol point of view has not once been accepted.
Shokhin (interjecting): Bryansk, Central Volga.
Lunacharsky: Central Volga changed its decision and passed a resolution that was not in your favour.
Shokhin: [Because] Lunacharsky came.
Lunacharsky: No, not because Lunacharsky came, but because the obkom did not confirm the decision.[61]

The Komsomol activists had probably alienated some potentially sympathetic obkom opinion by suggesting – as Komsomol speakers were wont to do when their arguments were rejected – that the adult party's dynamic impulse was thwarted by complacent and conservative bureaucrats. Shokhin, in a remark excluded from the published stenogram of the meeting but quoted by Lunacharsky as 'risqué', claimed that '*apparatchiki* were in charge of almost all the party meetings' and that 'our party's apparat is not linked with the proletariat, and only the Komsomol is linked with it'.[62]

A selective survey of provincial materials reveals that there was indeed a battle in progress, but the balance of forces differed from place to place. In the Northern Caucasus, with a well-established secondary-education system, Narkompros soundly defeated the local Komsomol – though it should be said that first Epshtein and then Lunacharsky appeared to reinforce the local education department's resolution. A Party Meeting held in Rostov in March 1929 is vividly described in the local education journal:

There were many unfamiliar faces. Agitprop workers came over *en masse* to the regional party meeting on education after the general regional party conference. They sat silently taking notes. . .The question [of the education system] was the basic and most controversial on the whole agenda of the meeting. Even before comrade Epshtein's paper, 'backstairs' discussions were going on. . .The representatives of the Komsomol regional committee hurried to distribute counter-theses [to those of the education department] among the delegates to the meeting. The temperature rose. Everyone expected a fight. . .The Komsomol grouped themselves in the front rows. . . [But] even during [Epshtein's] paper it was possible to judge which side was winning. Individual interjections from the Komsomol did not receive support from the majority of those attending the meeting.[63]

The Siberians also supported Narkompros' position on the general secondary school.[64] But it was defeated, on Komsomol initiative, in Smolensk;[65] and in Saratov – a centre of ideological radicalism – the education department itself opted for the 'Ukrainian alternative'.[66]

In the industrial and industrializing regions of the country, the educational debate was usually conducted in terms of the urgent local need for cadres rather than the Komsomol platform *per se*. Stalingrad, Orekhovo-Zuevo and Ivanovo-Voznesensk were all reported in early 1929 to be ignoring the general secondary school and setting up (or planning to set up) vocational schools.[67] In the Urals, a party meeting on education was persuaded by V. N. Yakovleva, of the Narkompros collegium, to vote for the Narkompros platform; but at the same time, the local economic authorities were making plans to use the general secondary school for the training of industrial technicians, electricians, agronomists and forestry experts.[68]

Since the Central Committee, as late as November 1929, was still clearly committed to retention of the existing secondary school, it is hardly surprising that the majority of local party committees took the same line in their public statements. It was equally natural that local party meetings on education, with a majority of professional educators among the delegates, should vote for the Narkompros line and against the Komsomol. But this certainly did not mean that the future of the general secondary school was secure. Local authorities had limited budgets, and their highest priority was industrialization. There was a finite limit on the number of pupils and teachers available for secondary education, and the industrial apprenticeship school, offering wages to pupils and higher salaries for teachers, was in competition with the secondary school. The technicum, in the same competitive situation but with less access than the apprenticeship school to central and local industrial budgets, was under great pressure to expand. Both the technicums and the new VTUZy needed extra teachers and classroom space.

In the mid-1920s, Shulgin had prophesied that the school would 'wither away'. Yet even he was surprised (though delighted) when the process of withering away of grades VIII and IX began in the winter of 1929/30. Neither Shulgin nor Bubnov could take any credit for this development, and in November 1929 the Central Committee was still unaware of it. The unwitting sponsor was Vesenkha USSR, which by the end of 1929 was experiencing an acute shortage of skilled workers for the industrialization drive.

In December 1929, Vesenkha announced that there would be an enormous extra enrolment in the apprenticeship schools in the new year, with further massive enrolments to follow. The target set for admissions in January 1930 was 57,000 (almost equal to the total number of students registered in all industrial FZU schools in 1928/29), but in fact it was exceeded: enterprises, especially in the industrial construction areas, had enormous labour needs, and the Siberian and Urals economic councils, for example, raised FZU enrolment norms by 200–300%.[69]

In earlier years, the great majority of entrants to the apprenticeship schools had had only primary education. But in 1930, almost a third of the new entrants had completed the 7-year school – perhaps 60,000 adolescents,[70] a number equal to 36% of the total contingent in grades VIII to X in 1928/29.[71]

'We are now seeing that in the industrial districts the apprenticeship school is beating down the secondary school', Shulgin wrote, 'as great numbers are leaving it for the apprenticeship school, and in many places secondary-school classes are being dropped.'[72] Elsewhere he commented with satisfaction that

The secondary school stands on the edge of a freshly-dug grave. It is so obvious. Students in their hundreds and thousands are leaving and, after all, this is only the beginning...[The apprenticeship school] will go on and on attracting students, not just for one year – and what will happen then? A new polytechnical school, our school, will grow. It was born in the factory, and it is there that it will grow to full strength.[73]

Although the suggestion was made that the remaining senior grades of the secondary school be converted into apprenticeship schools to meet the labour shortage (and extirpate remnants of bourgeois culture),[74] it did not gain general acceptance. Ten years of debate had inculcated the notion that, if the senior grades of the general school were to be reorganized, they were to be reorganized into technicums. In response to 'spontaneous developments', and even before the long-awaited Party Meeting on Education was held in April 1930 to adjudicate the debate on the education system, the Russian Narkompros and the Komsomol had agreed that such reorganization was inevitable.[75]

At the Party Meeting, both Bubnov and Skrypnik of the Ukraine made it clear that the reorganization was no cause for rejoicing.[76] Komsomol claims to have won an ideological victory were coolly received. Yet the mood was one of acceptance of a *fait accompli*. According to Stetsky, head of the Central Committee agitprop department, some unreconstructed liberal-educationists in the Russian Narkompros (apparently including Epshtein) were still trying 'to find a loophole so as to carry the fight onto other ground'.[77] But the only outspoken objection came from Orekhelashvili, of the Georgian Narkompros, whose position had already been defeated at the Caucasian Party Meeting on Education.[78]

It was resolved that grades VIII–X of the general secondary school were to be reclassified as technicums 'giving a complete qualification in a particular branch of labour'.[79] As technicums, in accordance with the recent reorganization of higher technical education,[80] they would pass out of the jurisdiction of the republican education commissariats into that of the all-Union authorities such as Vesenkha. But Vesenkha – which was the target of a number of malicious remarks at the meeting[81] – was described as showing indifference rather than unseemly eagerness to take over the schools. The expectation of the Narkompros representatives was clearly that a production-oriented reorganization of grades VIII–X would only occur on paper. In practice, buildings, teachers and pupils would be dispersed among existing technicums, rabfaks and VTUZy, and an integral part of the general education system would simply wither away.[82]

'Hare-brained scheming'

While experienced educational administrators like Epshtein and Skrypnik took a gloomy view of the collapse of the upper-level secondary school, the radicals were essentially optimistic rationalizers of events: if the old educational structure began to disintegrate, this was an encouraging sign that a new and better structure would soon emerge. But what would the new structure be like? The educational process would, of course, be closely linked with the processes of production. But for many radicals, including Shulgin, this was not enough. The child must participate in all aspects of adult collective life. Most importantly, he must become a political participant, since Soviet character, Shulgin believed, was formed in the process of class struggle.

'Socially-useful work', the concept which dominated educational thinking during the First Five-Year Plan, meant both practical work in production (or, more broadly, physical labour) and public activism. A child could be socially useful by gathering firewood, working in a factory, teaching peasants to read or distributing anti-religious literature. He could not, however, be socially useful by sitting in a classroom reading books or solving mathematical problems.

The concept and the activities associated with it were quite familiar to Soviet schoolchildren in the 1920s, but they were familiar mainly in the context of the Komsomol and Pioneer movements. During the First Five-Year Plan, the youth organizations continued to organize 'socially-useful work', and on a larger scale than before: the Komsomol, for example, mobilized its members for the campaign against illiteracy and for work on the construction of the new city of Komsomolsk on the Amur; the Pioneers organized campaigns against adult drunkenness and worker truancy from the factory.[83] These and other similar activities were noted by the Narkompros collegium in its first manifesto of Cultural Revolution.[84] Narkompros called on the schools to emulate them; and, to the extent that they did so, the previous distinction between formal learning in the school and socialization in the youth movements became blurred. Some Pioneer leaders even began to suggest that the youth movements should supersede the schools entirely.[85]

Shulgin did not accept this idea, but his plans for the reorganization of school life went a long way in the same direction. He proposed a complete transfer to the project method. This term, which was also current among Western educational theorists, had a special meaning in the Soviet context. The projects involved were not assignments for independent research but for work in political campaigns, the kolkhoz and the factory. Blonsky wrote in his memoirs that

V. N. Shulgin insisted that the school must work on the 'project method', and furthermore that the 'project' must be the same for all schools and all ages – consisting, for example, in the school's participation in carrying out the government's Economic Plan [*promfinplan*] for the whole country in a given year. I heard that he publicly and ecstatically said that when visiting one school he saw almost no pupils in it because they had all dispersed to various places to help carry out the Plan.[86]

Shulgin's Institute of Methods of School Work was pushing the project method as 'the only and universal method' as early as 1928.[87] But Narkompros took some time to respond, even after Shulgin's appointment to the collegium and methodological sector. Late in 1929, Narkompros recommended 'saturation of the existing "complex" themes with "socially-useful work" '.[88] But the advocates of complete transfer to the project method were unsuccessful in a Narkompros discussion held in February 1930.[89]

However, Narkompros reported receiving many enquiries from schools and teachers about revision of the programmes in the light of the present political and social situation.[90] Some local authorities were already taking their own initiatives. The Saratov education department, for example, had instructed schools to transfer to the project method, basing the projects on the Five-Year Plan and transforming classes into 'shock brigades' under the direction of a Pioneer leader or Komsomol.[91]

The project movement was greatly encouraged by a decision of the Congress on Polytechnical Education (which met early in the summer of 1930) to link even primary schools with neighbouring factories, kolkhozy and public utilities.[92] This was a measure which had been long advocated by the Komsomol and doubtfully received by Narkompros.[93] What it meant was that the factory or other enterprise would become the *shef* or patron of the school, giving it material support, introducing the pupils to the processes of production and, in the case of the older children, actually using their labour.[94]

As usual, the greatest attention was concentrated on the schools in industrial districts which were to be linked with factories, and these were henceforth referred to as 'factory 7-year schools' or FZS.

But the factories did not necessarily share the educationalists' enthusiasm. They did not want the children under foot in the shops, and they were unwilling to let the schools have discarded equipment *gratis* when it could be profitably disposed of elsewhere.[95] A few big enterprises like 'Dinamo' in Moscow took up the idea of *shefstvo* and incidentally gave support to the radical methodologists ('The Narkompros programme...did not suit us; we had to smash it', reported a spokesman for the Dinamo school. 'We had to bury the old Russian language programme, since in practice geography, social studies and Russian language all merged with each other.'[96]) The more typical situation was that the factories were prepared to sign a formal contract taking responsibility for the school, but no more. In Tula, for example, 'the pupils had to resort to staging demonstrations, in which they came to the factory gates with slogans, banners and songs, in order to gain access to production'.[97]

By the second half of 1930, all types of schools were required to attach themselves to an enterprise. This could cause real problems when there were not enough enterprises to go round, as is illustrated by an account from the city of Alatyr in the Chuvash Autonomous Republic. Alatyr had seven primary schools, one 7-year school, a pedagogical technicum and a 9-year school (which, by a typical anomaly, had not yet discarded its upper level). On the production side, it possessed timber mills, a rolling-stock repair shop and a neighbouring kolkhoz. The primary schools attached themselves to the timber mills, and limited their contact to occasional excursions. The 9-year school attached itself to the kolkhoz, and the 7-year school to the repair shop. None of the enterprises would supply materials or equipment, and for a long time the junior secondary-school pupils practised labour skills by dismantling the iconostasis of a disused church ('Two birds with one stone!' remarked the school's director. 'Polytechnicalism and anti-religious training!') Both 7-year and 9-year schools solicited production orders from their respective patrons. The 7-year school was unsuccessful, but the 9-year school finally received a paid commission from the kolkhoz to produce 500 rakes and 500 spade shafts.[98]

In new industrial areas and those with acute labour shortages, the schools – teachers as well as pupils – were sometimes mobilized by local enterprises. This happened in the Donbass, where children of one school worked in the mines.[99] Elsewhere, after arrests of technical personnel in the local factory, junior secondary-school teachers 'declared themselves mobilized and worked in the factory shops' – no doubt partly motivated by desire for industrial wages and rations, and dissatisfaction with what Krupskaya described as 'awful conditions' in the school.[100] The 'Edison' school in Stalingrad worked for a year on the project 'All hands to the weak link' (*Vse na proryv*), with four chemistry teachers working in the factory laboratory testing metals and eighty of the children working as draftsmen and bookkeepers. The school was described as a *tsekh* (workshop) of the factory, and its director was described as the *nachal'nik* (shop boss).[101]

In rural areas, the new project methods were often a cover for the time-honoured practice of using child labour in the fields. An example given as typical for Central Asia was the 7-year school in Bairam-Ali attached to a sovkhoz. One of the teachers reported:

For four months of the school year 1930/31, the collective of teachers and pupils in grades v–vii was torn away from study for work in the sovkhoz. The sovkhoz. . .uses the pupils and teachers of our school for seasonal labour. In autumn we picked cotton, and in spring took part in the sowing and then the covering of the cotton crop. The working day in the cotton field was six, eight or ten hours. Quite often there were three weeks without one day off.[102]

In the Northern Caucasus, a primary school 'considered a model in the implementation of polytechnicalism' declared itself a part of the kolkhoz and its pupils a part of the work force.[103]

An investigation of 1931, probably conducted in Moscow schools, reported that the Pioneers in the schools 'do anything but study'; 'a Pioneer in grade iv has 28 hours of study and 30–32 hours of social work in the ten-day week'.[104] Not all the social work involved physical labour. Children were used to sell lottery tickets and solicit subscriptions to the industrialization and collectivization loans ('In Moscow, Pioneer girls go along the corridors of the Hotel Paris knocking on doors and collecting money for tractors'[105]). Brigades of urban children went out to the kolkhozy to conduct political agitation.[106] In some villages, it was reported that 'children's kolkhozy' were being organized. 'They have their own entrance dues, their own administration, they buy rabbits or chickens with the kolkhoz capital, and think that this is just the way to link children's education with production', Stetsky commented disapprovingly. '. . .It is playing at being a kolkhoz.'[107]

The new methods left little place for teachers, classroom study and the acquiring of basic skills. The formal classroom lesson was 'one of the remnants of authoritarianism in our school', according to the 1931 programme for factory 7-year schools prepared by Narkompros'

Methodological Sector.[108] Under the project method, children would check into the school to receive their assignments, and then absent themselves for a shorter or longer period before reappearing to make their reports.[109] In Leningrad schools, teachers were found to be working with half a dozen of the duller students, while the brighter ones had been sent off to the factory, on fuel-collecting expeditions and so forth.[110]

Back in 1927, Narkompros had been instructed to 'stabilize' or cease constant revision of the textbooks recommended for schools. But during the Cultural Revolution, textbooks immediately came under attack, both for political mistakes and lack of contemporary relevance and for their inappropriateness to the project method. In March 1930, the presidium of the Teachers' Union denounced the principle of stabilization of textbooks, and suggested that instead of conventional textbooks primary schools should use 'loose-leaf books for reading and work assignments'.[111] As always, there was an absence of coordination between different arms of government: despite the Narkompros methodologists' objections on principle, the State Publishing House continued to issue and distribute conventional textbooks in 1930, although reducing its printing plan because of the paper shortage.[112] But from the beginning of the 1930/31 school year, a new kind of 'journal–textbook' was also available on subscription. Published ten times a year, it consisted of informational material on a variety of subjects interspersed with blank pages for the students' own jottings.[113]

In this, as in other aspects of Cultural Revolution in the school, there is a question of how widely the new methods were actually applied. The normal tendency would be for schools to use the textbooks they had until absolutely forced to buy new ones. Similarly, teachers accustomed to using traditional methods were likely to go on using them; and parents were likely to express indignation if their children were roaming the streets all day, and take steps to prevent it. 'Wilder things were said and boasted than actually done', Bubnov said after the counter-revolution in schools policy in the autumn of 1931;[114] and his remark was greeted with laughter and applause.[115]

Nevertheless, wild things *had* been said – not only in Narkompros but also in Vesenkha's education department, whose methodological instructions appalled the trade unions (according to their later account) as well as provoking an interdepartmental feud within Vesenkha.[116]

Narkompros reached the height of radical planning in its 1931 programmes – which were never, in fact, published – for the period of the Second Five-Year Plan. These described the school as a 'workshop of the factory', and anticipated a reduction of study hours in connection with the introduction of 'compulsory child labour in industrial and agricultural enterprises'. Compulsory child labour, beginning in grade v or vi (age 12 or 13) and paid for the enterprise, was to make it possible for the entire education system from primary school to VUZ to transfer to *khozraschet* (cost accounting), that is, to become economically self-supporting.[117]

The impact of Cultural Revolution on the pedagogical profession

Despite their involvement in Narkompros' methodological sector, the radical educationalists remained deeply committed to research. They were interested, above all, in observing the behavioural transformation accompanying the social and political upheaval of the First Five-Year Plan. The journals – Krupskaya's *Na putyakh k novoi shkole*, the new *Pedologiya* (with both Shulgin and Zalkind on the editorial board) and even Narkompros' conservative monthly *Narodnoe prosveshchenie* – were filled with the results of surveys on subjects as disparate as the counter-culture of the *besprizornye* and the impact of the literacy campaign on peasant family life. Researchers studied the ideology of schoolchildren and the sex life of students, investigated living standards and administered professional aptitude and IQ tests. It was the heyday of questionnaires, quantitative research and psychological testing.

Shulgin's Institute had always focussed on the ideology of schoolchildren, and its topics during the First Five-Year Plan included such subjects as the children's attitude to grain hoarding, the kolkhoz and 'the coming war of the bourgeoisie and the Soviet Union'. Although the researchers noted that from an ideological point of view 'all is not well [in the kolkhoz]', they clearly distinguished their role as scientists from the role of the political commissar. As scientists, they presented the children with multi-choice questionnaires containing not only politically 'correct' answers but answers which (as critics later pointed out) were 'counter-revolutionary' from the regime's standpoint.[118]

The Institute's most startling technique was the method of 'collisions', adapted from American progressive theory, in which the participants were offered a series of views on a controversial social or political question and asked to continue the debate. One such 'collision' suggested by the Institute was on the question of grain procurement: if one knew that a peasant in one's own village was holding back grain, was it right to inform on him or not?[119] Another example, used in schools in the Urals by the radical method-ologists of Perm, concerned the problem of antisemitism:

A factory director is being elected at a general meeting of the factory 'Zarya'. The candidacy of the Jewish activist Vainshtein is proposed. During the voting, three motions were proposed. Some said: 'Once it's an important job, you'll find a Jew there. There aren't many Jewish workers at the factory, and none at all in agriculture. Vainshtein should not be elected.' A second group said: 'Vainshtein works well, is socially active, and would lead the factory forward with great success. Vainshtein should be elected.' The third group suggested: 'There are other good workers at the factory besides Vainshtein. Why do we have to choose a Jew and upset the workers? We ought to look for a Russian worker.'[120]

In staging a 'collision', the researcher was told 'not to lead the discussion but let it develop' – that is, as a disapproving commentator pointed out, 'it was thought possible to allow the floor in this discus-sion to anyone at all, including the class enemy'.[121]

To agitprop officials, whose general responsibilities included education, this kind of educational experimentation was, at best, irresponsible. But 'collisions' were not the radicals' only ideological mistake. Shulgin's theory of the 'withering away of the school' was clearly related to the Marxist theory of the withering away of the state, which had been sharply rejected (at least for the foreseeable future) by Stalin at the XVI Party Congress in 1930.[122] In the spring of 1931, Shulgin acknowledged that his theory had proved 'dis-orienting' to teachers.[123] But Stalin's speech had done little apparent damage to the radicals: it was, in fact, in the year *after* the speech that Shulgin's ideas became most influential and widely disseminated.

The same paradox may be seen in the case of the pedologists. In 1930, when they held a large Congress on Human Behaviour in Leningrad, they were already running into political and ideological problems.[124] In the following year, the ideological problems became acute; and the pedologists plunged into political self-criticism and soul-searching about their professional identity.[125]

Yet it was just at this time that the profession finally achieved the long-desired breakthrough into the schools, which were told to employ pedologists as career counsellors, methodological advisors and aptitude testers.[126] In the following years, they extended their activity to include the identification of children who were 'mentally retarded, physically weak [or] deviating from the norm' and the supervision of a growing network of special schools for the handi-capped and problem child.[127]

In both these cases, enthusiasm for ideas that seemed 'scientific' and 'modern' was sufficiently powerful to drown the ideological criticisms. The pedologists, although totally discredited in ideological terms by 1932, were still flourishing in practice four years later;[128] and one reason was surely that local education departments were simply proud to possess such a visible symbol of scientific enlightenment (far in advance of the West!) as a regional 'pedological laboratory'.

Shulgin's triumph was of shorter duration since (as will be described in Chapter 10) the Narkompros methodologists became targets of Stalin's personal disapproval. But until the middle of 1931, despite known ideological errors, Shulgin's star too seemed to be rising. He had the support of the powerful proletarian writers' association, RAPP, led by Leopold Averbakh; and RAPP had to a large extent assumed the prerogatives of the now defunct Arts Administration of Narkompros as a patron and cultural arbiter. Averbakh himself wrote on education, and for a few months in 1931 even edited the Teachers' Union newspaper *Za kommunisticheskoe prosveshchenie*.[129] Under his editorship, the newspaper became a stronghold of the radical education theorists, with Shulgin in the place of honour. RAPP was also an enthusiastic advocate of the experimental 'journal–textbook' introduced by the Narkompros methodological sector.[130]

The educational press was almost completely monopolized by the 'left' in the first half of 1931, and the same was true of the educational publishing houses. In March of that year, 'leftist' orthodoxy was so firmly established in the leadership of the Teachers' Union that a critic of Shulgin's theory of 'withering away of the school' (Shumsky) was hardly given a serious hearing: 'Many comrades were astonished, looked away, and took me at best for a fool who didn't understand what was going on and bellowed out "Rest in peace" instead of "Your health".'[131]

8

Mass education and mobility
in the countryside

At the beginning of 1928, when the Soviet leadership endorsed coercive measures to extract hoarded grain from the peasantry, the regime and the peasantry entered a period of confrontation which was officially described as 'class war'. The decision to collectivize individual peasant holdings, taken towards the end of 1929, substantially increased hostility and the incidence of violence on both sides. Prosperous peasants, as well as those active in opposing grain procurements and collectivization, were labelled kulaks and class enemies. They were punished by measures ranging from punitive taxation and expulsion of children from school to physical deportation, and retaliated by arson and attacks on Soviet officials. But the regime's attempts to divide the peasantry on class lines were unsuccessful. The peasantry as a whole expressed its hostility to the new policies in the wholesale slaughter of livestock. Collectivization was widely regarded by the peasants as a second serfdom. Sometimes, harking back to an older tradition of grievance against state authority, they associated its perpetrators with Antichrist.

Yet for very large numbers of peasants the end result was not 'enserfment' in the kolkhoz but departure from the countryside. Some simply fled to the towns; others were taken into the industrial labour force by *orgnabor* (organized recruitment); and a substantial group entered the labour force after being deported from the villages as kulaks. In the years 1930–32 alone, 9.5 million rural inhabitants moved permanently to the towns,[1] with young males forming a large part of the migrant group. Despite a brief check on peasant migration in 1933, following an attempt to regulate the growth of the urban labour force and the introduction of passports, the high rate of departure from the countryside continued throughout the 1930s. Between the 1926 census and that of 1939, the urban population of the Soviet Union grew by almost 30 million,[2] mainly as a result of peasant migration.

The regime had not anticipated such massive growth of the

industrial labour force during the First Five-Year Plan; but by 1930 it was clear that the phenomenon of peasant movement into the labour force required new educational policies for the countryside. If large numbers of young peasants were to be upwardly mobile – and if, in addition, collectivization was to increase the demand for skills among those peasants who remained on the land – it was imperative that the peasant population should be literate and that all young peasants should receive at least primary education.

The campaigns against illiteracy and for universal primary education had proceeded at a rather desultory pace throughout the NEP period. In 1928/29, the campaign against illiteracy was enlivened by the participation of the Komsomol; but it was not until 1930, with the realization of the true magnitude of industry's labour needs, that the regime took decisive action. In the middle of that year, the XVI Party Congress resolved that liquidation of illiteracy and the introduction of universal primary education were 'a militant task of the party in the coming period'.[3] The relatively moderate mass-education goals of earlier versions of the Five-Year Plan were abandoned;[4] and the Congress initiated a drive for 100% achievement both in the liquidation of adult illiteracy and the introduction of universal primary education.

The campaigns for the mass education of peasants were carried out simultaneously with collectivization. As a result, the authorities often behaved in a coercive and threatening manner, and the peasants responded with resentment and sometimes violence. But, on the peasant side, the most belligerent opponents of the educational campaigns seem to have been older peasants and women – those whose probable fate was to remain in the kolkhoz. For the younger peasants, education was a ticket for escape and upward mobility; and this, despite the manifold contradictions of official policy, corresponded with the basic interests of the industrializing Soviet state.

'Class war' in rural education

From the beginning of 1928, the tensions of the grain procurement drive were reflected in the schools. The drive was directed against peasant 'hoarders' of grain – that is, those who were prosperous enough to hold back some of the autumn harvest in the hope that spring prices would be higher – and the authorities did their best to stimulate antagonism between poorer and richer peasants in the village. It was reported that

some comrades coming in for grain procurements recommend doing everything to encourage the incidents of persecution of kulaks' children that
occur in the school, using this persecution as a means of putting pressure on
the kulak parents who are maliciously holding back grain. Following their
advice, one has to observe how the class tensions among the children become acute, beginning with teasing the little children and usually ending
in a fight.[5]

As in the towns, many rural schools tried to raise the 'proletarian'
percentage (children of rural workers, poor peasants and agricultural
labourers) by expelling or refusing to admit other pupils. Not only
the 'kulak' children suffered by this policy, but also the children of
middle peasants and local artisans and craftsmen.[6]

The teachers were always vulnerable to an increase of social and
political tension in the countryside. They occupied an ambiguous
position between Soviet power and a resentful peasantry, and in
1928/29 the pressure was mounting from both sides. Often the
teachers tried to act as mediators: they 'say it is good to live with
everyone in this world – with the poor peasants and with the
prosperous ones as well'.[7] When they acceded to Communist
demands on questions such as the expulsion of kulak children, they
were likely to be ostracized in the village and face mutiny in the
classroom. 'They are pushing the school over the abyss by opposing
it to the family', teachers were reported as saying privately. 'The
people will drive us out of the school and out of the village if we
work openly [for Soviet power].'[8]

Local officials had always tended to bully the teachers, but in the
spring and summer of 1928 this tendency clearly intensified. The
power to hire and fire had been transferred from regional to district
level,[9] greatly increasing the possibility of retaliatory dismissals and
settling of personal scores. But added to this was the suspicion that
the teachers – as offspring of priests and kulaks, or as 'intelligentsia'
– were class enemies. In Smolensk, the regional authorities warned
the districts against indiscriminate purging of the local intelligentsia.
But in the districts, one speaker said, 'there is a mood to purge
everything, including the schools and the hospital'.[10]

'Mass dismissals' of teachers were reported in the summer of
1928,[11] despite a series of prohibitions from the central government.[12]
According to a possibly inaccurate report, the Teachers' Union was
sufficiently disturbed by this to draft a proposal giving security of
tenure to all teachers currently employed and making it illegal to
dismiss a teacher on social or ideological grounds.[13] Needless to say,
the proposal was quickly dropped. But the new level of antagonism

was illustrated by the fact that a union representative describing the teachers' plight to a conference of senior education officials from the provinces could scarcely get a hearing:

One teacher worked for ten years and recently graduated from the VUZ. He had served in the Red Army, and after the Army went back to school. Now it turns out that some relative of his was a priest, and he is being fired. So once you have a priest in the family, you have to be thrown out on your neck? Is that just? And you will find as many cases of this sort as you like. [Noises, protests in the hall][14]

The growing brutalization of rural life also affected the teachers. There was a remarkable increase in reported cases of rape, or undesired sexual intercourse forced on a female teacher by Soviet officials. The assumption of a Soviet *droit de seigneur* was not a new phenomenon: 'Officials passing through [the village] – education department inspectors, various representatives of Soviet co-operative organs – prefer "cultured surroundings" and invariably seek lodging for the night in the school. It has become a tradition.'[15] But observers found a qualitative as well as quantitative change in this epoch of class warfare. In one typical instance, local officials

specially went to Yablonskaya school to see teacher Orlova, the daughter of a kulak sentenced to eight years for anti-Soviet activity, and Kustova, the daughter of a priest. There they organized a drunken party and forced the teachers to sleep with them...[One of the officials] motivated his infamous suggestion with the statement: 'I am [Soviet] power; I can do anything', knowing that such statements would have particular effect on Orlova and Kustova, since they are of alien class origin. As a result of his tormenting, Kustova came close to suicide.[16]

The tensions between teachers, peasants and Soviet power were aggravated by the Komsomoi. In the autumn of 1928, the Komsomol began a 'cultural campaign' (*kul'tpokhod*) against illiteracy.[17] This campaign was primarily aimed at the adult rural population; and a great deal of the actual literacy teaching fell as an extra and unpaid burden on the village teacher. The Komsomol mobilized a 'Cultural Army' (in which Komsomols were clearly the officers, and teachers the conscripted soldiers), and as far as possible organized the drive against illiteracy as if it really were a military campaign. In one region, it was reported, 'they practised cultural-political recon-naisance [*razvedka*]...and almost used to get the Cultural Army out of bed at a signal to check their fighting capacity'.[18] The young Komsomol volunteers – most of them on short visits from the towns

– seemed constantly on the brink of treating the village as occupied territory, and its illiterate population as the enemy.

Soviet literacy campaigns had been associated with coercion since the Civil War;[19] they had been headed in the early 1920s by an anti-illiteracy 'Cheka'; and even during NEP it had been necessary to remind provincial authorities that attendance at literacy schools was voluntary.[20] In 1929, Krupskaya reported that the peasants feared that the current campaign would 'take the path of coercion'. She described a typical *kul'tpokhod* meeting as follows:

In the front rows sit the liquidators [of illiteracy], the organizers of the campaign and the *aktiv*...At the back and on the side, crowded shoulder to shoulder, stand the masses of those who are to be taught – tense, motionless, listening...They are waiting, tensely waiting: What does it mean? Is it serious, or is it just talk?[21]

The Komsomol 'cultural warriors' were also known as 'liquidators of illiteracy', and the literacy schools were called 'liquidation points' (*likpunkty*). This terminology acquired particularly sinister overtones after Stalin's announcement of the policy of 'liquidation of the kulaks as a class' at the end of 1929; but even before that time rumours abounded in the countryside that the campaign had some ulterior motive. Who could tell what awful fate might befall those driven by *kul'tarmeitsy* to a *likpunkt*? At the very least, the newly literate would probably have to pay extra agricultural tax.[22] But there were worse rumours: 'that pupils will be sent off to war'; 'that girls weighing 64 kilograms will be taken to China, that their plaits will be cut off and used as industrial raw material [*utylsyrye*], that pupils will be branded with the mark of Antichrist'.[23]

The literacy campaign was closely associated with the campaign against religion, in which the Komsomol was also particularly active. Orthodox priests, therefore, took the lead in conducting agitation against the *likpunkty*; and their warnings were reinforced by 'secret letters' carried by wandering people of God 'putting an anathema on old men and women who visited the Devil's encampments and acquired Satanic wisdom'.[24] Communists and Komsomols, cast in the image of the Mongol hordes, were also perceived as seducers (at least on the ideological plane) of peasant women. Men forbade their womenfolk to enter the *likpunkt*, while enthusiastic liquidators conducted covert propaganda in the village against male tyranny and persuaded the women to visit the *likpunkty* by stealth.[25]

The peasants' resentment and fear was often expressed in physical attacks on the teachers, especially those teaching in the *likpunkty* as well as the normal school. In Uzbekistan, for example, a literacy school was set on fire with the teacher and five women students inside it. In another case, acid was thrown in the face of a woman teacher heading a rural *likpunkt*.[26]

According to incomplete data collected by the Teachers' Union, 215 cases of 'kulak terror' (beatings, injuries, murder, stone-throwing) against teachers were registered between May and December 1929.[27] The courts, following the principles of class justice, punished social aliens more severely than social allies; but there was disagreement between the Russian Commissariat of Justice and its local organs over the category to which the teacher belonged. According to the central commissariat, local courts failed to understand the 'true class essence' of the attacks on teachers (whose own offences, even trivial ones, were usually severely punished): 'the necessary support is not given to persecuted teachers, and in cases where they are murdered, beaten or suffer other acts of violence, the investigation drags on in an inert and bureaucratic way'.[28]

To the peasants, however, the schools and *likpunkty* belonged to the state, and teachers were the state's servants. Violence against the teachers increased in the first months of 1930, as the peasants reacted to forced collectivization, the expropriation of the kulaks and the closing of churches. In the Tartar Republic, where half the churches and mosques had recently been closed, and homeless kulaks were terrorizing both officials and the newly collectivized peasants, Communists reported an absolute rejection of the Soviet regime and all its works in many parts of the countryside. For the Tartar peasants, teachers and Soviet officials came in the same category (a majority in both groups was probably Russian): they were demanding 'the closing of Soviet schools, the driving out of Soviet teachers, deprivation of the voting rights of Communists and Komsomols [and] their eviction from the village'.[29]

The impact of collectivization

The schools were immediately affected by the expropriation and subsequent deportation of the kulaks. In many cases, the kulaks' children had already been expelled from the schools. Now many of them were deported with their parents to distant parts of the Soviet Union. It is claimed by Soviet historians that, of the hundreds of thousands of kulak children deported with their parents to convict settlements (*spetsposelki*) in the North, the Far East and Siberia, 90% were attending school in the 1931/32 school year.[30] If true, this was certainly a remarkable feat, considering that most of the schools had to be created from scratch. But voting rights were not returned to the adult children of deported kulaks until 1933;[31] and it was not until 1938 that those who had been deported with their parents received the right to leave their place of exile.[32]

There were also kulak children who became separated from their parents and were not deported. These children, as well as many adolescents who had worked for the kulaks and lived in their homes, were often left destitute in the villages. Krupskaya reported that schools and teachers felt a responsibility towards the children, but were afraid of offering them shelter:

A young child's parents are arrested. He goes along the street crying... Everyone is sorry for him, but nobody can make up his mind to adopt him, to take him into his home: 'After all, he is the son of a kulak...There might be unpleasant consequences.' Here the issue is clear: we are not waging war with children but with adults. A child cannot choose his parents he has exploited nobody, has oppressed nobody, made nobody's life unbearable, conducted no intrigues. He is guilty of nothing. A child is a child...It is an unforgivable act to punish children for their parents, to persecute those teachers and kolkhozniks who take it on themselves to look after the kulaks' children.[33]

Among the victims of dekulakization were not only peasants but also teachers. According to a mid-1930 report, there were 'enormous numbers' of cases of dekulakization, confiscation of property and deportation of teachers. Desperate appeals were sent to Narkompros, the Central Committee of the Teachers' Union, and the teachers' newspaper. 'The teachers, not finding help or protection in local unions and education departments, are sending their complaints to the centre, and often using their last kopeks to come personally to the centre seeking protection.'[34]

In some cases, the teachers were evidently dekulakized as prosperous peasants, either because they were married to such peasants or had their own plot of land. But there were also cases of victimization of teachers who were personally unpopular in the village or had come in conflict with local authorities. In one reported instance, the widow of a Communist killed in the Civil War was dekulakized 'essentially because she had more than once driven the local "activists" – the secretary of the village soviet (a candidate member of the party), the local cultural official (also a party member) and the secretary of the local cooperative organization – out of the school where they intended to hold a drinking party'. Since she had no 'means of production' to confiscate, they took her clothes and cooking utensils and tore up her books.[35] Another woman teacher was dekulakized on the grounds that she was a priest's daughter: 'when she produced documents to show that she was the daughter of a peasant, they declared that "her mother visited the priest, and therefore it is possible that she is the priest's daughter" '.[36]

In the period of reassessment after Stalin's 'Dizzy with success' speech of March 1930, the Smolensk authorities found that 63 teachers had been wrongly subjected to dekulakization – almost one tenth of all the cases so classified in the region under investigation.[37]

But the majority of teachers, like the majority of peasants, were faced not with deportation but with the new kolkhoz. It was reported in 1930 that teachers' entry into the kolkhoz was 'a mass phenomenon, almost universal. In some [areas] it is voluntary, but in some the trade unions have published a mandatory resolution on compulsory entry.'[38] In one district in the Urals, 98% of teachers became kolkhoz members in 1930/31.[39] Nevertheless, some thousands of teachers fled from Russian schools in the spring and summer of 1930,[40] probably to avoid being forced into the kolkhoz.

The teacher's position as a kolkhoz member was ill-defined, especially if he had not previously held and cultivated a plot of land. One of the major problems was that the teacher received an individual salary from outside the kolkhoz, and was entitled to certain privileges such as vacations and pensions which were not available to other kolkhozniki. The kolkhozy were unwilling to allow him to use these privileges, and frequently insisted on taking a proportion of his salary. In theory, the kolkhozy had no right to make financial demands on the teacher beyond exacting 3% of his annual salary in entrance dues.[41] In practice, the new kolkhozy were desperately short of money and, according to Narkompros, claimed from 25% to 100% of the teacher's salary for the common treasury.[42] In addition, the kolkhozy often expected the teacher to do his share of work in the fields or serve as kolkhoz accountant, sometimes in addition to work in the school and sometimes in place of it.[43]

Rural schools were also drawn into a close relationship with the kolkhoz, though they continued to be supported on the budget of the local soviet, not that of the kolkhoz. At the end of 1930, all existing primary and 7-year schools in the countryside were formally attached (*prikrepleny*) to kolkhozy or sovkhozy,[44] and many apparently transferred the school plots and agricultural equipment owned by the school to the kolkhoz.[45] As Narkompros envisaged it, the school's relationship to the kolkhoz was similar to its relationship to the factory in the towns – a means of strengthening the 'production orientation' in education and breaking down the school's isolation from the life and work of the community as a whole. But the reality was often somewhat different. If the kolkhozy did not try to ignore the schools, they were inclined to regard teachers and pupils alike as part of the kolkhoz labour force.[46]

This was an extremely unpopular measure with those peasants who remained outside the kolkhoz, and some drew the natural (though incorrect) conclusion that the drive for compulsory and universal primary education was part of the state's general attack on the individual farm. In the words of one uncollectivized peasant,

It's not at all because they need to be taught that the children are staying in school. They don't want to let them work on their own farms. They want to harm the individual farm. All schoolchildren will work only on the kolkhoz. You feed your son, clothe him and give him shoes – and your son will be working for them.[47]

The Schools of Peasant Youth had also to be reoriented towards the kolkhoz, since their programmes had previously been designed to fit the context of individual, small-scale farming.[48] At a special meeting of Schools of Peasant Youth students late in 1929, it was reported that 'only a small place is allotted to collectivization in the programmes, and a still smaller place in the practice of the Schools'. The pupils did not know how to use a tractor because most of them had never seen one. Moreover, when they graduated they could not join the kolkhoz even if they wished because they were too young (the schools admitted students from the age of 12).[49]

The Komsomol was strongly in favour of turning the Schools of Peasant Youth into service schools for the kolkhozy; and Narkompros, despite many reservations, was forced to take appropriate action. In February 1930, the schools were renamed Schools of Kolkhoz Youth (still abbreviated to 'ShKM'), and Narkompros issued a new formulation of their functions. They were to be strictly specialized according to the agricultural nature of the area; the pupils were to work in the kolkhoz and be paid for their labour; the kolkhoz was to bear some of the costs of the school and to allow it the use of machinery, livestock and land for teaching purposes.[50]

These guidelines were appropriate for the large-scale modern farming which some enthusiasts thought would miraculously develop in the kolkhoz, but they bore little relation to the sullen poverty-stricken collectivized village which was closer to the normal reality.

The kolkhozy had no money to give the ShKM, little equipment or livestock, and absolutely no time or interest for the mutually enriching interaction with the schools envisaged by the Narkompros theorists.

During the First Five-Year Plan period, there was a spectacular increase in the number of students in rural secondary schools (from less than half a million in 1927/28 to well over two million in 1932/33[51]); and by 1931/32 almost all these schools had the official title of Schools of Kolkhoz Youth[52] and, in theory, offered a highly specialized agricultural training programme. In fact, however, they remained general educational schools,[53] whose graduates, as in the past, mainly took white-collar jobs in the countryside or went on to further education. The kolkhozy and sovkhozy, desperately in need of skilled personnel, were forced to obtain it by other means, chiefly by training the young adult peasants who had long ago dropped out of the general-educational system after only a few years of primary school.

The first and most immediate need of the new collective farms was not tractor-drivers and mechanics (though that need became acute within a few years) but accountants. This question was urgently raised at a meeting organized by the central kolkhoz authority, Kolkhoztsentr, in January 1930, when kolkhoz delegates expressed their distress at the insufficiency of existing training programmes. 'Where are the schools, where are all those whose special vocation it is to train and educate the masses of humanity?' asked one delegate. 'Where is the direction and assistance that [ought to come] from Narkompros, Kolkhoztsentr and the higher authorities in general?'[54]

The central authorities do indeed seem to have been caught off balance, since in the autumn of 1929 Gosplan had not even included accountants among the categories of skilled worker which the kolkhozy would need.[55] Yet the new collectives literally could not function without them: early in 1930, a commission of the Finance Commissariats and Rabkrin acknowledged that kolkhoz financial affairs were in a 'catastrophic state', with the kolkhoz administrations unable to calculate what each member had earned by his labour.[56]

In April, the Orgburo of the Central Committee took note of the crisis. The first step was the mobilization of urban accountants to the kolkhozy, to meet a need which was now estimated at 100,000 for the current year. Kolkhoztsentr, the Red Army, the Union of Soviet Trading Employees and Narkompros were all given urgent directives to send accountants immediately, and to train a much larger group for kolkhoz work by the end of the year. The Komsomol alone was to provide 20,000 accountants, half recruited in the towns and half in the villages; and it had to find a further 100,000 Komsomols to act as accounting clerks (*uchetchiki*) for individual kolkhoz brigades.[57]

But this could only be an emergency measure, for even in the comparatively short run the rural population would have to produce its own skilled personnel. In mid-1930, the XVI Party Congress resolved that the chief organizational tasks of the kolkhoz movement were: '(a) to organize a system of promotion to leading work of personnel from among the kolkhozniki themselves; (b) to organize mass short-term training of kolkhoz personnel under the sovkhozy, Schools of Kolkhoz Youth, VUZy, agricultural technicums, secondary schools and Machine-Tractor Stations; (c) to draw kolkhoz youth more widely into agricultural VUZy and technicums'.[58]

During the First Five-Year Plan, short-term courses provided the bulk of the new accountants, mechanics and tractor drivers required by the kolkhozy. These courses were organized by many different organizations (tractor drivers, for example, were trained by the kolkhoz organizations, the sovkhozy, Khlebotsentr, Traktorotsentr and local branches of the Commissariat of Labour) on an *ad hoc* and improvised basis. Most of the courses lasted for only a few months – in some cases, only a few days – and the skills imparted were minimal. In one region, general courses were set up for kolkhoz 'organizers': those who did well were sent out as kolkhoz chairmen, while those who did poorly became kolkhoz accountants. It was universally reported that the new tractor drivers could barely drive their machines and were quite unable to service or repair them.[59]

However, the deficiencies of the training should not obscure the fact that a large proportion of the young rural population was acquiring elementary skills and being forced to put them into practice. Kolkhoz requirements made such training imperative. But in the broader perspective, as we shall see later in this chapter, the kolkhoz was not the only beneficiary, nor even the main one.

Campaigns for adult literacy and universal primary education

The party leadership first turned its attention to questions of adult literacy and primary education in 1930, as the full implications of industrialization for labour and mass education became clear.

But for a number of years before 1930 the education authorities had been trying to draw attention to the problems which existed in this area. Despite the claims that were sometimes made for Soviet achievements in mass education during the first ten years, these achievements were largely based on pre-war investment and the expansion of literacy among young males as a result of military service. But war had also had a disruptive effect, particularly on the literacy of those who were at primary-school age at the beginning of the 1920s. During NEP, the Soviet growth rate in primary education was almost certainly lower than that which would have been predicted for the Tsarist regime on the basis of the very rapid growth of the immediate pre-war years.[60]

According to the 1926 census, 51% of the Soviet population aged nine years and over was literate.[61] This represented a 12–13% increase on the literacy of the population of the Russian Empire at the outbreak of World War I,[62] though it is doubtful that Soviet literacy campaigns (except perhaps those undertaken in the Red Army) had added much to the natural increase in literacy arising from the expansion of mass education in the last decades of the Tsarist regime. But it remained a low aggregate figure, with literacy very unequally distributed between men and women and urban and rural dwellers. In the age group 16 to 50, 88.3% of urban males were literate in 1926. But the literacy of rural males was twenty percentage points lower, and only a third of rural women in the age group were literate.[63]

The comparatively low literacy of the adolescent age groups in 1926,[64] caused by Civil War disruption of primary education, was particularly worrying. In the late 1920s, the number of illiterates reaching maturity each year was approximately equal to the number of adults who were taught to read and write in the literacy schools during that year;[65] and in regions with traditionally high literacy, the proportion of illiterates was actually rising.[66]

By the end of NEP, there were two million more children in primary schools than there had been in 1914/15; and it was sometimes claimed that primary education was almost universal for the 8–11 age group, in contrast to the 51% of the age group in school in 1915.[67] But this claim was extremely shaky, since the primary schools – as well as the literacy schools for adults – were partly serving the adolescents who had earlier been deprived of basic education. According to Gosplan's estimate, based on the 1927 schools census, 34.5% of all pupils in primary schools were above the normal age for grades I–IV.[68] This suggests that in fact about

50–60% of children of primary-school age were in school during the last years of NEP[69] – probably an improvement on the pre-war situation, but not very impressive considering the unusually small size of the age group.

On 25 July 1930, following the decision of the xvi Party Congress, the Central Committee directed that three years of primary education were to become compulsory in the countryside from the beginning of the next school year (1930/31). In the towns, where four years of primary schooling was already the norm, grade v was to become compulsory from the coming year, and grades vi and vii in the two following years.

The central Committee's resolution thus recognized the comparative backwardness of the countryside, but indicated an urgent desire to liquidate it in the shortest possible time: grade iv was to become compulsory for rural children from 1931/32; and by the end of the First Five-Year Plan, the 'basic mass of kolkhoz youth' was to be enrolled in the Schools of Kolkhoz Youth (rural grades v–vii). The special problem of adolescent illiteracy was also recognized in the directive to establish compulsory courses of one to two years for all 11–15 year olds who had not received primary education.[70]

As the Central Committee noted, implementation of this decision presented 'the most formidable difficulties'. These difficulties were psychological as well as organizational and economic. Over the past few years, local authorities had become accustomed to a quite different approach to the school – one which emphasized social discrimination in admissions and encouraged the exclusion of 'socially-alien' pupils. In the Turkmenian Republic, to take the most extreme example, the social composition of urban primary schools had just been drastically improved by excluding 5,000 children of white-collar and 'alien' parents, who made up a quarter of the total enrolment.[71] This was not typical on a national scale; and enrolments in rural primary schools had actually increased over the past two years.[72] But every village school had had to deal with its 'kulak' pupils, and it had been widely assumed that excluding them was the way to win praise from higher authorities.

Even if local officials were able to rid themselves of a class-discriminatory approach to education, there remained the problem of actively involving them in the drive for universal primary education. The task of collectivization had absolute priority in the countryside; and local authorities who failed to cope with it were in serious trouble. The educational campaigns had to take second place – and, given the magnitude of the collectivization problem, this might mean that they were neglected entirely. As one president of a village soviet remarked, 'however much fuss they make about compulsory primary education and the campaign against illiteracy, all the same they won't put you in prison for weakness on this front'.[73]

Another type of difficulty was to be encountered in the attitudes of the peasants themselves. Peasants often set fire to kulaks' houses which had been appropriated for use as schools or *likpunkty*; and fresh rumours were circulated about the danger of attending Godless schools. In one village, half the children left the school because of the rumour that all schoolchildren would be stamped with the mark of Antichrist. In another, the rumour was reported that 'fifty kilometres from here, God sent a terrible storm that carried all kolkhozniki and Pioneers with their possessions, animals and harvest to destruction at the ends of the earth, but the church remained'.[74]

These were, no doubt, expressions of general grievance against the Soviet regime as much as specific grievances against the school, since lack of access to primary education had been a common peasant complaint during NEP. But the peasants had also assumed that, when schooling finally became universal and compulsory, there would be a material *quid pro quo* for the parents. Compulsory schooling, Narkompros had suggested and hoped, would oblige the state to provide not only free textbooks and writing materials but also free hot lunches, shoes and clothing for the children.

With the introduction of compulsory primary education in 1930, the government recommended 'a significant increase' in material aid of this kind, but only in regard to children of the lowest paid workers, agricultural labourers and poor peasants.[75] The Siberian authorities stated that children of persons without voting rights and kulaks should even be made to pay for paper and textbooks, which were traditionally provided free (if available) to schoolchildren.[76] This may have been a local deviation; but scarcity was a general phenomenon, and socially-discriminatory allocation was officially recommended. The central journal of the campaign for compulsory primary education condemned the 'right opportunism' of school authorities which distributed whatever supplies of clothing and shoes they received equally among all the children.[77]

Peasants objected both to discriminatory allocation and to the inadequacy of supplies. They claimed (in what officials regarded as an attempt to sabotage the campaign) that they could not send their children to school until they were provided with shoes and clothing. 'Once it's compulsory to teach the children, then it's compulsory to clothe them as well.' 'Once we can't make decisions about our own children, then you provide for them.' A variant reported in a number of villages was protest *against* the provision of hot lunches in the school: 'We don't need hot lunches – they will make us pay for it in taxes.'[78]

This last comment was essentially accurate. Despite the great expansion of mass education required by the decisions of 1930, subsidies from the all-Union and republican governments for this purpose over the next few years were negligible: in 1932, 99.5% of all expenditure on general-educational schools came from local sources.[79] The peasants contributed directly through two new kinds of taxation. The first was village 'self-taxation' (*samooblozhenie*), introduced in 1928 and primarily used for cultural purposes.[80] The second was the new special tax for cultural and housing purposes (*kul'tzhilsbor*) collected by the central government in 1931 and 1932.[81] The proceeds were transferred in their entirety to the urban (*raion*) and village soviets; and in rural areas they were to be used purely for educational purposes, and in particular for primary education.

The literacy campaign, similarly, was to be financed almost entirely on the local budget and by voluntary labour and contributions.[82] With this kind of financial base, the question of campaign organization became crucial. Organizational leadership would not come from the peasantry, and was unlikely to come from local party or soviet authorities preoccupied with other tasks. It would be provided, the Central Committee hoped, by voluntary organizations like the Komsomol's Cultural Army, using *kul'tpokhod* methods to mobilize popular participation and support.[83]

As described in the previous chapter, the *kul'tpokhod* challenge to the 'bureaucratic' education departments in 1929/30 had not succeeded; but the leadership was nevertheless impressed with *kul'tpokhod* achievements in the literacy campaign. In the Urals, Bubnov told the XVI Party Congress in the summer of 1930, a Cultural Army of 45,000 had taught more than three times the number of illiterates taught in Narkompros' own literacy schools. Under *kul'tpokhod* methods, training of one illiterate cost less than three roubles, compared with twelve to seventeen roubles in the literacy schools. The *kul'tpokhod* had shown how much could be done without an increase in the central educational budget. In future, the *kul'tpokhod* would be the 'universal method' for carrying out urgent tasks in the cultural sphere – not only the literacy campaign, but the campaigns for agronomic and technical literacy, kindergartens, libraries and universal primary education.[84]

In practice, *kul'tpokhod* methods meant two things: fund-raising from local organizations and recruitment of volunteer labour. In Saratov, for example, Broido (the local *kul'tpokhod* organizer) had enlisted the support of the Lower Volga party committee to obtain financial support from the local soviet; and he had also managed to secure 20% of the local trade unions' cultural fund and 15% of the local subscription to the industrialization loan for the literacy campaign. In addition, the Saratov Komsomol had raised a considerable sum in voluntary contributions from individuals and organizations and the profits from lotteries, the sale of elementary readers and other activities. For the actual teaching of literacy, the Saratov *kul'tpokhod* had mobilized a large number of unpaid volunteers, most of whom were VUZ and secondary-school students, housewives and Soviet employees.[85]

The same techniques were used in the later versions of the *kul'tpokhod* (which, around 1930, acquired the new name of *kul'testafeta* or cultural relay-race,[86] linking it with the movement for 'socialist competition'). Campaign activists were both fund-raisers and watchdogs over local authorities, who might need to be badgered and harassed into fulfilling their cultural responsibilities. It was their duty to see that premises were provided and maintained for school purposes, that the necessary supplies and equipment was available, and that local volunteers were found not only to teach but to mend roofs, bring in firewood and so on. Participants in the Stalingrad *kul'testafeta* of 1930, for example, were instructed to raise 200,000 roubles in contributions for the literacy campaign and 375,000 roubles for primary education, as well as making practical preparations for the new schools and classes that would be organized locally. They were also to conduct explanatory work on the theme: 'You can't introduce universal primary education and polytechnicalism on state budgetary funds.'[87]

In the countryside, there were fewer potential volunteers for literacy teaching than in the towns. This deficiency was partly made up by bringing in outside volunteers like urban Komsomols and students on vacation. But the village schoolteachers took a great part of the burden. 71% of all teachers also taught in the literacy schools; and Bubnov said in 1930 that the average teacher 'spends 30% of his working time in the [regular] school and 70% outside it'[88] (though literacy teaching was only one of the unpaid extra duties which the teacher was called upon to perform).

After the first wave of clerical hostility to the literacy campaign, it became relatively common for priests and members of their families to teach in the literacy schools. Baptists were also active, though their interests were no doubt somewhat different from those of the state: after the adoption of the Soviet slogan for 'socialist competition', Baptists of the Northern Caucasus were reported to have challenged the sectarians of Siberia to a contest in acquiring influence over the illiterate masses.[89]

In many cases, the volunteer teachers knew little more than their pupils. In the Tambov area in 1930, 14,860 out of a total 16,942 literacy teachers were peasants who, as one of them put it, were not 'strongly literate' but 'teach their comrades, pass on to the pupils what they themselves know'.[90] In the primary schools, senior pupils sometimes served as teachers for the junior groups. Universal education, according to one report, 'is being introduced through the resources that exist in the countryside – in crowded izbas, with the aid of the first textbooks that come to hand, with the aid of personnel such as pupils of grades III and IV of the primary school'.[91]

From 1930, however, the number of regular teachers in the countryside increased rapidly, as did the proportion of young teachers and Komsomol members in the profession as a whole. Between 1927/28 and 1932/33, the number of teachers in rural schools (primary and secondary) throughout the Soviet Union more than doubled, increasing by over 230,000; and, despite the increase in the number of pupils, there was actually a slight improvement in the teacher–pupil ratio in rural schools during the First Five-Year Plan.[92]

The new teachers differed from the old in their youth and Komsomol membership, and this almost certainly implied a different and more positive attitude to the Soviet regime. Between 1931 and 1933, 50,000 Komsomols were mobilized to teach in the schools; and by 1936, a third to a half of all primary teachers were Komsomol members.[93] Many of the new teachers, including the Komsomols, lacked formal teaching qualifications. Of 187,281 teachers in Russian primary schools teaching classes in all subjects at the beginning of 1935, more than a third had only primary or incomplete secondary education, and another quarter had finished general secondary school but did not hold a teaching diploma from the pedagogical technicum.[94] At the beginning of 1934, the Teachers' Union had 327,000 members (27%) in the 16–23 age bracket; and by 1936 – with 40% of all teachers under 28 years of age – the teaching profession consisted largely of 'Soviet youth, which has proved its enthusiasm and devotion to cultural revolution'.[95]

The achievements of the First Five-Year Plan in increasing access to primary and junior secondary education were extremely impressive: total numbers in grades I–VII (including the preparatory year introduced before grade I) grew from 11 million in 1927/28 to 21 million in 1932/33, almost 8 million of the increase occurring in rural grades I–IV.[96] It was officially, and apparently accurately, claimed that by 1931/32 95% of the 8–11 age group were already in primary school.[97] In addition, about three million adolescents who had previously missed primary education were studying either in the normal primary schools or in special courses created according to the Central Committee's directive of 1930.[98]

There was, however, a darker side to the picture: the schools were hopelessly overcrowded. School accommodation had been a problem even during NEP, as a result of poor maintenance, little new construction, and the failure of the army and other institutions to return the school buildings that had earlier been requisitioned for other uses. In the late 1920s, it was found that only 55% of schools in the RSFSR were in premises built for the purpose, while 23% were in converted barracks or similar accommodation and 22% in rented premises.[99]

School building continued to lag during the First and even the Second Five-Year Plans; and the result was that many schools had to transfer to a 2- or 3-shift system. The problem was most serious in the towns: in the working-class district of Sormovo (Nizhny Novgorod), for example, Narkompros noted that 'the universality and general accessibility of the school network has been achieved at the cost of worsening conditions of work within it (three shifts, accommodation of classes in basements and buildings which are over-crowded and ill-adapted to the purpose)'.[100] But in rural areas, too, 30% of primary schools were working more than one shift in 1933/34;[101] and despite a series of government and party resolutions deploring the situation, the shift system was still in operation in the summer of 1938 in 77% of urban and 43% of rural primary schools in the USSR.[102]

In the sphere of adult literacy, the First Five-Year Plan achievement appears to have been less impressive, and the official claims seriously exaggerated. In assessing the degree of Plan fulfilment, the Gosplan statisticians claimed that the literacy of the population of the USSR had risen to 90%, as a result of the training of more than 45 million adults in the literacy schools.[103] This was pure wishful thinking, since attendance at literacy school (even if these figures could be regarded as reliable[104]) was no guarantee of permanent or even temporary literacy. No criteria of literacy were indicated in presenting these results; and no allowance was made for subsequent regression to illiteracy, though earlier reports had suggested that up to two-thirds of the rural adults taught to read and write each winter had forgotten their new skills by the end of the summer harvesting.[105]

At the beginning of 1939, the first published Soviet census since 1926 found that 81% of the population aged 9 years and over was literate, in the sense of being able to read or write.[106] For the First Five-Year Plan figures to have been correct, we would have to assume a 9% *drop* in literacy over a six-year period in which all normal indicators – urbanization, the mortality of the oldest and least literate age groups, the extension of primary education and a large-scale programme of adult literacy training – would suggest that literacy ought to have been rising at a rapid rate.

The most reliable guide to the actual increase of literacy by the end of the First Five-Year Plan (1932/33) is provided by the 1926 and 1939 population censuses – though even here we have the problem that in 1926 the criterion of literacy was ability to read (effectively based on the statements of heads of households to the census-takers), and in 1939 the criterion was ability to read *or* write.[107] Since 1932/33 lies midway between the two censuses, we could expect literacy at that time to be about halfway between the 1926 census (57 million literates, or 51% of the 112 million of the population aged 9 years and over) and the 1939 census (109 million literates, or 81% of the 135 million of the population aged 9 years and over).[108] That would put it in the vicinity of 83 million literates, or about 68% of an estimated population of 122 million aged 9 years and over.[109]

According to the revised estimates of 1940, the numbers of adults taught in the literacy schools (not including semi-literates) were approximately equal in the periods of the First and Second Five-Year Plans;[110] and the average number taught per year in the second decade of Soviet power was four to five times as great as in the first decade.[111] Many peasants became literate after moving to the towns and entering the industrial labour force.[112] But there was also a substantial rise in the literacy of the rural population between 1926 and 1939. In the rural population of the RSFSR aged 9–49, 73% of males and 39% of females were literate in 1926. But by 1939, 95% of rural males in this age group and 79% of rural females were classified as literate.[113]

Education and peasant mobility

For peasants, collectivization did not necessarily mean entry into the kolkhoz. It might mean deportation or, on the other hand, voluntary departure into the urban labour force. For every three peasant farmers who entered kolkhozy during the First Five-Year Plan, one became a worker or white-collar employee.[114] Among young peasants, the proportion becoming upwardly mobile as a result of collectivization and the industrialization drive must have been much higher, for about 70% of the new industrial workers in the period 1929/32 were under 24 years of age.[115]

Thus all rural education programmes had, in practice, a dual function. They were not only training personnel for the countryside but also for the towns and industrial construction sites, and often the second function turned out to be the most important one. The Schools of Peasant Youth, for example, were formally reorganized as kolkhoz training schools during the First Five-Year Plan. Yet about two-thirds of their graduates had always left the countryside or taken white-collar jobs rather than going into agricultural work,[116] and it is unlikely that the proportion remaining on the land increased after collectivization. Indeed, the same government resolution which, in 1930, described the function of the Schools of Peasant Youth as 'primarily training cadres for practical work in the agricultural sphere (in kolkhozy and sovkhozy)', also noted that the schools must serve as a channel for peasant recruitment into the agricultural technicums and VUZy.[117]

The drive for universal primary education in the countryside was undoubtedly related to industrial as well as kolkhoz and sovkhoz needs. This was evidently the factor uppermost in Stalin's mind in February 1929, when he startled Lunacharsky by his intervention in the current debate on whether three or four years schooling should be made compulsory: according to Stalin, *five* years was more appropriate. 'From his point of view', Lunacharsky reported, 'the 4-year school leaves us trailing behind the European countries and even the most Asiatic countries, and there is no guarantee that the workers [*rabotniki*] who graduate from our 4-year school will be good material for our socialist construction.'[118] Earlier, Stalin had noted the importance of the apprenticeship (FZU) school in raising the general educational level of new industrial recruits, 'especially taking into account the flood of rural elements into industry'.[119] The education system, in other words, had to be geared for the training of peasant children and adolescents who would in the future become workers.

It was only at the end of the First Five-Year Plan period that peasants became an important group in the apprenticeship schools (in 1932, 41% of all FZU students were peasants[120]), but FZU apprenticeship was the elite form of entry to industry. Peasants constituted the great majority of those who entered the labour force as construction workers and unskilled labourers in the factories throughout the First Five-Year Plan.[121] Of the 101,000 new workers admitted to the Central Institute of Labour's courses at the beginning of 1931, two-thirds were peasants and rural artisans.[122]

Even the deported kulaks participated, however involuntarily, in the general movement of peasants into the industrial labour force. Almost 60% of more than a million peasant deportees (including families) were working in industrial enterprises and on the new construction sites at the beginning of 1935, and some of these received training at the enterprise and took the examinations for the State Technical Minimum.[123] At Magnitogorsk, according to John Scott, about 18,000 former kulaks were working as unskilled labourers under GPU guard: they received the opportunity for education, though separately from the other workers; and those who showed aptitude and willingness to work won an earlier transfer from the status of convict to that of regular worker.[124] (Those released in the 1930s, however, were normally still obliged to remain working in the place to which they had been exiled.)

While there were also restrictions on the movement of kolkhoz peasants – imposed initially by the kolkhozy themselves, and from 1933 by the passport system – this did not mean that peasants ceased to be mobile. Industrial recruitment had priority over kolkhoz needs; and throughout the 1930s one to two million peasants, mainly young adults, were recruited from the kolkhozy into the industrial labour force each year.[125]

This 'organized recruitment' process was probably a good deal less organized than some Soviet historians have suggested. Many of those who departed were young peasants who had just acquired elementary mechanical or technical training in the short courses for kolkhoz and sovkhoz personnel – a situation which was enormously frustrating for the kolkhoz and sovkhoz authorities, but no doubt facilitated the peasants' entry and assimilation into industrial work.

No matter how many peasants were trained in the kolkhoz and sovkhoz courses, the countryside was always left with a deficit. Between 1929 and 1932, the kolkhozy trained 3 million peasants in various skills, and the sovkhozy trained 1.5 million;[126] 80% of those trained were in their late adolescence or early 20s;[127] and only a very small proportion seem to have stayed in the countryside. Of 41,000 tractor drivers trained by the grain sovkhozy in 1930/31, for example, only 2,500 remained in the sovkhozy by February 1932. Over the years 1931–33, 99,000 tractor drivers were trained for the sovkhoz system as a whole, but only 16,000 of them were still working in sovkhozy in 1934.[128] The situation was the same with regard to kolkhoz accountants and even kolkhoz chairmen: the training which was supposed to equip them for work in the kolkhozy often in fact proved a prelude to their departure for other and more attractive positions in the towns.

Many young peasants left to continue their education. The social selection process of the First Five-Year Plan period gave absolute priority to working-class applicants. But kolkhozniki and their children were also considered desirable entrants, ranking above individual peasant farmers (*edinolichniki*) because of the socialized nature of kolkhoz production. Particular efforts were made to enrol peasant students in the agricultural VUZy, rabfaks and technicums. In 1929, Narkompros set up preparatory departments attached to the agricultural technicums for the training of workers, agricultural labourers and poor peasants: stipends were available, and the admission requirement of two years general schooling could be lowered at the discretion of local authorities.[129] From 1930, agricultural labourers, poor peasants and kolkhozniki had equal priority with workers in admission to agricultural VUZy and rabfaks; and these schools were required to aim for a 75% quota of workers *and peasants*, instead of the pure working-class quota demanded of industrial schools.[130] In practice, peasants made up 42% of students in agricultural VUZy and 50% of those in agricultural technicums in 1931. They were also strongly represented in pedagogical VUZy (31% of students in 1931) and pedagogical technicums (43%).[131]

While many pedagogical graduates actually returned to the countryside to teach, only a minority of the agricultural graduates went to work in kolkhozy and sovkhozy. Of 153,000 graduates of agricultural VUZy and technicums working in the civilian economy at the beginning of 1941, only 22% were working in kolkhozy, sovkhozy or other agricultural enterprises, and 36% had found themselves administrative jobs in the apparats (soviet, economic, cooperative, party etc.).[132]

Work in the countryside was unattractive, both in material and socio-cultural terms, and those peasants with the opportunity to escape through education or army service were likely to do so. This was later to be a real problem for the Soviet regime, but at the beginning of the 1930s the young peasants' escape must have been regretted only by the kolkhozy and sovkhozy, not by the central political and planning authorities.

During the first stages of the industrialization drive, the important thing was that large numbers of peasants should move upward into industrial and white-collar jobs, and that they should acquire some kind of education in the process. From a state planning standpoint, it was more or less immaterial whether the future skilled worker or office accountant had been trained in an urban vocational school, or during compulsory military service (which had always been a major channel of peasant education and mobility), or in a kolkhoz training programme. Whatever training the peasant *vydvizhenets* had received, it was likely that he would have to be retrained and further educated on the job – and this process of 'raising of qualifications' was in fact to become one of the main educational preoccupations of the later 1930s.[133]

On paper, many forms of education during the First Five-Year Plan were characterized by extreme specialization. In practice, this seems usually to have been a euphemism for training at an extremely low level. The real educational strategy of the period had little to do with specialization. It was to educate as many peasants as possible in the shortest possible time, using any pretext for training and whatever resources were locally available. Once minimally trained, the peasant in effect found his own level in the expanding range of opportunities in agriculture, industry and white-collar employment.

9

The making of a proletarian intelligentsia

During the First Five-Year Plan, the Soviet leadership undertook a massive programme for the promotion (*vydvizhenie*) of workers and Communists to higher education. This programme was justified by the threat from 'bourgeois wreckers', the need for the proletarian dictatorship to create its own intelligentsia, and the imperatives of the industrialization drive. Bolsheviks must 'master technology' in order to rule, Stalin said; and, if they doubted their ability to learn chemical formulae, they should remember that 'there are no fortresses Bolsheviks cannot storm'.[1]

This was not the first effort to introduce former workers into the intelligentsia through higher education. But it was the first time such a campaign had been a top priority task for the Communist Party; the first time tens of thousands of factory workers and Communists already holding responsible administrative positions had been 'mobilized' for full-time study; and the first time that the regime's chosen students had been sent *en masse* to study engineering.

The new policy produced an upheaval in all higher education, including even the military VUZy,[2] but its greatest impact was on the engineering schools. The VTUZy now had a double responsibility. On the one hand, they were training the 'Red specialists' needed to replace the old, untrustworthy, 'bourgeois' engineers. But, on the other hand, the VTUZy – together with the new Industrial Academies[3] – were also training the workers and Communists who were to become the industrial managers, administrators and political leaders of the future. They had become the major training institutions for that select body of young Communists which the party leadership during NEP had called its *smena* or replacement.

In discussing this radical reorientation of policy, our first question must be why such a difficult and expensive task as the *vydvizhenie* was ever undertaken. It was surely not, in any direct sense, a response to the imperatives of industrialization. The First Five-Year Plan industrialization drive created an acute need for engineers and technicians. But it created an equally acute need for experienced skilled workers, who were exactly the group being pushed upwards into higher education and specialist and managerial jobs. At the same time, the campaign against 'bourgeois specialists' which was the corollary of proletarian *vydvizhenie* deprived industry of the services of experienced engineers, although there is no evidence that these engineers as a group had actually engaged in wrecking or were likely to do so in the future.

The idea of a massive *vydvizhenie* of workers and Communists – first expressed in Central Committee discussions of April–July 1928 – apparently came from Stalin and Molotov.[4] This puts its institutional location in the Central Committee secretariat, and suggests that the policy's rationale is not to be found in the security or economic sphere but in that of party organization and cadres. It is probable that the cadres problem with which Stalin and Molotov were primarily concerned was that of the administrative competence of Communists recently recruited from the working-class and peasantry.

Since 1924, the party had recruited very heavily from the working class; and the policy of expansion through large-scale working-class and peasant recruitment was to continue throughout the period of the First Five-Year Plan. Even in 1927, with much of this recruitment still in the future, the party census showed 30% of party members to be currently workers by occupation, and 56% to have been workers at the time of party entry. From this second group of ex-workers came 42% of Communists currently in white-collar jobs and 43.9% of those in responsible administrative and specialist positions (*na rukovodyashchei rabote*).[5] Almost half the party secretaries at regional (oblast, guberniya and krai) level had joined the party as workers.[6]

The party's social base was reflected in the educational level of its members. If the Old Bolshevik party leadership had a cultural and educational level closer to that of the intelligentsia than to the industrial working class, this was not true of the party as a whole. In 1927, only 8.7% of all Communists and 4% of working-class Communists had higher or completed secondary education. Communists in white-collar jobs averaged only four to five years schooling.[7]

Even more disturbing was the fact that a low educational level was as characteristic of the party's administrative cadres as of its rank-and-file. Within the white-collar group, only a few special categories – economists and planners, senior officials in the central apparats in Moscow – stood distinctly above the educational level of the party as a whole. Seniority in position was often inversely correlated with education. Heads and deputy heads of Soviet, party and other institutions in the RSFSR were somewhat more likely to be former workers than those in more junior responsible positions in the same institutions, and their educational attainments were correspondingly lower: directors of industrial enterprises and their deputies, for example, averaged little more than three years schooling. At the beginning of 1928, 70.3% of all Communist directors in industry were former workers, and 82.3% of Communist directors had only primary informal (*domashnee*) education. Among the much smaller group of non-party directors, the percentages were almost reversed; 95.1% of this group were of white-collar origin, and 82.7% had secondary or higher education.[8]

Stalin's main concern was with the Communist industrial directors and, in general, with those Communists who would be responsible for leading the industrialization drive: he repeatedly stated that lack of education and specialized knowledge undermined the Communists' authority and their ability to direct the industrialization process.[9] But the forms of elite training for Communists existing during NEP did little to solve this problem. The Communist Universities and the social science faculties of the old universities offered a theoretical training to a relatively small number of Communists; and graduates of these institutions had tended to gravitate towards journalism or agitprop work, showing a much greater interest in political faction-fighting and theoretical polemics than in any kind of practical administrative work.

During the First Five-Year Plan, the stress on technical training for Communists reduced the importance of the Communist Universities, and of the social science sector of higher education as a whole. In fact, an entirely new function was found for the Communist Universities, and one which clearly indicated their loss of prestige: they were transformed in 1932 into training schools for kolkhoz and MTS personnel,[10] putting their students firmly on a career track which led out of the big cities and into an area of party work which was both arduous and poorly rewarded.

The shift of emphasis to engineering occurred simultaneously with the beginning of large-scale recruitment of workers and Communists to higher education in 1928. Clearly the engineering emphasis must be related first and foremost to the industrialization drive, while the proletarian *vydvizhenie* corresponded to the recruitment pattern already established for the Communist Party and was part of the same strategy of elite formation. But, if one considers the implications of recruiting adult workers to higher education, it is hard to imagine a more appropriate and acceptable form of training than engineering, even leaving aside the question of industrialization imperatives. For workers and former workers, engineering was the most familiar 'bourgeois' profession, and its skills were surely the most easily comprehended and mastered. The training which the VTUZy offered in the First Five-Year Plan period was modelled as closely as possible on the training that a skilled industrial worker promoted within the enterprise to a specialist position would receive on the job. In practice, working-class *vydvizhentsy* often refused mobilization to a non-engineering school, expressing either apprehension or contempt for professions not directly related to industrial production. The Komsomol secretary at the Moscow Instrument Plant flatly rejected a request to recruit young workers for study in pedagogical and medical schools: 'Our boys won't go to those VUZy', he said, 'and that's that.'[11]

Mobilization of the Thousands

The Central Committee plenum of July 1928 ordered a special mobilization of 1,000 Communists for study in the engineering VTUZy, beginning in September 1928. But the emphasis was not only on the recruitment of Communists but also on the recruitment of adult workers; 65% of the new enrolment in the VTUZy (including the Communist Thousand) were to be workers or children of workers. In addition, there was to be an extra enrolment of 3,000 workers to the rabfaks over the next two years, and an expansion of the network of evening rabfaks to provide VTUZ preparation for workers still at the factory.[12]

The first Communist Thousand was selected under Central Committee supervision. The maximum age was 35, and those selected were required to have not less than 4 or 5 years experience of responsible work in the party, soviet, or trade union apparats or in industry.[13] In fact, 60% of those selected were over 30, and 79% were of working-class origin. Most had served in the Red Army during the Civil War, and only 20% had joined the party after 1922; 40% had only primary education, and 21% incomplete secondary. The group included the president of the Precision Engineering Trust, the deputy head of the agitprop department of the Moscow party committee, the editor of the party journal *Zarya vostoka*, the liaison officer between the Komsomol Central Committee and the Red Army political administration, and the head of the appointments department of the Komsomol Central Committee.[14] The largest single group of the Thousand went to Moscow Higher Technical School, and substantial groups also went to other Moscow engineering schools – the Mendeleev Chemical Institute, the Institute of Transport Engineers, the Lomonosov Mechanics Institute and (despite Narkompros' objections) the Kagan-Shabshai Electrotechnical Institute.[15] The only non-engineering VUZ to receive more than a handful of Thousanders was the Plekhanov Economics Institute.[16]

This was the first in a series of party Thousands sent to higher education during the First Five-Year Plan. The majority of the Thousanders went to study engineering, and a smaller group to agriculture and education. It should be mentioned – though this lies outside the scope of the present book – that the same policy was followed with regard to the military VUZy; 8,000 party Thousanders were mobilized to military VUZy in 1931 and 1932, and 93% of the group were of working-class origin.[17]

The trade unions also recruited a series of worker Thousands for study in the VUZy. The first trade union Thousand, recruited in Moscow in 1928/29, consisted mainly of non-party workers with a minimum of five years experience in production.[18] The Moscow trade unionists were jealous of working-class prerogatives in the selection of candidates: lists were drawn up at workers' meetings at the factory, and attempts by local party officials to change them provoked a strong protest from a member of the Moscow Council of Trade Union.[19] The Moscow workers, whose representatives had often complained about 'socially alien' students in higher education,[20] responded enthusiastically. The mobilization 'met with wide acclaim from the worker masses', Bauman said in 1929. 'You can imagine the mood of the young and sometimes even middle-aged workers, who until now had no chance to study.'[21]

The composition of later trade union Thousands varied according to the region in which they were recruited. The Ukrainians, for example, were mainly Communists with many years industrial experience; while the Leningrad group included a rather large number with less than five years experience on production, many of whom may have been secondary-school graduates from white-collar families. But on the whole the trade union Thousanders seem to have been real workers: of the total of 8,145 who had entered VTUZy by the spring of 1931, 48% had 5–9 years industrial experience and

23% 10 years or more. Communists and candidate members of the party made up 59% of the group, Komsomols 13%, and 28% were non-party.[22]

The majority of party Thousanders apparently went directly to VUZ, but almost all the trade union Thousanders needed preparatory courses.[23] Since no thought had been given to the problem in advance, the trade unions and other organizations scrambled to establish 6–12 month courses, using whatever funds, teachers and premises were available. In 1930 alone, the trade unions claimed to have put over 55,000 workers and agricultural labourers through such courses and sent them on to VUZy and technicums.[24]

The traditional preparatory institutions, the rabfaks, were not used to train the Thousanders, because their 2- or 3-year courses were considered too long in view of the urgency of the task. This meant that the rabfaks suffered a decline in prestige during the First Five-Year Plan period, even though the number of students in them increased: they were increasingly recruiting young students with very little work experience, while the 'real workers' were going through other channels.[25]

Dimensions of organized worker and Communist recruitment to higher education

The official Thousanders were only a part of the total *vydvizhenie* to higher education, though it is the part which is easiest to quantify. Just under 10,000 Thousanders were sent by party organizations in the years 1928–31, while the trade unions sent 9,400 (or, by another count, 9,700) worker Thousanders to engineering VTUZy.[26] All told, the mobilization of the Thousands (excluding the special mobilizations of Communists to military VUZy and farm labourers to agricultural schools) provided almost 20,000 adult students for higher education.

The Thousanders, who had slightly higher stipends and better living conditions than other students, were the aristocrats of the *vydvizhenie*. But their path was followed by tens of thousands of other adult workers and Communists from the factories and the administrative apparats. The VUZy actively recruited such students, because they had proletarian and Communist quotas to fill. The adults came, despite the strain and hardship involved, out of enthusiasm for a new opportunity or simply out of ambition: the future belonged to young workers and Communists, Stalin said, but those who were unwilling to study would disqualify themselves from future leadership positions.[27]

A *vydvizhenets* may be defined as an adult student entering higher education after at least five years work experience. The term was normally applied to persons who had not completed secondary education and were of lower-class origin. From the regime's standpoint, the most important of the *vydvizhentsy* were the Communists and former workers; and it is this group whose numbers we shall try to estimate.

During the First Five-Year Plan period, over 110,000 Communists – equivalent to almost one in ten of all party members and candidates in 1928 – entered higher educational institutions.[28] Almost two-thirds of them went to engineering schools;[29] and about half had entered the party as workers.[30]

It is much more difficult to calculate the number of adult workers entering higher education in this period. According to the official statistics (see Table 2), the number of working-class students in Soviet VUZy rose by almost 200,000 between 1927/28 and 1932/33. By the end of the First Five-Year Plan, there were 151,000 students classified as working-class in the engineering VTUZy alone, and an additional 85,000 in other types of higher school.

But these figures have to be treated with caution. They were no doubt inflated because of the pressure to meet high proletarian quotas (which encouraged students to disguise their social origins and VUZy to accept doubtful claims to proletarian status); and they also included many students who were not *vydvizhentsy*, among them school-leavers who had spent a few years in the factory in order to get into VUZy as 'proletarians', FZU graduates and children of working-class families coming straight from school.

However, we know that about half the 110,000 Communist *vydvizhentsy* were former workers, and on this basis it is possible to make an approximate estimate of the number of *vydvizhentsy* who were former workers but not party members. According to a survey of leading cadres and specialists taken in November 1933, 9,480 of the First Five-Year Plan graduates already holding responsible jobs were Communist former workers, and 7,530 were non-party former workers.[31] This gives us a ratio of 56 Communists to 44 non-party in the working-class group. Thus, if 56,000 Communist *vydvizhentsy* in the First Five-Year Plan were former workers, we should expect that there were about 44,000 worker *vydvizhentsy* who were not party members.

Our conclusion, then, is that the total working-class and Communist *vydvizhenie* to higher education (excluding military) may be estimated at 150,000 or above – 110,000 Communists, half of whom were former workers, together with more than 40,000 former workers who were not Communists. That means that almost a third of all students in higher education in 1932/33 were *vydvizhentsy* (and in the engineering schools, which attracted most Communists and former workers, the proportion must have been considerably higher).

TABLE 2

Total enrolment of students in higher education, with working-class percentages, 1927/28–1932/33

	Numbers in all Soviet VUZy and VTUZy	Working-class %	Numbers in industrial–transport VTUZy	Working-class %
1927/28	159,800[1]	25.4[2]	45,200[3]	38.3[4]
1928/29	166,800[5]	30.3[6]	52,300[5]	43.1[7]
1929/30	191,100[5]	35.2[6]	62,800[5]	46.4[4]
1930/31	272,100[5]	46.4[2]	130,300[5]	61.7[4]
1931/32	394,000[5]	51.4[8]	197,300[5]	63.7[8]
1932/33	469,800[5]	50.3[2]	233,400[5]	64.6[2]

Sources:
[1] *Sotsialisticheskoe stroitel'stvo SSSR* (Moscow, 1934), p. 406.
[2] *Ibid.*, p. 410.
[3] A. E. Beilin, *Kadry spetsialistov SSSR. Ikh formirovanie i rost* (Moscow, 1935), p. 74.
[4] *Podgotovka kadrov v SSSR 1927–1931 gg.* (Moscow, 1933), p. 19.
[5] N. de Witt, *Education and Professional Employment in the USSR* (Washington DC, 1961), pp. 638–9.
[6] *Narodnoe khozyaistvo SSSR* (Moscow–Leningrad, 1932), pp. 534–5.
[7] *Novye kadry tyazheloi promyshlennosti* (Moscow, 1934), p. 49. For the years 1929/30–1932/33, this source gives higher working-class VTUZ percentages than those cited, but they appear less reliable.
[8] TsGAOR 5451/15/715, p. 18: Sector of Industrial Cadres, VTsSPS – Table on Social Composition of Students in Higher Education. This source gives the same working-class percentages in all VUZy and VTUZy alone for 1927/28 as sources (2) and (4).

Although this group was of peculiar political interest to the regime, it should not be forgotten that the First Five-Year Plan expansion of higher education gave many other adults of lower-class origin and incomplete secondary education the opportunity to enter the VUZy. The simple expansion of numbers meant that two out of every three students in Soviet VUZy in 1932/33 were students who could not have entered during NEP, and only one of these two 'new' students was a working-class or Communist *vvdvizhenets*. Peasants, teachers and low-grade officeworkers filled many of the newly-created places in agricultural and pedagogical VUZy. The pre-dominance of *adult* students from all social backgrounds is indicated by the age breakdown: in 1931, two-thirds of all students in Soviet higher education were aged 23 and over; 16% were over 29; and of the over-29 age group (65,000 students), 46,000 were in non-engineering schools.[32]

Impact of the new policy on higher education

Between 1928 and 1931, the VTUZy were pushed with ever-increasing force towards shorter courses, narrower specialization and greater practical work on production. The same pressures were put on the non-engineering schools, though the results were less closely monitored. The professors, of course, protested; and in high-prestige VTUZy like Moscow Higher Technical School they won some support both from the administration and the Communist students.[33] But objections that the new policies would lower educational standards were swept aside. As the head of Vesenkha's technical-education administration explained with regard to the principle of narrow specialization:

The 'broad engineer' is a toga in which the old professors are draping themselves to protect their own set-up...If we leave even one little loop-hole, if we leave even one crack for any kind of experiment with the development of the so-called broad engineer, we will destroy the whole reorganization [of the VTUZy].[34]

The VTUZy were required to attach themselves to industrial enterprises, which would provide the facilities for continuous practical work throughout the school year, for which the students would be paid by the enterprises. By the end of 1929, the desired ratio of practical work in production and theoretical work in the VTUZ was 1:1. To make up the theoretical deficit, the VTUZy were allowed to transfer some school subjects to the enterprise, where they would supposedly be taught informally by the engineers. The same system was applied, at least on paper, in the non-industrial VUZy. The practical work of a pedagogical student, for example, would be conducted in a school or local education department; that of an economics student in an accounting department or planning agency. In practice, non-industrial practical work seems often to have meant clerical work in an office.[35]

The introduction of continuous industrial practical work caused a seemingly endless series of problems between educational and industrial authorities. It was reported in 1929 that 'almost every [industrial] organization is intentionally or unintentionally making difficulties. If the trust agrees to take students for practical work, the factory is against it. If the factory agrees, of course the enterprise will not take them.'[36] There were complaints that students were not being placed according to their specialization, not being given space on the shop floor or shunted off to the factory office to do clerical work or run errands. But there were also complaints that factories short of engineering personnel were stealing the students altogether from the VTUZy.[37] This latter practice was particularly noted in 1929, when the trusts also developed a dubiously legal system of *kontraktatsiya*, by which the students accepted stipends well above the state norm from the trusts in return for an undertaking to work for them after graduation. It was reported that various trusts engaged in 'wild competition' for students of the more desirable VTUZy. But their enthusiasm declined as it was noted that the students could not be made to honour their commitments to work for the contracting agency after graduation; and in the autumn of 1930 a government decree forbade the signing of new contracts.[38]

Despite a brief upsurge of interest in the German type of 'broad engineer' fostered by Gosplan and the German 'Technical Week' held at the beginning of 1929,[39] the ideal of narrow specialization continued to gain ground. The narrow engineering profile was believed to be both ultra-modern (because American) and ultra-socialist (because appropriate to an economy planned to the last detail). But what lay behind these rationalizations was the knowledge that Soviet engineering students had neither the time nor the educational background to assimilate very much theory, and the hope that practical experience and proletarian instinct would compensate for lack of book learning. 'Do we really need such large numbers of highly qualified specialists as Gosplan indicates?' asked one discussant after a Gosplan report. 'Take Dneprostroi: there are more than 1,000 engineers working there, which is completely unnecessary; and they are all learning from [the American engineer] Cooper who, if you give him an equation to solve, will not be able to do it, because he is not an engineer in our sense of the word.'[40]

Courses in the old VTUZy were reduced to a maximum of 4 years, while the 'new-type VTUZy' offered 3-year courses.[41] But when the shock-work (*udarnichestvo*) movement developed in industry, it became common for Communist students, in particular, to undertake to complete their studies in less than the normal time. The party organization in the Lenin Agricultural Academy set Communist students the task of graduating in under two years. In the machine-building and planning sections of the Moscow Power Institute, 'students – old party members – were expelled from the ranks of the Communist Party for refusing to agree to leftist demands for a sharp reduction of the term of study in the Institute'. Students of the Grozny Oil Institute actually appealed to Sovnarkom USSR for protection against the Oil Trust's demands that they complete the 3-year course in two years, noting that 'they are trying to make us not into engineers but into uneducated involuntary wreckers of industry'.[42]

Apart from the instructions on practical work, the party leadership gave no directives on the reorganization of teaching methods in the VUZy. But the radical methods currently being applied in the schools[43] had their counterpart in higher education. Lectures were regarded as hopelessly old-fashioned; and in any case the demands of continuous practical work made it impossible to enforce attendance. The so-called 'brigade-laboratory method', involving group work on projects under the supervision of a professor, was officially endorsed by Narkompros in 1931.[44] The old rabfak practice of collective testing (*kellektivnyi uchet*) replaced formal examinations. The resulting disorganization is vividly described in the jubilee history of the Plekhanov Economics Institute:

Each brigade, consisting of five or six persons, had its own study plan and its own timetable. All this required a colossal number of separate classrooms. The supply of auditoria was completely inadequate. A breakdown of classes occurred.

No account was taken of the student's allocation of time. There were a large number of gaps between classes. In testing knowledge, it was difficult to establish the individuality of each member of the brigade. The more competent students, on whom fell responsibility for the success of the whole brigade, carried an enormous workload.[45]

Equal confusion reigned in the administration of higher education. In November 1929, after hearing a report from Kaganovich, the Central Committee plenum resolved that 'the experiment of transferring VTUZy into the jurisdiction of Vesenkha had completely justified itself'.[46] Early in the new year, it was decided to divide all the existing higher schools into highly specialized professional institutes, and transfer them to the administrative control of the government agency or branch of industry which would employ their graduates. An All-Union Sovnarkom commission headed by V. V.

Schmidt was created to supervise the reorganization, which was conducted in the spring and summer of 1930.[47]

This was a more complete defeat for Narkompros than its former leadership had envisaged even in the bitterest moments of struggle with Vesenkha over control of the VTUZy. The new policy was clearly in part a rebuke to the education commissariats for their 'rightist' associations and allegedly incompetent management of higher education. But it also reflected a strong anti-generalist philosophy in the educational world, expressed in the late 1929 discussions on whether universities and polytechnical institutes were survivals from a pre-modern mode of educational production.[48] Under the new order, the VTUZy were to be split up into narrowly specialized schools under the control of specific branches of industry (coal, oil etc.), with little central coordination from Vesenkha. The universities were similarly to lose their corporate identity, with law and medical schools going to the Commissariats of Justice and Health, economics departments going to Gosplan and the Commissariat of Finance, and so on.

The reorganization of higher education produced an instant increase in the number of VUZy – from 152 in 1929/30 to 537 in 1930/31.[49] It also created an incredible diversity of administrative bodies with some responsibility for higher education. Some government institutions flatly refused to take on the new responsibilities;[50] others – like the Bread Trust of the All-Union Commissariat of Supply, which must have been disconcerted to find itself master of the new Odessa Technological Institute of Cereals and Flour – coped as best they could with their new charges, or simply ignored them. The education commissariats retained 'general methodological leadership' over all higher education. This situation caused disssatisfaction not only to Narkompros but to Vesenkha, which wanted its own department (Glavpromkadrov) to have methodological control over the engineering schools; and when N. P. Gorbunov, as secretary to Sovnarkom, signed its resolution on this question, he felt such distress at its organizational implications that he distributed a personal letter of protest to all Sovnarkom members.[51]

The new VUZy were, for the most part, schools or departments of a former VUZ; and one of the notable disadvantages of the reorganization was that five or six independent institutes (each with its own administrative staff) often had to share the same buildings, laboratories and libraries. Sometimes one of the new institutes succeeded in taking over most of the old VUZ property, leaving the rest destitute. When the Voronezh Agricultural VUZ, for example, was split into six separate institutes, the new Chemical–Technical Institute managed to monopolize all the laboratory facilities, while the Poultry Institute acquired only 'eight small benches, a corridor and one lecture room (shared with the Mechanization Institute)'.[52]

The education commissariats retained administrative control over the pedagogical VUZy; an undistributable residue of pure science, mathematics and arts schools; and, in addition, such medical and law schools, geography departments and so on as had been rejected by other government agencies. The Russian Narkompros preserved the major universities under the old title (though bereft of many of their former schools and departments). But in the Ukraine the universities were disbanded, leaving a number of small, specialized institutes, most of which were still under the jurisdiction of the Ukrainian Narkompros.

Purging and expansion in higher education

Professors were an obvious source of potential opposition to large-scale *vydvizhenie* and higher educational reorganization, and the authorities quickly took steps to neutralize them. The Shakhty trial put all members of the 'bourgeois intelligentsia' under suspicion; and the professors, as was pointed out, were not just 'bourgeois' but 'feudal' in political attitudes and social origin.[53] Relatively little publicity was given to professorial objections to the reorganization of higher education, but the press found many examples of arrogant, aristocratic and anti-Soviet behaviour among the faculty. It was reported, for example, that a priest had been called in to bless the new premises of the Leningrad Institute of Experimental Agronomy; that a professor in the Urals had told his students that Communist despotism was economically less effective than enlightened capitalism; and that a medical researcher investigating 'reactive psychoses in conditions of class war' had found collectivization to be a cause of peasant psychosis.[54]

The main disciplinary measure taken against the professors was enforcement of the legal requirement, previously ignored, that all VUZ faculty members whose tenure had expired should seek re-election. The re-election campaign was organized by Vyshinsky, newly appointed head of the Narkompros administration of higher and technical education. Vyshinsky apparently did not want to fire large numbers of professors.[55] But he hoped that ambitious junior faculty would be persuaded to challenge and criticize their senior colleagues in a public forum, with the radical students providing a properly intimidating atmosphere of proletarian Cultural Revolution.

Vyshinsky's colleagues in Narkompros were clearly unenthusiastic about this policy;[56] and the first elections (*perevybory*), held in the summer of 1929, were confined to a small number of prominent VUZy.[57] The faculty showed considerable professional solidarity, and even the students' criticism seems to have been restrained. The press singled out a few individuals for censure, including Poyarkov, a professor at the Plekhanov Economics Institute, who was described as a projector of socially-alien students, an anti-semite and 'a notorious woman-hater'. But after Poyarkov was attacked, the electrical engineer who had been after his job withdrew his candidacy.[58]

In the short run, at any rate, outside attempts to exploit professional jealousies tended to be counter-productive. When a Communist historian of Leningrad University was commissioned to attack his colleague, Academician Tarle, he 'could find nothing better than to warn the Academician of his forthcoming attack on him, apologizing in advance for what he called his "involuntary criticism"'. This was considered a clear choice of professional over Communist loyalty, and the historian was expelled from the party as 'a two-faced deserter from the Marxist front'.[59]

The elections drew few outside candidacies; and only in the Northern Caucasus – home of the Shakhty wreckers – was there a report of 'workers and engineers' gathering from distant areas to participate in elections at the Don Polytechnical Institute. In Moscow, the greatest student participation was reported in the Timiryazev Agricultural Academy: there was considerable discussion on whether an alternative candidate should contest the chair held by the distinguished Academician Pryanishnikov, since the students disliked his ideology but conceded his knowledge of agrochemistry and fertilizers; and a negative verdict was returned in the case of a Christian professor of meteorology ('It is clear that a church-going professor cannot explain and predict weather manifestations from a materialist point of view.').[60]

As a result of the first round of professorial elections, which involved 312 professorial posts and 750 at lower level, 65 professors lost their jobs, and the same fate befell 154 junior faculty.[61] A similar proportion – around 20% – dropped out or were expelled from the Section of Scientific Workers in a re-registration of members conducted in 1930.[62] But we should not conclude from these figures that a sizeable group of the old professoriate was permanently, or even temporarily, driven out of the profession. Poyarkov, the woman-hater, for example, lost his job at the Plekhanov Institute, but probably retained at least one of his other full-time teaching positions (at Moscow Higher Technical School and Ivanovo-Voznesensk Polytechnical Institute). Professor Solosin, fired from Smolensk University for being 'anti-Marxist and non-scientific', not only immediately found himself an academic job but was appointed deputy rector in his new university.[63]

The expansion of higher education meant that professors were in a sellers' market; and the fragmentation of control under the structural reorganization of 1930 meant that a great number of authorities were competing for a quite small number of qualified personnel. The number of teaching positions in higher education rose from 18,000 in 1927/28 to 47,000 in 1930/31 and 57,000 at the beginning of 1933. The actual increase in personnel was less, because most professors held more than one job. But in the first two years of the Five-Year Plan alone, the total number of VUZ teachers grew by 10,000.[64]

This was a period in which, as one indignant witness reported, 'anyone could become a professor'.

Old professors with world reputations, carrying the weight of decades of work in the VUZy and dozens of major works, engineer–*praktiki* from the factories, young people fresh from college classrooms, secondary-school teachers tempted by better material conditions and, finally, outright confidence men and frauds – all of them...bore the same title of professor or *dotsent*, had the same position in society and enjoyed equal material benefits![65]

Because of the chaotic conditions in the VUZy, many old professors preferred to move their base to one of the new scientific research institutes which proliferated in all fields during the First Five-Year Plan,[66] but they almost invariably continued to teach courses and draw a salary at the VUZ.

In 1930/31, there were 18,454 VUZ positions carrying the title of professor or *dotsent*. Just over half of the holders of these positions counted VUZ teaching as their basic occupation, while the rest were either basically employed in scientific research institutes (4,023) or practising their profession as engineers, economists, doctors and so on (4,787). In the engineering VTUZy, almost a quarter of all full professorships and a third of all *dotsent* positions were held by factory engineers.[67]

Although the proportion of Communists among VUZ teachers

rose to about 13% in 1930/31,[68] Communist influence in higher education was most objectionably manifested (from the professorial point of view) in the growing body of graduate students. At the beginning of the First Five-Year Plan, there were less than a thousand graduate students in all Soviet higher schools, and probably not more than a hundred of them were Communists or Komsomols. By January 1933, the total number of graduate students had risen to over 10,000, of whom 50% were Communists and 20% Komsomols.[69]

From 1929, entrance to *aspirantura* (graduate studies) was possible without a degree,[70] and, 'as a general rule, the selection of graduate students [was a process] in which the academic community of the VTUZy did not participate'.[71] This was an enormous cause of resentment, since the professors were forced into close contact with students whom they regarded as unqualified and unsuitable for academic life. The uneasy relationship of the old professor, his chosen 'bourgeois' successor and assistant, the naive *vydvizhenets* and the intimidating Communist graduate student was vividly portrayed in a contemporary play by Afinogenov, *Fear* (1930).

At undergraduate level, the new recruitment policies introduced in the autumn of 1928 had the immediate effect of drastically reducing the number of places available to 'bourgeois' students competing on the free enrolment. The situation was particularly bad in the high-prestige VTUZy of Moscow, to which many of the new proletarian and Communist students were sent. At the beginning of the 1928/29 school year, Moscow Higher Technical School had only 43 places open to competition, while the Mining Academy and the technical departments of the Plekhanov Economics Institute had a mere 14 each.[72] There were cases of suicide among middle-class parents, according to Lunacharsky; and the more accessible Communist leaders were deluged with requests for intervention on behalf of individual applicants.[73]

But the atmosphere was threatening to students with the wrong class background. Alarmist stories appeared in the press on children of kulaks, priests and merchants who had managed to worm their way into Soviet higher schools.[74] Local party committees, taking their cue from the Shakhty trial, began to conduct purges of the student body.[75] In contrast to the situation in 1924, these purges were not the product of an explicit directive from the party Central Committee, though in the Smolensk Archive we find evidence that least one Central Committee *rapporteur* on the July plenum encouraged a local purge.[76]

The Ukrainian party's Central Committee, however, tried to discourage the purges, as did the Russian and Ukrainian education commissariats.[77] As in 1924, the commissariats reinstated students who appealed their expulsion by local organizations; and the Smolensk (now Western Oblast) party committee once again complained to the agitprop department of the Central Committee that it had encountered 'opposition from Narkompros on the matter of purging socially alien students'.[78] Vyshinsky reported that similar complaints were being sent by local organizations to Rabkrin.[79]

In statistical terms, the purges had some ascertainable impact on the composition of the student body in the 1928/29 school year.[80] But in subsequent years, although purging sporadically continued, the effects were cancelled out by the enormous increase in the total number of students in higher education. Between 1927/28 and 1932/33, student numbers grew from 159,800 to 469,800 (see above, Table 2) – an increase of almost 300%. Over the same period, the percentage of students who came from white-collar backgrounds dropped from 51% to 33%,[81] but in absolute terms this meant a rise in numbers from 81,000 to 145,000. Even the number of socially-alien students ('others') increased by more than 6,000 between 1928/29 and 1930/31.[82]

It is probable, moreover, that these figures substantially under-represent the real size of the white-collar and alien contingent, since there are many reports of students using false documents of social origin. According to one such report, in 1928/29 'about 30% of the first-year students [in the Second Moscow University] turned out to be persons deprived of voting rights'[83] – most of them clearly having entered with false documents, as it was a year of strict social selection in admissions. It was not always necessary even to forge the documents:

It is striking how easy it is to get documents on social position from the village soviets and local executive committees, which give out endorsements that 'The bearer of this is a poor peasant' with criminal light-mindedness and irresponsibility to almost anyone, starting with middle peasants and ending with kulaks and merchants. The village soviets and local executive committees give statements to priests affirming that they are 'grain-sowers'.[84]

All higher schools needed students, and there was apparently no central blacklist of students who had been purged. Thus the obvious thing for a purged student to do was to apply to another VUZ, probably in a different town, and begin his student career anew.[85]

But the purged students were not the only ones in transit. The 1930 reorganization of higher education provoked a mass migration, as students tried to determine which of the new VUZy would be best funded and have the most dormitory space. There was a constant tendency for students initially accepted by non-industrial schools to transfer to the higher-prestige engineering VTUZy – a very sound decision in terms of career opportunities which was made by the young Leonid Brezhnev, among many others, when he left the Timiryazev Agricultural Academy during the 1930/31 school year, returned to his home town of Dneprodzerzhinsk and subsequently re-enrolled as a worker student at the local Metallurgical Institute.[86]

Training in the factory

The administrative reorganization of the education system conducted in 1929/30 brought a great part of the educational network directly under the jurisdiction of industrial authorities and on to the industrial budget. Industry took over total responsibility for the apprenticeship and trade schools, the industrial technicums (including those formed from the liquidation of grades viii–x of the general secondary school) and the VTUZy. There was a vast increase in the number of students being trained for industry, since not only did the total number of students in secondary and higher education rise sharply, but so did the percentage of all students who were in engineering schools. In 1928/29, there were 645,000 students in all types of secondary education above the level of grade vii, and 41% of them were being trained for industry (including building and transport). Three years later, the total number of students had risen to 1,724,000, and the industrial share to 60–70%.[87] Over the same period, the total number of students in higher education increased from 167,000 to 394,000, while the share of the engineering VTUZy rose from 31% to 50%.[88]

But in addition to this, the enterprises were forced to organize a massive programme of training on the job and in the factory. According to official figures, the industrial labour force grew by 3 million in the First Five-Year Plan period, while the numbers of construction workers increased by almost $2\frac{1}{2}$ million; 2 million workers became skilled or semi-skilled, and at the big factories 'about a third and sometimes a half of the total number of workers' were involved in some type of training programme.[89]

The traditional form of labour training was on-the-job apprenticeship (in contemporary Soviet terminology, *individual'no-brigadnoe*

uchenichestvo); and during NEP this had been the form preferred
by Vesenkha. The alternatives were the factory–apprenticeship
school (FZU), supported by Narkompros and the Komsomol because
it gave general education as well as apprenticeship training, and the
short courses organized by Gastev's Central Institute of Labour,
which had the endorsement of the trade union leadership.

In 1927/28, Narkompros and the Komsomol raised an outcry
about Vesenkha's interest in Gastev's methods and hostility to the
apprenticeship school.[90] But both the circumstances and Vesenkha's
attitude changed rapidly. By the middle of 1929, it had become clear
that industry had two major problems involving labour. One was the
acute shortage of skilled workers, which created a much greater
demand than the existing forms of training could meet.[91] The other
was the influx of inexperienced and often illiterate peasants into the
industrial labour force. The peasants lacked industrial skills, but
above all they were deficient in 'culture' and 'social consciousness' –
that is, they needed to learn how to live in a town or workers'
barracks and how to adapt to the discipline of a factory. Given the
multitude of pressures and demands on the skilled workers, informal
apprenticeship no longer seemed a satisfactory answer to the problem
of assimilation. Some industrial spokesmen advocated the 'conditioning' methods of the Central Institute of Labour, while others began
to think in terms of formal education and the apprenticeship school.[92]

In June 1929, Vesenkha announced its conversion to the principle
of the factory apprenticeship school. Kuibyshev, in language reminiscent of that earlier used by Narkompros, said that the school must
be supported because

carrying out the grandiose tasks of reconstruction of industry anticipated
under the Five-Year Plan is possible only with cadres of workers who are
politically conscious and possess social initiative. Therefore it must be
emphasized that the skilled (and also the unskilled) worker in the reconstruction period must be regarded not only as an executant of his specific
industrial function but as a conscious creator and organizer of the whole
industrial process.[93]

The whole FZU network was to be expanded; and, in addition to
the apprenticeship schools training skilled workers, there were to be
2-year apprenticeship schools for the 'mass professions' (that is, for
unskilled and semi-skilled jobs), to be known as ShUMP.[94]

This was a real change of policy on the apprenticeship schools, for
their expansion in the following years was remarkable. In 1928/29,
there were 120,000 pupils in industrial and other apprenticeship

schools (building, transport, forestry, sovkhoz and so on) and 152,000 in the mainly artisan trade schools. In 1931/32, after the merging of the apprenticeship and trade school network, the numbers in 'FZU and FZU-type schools' had reached over a million.[95]

This does not mean, however, that the apprenticeship school actually became the major source of skilled and semi-skilled industrial labour. Of the two million workers who acquired some skills during the First Five-Year Plan period, only 300,000 were apprenticeship school graduates.[96] The rest were trained in the short-term courses of the Central Institute of Labour or on the job.

The bases of the Central Institute of Labour were particularly important in the early years of the First Five-Year Plan in the retraining of the unemployed; and they also played a large role in the training of construction workers – often peasants entering the urban labour force for the first time. In both these cases, the Institute worked under contract to the Commissariat of Labour, making its share company 'Ustanovka' 'a highly profitable enterprise'[97] which basically financed the Institute's research on the scientific organization of labour and the production process. 'Ustanovka' had 1,700 training bases for the construction industry in 1931; and in 1932 the Commissar of Labour stated that during the First Five-Year Plan period '750,000 workers were trained according to the methods of the Central Institute of Labour in the Labour Commissariat system'.[98]

The industrial authorities normally turned to Gastev's methods when there was an acute crisis in a particular branch of industry; and such crises occurred regularly whenever one of the big new enterprises went into production for the first time, and it was discovered that labour needs had been vastly underestimated.[99] But the enterprises were often dissatisfied with the quality of the trainees, whose preparation on the base did not familiarize them with the actual conditions on the shop floor.[100] In the autumn of 1931, the Central Committee transferred the Institute of Labour and 'Ustanovka' to the control of Vesenkha, and directed the Institute to concentrate its energies not on direct labour training but on research and consultation on questions of industrial rationalization and scientific organization of labour.[101]

This directive was in part a response to the development of a more formal system of on-the-job training within the enterprises themselves. At the end of 1929, it had been officially recognized that the regular specialized-education system, despite its dramatic expansion, could not meet industrial demands for workers and technical personnel; and the November plenum of the Central Committee resolved that 'industrial enterprises and sovkhozy, especially those that are the most technically equipped, should transform themselves into a kind of school for the mass training and retraining of skilled workers, foremen, technicians and engineers'.[102]

The enterprises were already training their own workers and even technical personnel,[103] but the Central Committee's resolution raised the status of in-factory training, allowed the enterprises to claim the title of *zavod-VTUZ* and, with the approval of the central industrial authorities, to award degrees and diplomas.[104] For the radical educational theorists who wished to see a merging of education and production,[105] the Central Committee's recognition of the *zavod-VTUZ* was a milestone on the road to socialism. Some of the enterprises had the same reaction, regarding the *zavod-VTUZ* title as a mark of status, and establishing courses for engineers even when they were not really necessary. Others, in a period when cost accounting was a very peripheral concern for the big industrial enterprises, spent lavishly on their training programmes (in the words of a Dneprostroi representative, 'we spend as much as we have to – money is no problem for us').[106]

The *zavod-VTUZ* programme was really a luxury undertaking which could be afforded only by enterprises with a relatively abundant supply of skilled labour – the Automotive Plant in Moscow and the Stalin Metallurgical Factory in Leningrad, for example. Initially, these plants did not even include labour training in the *zavod-VTUZ* structure, but in effect created their own secondary and higher schools within the enterprise. In 1930, the *zavody-VTUZy* normally offered three courses, all of them weighted towards general education rather than narrowly specialized training. The lowest course, attended by skilled workers, gave the equivalent of a grade VII programme in the normal school. The middle course was at technicum level; and the highest – for students who were probably already *praktiki* holding technicians' and engineers' jobs – was on the level of the VTUZ.[107]

But most enterprises needed skilled and semi-skilled workers more than they needed engineers. In 1931, all factories were obliged to provide new worker recruits with compulsory introductory classes on the production process;[108] and a number of the new enterprises set up elaborate training programmes extending from elementary lectures for novices to advanced technical courses.[109] According to a rather irritated trade union report of 1931, it was impossible to tell how many workers were actually involved in factory training programmes because of Vesenkha's slipshod collection of data.[110] The number, in any case, was large and growing.[111] While the *zavod-VTUZ* began to disappear from the scene from 1931, when the regular technicums and VTUZy expanded their evening courses, enterprise programmes for the 'raising of qualifications' of the work-force became a permanent part of Soviet industrial life.

Training in the factory and upward mobility

Internal *vydvizhenie* – the promotion of skilled workers to positions as foremen and masters, who in their turn might become technician- or engineer-*praktiki* without holding formal diplomas or degrees – had traditionally provided industry with a large proportion of its specialist cadres. This remained the situation during the First Five-Year Plan period and beyond, despite the vast expansion of secondary and higher technical education. Between 1931 and 1934, the output of engineering VTUZy and technicums was actually greater than the total increase in numbers of engineers and technicians working in the enterprises;[112] yet more than a third of the new engineers and well over half of the new technicians in the enterprises in the same years were *praktiki* without formal qualifications.[113]

In the early 1930s, however, the enterprises unwittingly sponsored another form of upward mobility through the apprenticeship schools and factory courses. A worker graduating from the lowest course of the *zavod-VTUZ* was credited with the equivalent of seven years general schooling, and this made him a desirable entrant for the technicum and even for the VTUZ. Many young workers took the opportunity to move on to full-time education, but workers were not the only ones to use the factory courses for this purpose. Clerical employees of the enterprises went through the programmes of the *zavod-VTUZ*, and it was reported that at some enterprises 50–75% of students in the middle-level (technicum) courses were 'adolescents, graduates of the 7-year school'.[114] 'In practice', a Soviet historian concludes, '...[the courses] were nothing other than an unusual kind of preparatory school...for subsequent entry to rabfaks, technicums and VTUZy.'[115]

The factory apprenticeship school, in which industry made such a heavy investment during the First Five-Year Plan, functioned even more blatantly as a channel to higher education. With the collapse of the upper level of general secondary school, the apprenticeship school – at least in the major cities – took over not only students and teachers from the old secondary school but also its position as the major institution offering general education beyond grade VII level. In 1930 and 1931, about a sixth of all FZU pupils came from white-collar families;[116] and they had presumably entered the school not because they wanted to become industrial apprentices but because they wanted to qualify as 'proletarian' entrants to technicum or VUZ. Many of the working-class students, who remained the core of the student body in the apprenticeship schools,[117] evidently developed similar aspirations towards higher education.

Up to 65% of study time in the apprenticeship schools went to general educational subjects, and there was an effort to model the schools' programme on that of the old grade IX of general secondary school. The curriculum included Russian language, social studies, natural science, chemistry, technical physics and mathematics; and the 3-year apprenticeship schools also taught a foreign language.[118] Within the schools, both teachers and pupils had their eyes firmly fixed on higher education, or so it was reported by one Moscow-based writer in an educational journal. When he argued at one apprenticeship school for a greater emphasis on industrial training,

the pupils spoke sharply against it, saying that if they did not work through logarithms none of them would get accepted in any VTUZ. Such opinions were supported at that school, as in almost all other schools, by the large number of methodologically competent teachers of general educational subjects. They were opposed by the teachers of special [i.e. vocational] subjects...who, as everyone knows, had little influence on the internal life of the majority of schools.[119]

Although a formal instruction existed obliging graduates of the apprenticeship school to work for three years in industry after finishing the course,[120] it may have been more honoured in the breach than the observance. Sovnarkom itself directed technicums to recruit apprenticeship graduates in 1931;[121] and at the 'Serp i molot' plant in 1933 only 210 out of 900 FZU apprentices registered for work at the plant after graduating.[122]

In 1932, 35% of students admitted to the VTUZy and technicums of heavy industry were former FZU pupils – a group numbering around 57,000, in a year when the industrial apprenticeship schools graduated somewhat under 88,000.[123] This calculation may exaggerate the loss to industry. But other data seem to confirm a high attrition rate; and even in 1934, when great efforts had been made to reduce it, the new Committee on Higher Technical Education noted that a 'considerable number of young people go from the FZU schools to the rabfaks and technicums, and then straight to the VUZy and also into graduate school'.[124]

It is difficult not to be impressed both by the scope of the educational expansion and *vydvizhenie* of the First Five-Year Plan period and by the reckless and extravagant manner in which it was accomplished. An enormous network of apprenticeship schools was set up to provide industry with skilled labour – but it turned out that many of the graduates preferred to go on to further education, and the apprenticeship schools became in effect general secondary schools. The VTUZy and technicums were vastly expanded to provide industry with the needed engineers and technicians – but it turned out that a substantial proportion of the graduates chose further education or administrative and office jobs, so the enterprises had to set up their own independent training schemes for *praktiki*. Such examples could be multiplied almost indefinitely.

Shturmovshchina produced waste, and policies conceived at 'Bolshevik tempo' produced contradictions. As a byproduct of the policy of *vydvizhenie*, the VUZy spent an enormous amount of time purging the student body and checking social credentials. But this activity was almost meaningless in a situation of wild higher-educational growth, because the student simply moved to another VUZ. The infatuation with narrow specialization profiles led to a structural reorganization of higher education which was inherently unworkable and merely slowed down the production of specialists. The stress on practical work forced students to spend half their time on production; but at the same time the *vydvizhenie* brought into the VTUZy students who were already familiar with production processes and needed above all to learn theory.

The reorganization of education at all levels was intended to bring the schools into closer contact with production. What this meant in practice was that industry became financially responsible for the schools: by the end of the First Five-Year Plan, the greater part of all costs for education beyond grade VII was subsumed in the industrial budgets. It could hardly be argued that industry was getting a satisfactory short-term return on its investment. The direct beneficiaries were the education system and the administrative apparat.

However, it may well be that there are no rational ways of achieving radical change; and at least two kinds of important radical change were produced. First, the society and its schools were abruptly forced to acquire a technical orientation. Whatever the loss in educational quality and breadth, the Soviet Union did avoid a pitfall of other developing nations in the twentieth century – over-production of lawyers, under-production of engineers, and elite preoccupation (similar to that of the Soviet *smena* in the 1920s) with intellectual debates and political faction-fighting.

Second, the Soviet Union created its future elite on a largely working-class base. Party membership and higher education were the two main channels into the elite, and, from respectively 1924 and 1928 until 1932, workers predominated in both. First Five-Year Plan educational policies greatly facilitated working-class *vydvizhenie*; and the process continued throughout the 1930s as a natural result of industrialization and the expansion of the administrative and specialist elite. Mass upward mobility would certainly have occurred without regime intervention, but the policies of the 1920s and early 1930s firmly linked Soviet power with the increasing opportunities open to young workers and peasants.

The products of many actions of the leadership during the First Five-Year Plan were accidental and unplanned. But this was not the case with the policy of working-class *vydvizhenie*. The policy and its objective – the creation of a new elite, or 'proletarian intelligent-sia' – were clearly stated in 1928. If one assumes that Stalin saw it as a breakthrough policy that would not be indefinitely continued, the objective was successfully reached. This was a major political achievement, and its impact on the nature of the Soviet regime and leadership was lasting.

PART III

The restoration of order: new policies in education, 1931–1934

The policies which came under the general heading of Cultural Revolution – harassment of the old intelligentsia and massive recruitment of workers and Communists to higher education – were introduced in 1928 and reached a peak of intensity in 1930/31. But by the middle of 1931, there were signs that the Cultural Revolution had run its course. The pool of willing and even partially qualified worker and Communist applicants for higher education showed signs of drying up. The industrial enterprises were resisting further inroads on their skilled labour force; and the industrial leadership was actively campaigning for an end to the persecution of the old engineers. In the summer of 1931, the 'bourgeois intelligentsia' was formally rehabilitated in a speech by Stalin. In the autumn, the organized recruitment of workers to full-time study in the VTUZy was quietly abandoned.

Cultural Revolution, however, had meant more than proletarian *vydvizhenie* and the harassment of bourgeois specialists; and the restoration of order in education and cultural life was consequently a complex and many-faceted process. It is likely, indeed, that the party leadership only became fully aware of the dimensions of the cultural upheaval it had sponsored when the time came to reverse the policy.

Cultural Revolution had meant, in the first place, the establishment of 'proletarian hegemony' in the cultural professions by groups of militant Communist intellectuals. These activists, who were greatly disliked in their professions, had dispatched the 'bourgeois' and 'rightist' enemies by 1931, and were in the process of splitting into warring factions. They had ignored a number of warning signals from the leadership, and failed altogether to respond to its pleas for *practical* support of the industrialization and collectivization effort. To an impartial eye, as well as to Stalin's, they were serving no useful function; and their political and professional enemies were legion.

In the second place, the cultural upheaval had produced a complete, and in many ways remarkable, structural and financial reorganization of the education system. Industry was maintaining the greater part of all secondary and higher education. The senior grades of general secondary school were gone, and there was no direct path from the 7-year school to VUZ. The enormously expanded FZU apprenticeship school was providing more candidates for further education than apprentices. The old VUZy had been split up into highly specialized institutes, subordinate to a bewildering variety of state and economic agencies. The old universities retained only a marginal existence, with the teaching of pure science restored only after protest from the scientific community, and the humanities and social sciences apparently heading for complete extinction. The situation was scarcely compatible with a rapprochement between the regime and the scientific and professional community, and probably intolerable for industry on any long-term basis.

The third aspect of Cultural Revolution was methodological 'hare-brained scheming' in education. For some years, this apparently passed unnoticed by the party leadership. But it was a cause of disorder and indiscipline in the schools, and contributed to the general lowering of education standards. Protests came from teachers, parents, and the admissions boards of technicums and VUZy. The radicals responded only by moving further to the left. With the rehabilitation of bourgeois specialists, the professors added their voices to the chorus of criticism. When the party leadership finally became aware of the situation, it had no reason to support the educational radicals and many reasons to repudiate them.

The process of restoring order followed two distinct lines, parallel to a great extent but separate. Industry – led by Vesenkha and (from 1932) its successor, the Commissariat of Heavy Industry – initiated the rehabilitation of the bourgeois specialist and subsequently supervized the reorganization of higher technical education, which served as a model for other professional schools. It also reorganized the system of factory apprenticeship schools. The development of pure science was fostered by an informal alliance of the industrial leadership and the scientific community; in institutional terms, this was expressed in the cooperation between the Commissariat of Heavy Industry, the Committee on Higher Technical Education under TsIK and the Academy of Sciences.

The party Central Committee organized the reform of primary and secondary education and the purging of the Communist cultural militants. Until 1936, it remained aloof from questions of higher education, with the one notable exception of history. Stalin, who was the driving force behind the Central Committee's involvement in education, took a strong personal interest in the revival of history teaching in schools and universities; and in history, as in the industrial reorganization, 'bourgeois specialists' were co-opted. But in contrast to the industrial leaders, whose role was almost that of patrons of the old intelligentsia, Stalin and the officials of the Central Committee secretariat acted as stern ideological overseers of both 'bourgeois' and Marxist historians.

It has been suggested that Stalin and Molotov favoured a continuing emphasis on proletarianization and practical orientation in higher education, and that in 1932 they were essentially defeated by the industrialists on this question.[1] To this author, the argument is not wholly convincing: it was Stalin, after all, who sponsored the rehabilitation of the old specialists and the academically oriented restoration of order in the schools in 1931; and after the Great Purges of 1937/38, which swept away almost the entire industrial leadership of the early 1930s, Stalin showed not the slightest inclination to return to the educational policies of the First Five-Year Plan.

Yet one certainly senses some tension in the political leadership over the new policy orientation – most notably a tension between Molotov, now head of the All-Union Sovnarkom but formerly a very influential party secretary, and Ordzhonikidze, the Commissar of Heavy Industry for the USSR. Ordzhonikidze's Commissariat, nominally subordinate to Molotov's Sovnarkom, in fact enjoyed considerable autonomy in its own sphere during the first half of the 1930s; and its sphere was evidently wide enough to encompass science and higher education. This situation, coupled with a widely observed decline in Molotov's political influence in the years 1932–34, might well lead to conflict. In addition, as we shall see, Molotov and Ordzhonikidze seem to have had a longstanding disagreement on the importance of 'vigilance' and the use of police repression.

It was Stalin's habit to encourage such conflicts among Politburo members, but also to stand above them. He may well have had reservations about the manner in which the industrialists conducted their educational reforms, not only because of the tinge of Old Bolshevik 'liberalism' but because of the prominent part played by two of his former political opponents, Bukharin and Krzhizhanovsky,[2] in establishing links between the industrial leadership and the scientific community. But, on the other hand, he did not draw Molotov into the reorganization of school education, which would normally have been the business of Sovnarkom rather than the Central Committee secretariat; and later snubbed him by inviting Kirov and Zhdanov (but not Molotov) to participate in the revision of the history texts.

Whatever the antagonisms within the political leadership, there was a basic coherence to the policies of 'restoration of order' which were applied in different cultural spheres; and these policies were to remain essentially unchanged for the remaining twenty years of Stalin's rule.

The end of organized worker recruitment to higher education

By 1931, many of the new industrial enterprises which had been under construction during the past few years were either beginning production or scheduled to do so in the new future.[3] During the construction period, the most acute need had been for unskilled labour. But it was now necessary to find skilled workers for the new plants, and this question dominated the discussions not only of the industrial authorities and the trade unions but also of the party leadership.[4]

In the early years of the Five-Year Plan, skilled workers had been 'mobilized' at the factory for a great variety of purposes, ranging from the organization of kolkhozy and full-time study in higher education to less important campaign tasks like the purging of government commissariats. In October 1930, the Central Committee had declared a two-year moratorium on the *vydvizhenie* of skilled workers to administrative work in the Soviet apparat.[5] But stronger measures were needed; and in March 1931 the Central Committee absolutely prohibited the further mobilization of workers for current political campaigns, directed that those who had been sent to administrative work in the past six months be returned to production, and forbade the enterprises to give workers time off during the working day for any kind of outside activity including education.[6] By May, 31,000 skilled workers and administrative and technical personnel had been returned to production, but the Central Committee still issued a stern warning to authorities remaining in violation of the March decree.[7]

This was not in itself a prohibition of worker *vydvizhenie* to higher education. But the campaign for educational *vydvizhenie* was developing its own problems. The trade union Thousanders were supported on a 50:50 basis by the enterprises where they had formerly been employed and the trade unions. But neither industry nor the trade unions were happy with this situation. The unions claimed that the enterprises were not paying their share, and at the same time protested against their own financial burden. In the autumn of 1931, the unions announced that when the two million roubles currently remaining in their education fund was exhausted they would be quite unable to continue meeting payments to the Thousanders.[8]

Other difficulties were discussed at meetings of trade unionists and industrialists in Leningrad and Moscow in November 1931. If you go to a factory and try to recruit a skilled worker for study in the VTUZ, said one speaker, 'the factory administration cries out that we have no such worker, we can't release him from his job, because then we will have a breakdown in the Plan'. Workers were reported to be unwilling to give up high-paying jobs for a miserly student stipend. Skilled workers were now fleeing in panic at the suggestion that they should enrol in any kind of study programme: 'this is explained by the fact that there are comparatively few skilled workers left in the plants, and they are so loaded down with over-time and all kinds of piecework assignments that they simply do not have time to study'.[9]

In the autumn admissions of 1931, VUZy were instructed to enrol workers in the new evening courses (*ucheba bez otryva ot proizvodstva*) rather than as full-time day students.[10] This marked the first step in the retreat from an active policy of worker *vydvizhenie* and socially discriminatory selection of students. The regime continued to encourage workers to study as evening students in the VUTZy and technicums. But in 1932, the Central Committee deplored the age gap between students in secondary and higher education,[11] thus by implication criticizing the practice of recruit-ment of adults to full-time study in the normal VUZy.

There was still sufficient doubt on the question of social selection for the Commissariat of Heavy Industry to announce social quotas for its forthcoming VTUZ admissions in June 1932.[12] But quotas had been abandoned by August;[13] and in the autumn admissions of 1932, only national minority students retained special entrance privileges, and all VTUZy in heavy industry reintroduced entrance examinations. Factory workers who applied for full-time study were to be directed to enter the evening divisions of the VTUZy.[14]

Rehabilitation of the bourgeois specialists

The rehabilitation of the bourgeois specialists was announced by

Stalin on 23 June 1931. He presented the new policy in laconic and neutral terms.

It turns out [he said]. . .that one cannot lump all specialists and engineers and technicians of the old school together. Taking account of changing circumstances, it is necessary to change our policy, and treat those specialists and engineers and technicians of the old school who have definitely turned to the side of the working class with maximum care [*proyavit' maksimum zaboty*].[15]

In the same speech, Stalin promised a continuation of the effort to create a 'workers' intelligentsia'. Young Red specialists could still expect responsible jobs after graduation, and the enterprises would continue to promote technician- and engineer-*praktiki* from the ranks of industrial labour. But the emphasis was on industrial efficiency, discipline and incentives. Among the famous 'six conditions' for industrial growth that Stalin outlined were organized recruitment of labour; wage differentials to increase productivity and encourage workers to remain in the same factory; individual and group responsibility within the factory for machines and production quality (the elimination of 'facelessness' or *obezlichka*); and strict observance of *khozraschet* (cost-accounting) in the enterprises.

The new policies, however, were not of Stalin's own devising; and Stalin's change of position almost certainly reflected increasing pressure from the industrialists for a new approach towards specialists and industrial organization. In the six months before Stalin's speech, all of the 'six conditions' had been extensively discussed in *Za industrializatsiyu*, the newspaper of the All-Union Commissariat of Heavy Industry.[16] Stalin's speech was, in effect, an endorsement of the emerging industrial consensus and a summary of policy changes which the enterprises were already introducing.

In the two weeks before the published report of Stalin's speech to the industrialists,[17] *Za industrializatsiyu* ran a series of articles under the heading 'Immediately correct distortions of the party and Soviet line in regard to specialists!' The issue was harassment of engineers by Soviet courts. Local prosecutors were liable to attack 'bourgeois specialists' even if they appeared in court as witnesses rather than accused. They were almost invariably held responsible for industrial accidents. They were frequently tried 'under article 99 [of the Criminal Code], which some judicial workers, overcome by administrative ecstasy, interpret as if it gave them the right to bring specialists to trial. . .[*sic*] for anything at all'. *Za industrializatsiyu* directed the attention of the Chief Prosecutor of the RSFSR to four cases of unwarranted criminal sentences imposed on engineers and technicians.[18]

This was not the first indication that the industrial leadership wanted to protect its specialists from the Soviet judicial and security organs. The 'Industrial Party' trial of a group of leading specialists, held late in 1930, had received a rather chilly reception in Ordzhonikidze's Commissariat of Heavy Industry. Instead of pointing out, as Molotov had done, that 'for some comrades the Shakhty lesson proved insufficient',[19] Ordzhonikidze chose to interpret the trial as a sign that specialist 'wrecking' was a phenomenon of the past. The trial, Ordzhonikidze told the First All-Union Conference of Industrialists early in 1931, was a virtual guarantee of the future loyalty of bourgeois specialists, since it had made them aware of the consequences of passively disaffected 'neutrality'.[20] Bourgeois specialists were among those given places of honour at the Conference and in *Za industrializatsiyu*'s reports of it.

The industrialists' first priority was to rescue their specialists from the GPU and the courts. But their objective was not only to protect the specialists as individuals. A particularly indignant report from the Ukraine emphasized the damage to industrial initiative and discipline caused by the anti-specialist campaign:[21]

They don't *like* taking risks in production in the Donbass. It has become a *rarity*, and many specialists *avoid* it with the greatest care. Even in those cases where a quite responsible specialist introduces a valuable suggestion, ...he waits until *somebody* takes the initiative in implementing the suggestion or measure. The only form of initiative that is permissible in the mine is action 'on *orders from above*'...

The engineering and technical workers are losing all their authority, and many have already lost it. What is the reason for this? Who took on himself the unnecessary mission – bordering on the crudest political error – of compromising the specialists?

The industrialists' constant theme was that undermining the authority of the engineer and shop head had meant destroying the structure of authority and discipline within the plant. With this went the implication (quite absent from Stalin's speech of 23 June) that only the traditional hierarchical system of authority, in which the chief engineer commanded the respect of lower technical personnel and the plant administration, and workers obeyed the foremen and shop heads, could guarantee the effective functioning of industrial enterprises.

The industrialists were anxious to increase material incentives and salary differentials for engineering and technical personnel. This was not one of the themes of Stalin's speech of 23 June (his attack on *uravnilovka*, or vulgar equalitarianism, was put in a context of *workers'* wages), but it had been discussed at the February Conference of Industrialists and aroused a very favourable response.[22]

There had not, in fact, been any real equalization of wages and salaries during the first years of the First Five-Year Plan, although in 1928 and 1929 the differential between the average worker's wage and the average salary of industrial employees and engineering–technical personnel had been slightly reduced.[23] However, the competing demands of industrial enterprises – including the new construction sites, which offered very large bonuses to attract engineers and skilled workers from the big cities – had created an irrational and arbitrary differentiation of wages and salaries.[24]

In 1930/31, engineering–technical salaries rose in relation to workers' wages; and in 1932 the differential reached its highest point for the entire Soviet period from 1917 to the present, surpassing the peak level of NEP.[25] At the same time, the bourgeois specialists were beginning to receive symbolic as well as material rewards. In August 1931, Orders of Lenin were awarded to a number of specialists conducting industrially relevant scientific research.[26] Among the recipients was Professor S. V. Lebedev, Kirov's protégé in Leningrad,[27] who was honoured for his work on the production of synthetic rubber.

The industrialists were also strong supporters of a general improvement in the specialists' standard of living. This did not mean that during the first years of the Five-Year Plan the specialists as a group had lost their previous privileges.[28] But there were some very delicate problems involving housing. Engineers released from prison were likely to find that they had lost at least part of their old apartments. During the anti-specialist campaign, the courts had tended to decide against all specialists in disputed housing cases. Engineers 'mobilized' to work on distant construction sites often refused to leave, because they did not trust local authorities to protect their housing rights, even if their families remained behind in the old apartments.[29]

At the beginning of August 1931, TsIK and Sovnarkom USSR passed a resolution to improve the living conditions of engineering and technical personnel.[30] The resolution, which guaranteed the specialists only an *equal* priority with industrial workers in access to housing, rations and VUZ admissions for their children, was almost meaningless, since in most respects the specialists already possessed equal priority in theory[31] and greater privilege in practice.

But the resolution was interpreted as an instruction to provide the specialists with special facilities at the plants and privileged separate housing at the new construction sites. In Armenia, for example, a commission for implementation of the resolution instructed big enterprises to open special dining-rooms for engineering and technical personnel, and to construct special apartment houses for them.[32] Similar reports came from other republics (John Scott has vividly described the housing hierarchy that developed in Magnitogorsk[33]), and in 1932 the building of special apartment houses for specialists was explicitly endorsed by the Soviet government.[34]

Reorganization of higher technical schools

The industrialists desired the services of the old engineers and were ready to pay for them. This was not because they had any animus against the young Red specialists, whom they regarded with pride and hope, but because they realized that the young engineers were too inexperienced for the jobs which, in many cases, had been thrust upon them. As Ordzhonikidze described the problems of the metallurgical industry early in 1932:

There turned out not to be enough experienced engineers who would understand metals, understand the blast furnace, keep watch on the furnace and know when something is happening and what it is. Comrade V. Mezhlauk, who for many years headed the metallurgical industry, was at the Dzerzhinsky plant last summer, and wrote to me that the most responsible positions in the shops of the plant were held by young engineers, fresh from the school bench – fine lads, enthusiasts, who will make good engineers in a year, or two or three. There is no doubt of that. But today they are learning, and their learning is quite hard on the furnaces.[35]

However, industry remained relatively satisfied with its VTUZy until after the summer of 1931, when the first large batch of First Five-Year Plan engineering students (including the first of the Thousanders) graduated.[36] This satisfaction was quickly dispelled in the following months, as a stream of complaints came in about the quality of the new engineers. One type of complaint – coming from the young engineers themselves, and strongly supported by the former professors – was that they lacked basic theoretical grounding in such subjects as mechanics, physics and mathematics.[37] The other type, coming from the enterprises, was that the graduates lacked 'production skills'. This came as a particular shock, considering the 1:1 ratio established in the VTUZy between theoretical and practical work. Even graduates of Kagan-Shabshai's Institute, the prototype of the 'new type of VTUZ', were criticized for lack of familiarity with production.[38]

The problem of young specialists was raised at the XVII Party Conference,[39] and freely discussed in the industrial press in the first half of 1932. By July, a consensus appeared to have been reached on the need for radical change in the system of higher technical education. Writers began to refer to the 1928–30 reform of VTUZ methods with barely disguised scorn. There were criticisms of narrow specialization, and even of practical work in production – the panacea which Stalin himself had recommended in 1928. It was incredible, wrote one commentator, that Vesenkha should have been so carried away with the idea of practical work in industry that they had actually disbanded the VTUZ laboratories and workshops. The plants were not competent to direct the students' work, and in any case did not want students wandering in and out of their shops. Was it really necessary for students to spend so much time on production? 'Couldn't polytechnical practical work be carried out through excursions to production or in the the process of work in the laboratory and workshop of the VTUZ?'[40]

Some of these criticisms were expressed by 'bourgeois specialists', whose opinions the industrialists solicited and treated with respect. This prompted the first revival of overt group spirit among the specialists since 1927. The professors' journal, *Front nauki i tekhniki,*[41] had been converted during the Cultural Revolution into a 'militant organ of the progressive Soviet intelligentsia', and as such had almost ceased to express a distinct professional interest. But in the middle of 1932, it reverted to its former self and began a devastating indictment of the 1928–30 reforms.

The first sign of change was the publication of an article 'On the quality of higher technical education in the Union' by Yan Shpilrein, a 'bourgeois' professor of electrical engineering who only six months earlier had been attacked by name by Vyshinsky for opposing the reform of higher education.[42] Shpilrein listed all the basic objections of the old professors to the changes of recent years. Essential theoretical subjects like chemistry had been neglected; students entered without adequate academic preparation and were not properly tested at the VTUZ; professors were given no voice in the administration or even in the selection of graduate students; lectures were almost outlawed; and the 'laboratory-brigade' method made systematic teaching impossible. The coming reorganization of higher technical education, Shpilrein told his colleagues, 'must not take us unawares. We must take a business-like part in carrying it out.'[43]

The official outline of the reorganization came from TsIK in September 1932.[44] The decree, which applied to all VUZy and technicums, stated that 80–85% of study time should be allocated to basic theoretical and technical subjects. Lectures should be reintroduced, and the 'laboratory-brigade' method phased out. Entrance examinations were to be compulsory for all students; and students should be individually examined throughout the course. Academic criteria should be applied in the appointment of faculty; and new salary scales would be introduced, differentiating according to academic status and seniority.

Although the TsIK resolution applied to higher education as a whole, the body created to implement it – the Committee for Higher Technical Education under TsIK USSR – was responsible only for the industrial VTUZy and technicums. The Committee's staff was small[45] (it used GUUZ, the Commissariat of Heavy Industry's education sector,[46] as an executive apparat), but striking in composition. Besides the chairman, Krzhizhanovsky, two Academicians were members of the Presidium. The deputy chairman was Khodorovsky, Vyshinsky's predecessor at Narkompros; and Pinkevich, an early target of Shulgin's attacks in the pedagogical field, headed the teaching and methodological sector.[47]

Krzhizhanovsky combined his chairmanship of the Committee with the position of vice-president of the Academy of Sciences; while the other leading Communist Academician, Bukharin, headed the department of scientific research in the Commissariat of Heavy Industry.[48] They relied on the same body of expert advice, much of it from the Academy of Sciences; and the professors' and Academicians' opinion were almost as often to be found in the pages of industry's newspaper *Za industrializatsiyu* as in the journal of Krzhizhanovsky's Committee, *Vysshaya tekhnicheskaya shkola*. Relations between the Commissariat, the Committee and the academic and scientific community were not only courteous but positively warm.[49]

The professors had reason for gratitude, since the reorganization of higher technical education carried out by the Committee and the Commissariat met their requirements in virtually every respect. It was acknowledged that the professorial title denoted 'status, not office',[50] and the status must be conferred with the consent of the profession. Commissions were immediately established to review the claim of existing VUZ faculty to the titles of professor and *dotsent* and the academic status of *doktor* and *kandidat nauk*.[51] Some of the young professors appointed in recent years survived the review (among them L. V. Kantorovich of the Leningrad Institute of Means of Communication), but many VUZy were left 'almost without a single professor', and even the high-prestige VTUZy of the Commissariat of Heavy Industry had a deficit of 282 professors in 1934.[52] The graduate student body was subjected to a similar review, which in the VTUZy of heavy industry resulted in the removal of 500 graduate students in engineering, who were sent to work in the enterprises.[53]

Revision of the curriculum began immediately after the TsIK resolution. Theoretical subjects were restored, industrial practical work drastically cut down, and (in 1933) new broad specialization profiles established for the VTUZy. Diploma work – abolished during the Cultural Revolution – was reintroduced, to the distress of many of the students; and it was even required of the graduating class of 1932/33, so that their graduation was delayed for six months.[54]

The network of VTUZy and technicums was reviewed, and those that failed to meet the new academic standards were downgraded, merged or closed.[55] Students also were subjected to an academic purge, and sub-standard VTUZ students were transferred to the evening divisions of the VTUZy or sent to technicums.[56] Examinations were reintroduced for entering students; and, from 1933, full-time VUZ students were mainly recruited from the graduates of rabfaks and technicums, with the normal secondary school playing an increasingly large part as grades VIII–X were re-established during the 1930s.[57]

Even the radical *Krasnoe studenchestvo* reflected the new ethos of serious study, and began to instruct its readers on the technique of reading books and taking notes.[58] The journals also carried many articles on 'How to give a good lecture' – among them one by Professor Reformatsky, a veteran of 45 years teaching in the higher school, who wrote of the revolutionary methodology of the past few years as a folly born of youth and inexperience.[59] Reformatsky's advice to the young exemplified the spirit of the new VTUZ reform: learn the traditions of the profession from those who have won professional honour and respect, and in time you too will become wise.

The Central Committee and the schools

Even before industry became concerned about the VTUZy, the Central Committee had started to undo the effects of Cultural Revolution in the schools. The reason for the Central Committee's involvement was, apparently, Stalin's personal interest and his lack of confidence in Narkompros. Stalin's interest, according to Kaganovich, was aroused almost by chance. Somebody called his attention to the fact that 'teaching in one school was going badly and the training of the children was poorly organized'. He discovered that there was no discipline in the school, very little formal teaching by subject and no regular textbooks. He also presumably became aware of Shulgin's theory of the 'withering away of the school', a close relative to the theory of the imminent 'withering away of the state' which Stalin had condemned a year earlier.[60] Out of these discoveries, Kaganovich said, 'emerged the whole complex of questions about the school; and a decision about the school – which later the educational workers themselves justly called a historic decision – was made'.[61]

There was, of course, a somewhat broader context in which the decision was made. Others beside Stalin were disturbed by the disorganization of school life and the fact that pupils were not receiving a systematic general education. The enterprises disliked their new role as school guardians, and the VTUZy and technicums were complaining of the inadequate preparation of entering students. By the summer of 1931, there was talk of the need to re-establish the old grades viii–x of the general secondary school.[62] Bubnov rejected any idea of returning to the 'old academic school' but acknowledged the deficiencies of the new one:

It must be said with the greatest severity that the 7-year school is not giving an adequate educational preparation for the technicums. Not long ago there was a meeting of technicum representatives on the level of knowledge and skills possessed by the adolescent contingents entering the technicums. The general opinion at that meeting was that there was no doubt that we have an unsatisfactory situation, and that this has to be recognized.[63]

Bubnov himself might have acted more decisively had he not firmly believed himself to be an executor rather than a maker of policy. His natural inclinations were towards order and firm discipline.[64] By 1931, he was certainly aware of a lack of neatness and orderly procedure in the school; and he had begun to rely less on Shulgin and more on the relatively conservative Epshtein, a survivor from the old Narkompros leadership.[65] But he knew that Lunacharsky's chief failing, in the eyes of the leadership, had been his assumption of an independent policy-making role for the commissariat. Bubnov therefore took no initiatives, but rather attempted to instil soldierly discipline by personal example and exhortation. His subordinates regarded him as a hard taskmaster, but his requirements seem to have been more those of a drill sergeant than a commanding officer. On visiting a school, according to one observer, Bubnov 'acquaints himself with all the corners and all the "trivia" of school life. He carefully inspects the peg on which the overcoat is hung, and notes that galoshes must not be kept above it, since dirt from them will fall on the coat.'[66]

Bubnov may have had a hand in framing the Central Committee's resolution of 25 August 1931 'On the elementary and middle school',[67] but his role was minor. The resolution was far more outspoken than any earlier criticism from Bubnov. On the theoretical level, it repudiated the theory of 'withering away of the school' and denounced the project method. On the practical level, it found that the school's 'basic failing' was that it 'does not give a sufficient amount of general knowledge, and does not adequately solve the problem of training fully literate persons with a good grasp of the bases of the sciences (physics, chemistry, mathematics, native language, geography and so on) for entrance to technicums and higher schools'.

The core recommendation was that the teaching of physics, chemistry and mathematics, in particular, 'must be based on strictly delineated and carefully worked-out programmes and study plans', and classes should be organized on a firm timetable. Narkompros was to work out systematic programmes in the basic subjects and see that the schools followed them.[68]

Many people welcomed the Central Committee resolution as a return to the 'old school'.[69] This interpretation, though not far from the truth, was too much for Narkompros and the progressive educationalists to swallow. Editorialists in the educational press struggled to work out the Central Committee's real meaning. Surely it was not endorsing old-fashioned classroom teaching of individual subjects? It could not mean 'that our school must return to the work methods of the old, scholastic, academic school', concluded one of the educational journals. It *must* mean, despite the condemnation of the project method, that 'our school should apply all the variety of activity methods already proved in practice (research, laboratory and excursion methods)'.[70]

There were mixed reactions from the provincial education departments. The Central Black Earth region succumbed (in Narkompros' view) to 'rotten liberalism' and attempted 'to go back to the bourgeois school'. But in Nizhny Novgorod and Ivanovo-Voznesensk, children continued to be taken out of school to work on the flax and potato harvest; the project method remained in use in Kazan; and the West Siberian education department issued a circular 'blatantly distorting the Central Committee's directive' by recommending 'mass application of the project method,. . .as if entering into a polemic with the Central Committee resolution'.[71]

The Russian Narkompros (unlike those of the Ukraine and Belorussia[72]) accepted the reinstatement of teaching by subject, and circulated new subject programmes to the schools in January and February of 1932.[73] The new programmes, and the methodological instructions which followed, were apparently extremely long and confused. The schools were told, for example, to teach grammar. But, while the teachers may have known how to do this, the Narkompros methodologists did not. The definition of a sentence offered by Narkompros to Russian teachers of grade v was 'a unit of communication expressing objective reality through class consciousness'.[74]

The Central Committee resolution had formally upheld the polytechnical principle, with abundant quotation from Lenin, and approved the linking of schools with particular factories and kolkhozy. But the implication of the resolution was that schools and factories should keep to their own metiers. Narkompros accordingly issued instructions which tended to withdraw the children from 'productive practical work' in the enterprise and reduce the enterprise's responsibility for the school to a more or less nominal supervision.[75] At the same time, Narkompros and the Komsomol Central Committee issued instructions aimed at discouraging the involvement of Pioneers and schoolchildren in outside 'social work' which distracted them from their studies: no meetings were to be held after 8 p.m., and the children's free days 'must be used entirely and only for recreational purposes (walks, skiing, skating etc.)'.[76]

However, the Central Committee was not satisfied with the response to its resolution. When Bubnov, rather plaintively, tried to get credit for at least carrying out instructions on the school reform, he received a sharp rebuff from Kaganovich:

Bubnov: All the same, did we get something done or not?
Kaganovich: Yes, comrade Bubnov, you got something done – after the Central Committee raised the question in very acute form and carefully supervised the implementation of its resolution.[77]

In fact, the Central Committee had to supervise the implementation not of one resolution only but a whole series – a supplementary resolution 'On the study programmes and regime in the elementary and middle school', issued exactly a year after the first one, followed by resolutions on textbooks, the teaching of history and geography, construction and equipment of schools and so on.[78] It became necessary, for the first time, to create a separate department of schools in the Central Committee apparat.[79]

In its 1932 decree,[80] the Central Committee clarified its attitude to activity methods in the schools. The 'laboratory-brigade' method was repudiated; classroom lectures by the teacher were established as the basic Soviet teaching method; and the students were to be regularly examined on each academic subject. This amounted to a rejection not only of the extreme progressivism of the Cultural Revolution but also the more moderate progressivism of the 1920s.

One of the basic concerns of the 1932 decree was school discipline. Parents, as well as Komsomol and Pioneer organizations, were to be drawn into the struggle for order and discipline in the schools. Persistent offenders – those who 'misbehaved and insulted teaching personnel, violated the instructions of the school administration or the teachers, broke school rules, destroyed or stole school property' – were to be expelled from the school without right of re-entry for a period of one to three years.

But even after two resolutions, it turned out that a crucial point had been overlooked. The Central Committee had never explicitly stated that teaching by subject meant teaching by textbooks, although this was almost certainly its assumption from the beginning. In 1931, Narkompros had realized that its 'journal-textbooks' might not be exactly what the Central Committee had in mind. But since there was no explicit prohibition, it was decided 'not to prejudge' the textbook question and keep the journal-textbooks in circulation for the time being.[81]

This was a mistake. Once again, it was Stalin who caught Narkompros out; and the 'saga of the textbook' evidently became a Politburo anecdote. This is how Kaganovich, urged on by Postyshev and Stalin, told the story to the XVII Party Congress in 1934:

Kaganovich: The Central Committee found out that the children did not have textbooks. Comrade Stalin came and asked: 'How are things with the textbooks? Find out what is happening.' Then the Politburo established that we did not have any permanent textbooks.
Stalin: They changed every year.
Kaganovich: Right, the textbooks were changing every year...The 'leftist' theorists of the withering away of the school argued that if we kept the

same textbooks for a few years we would be dragged backwards, not noticing that for want of textbooks the children were half illiterate.

The name 'loose-leaf' textbook is not a malicious tag or a joke, but the official Narkompros name for that kind of 'textbook'...The 'loose-leaf' textbook really was a collection of separate pages on all the sciences lumped together, or, as they put it, 'in a complex'...

Just let a student try to get any firm systematic knowledge on the basis of 'loose-leaf' textbooks.

Each year Narkompros issued an enormous number of textbooks. Money was spent and mountains of paper wasted on the 'loose-leaf' textbooks, yet each year we still had no stable textbooks...

Stalin: Now the textbooks are stable.[82]

The last comment was somewhat premature, although the Central Committee had certainly made its wishes plain. Its resolution 'On textbooks for the elementary and middle school' (February 1933)[83] deplored not only the absence of textbooks but the fact that the Narkompros and Teachers' Union leadership 'apparently consider this a sign of [their] own revolutionary achievements'. Stable textbooks were to be prepared in all the basic subjects; and, with the exception of *kraevedenie* (study of the local region), they were to be uniform throughout the USSR.

There remained the problem of restructuring the educational system. As a result of the upheavals of the period of Cultural Revolution, the general (7-year) school did not give access to higher education, and the gap was bridged by preparatory courses, rabfaks, technicums and industry's apprenticeship school. This had some rationality in a period of adult *vydvizhenie*, but nobody except the Komsomol really considered it appropriate as a long-term solution. It was peculiarly inappropriate from the standpoint of the industrialists, since industry bore the costs of the vocational schools without directly reaping the benefit.

In August 1932, the Central Committee directed that grades VIII, IX and X should be re-established in the normal school, in accordance with the 1919 party programme 'and also with the aim of raising the standard of general-educational and polytechnical training of secondary school pupils as quickly as possible, expanding the contingents trained for higher school and eliminating the age gap between middle and higher school'.[84] Grade VIII was to be re-established from the beginning of the 1932/33 school year.

This decision had important consequences for the apprenticeship school (FZU). If the apprenticeship school was no longer to function as a major channel to higher education, it was no longer necessary for it to offer, in effect, a course of general secondary education. It could be redefined as a strictly vocational school (as was already happening with the workers' courses offered at the factories[85]), and its graduates could be firmly directed into the industrial labour force.

Thus in the summer of 1933, the All-Union Commissariat of Heavy Industry decided 'to reconstruct the existing network of FZU schools. . .into sharply delineated professional schools training semi-skilled [*massovykh kvalifikatsii*] workers *exclusively* for production'.[86] In September, TsIK and Sovnarkom USSR issued a similar resolution, instructing all apprenticeship schools 'to cease the practice of transferring graduates to educational institutions (technicums, VUZy and VTUZy)' and obliging apprenticeship students to work in production for not less than three years after graduation. Courses in the apprenticeship school were to be reduced to six or twelve months, and 80% of study time was to be spent directly in production.[87]

Many of the FZU students apparently left for the general secondary school in 1932/33 and 1933/34,[88] and there was a very striking drop in the total enrolment. This fell from 959,000 in 1932/33 to 261,000 in 1934/35[89] – the first year in which enrolment in grades VIII–X of the general secondary school exceeded that in the apprenticeship school.

At the same time, the general secondary school was growing by leaps and bounds. By the 1935/36 school year, there were 303,000 children in grade VIII (about a quarter of the numbers in grade VII in the same year), 137,000 in grade IX and 51,000 in grade X. The expansion of upper-level secondary school continued throughout the 1930s, both in rural and urban areas. By 1940/41, grades VIII–X had a total of 2.4 million pupils. This was just over a fifth of the numbers in grades V–VII in the same year. But the rate of expansion of the secondary school system as a whole may be judged from the fact that the contingent in grades VIII–X in 1940/41 was actually larger than that in grades V–VII ten years earlier.[90]

Condemnation of the radical theorists

In the early months of 1931, Bubnov initiated a discussion on pedagogical theory.[91] Like other theoretical discussions of the period, it amounted to a condemnation of the 'right' and the 'left' deviation. Attacks against 'leftism' were at first directed at the political Oppositionist Vaganyan, although Shulgin's theory of the withering away of the school was sometimes included. Krupskaya's journal *Na putyakh* did not participate in the discussion since, as she bluntly stated, she found it 'very scholastic and boring'.[92]

In April, Bubnov provoked a confrontation with Shulgin and Krupskaya. Shulgin, he said, was insubordinate, showed 'theoretical arrogance' and refused to give his mistakes 'the correct political evaluation'.[93] Yet Bubnov's attitude to Shulgin still seems to have been basically friendly (he remarked that he was 'very sad' to see someone with 'a fine past' heading for trouble). Krupskaya concluded, probably correctly, that the attack was really directed against her. She responded with a very indignant written protest invoking Lenin's authority on the side of the 'leftists':[94]

All my life I have fought rightists, and will go on fighting them. For me, the words 'the greatest danger is from the right' are not simply words: they are filled with living content...As for the leftists, in particular Shulgin and Krupenina, Ilyich wrote that one must do everything to welcome those who fight against the old school. And I must say that in the struggle against the old school I did form a bloc with...Shulgin.

By August, Bubnov had proposed liquidating Shulgin's Institute, a suggestion which Krupskaya and Shulgin took rather badly.[95] He presumably already knew the contents of the resolution on the schools in preparation in the Central Committee; and, while he was not prepared to condemn the educational revolution of the past three years *in toto*, he conceded that Shulgin's ideas had done considerable damage. 'The theory of "the withering away of the school" has a very nimble nature', he said. 'It gets in everywhere. It gets into the question of activity methods, including the "project method". It also gets into the question of self-government in the school, the role of the Pioneers, and so on.'[96]

After the publication of the Central Committee resolution, Shulgin's Institute was dissolved; and Shulgin was removed from the Narkompros collegium and persuaded 'under very great pressure' to repudiate the theory of 'the withering away of the school'.[97] He then departed, probably under the auspices of the association of proletarian writers, RAPP, to write a novel about the Stalingrad Tractor Factory,[98] and took no further part in educational life.

Krupskaya was not so easily disposed of. She treated the Central Committee resolution as a public relations defeat for the progressive educationalists and a victory for 'those who are now organizing a campaign for the old school'.[99] She was belligerent and rude in a discussion on the resolution organized by the Teachers' Union, describing the resolution 'in a caricature way' and refusing to criticize Shulgin in the appropriate terms. Shumsky, the new president of the Union, was greatly embarrassed by her behaviour (after all, as he pointed out, the teachers 'listen to every word of Nadezhda Konstantinovna as if it were a directive'), and became almost plaintive in his appeals:

Nadezhda Konstantinovna told us here that in the process of her work with comrade Shulgin she had 'had to notice that he had a certain, so to speak, anarchist tendency. A tendency to jump over things, to underestimate organizational questions...' But is that really all that needs to be said, when it is a question of the most vicious distortion of the teaching of Marx and Lenin?[100]

Shortly after the publication of the Central Committee resolution 'On the elementary and middle school', Stalin published a very unusual letter to the editors of the party history journal *Proletarskaya revolyutsiya*.[101] The letter – formally an attack on a particular article dealing with Lenin's relations with German Social Democracy – was in effect a condemnation of the abstract theorizing of the Communist intelligentsia as a whole. Its appearance prompted an outburst of organized discussion and *samokritika* (self-criticism) in the Communist Academy, the Institute of Red Professors and all the militant Communist groups that had established 'proletarian hegemony' in the professions during the Cultural Revolution.

In the educational sphere, *samokritika* was required of the pedagogical left and the pedologists. Krupskaya had to apologize on behalf of the Communist Academy's Society of Marxist Pedagogues for failing to join the struggle against left deviation. She did so with characteristic lack of grace.

It was decided that the collegium of Narkompros would lead the front in the discussion [against the left], and the Society would play only a peripheral role on that discussion. This decision, however, inhibited the Society in its struggle on the two fronts. It was undoubtedly a mistake. It was impossible to bypass the struggle on the pedagogical front, *however scholastic and inbred that discussion may have been.* [My emphasis added][102]

Scholasticism was indeed the dominant trait of the discussions that followed Stalin's letter to *Proletarskaya revolyutsiya*, but it was scholasticism with peculiarly vindicative political overtones. It was already customary to denounce intellectual trends for Bukharinism, Trotskyism and Menshevism. But the unmasking within the party of a 'right–left bloc' led by Syrtsov and Lominadze[103] added a new dimension of intellectual absurdity. 'Right–left' tendencies were noted in various sectors of the Communist Academy; and Ernest Kolman (who, curiously enough, was later to emigrate from the Soviet Union in 1976 in protest against the Brezhnev regime's denial of civil rights) denounced the pedologists for their 'right–left/ mechanist–idealist' deviation.[104]

The pedologists were tarred by their association with Shulgin. They were in a very awkward position, since it was known that they were in disgrace and must apologize before it was known what they should be apologizing for. Thus a self-critical editorial in *Pedologiya* simply apologized for every possible intellectual sin – 'ultra-biologism', 'autogeneticism', 'mechanical Lamarckism' and 'mechanical reflexological positions', not forgetting to add that 'one must not gloss over the significance of idealist Freudian–Adlerian and Sternian distortions'.[105]

Krupskaya observed the self-critical frenzy of the Communist intelligentsia with a very jaundiced eye. Manuscripts of *samokritika* and denunciation poured into the editorial office of *Na putyakh*, but Krupskaya refused to publish them. Her disgust was expressed in a critique of one manuscript attacking the educationalist Medynsky (of whom, as it happened, Krupskaya herself had a low opinion):

It takes some quotations (and not too many of them at that) out of context, and follows up with stubborn, malicious, 'true-believing' statements that the author is not a Marxist and didn't say this or that. What incantations! Medynsky cited Plekhanov. . .Lord have mercy! Lord have mercy!. . . Medynsky cited Kautsky. . .Lord have mercy! 44 pages of incantations,. . . [and] not one single idea about how the history of pedagogy ought to be written, not one. Well, to hell with them [*Nu, ikh!*]. It can't be printed in *Na putyakh*.[106]

In the course of the discussion on Shulgin and the pedologists, the nature of their offence began to emerge more clearly. They were observers and not active transformers of life. They overestimated the role of the environment and underestimated the role of consciousness in determining human behaviour. In the words of a repentant pedologist, they believed that

revolutionary interference in the course of events. . .would be counterproductive to progress. . .The fact that subjectively we considered our theory revolutionary has no relevance. By excluding the purposive [*tsele-polagayushchaya*] activity of man, his interference in the course of events, we automatically excluded also the necessity of educative work, thus creating the anti-Leninist theory of 'the withering away of the school'.[107]

In many ways, this was a reasonable characterization of the radicals' position. But it had the curious result of forcing Marxists to apologize for taking account of the influence of the social environment. In one of her last public outbursts, Krupskaya registered her protest. 'In the criticism that is appearing, they write: "What kind of people are these? They are talking about the influence of the environment!".. .But does that mean that the environment has no influence? If we said that, we would stop being Marxist.'[108]

The teaching of history

As Krupskaya suggested, the drive against Cultural Revolution and the theories associated with it often came close to being a repudiation of Marxist scholarship. The 'Great Retreat'[109] from Cultural Revolution was carried out by an alliance of the party leadership and the bourgeois specialists against the Communist intelligentsia. Almost inevitably, Marxist scholarship was a casualty; and this was nowhere so clear as in the denunciation of Pokrovsky's Marxist school, which had dominated the theory and practice of history during the Cultural Revolution, and the development of a new genre of Soviet 'patriotic' history in the 1930s.

However, even in this extreme case the leadership surely saw itself as restoring order and normality rather than repudiating Marxism. The initial involvement of the Central Committee (prompted, as in the case of the schools, by Stalin) was not an act of ideological assertion. It was a continuation of the 'saga of the textbook' – one of the many aspects of the Central Committee's struggle to re-organize the primary and secondary school.

History was not taught as a separate subject in the schools of the 1920s,[110] and the same was true of geography and literature. Strictly speaking, therefore, these subjects were not victims of the cultural revolutionaries' 'hare-brained scheming', but of an earlier brand of educational progressivism and (in the case of history) Pokrovsky's personal prejudice.

But the Central Committee's 1931 resolution 'On the elementary and middle school' listed history and geography among the basic subjects requiring systematic teaching.[111] The reference was casual, and it is quite possible that the drafters of the resolution were simply listing as 'basic subjects' those that they themselves had learned at school rather than making any political or ideological point. In its resolution of 1932, the Central Committee noted that history programmes had still not been written, and urged a more historical approach to the teaching of literature, geography and social studies.[112] The chronological approach in this area was a counterpart of the 'systematic' treatment of mathematics and the sciences which the Central Committee recommended at the same time.

The resolution abolishing 'journal-textbooks' and directing that regular textbooks should be prepared for all basic subjects followed in 1933. A year later, the Central Committee and Sovnarkom USSR jointly issued decrees on the teaching of geography and history in the schools.[113] In a follow-up resolution, the Central Committee again recommended 'chronological historical sequence in the setting out of historical events, firmly fixing in the minds of the pupils important historical events, historical personages and dates'. Without criticizing Pokrovsky by name, it attacked 'abstract sociological schemes' and 'abstract definition of socio-economic formations' in the writing of history.[114]

In practice, systematic teaching of history in the schools posed much more formidable problems than the systematic teaching of the sciences, as the Central Committee was beginning to recognize. Pre-revolutionary textbooks could, at a pinch, be used in science but not in history. The great majority of potential history teachers (currently, teachers of social studies) had graduated from school during NEP and from technicum or VUZ during the Cultural Revolution,[115] which meant that they had never learnt history. Finally, the history departments of the old universities had disappeared in the VUZ reorganization of 1930.

Of all higher schools, the universities probably suffered most during the Cultural Revolution. All the provincial universities were dissolved in 1930, and even the great universities of Moscow and Leningrad survived only in truncated form. Narkompros, as Bubnov later said, had been unable to offer adequate resistance to those who wanted to abolish universities altogether.[116] In April 1931, after a protest from the scientific community against the disintegration of university schools of physics and mathematics, the Central Committee decided that universities were a necessary institution[117] – but only for the purpose of teaching pure science and mathematics and training future professors.

When the universities reopened in the 1931/32 school year, they taught almost nothing but science. The humanities and social sciences were studied in a few specialized institutes in Moscow and

Leningrad and within the Communist Academy system. But from 1931 to 1934 the single non-scientific department in a university of the RSFSR was the department of oriental studies in Vladivostok. In the USSR as a whole, history was formally taught in a university only in Erevan and (from 1933) Dnepropetrovsk and Samarkand.[118]

In 1934, the Central Committee re-established the historical faculties of Moscow and Leningrad University.[119] The main purpose of this was to facilitate the writing of history textbooks for the schools. But it also, probably intentionally, reinforced the weight of the old 'bourgeois' historians against that of the dominant group, the Marxists in the Communist Academy.

The Marxists at this point were involved in bitter faction-fighting. The contenders were Pokrovsky, who dominated the general historical field, and Yaroslavsky, who was primarily concerned with party history. Each group repeatedly complained about the behaviour of the other to the Central Committee, urging its intervention to settle disputes.[120] The Central Committee had not intervened on behalf of either faction before 1934. But in 1931 Stalin had, in effect, declared a plague on all the houses of Soviet Marxist historians in his letter to the editors of *Proletarskaya revolyutsiya*.

Nevertheless, when the Central Committee called for outlines of textbooks on the ancient, medieval and modern history of the USSR and the world,[121] it was the Marxist historians who provided them.[122] Stalin retired for his summer vacation with Zhdanov and an unwilling Kirov[123] to assess the results. He came back with what, it should be emphasized, was essentially a schematic Marxist critique of the schematic Marxist outlines offered to him.[124] His comments were, for the first time, overtly critical of the Pokrovsky school. But this was obviously not his only concern. He had been re-reading the classic pre-revolutionary historians – Solovyev, Klyuchevsky, Platonov, Presnyakov – to see, among other things, how one wrote a standard narrative history. In Stalin's opinion, the Marxists' outlines had some ideological deficiencies, but the worst thing about them was that they were too long, too confused and (in the manner popularized by Pokrovsky) lacked names, dates and a clear account of the sequence of historical events. Stalin wanted the historians to give a traditional presentation of a revolutionary Marxist worldview. He wanted 'real' history textbooks for the schools – in other words, textbooks which poorly trained teachers could understand and on which students could be examined.

These simple objectives turned out quite difficult to achieve. Stalin could not create a Marxist Klyuchevsky by an act of will; and the historians, intimidated by the criticism of 'abstract sociological schemes', became extremely wary of offering any generalizations at all. The textbook writers of the 1930s overwhelmed the student with specifics: the grade x text on the history of the USSR, for example, included in its first hundred pages 227 names, 361 dates and 190 assorted statistics, together with a wealth of quotations from the works of Lenin and Stalin; and the grade v text on ancient history included 26 names in two pages, 20 of them being the names of Greek gods and goddesses.[125]

The destruction of the Pokrovsky school[126] meant that those Marxist historians who survived the stormy passage of 1934–37 preferred editing and acting as patrons of selected 'bourgeois' historians to writing.[127] It left the old specialists dominant in their profession, and they were the ones who finally did most of the work on the textbooks.[128] But their situation was less happy than that of their counterparts in the VTUZy, rehabilitated under the protection of the Commissariat of Heavy Industry. Their profession had been corrupted by the malice and intrigue of the previous years, and it was further corrupted by the attacks on the Pokrovsky school which the party leadership sponsored and the old specialists joined. The old historians, who were not Marxists, had to write 'Marxist' history; and they had to write under uncomfortably close scrutiny from the party leadership, in a period when those close to the leadership were not only peculiarly privileged but peculiarly liable to arrest. These circumstances produced not only poor Marxism but poor history – and it was probably small comfort to the 'bourgeois' historians to note that Stalin's own effort at writing a conventional history textbook[129] turned out, in purely professional terms, even worse.

11

The 'New Class': social mobility and education under Stalin

At the most practical level, the restoration of order which followed the Cultural Revolution meant a restructuring of the education system. In the new system that emerged in the 1930s, general secondary education led to higher education, and the VUZy recruited primarily from the secondary school. Vocational secondary education led to employment, and graduates of the FZU apprenticeship schools normally went directly into industry as workers.

In any other context but that of the Soviet Union in its first two decades, an education system of this type would be totally unremarkable. But, until the mid-1930s, Soviet higher schools had *not* recruited primarily from general secondary schools, and FZU apprentices had *not* normally become workers in industry. The peculiar characteristics of the Soviet education system before that time – entrance to higher education through rabfaks and preparatory courses; semi-vocationalization of general schools, accompanied by an involuntary conversion of vocational schools to serve general-educational functions – were the products of revolutionary ideology, filtered through a mesh of conflicting institutional policies and priorities. They sprung from a general suspicion of inherited 'bourgeois' schools, and the desire to use education to create a new working-class elite.

When we find commonsense structural considerations superseding ideological ones, as they increasingly did after 1931, certain basic questions have to be asked. Had the regime abandoned the idea of actively promoting upward mobility from the working class, and, if so, were the channels of upward mobility closed in the later part of the Stalin period? Was the earlier effort to create a working-class elite successful? Had the objective danger from 'bourgeois' institutions and 'bourgeois' specialists diminished in the 1930s, or did the regime finally succumb to the ethos of the old educated and privileged classes?

Educational opportunity in the Stalin period

'A son does not answer for his father', Stalin is quoted as saying;[1] and the policy change of the later 1930s summarized in the remark had great significance for victims of social discrimination and those who had had to make public repudiation of fathers who were priests or kulaks.[2] At the end of 1935, social criteria in selection for higher education were formally dropped,[3] after losing most of their practical meaning two years earlier. In 1936, the new constitution proclaimed the equality of all citizens regardless of class. Stalin explained that although Soviet society still contained classes – the peasantry, the working-class and an additional stratum (*sloi*), the intelligentsia – it no longer contained class antagonisms.[4] The new Soviet intelligentsia was as loyal and committed to Soviet goals as the working class and peasantry, for the majority of its members were no longer offspring of the old privileged classes but of the toiling masses. Specialists were no longer 'Red' or 'bourgeois', but simply 'Soviet'.

If all classes and strata were now equal in educational opportunity, some were inevitably more equal than others. Urban children had more chance of getting a secondary education than rural children. Children of white-collar and professional families were more likely to pass the VUZ entrance examinations than the children of workers. As had been argued by Soviet Communists in the 1920s, the absence of discrimination is in fact discrimination in favour of social groups with greater inherited culture, financial resources and motivation to seek education for their children. This kind of automatic discrimination existed during NEP, even when official policy was discriminatory in the opposite sense. It must also have existed in Stalin's Russia, when the authorities not only dropped the policy of countervailing discrimination but even ceased to collect data on social origin and parents' occupation.[5]

The last published breakdown of social composition of students in higher education – 1 January 1938 – showed a rise in the white-collar proportion and a substantial decline in the proportion of working-class students. Workers and their children now constituted 33.9% of students, still well above their representation in the total population (26%), but far below the working-class percentage in higher education during the First Five-Year Plan. Peasants and their children, at 21.6% of students, continued to be under-represented in population terms, though no more so than at the beginning of the

1930s. The white-collar and professional group – 17% of total population – provided 42.2% of students in 1938.[6]

In the immediate pre-war years, changes in the educational structure appeared to encourage the entrance into higher education of white-collar and professional children and discourage those from other social strata. Rabfaks ceased to exist in 1940.[7] At the same time, tuition fees were established for VUZy, technicums and grades VIII–X of the secondary school, which was now almost the only channel to higher education. No stipends were available for secondary school, and VUZ and technicum stipends were awarded on the basis of academic merit, not financial need.[8] From 1940, urban and rural adolescents aged 14 and over were liable for conscription to vocational Labour Reserve Schools[9] – unless they were already enrolled in the fee-charging general secondary schools and technicums.

However, before we conclude that Stalinist educational policy both intentionally and successfully closed the door to upward mobility through education, some other factors need to be taken into account.[10] In the first place, we have to consider whether the hypothetical alternative of continued proletarian recruitment was a real one. The First Five-Year Plan *vydvizhenie* was most effectively and importantly a movement to educate young adults. But the ranks of young adults belonging to the category of 'real' workers – those from working-class families, or with a number of years' experience in production – had been greatly depleted by the promotions of the First Five-Year Plan period. The industrial working class had, at the same time, absorbed an enormous influx of inexperienced recruits from the peasantry. But these new workers, constituting a majority of the industrial working class in the first half of the 1930s, were scarcely ready for a further mass promotion into the intelligentsia.

In the second place, numbers of professional and managerial jobs continued to increase at a very rapid rate, as did white-collar jobs as a whole. This meant that large-scale upward mobility was inevitable, whatever the intentions of the regime. In the whole Soviet population of 1926, there were fewer than four million persons classified as employees and professionals, and they had an average of 1.5 dependents. This group alone could not possibly have generated the fourteen million employees and professionals disclosed by the 1939 census.[11]

The third factor to be taken into account is that movement into the intelligentsia is not the only possible type of upward mobility. Faced with a perennial shortage of skilled workers and a continual influx of peasants into the labour force, the regime had to encourage internal promotion within the working class. One way of doing this was through the Stakhanovite movement and the system of bonuses and wage differentials. Another way was through the Labour Reserve system, established on the basis of the old FZU school network. The Labour Reserve system has sometimes been regarded as restricting the mobility of working-class children,[12] but this conclusion is highly dubious. Most of the Labour Reserve students were peasants;[13] and for peasant children – as for those of labourers and unskilled workers – the acquiring of a trade skill in itself constituted upward mobility.

The children of skilled workers probably did not normally attend the Labour Reserve schools. The existence of tuition fees for upper-level secondary schools and technicums should not have prevented the children of skilled workers from attending them: the fees were quite low, and in any case the average industrial worker by the end of the Stalin period earned more than the average white-collar employee.[14] Skilled working-class respondents in the post-war Harvard project perceived the Soviet system as one which provided ample opportunities for upward mobility through education.[15] This would hardly have been the case if their children's access to general and specialized secondary education had been significantly restricted in the late 1930s.

The last, and probably most important, factor is the expansion of schools and training institutions in the periods of the Second and Third Five-Year Plans (see Table 3). In 1938/39, the number of pupils in grades v–vii was more than three times that of 1931/32 and more than twice that of 1933/34. Senior secondary education (including grades viii–x of the general school, rabfaks, FZU schools and technicums) suffered a temporary contraction in the reorganization of 1933, but there was a subsequent substantial increase in the availability of all types of upper secondary education, and particularly of *general* secondary education, to adolescents. (The First Five-Year Plan *vydvizhenie* had produced a big expansion of technicums and rabfaks, but at the same time put adolescents in competition with adult *vydvizhentsy* for places in secondary education.)

There was a comparable expansion of part-time training programmes for adults. A compulsory State Technical Minimum for a wide range of industrial jobs was introduced;[16] and courses were established to train workers and foremen (the first- and second-level Technical Minimum courses, the Stakhanovite courses and the courses for 'masters of socialist labour') and raise the qualifications of

TABLE 3

Numbers of students in various types of secondary and higher schools, selected years, 1926–1939

	1926/27	1931/32	1933/34	1938/39
Secondary school grades v–vii				
urban	696,145	1,296,977	1,403,378	3,203,341
rural	362,933	1,516,666	2,680,210	5,576,708
total	1,059,078	2,813,643	4,083,588	8,780,049
Secondary school grades viii–x				
urban	118,304	892	123,593	855,089
rural	17,976	35	15,084	548,757
total	136,280	927	138,677	1,403,846
FZU schools (including trade schools)	244,600	975,000*	400,000	242,200
Rabfaks	45,702	285,019	271,104	107,877
Technicums	180,600	707,300	588,900	951,900
VUZy (including Com. VUZy, Industrial Academies, etc.)	168,000	405,900	458,300	602,900
Total in secondary and tertiary education	1,834,260	5,187,789	5,940,569	12,088,772

* A higher figure (1,099,000) is to be found in TsGAOR 5451/15/715, p. 42: VTsSPS, Sector of Industrial Cadres (1932).

Sources:
Kul'turnoe stroitel'stvo SSSR (Moscow, 1956), pp. 122–3, 201.
Kul'turnoe stroitel'stvo SSSR (Moscow, 1940), pp. 100 and 107.

engineering–technical personnel and industrial managers.[17] In 1938, in industry and building alone, 4.3 million workers went through various forms of courses, and 570,000 engineering–technical and managerial cadres were trained or retrained.[18] It was calculated that 'by the end of the Second Five-Year Plan, 1,200,000 Muscovites were drawn into training programmes [i.e. both formal schools and courses in the enterprise or place of work], that is, a third of the population of the capital. Not counting children of pre-school age and the elderly, every second inhabitant of Moscow was studying.'[19]

The end of the First Five-Year Plan *vydvizhenie*, therefore, was by no means the end of large-scale upward mobility through education, promotion on the job and training programmes. More 7-year schools meant increased opportunity for the children of peasants and unskilled workers to move into skilled industrial or office jobs. More places in upper-level secondary school and technicum meant more opportunities for children of skilled workers and office employees to acquire specialist qualifications. For adults, training programmes on the job reinforced the opportunities for promotion and raising of status. It was a less dramatic pattern than that of the First Five-Year Plan period, less politically significant in terms of abrupt elite transformation, but in no sense restrictive of upward social mobility.

Upward mobility and the new Soviet elite

'The Soviet intelligentsia is yesterday's workers and peasants and sons of workers and peasants promoted to command positions', stated the xviii Party Congress in 1939.[20] This is a claim that Western scholars have not usually taken seriously. The Soviet regime in 1939 was clearly moving away from policies which discriminated in favour of the working class and peasantry in educational and party admissions. Publication of systematic statistics on social origin had ceased. Even speakers at the Congress who made the claim provided only fragmentary evidence to substantiate it. One obvious possible inference to be drawn was that the claim was largely fraudulent – that, as Trotsky implied in *The Revolution Betrayed*, the new men in command positions were offspring of the old bureaucracy and bourgeoisie.[21]

This hypothesis, however, has been no better substantiated than the official Soviet one, and there are a number of reasons for finding it implausible. As has already been pointed out, the expansion of the white-collar sector between the 1926 and 1939 censuses could not have occurred without very substantial lower-class recruitment. Moreover, this lower-class recruitment was not restricted to low-status white-collar jobs. 'Command positions' were most accessible to Communist Party members and persons with higher education. But the great majority of party members in the late 1930s had entered the party in the years 1924–32, when the admissions policy was heavily weighted in favour of workers and, to a lesser extent, peasants (there were virtually no admissions in the years 1933–36, and relatively few even in 1937, after the official reopening of the party to new members). Similarly, the great majority of persons with higher education in the late 1930s were graduates of the First and Second Five-Year Plan period who had entered during the years of *vydvizhenie* and socially discriminatory admissions. This not only suggests that a high proportion of the new men in command positions were of working-class and peasant origin. It also implies that a substantial number were former workers who had risen during the *vydvizhenie* of the First Five-Year Plan.

Although the term 'intelligentsia' was often very broadly defined in the 1930s, a key group within it consisted of qualified specialists – graduates of higher and secondary specialized educational institutions. Their numbers grew spectacularly between 1928 and 1937. In January 1928, there were just under half a million graduates of VUZy and technicums employed in the national economy (excluding the military sector). By December 1937, there were 2.2 million, of whom 77% were graduates of the First and Second Five-Year Plan period.[22] Although no social breakdown is available for these graduates,[23] we can form some impression of their likely social composition by looking at the data on VUZ and technicum students in 1932/33, the mid-point of the period. In that year, 67% of VUZ students and 81% of technicum students were classified as working-class or peasant.[24]

Specialists *without* formal qualifications were an almost equally important component of the intelligentsia, constituting 42% of all those holding specialist jobs in 1937.[25] The two largest groups of such specialists in 1937 were teachers without pedagogical degrees or diplomas and industrial *praktiki* working as plant engineers and technicians – the first group probably largely peasant, the second largely working-class. Traditionally, the route of promotion on the job was more accessible to workers and peasants than that of formal education, and this is likely to have remained true even during the First Five-Year Plan. Among 483,676 industrial administrators and specialists in November 1933, 105,440 were former workers who had been promoted from work at the factory bench during the First Five-Year Plan. Only 55,036 were VUZ graduates of the First Five-Year Plan period, and in this group (most of whom would have entered higher education during NEP), former workers constituted little more than 20%.[26]

The only social breakdown available for any group of specialists (with and without educational qualifications) in 1937 applies, oddly enough, to the officer corps of the Red Army, in which 75% are stated to have been of working-class or peasant origin.[27] But some additional data are provided by Soviet sociological studies conducted in the post-Stalin period. A survey of engineering–technical personnel at a Sverdlovsk industrial plant in the 1960s, for example, found that in the cohort aged over 50, 55.2% were of working-class origin and 27.4% of peasant origin.[28] Another Soviet survey, this time of the population of the city of Kazan, found that 74.6% of those who had entered employment before 1942 in jobs requiring higher education were of working-class or peasant origin.[29] Despite the inadequacies of the data, it is reasonable to assume that about three-quarters of those holding specialist jobs in the late 1930s came from working-class and peasant families.

However, the most striking characteristic of the new Soviet intelligentsia was that a substantial proportion of its members not only came from lower-class families but had been upwardly mobile *as adults* from manual occupations. Adult *vydvizhentsy* were particularly prominent in the administrative group (although there were also many *vydvizhentsy* among the practising specialists), and statistics on party membership provide the best available data. In 1933, the great majority of Communists currently in white-collar jobs had entered the party as workers (59%) or peasants (22%). This meant that over 800,000 full and candidate members had been upwardly mobile into the white-collar group since joining the party.[30] But this is a minimum figure, as it excludes both Communists who were officers and employees in the Red Army and Communists who were full-time students (the latter numbering 233,000 in 1933[31]). According to one Soviet source, in the years 1930–1933 alone a total of 666,000 Communists who had entered the party as workers moved into white-collar and administrative jobs or went to full-time study.[32]

About a quarter of the Communists in white-collar positions came into the elite category of 'leading personnel and specialists' in November 1933. In this group, the proportion of former workers was 52%.[33] Less than a third of the Communist leading personnel had completed higher or secondary specialized education, but the recent influx of Communists into higher education was already making an impact, even though the big classes admitted in the years 1930–32 were still in school. Of the pre-1929 graduates in the survey, 14% were Communists. But among the graduates of 1929–32 (almost half the total), Communists constituted 28%.[34]

The exchange of party cards at the beginning of 1937 gives us a basis for assessing the results of Communist mobilization to education during the First Five-Year Plan, although it should be remembered that the large numbers of Communists admitted to VUZy in 1932 had yet to graduate. If we compare the 1937 data with those of the party census ten years earlier, we find a spectacular increase in total numbers of Communists with higher education, in the proportion of them trained in engineering, and in the proportion of them who had been workers at the time of entering the party.

In January 1937, there were 105,000 Communists with completed higher education, or more than ten times the number shown by the 1927 party census.[35] In 1937, 45% of all Communist graduates had received higher *technical* education, compared with 7.8% ten years earlier.[36] In 1937, 47.3% of Communist specialists with higher education had entered the party as workers and 10% as peasants, whereas in 1927 (when the total number of graduates was much smaller) a mere 7% had entered the party as workers and 1.5% as peasants.[37]

These radical changes must be attributed almost entirely to the First Five-Year Plan policy of recruiting Communists to higher education, since only a few thousand specialists were admitted to the party in the years 1927–32 and there was a moratorium on party admissions from the beginning of 1933 until November 1936. Of course, the strictly quantitative aspect of the changes should not be exaggerated: the majority of specialists, even in engineering, were still non-party in 1937, and graduates still constituted a very small group in the total party membership. But the political importance of the group was out of all proportion to its actual size. The *vydvizhentsy* combined technical expertise, party status and, in Stalin's view,[38] special qualities of political reliability which made their rapid promotion highly desirable for the regime.

When Stalin had described the purposes of the First Five-Year Plan *vydvizhenie* in his speeches of the time, he had emphasized the importance not only of training Communist and working-class specialists but also of producing the 'leading cadres' of the future. Whether by accident or design, the First Five-Year Plan *vydvizhentsy* had scarcely managed to graduate before that future became the present. The Great Purge of 1937/38 removed almost the entire top stratum of industrial managers and party and government personnel; and the *vydvizhentsy* – typically in their 30s, Communists with working-class background or with experience of work on production, newly graduated from engineering school, working as plant engineers, and often simultaneously completing diploma work or dissertations – stepped or stumbled into their places.[39]

As illustrations of the astonishing, and indeed shocking, opportunities for promotion opening before the *vydvizhentsy* in 1937/38, we may take the cases of P. K. Ponomarenko and A. S. Chuyanov. In 1938, when at the age of 36 and 33 both were working in junior positions in the Central Committee apparat, they could already look back on careers of great upward mobility and achievement. Ponomarenko, the son of a poor peasant, had fought in the Civil War, worked briefly as a fitter, joined the party in 1925 and spent the latter years of NEP in Komsomol and party work. Around 1928, he was sent to the Moscow Institute of Transport Engineers. After graduating in 1932, he worked in command posts in the army and as party secretary of a scientific research institute, before being transferred to the group of promising young cadres in the Central Committee apparat at the beginning of 1938.[40]

Chuyanov's parents were unskilled workers at a grain collection point. Before the October Revolution his father had contact with the Bolsheviks but did not join them because, as he explained to his son, 'I'm illiterate, dead wood, and they don't take such people.' His uncle became a military commissar who, around 1924, sponsored his nephew for party membership and got him a job in the Komsomol apparat. In 1927, Chuyanov took the examination to enter the third year of rabfak but failed. He spent the next year in a VUZ preparatory course, but it turned out that he never had to take the examination because in 1929 he was selected as a Party Thousander and sent to one of the Moscow VTUZy. Graduating in 1934 from the Moscow Chemical–Technological Institute of the Meat Industry, he went to work as a plant engineer and simultaneously entered graduate studies (a proposal arising from his student research had already been accepted by the meat industry administration). After finishing his graduate work in 1937, he was appointed to the Central Committee apparat.[41]

One day in 1938, Ponomarenko and Chuyanov were summoned by Andreev, then Central Committee secretary for cadres. Ponomarenko went in first, and after thirty minutes, as Chuyanov relates it, 'came out of the office thoughtful and stern. He said to me quietly: "I'm going to the Belorussian Central Committee." And went away without pausing.' He had been appointed first secretary of the Belorussian Communist Party.

Chuyanov then went in to Andreev, who informed him – to his considerable shock – that he was being recommended for the job of first secretary of the Stalingrad region:

'I haven't much experience of party work.'
'You'll get the experience. You have recently graduated from VUZ,

you are in graduate school, you know agriculture, and you also know the fishing industry...So your candidacy is quite appropriate.'

At that moment a messenger from the Politburo came in and handed over some package. Opening it, Andrei Andreevich [Andreev] said:

'Here is the Politburo decision.'

I was struck dumb by these words, not knowing what to say.

'Well then', said Andrei Andreevich, 'regard yourself as the future secretary of a party obkom. You can't wear your old student suit.'

Telephoning the Central Committee business manager, he said:

'Comrade Chuyanov is coming over. He needs to be clothed and shod as a future obkom secretary, at Central Committee expense. He has no money.'

And, turning to me again:

'You'll have to leave today, without going home...Phone your wife and have her come to the station, give her your old suit...'

...My wife was waiting at the station with our six-year-old son Vladimir.

'Why the hurry, so you can't even look in at home? Did something happen?'

'Nothing happened', I answered. 'That's just the way it has to be.'[42]

Vydvizhentsy working as plant engineers experienced similarly rapid promotions, though they were normally moving up the hierarchy within one institution. A report from the Commissariat of Heavy Machinery of late 1939 or early 1940 on the replenishment of leading industrial cadres cited the examples of Peshchany and Zaltsman, both newly appointed directors of important enterprises: Peshchany, a 1932 VTUZ graduate, had been successively section head, production head, shop supervisor and deputy chief engineer at the New Kramatorsk plant before being appointed director of the Old Kramatorsk plant; Zaltsman, graduating in 1933, was successively foreman of the repair shop, senior foreman, deputy supervisor and supervisor of the turbine shop before being promoted in 1937 to chief engineer of the Kirov (formerly Putilov) plant and in 1939 to director.[43]

Other new industrial directors and leading industrial personnel were even more recent VTUZ graduates. V. E. Arsenev graduated in 1937, aged 27, from the Leningrad Industrial Institute, began work as a metallurgical engineer at the Kirov plant, and within two years was head of its metallurgical department.[44] D. E. Morozov, a son of poor peasants who began factory work at the age of 13, was sent as a Party Thousander to the Leningrad Shipbuilding Institute. After graduating in 1934 or 1935, he became a shop head at Petrozavod, and was promoted to director in 1937. S. Ya. Padalko, an older *vydvizhenets*, Civil War veteran and former steelworker, was sent to

VTUZ in 1930, aged 32, and graduated as a chemical engineer in 1934. In October 1937 he was transferred from the relatively junior position of shop head in the Gorlovka chemical plant to become director of the important Berezniki Chemical Complex.[45]

Rapid promotion did not, of course, ensure permanent membership of the political and managerial elite; and we should consider the possibility that the First Five-Year Plan *vydvizhentsy* were not only beneficiaries of the Great Purge but also victims of it. However it appears that, although not all those promoted to top jobs during the purge or immediately after it kept those or equivalent positions,[46] the *vydvizhentsy* with higher education survived the purge years almost intact. We can draw this conclusion because of the existence of a January 1941 survey of 'leading cadres and specialists' in the Soviet Union, a summary of which has recently been published from the Soviet archives.[47] During the First Five-Year Plan, a total of 170,000 specialists graduated from all Soviet VUZy (excluding military). The VUZ output in the Second Five-Year Plan was 370,000.[48] In the 1941 survey, despite the exclusion of military, security and party personnel, the group of leading cadres included 152,000 First Five-Year Plan graduates, or 89% of the total. Only 72% of the Second Five-Year Plan graduates were among the 1941 leading cadres.[49] But this should probably be explained not in terms of the purges but as a result of army call-up, continued study in graduate school and the fact that the big graduating class of 1937 had not all achieved the rank of 'leading cadres' within $3\frac{1}{2}$ years of graduation.

Some of the *vydvizhentsy* were thrown into top jobs and failed to cope with them; others remained in the same position for a number of years (Chuyanov, for example, was first secretary of the Stalingrad obkom until 1946); and a third group simply continued to rise. The most common pattern seems to be promotion from director of an industrial enterprise to a major government position. V. A. Malyshev, for example, graduated from the Bauman Mechanical Machine-building Institute in 1932; went to work at the big Kolomna locomotive plant, where he rose in five years from a junior position as designer to director; and in 1939, at the age of 37, was appointed head of the Commissariat of Heavy Machinery of the USSR. A. N. Kosygin, a 1935 graduate of the Leningrad Textile Institute, was director of a textile factory by 1937, and by 1939 (at the age of 35), head of the Commissariat for the Textile Industry of the USSR. A. I. Samokhvalov, a Party Thousander, graduated from the Leningrad Metallurgical Institute in 1933, became director of the Volkhov Aluminium Plant in 1937, and was appointed head of the Commissariat for Precious Metals of the USSR two years later, at the age of 36. D. F. Ustinov, a 1934 graduate of the Leningrad Military-Mechanical Institute, rose from rank-and-file engineer to director of the Leningrad 'Bolshevik' works in the six years after graduation, and in 1941, at the age of 33, was appointed Commissar of Armaments for the USSR.[50]

Other *vydvizhentsy* followed their path into the top political leadership in the post-war years. In the Central Committee elected in 1952, there were 37 First Five-Year Plan *vydvizhentsy* – that is, persons who entered higher education during the First Five-Year Plan as adults with work experience, many of them with working-class or peasant background – out of a total of 104 members on whom there is educational data.[51] Twenty-three of the 37 *vydvizhentsy* were sent to VTUZ or Industrial Academy; and among them were two of the Soviet Union's future leaders, both of working-class origin and with experience as workers and in the apparat before entering higher education. Nikita Khrushchev, born in 1894, was one of the older *vydvizhentsy* whose party experience went back to the Civil War. In 1929, at the age of 35, he was sent from party work to the Moscow Industrial Academy, where he led the fight against the Right Opposition[52] before being appointed secretary of a Moscow raikom in 1931. Leonid Brezhnev, born in 1906, was both younger and better educated. During NEP, he graduated from a technicum and worked as a land surveyor and soviet official. He entered the Dneprodzerzhinsk Metallurgical Institute in 1931, the year in which he joined the party. After graduation, he worked for a few years as an engineer before becoming department head and, in 1939, secretary of the Dnepropetrovsk obkom.[53]

The preponderance of *vydvizhentsy* in the Soviet government of 1952[54] is particularly striking. Out of 115 ministers and deputy ministers on whom there are educational data, 50% (57) were First Five-Year Plan *vydvizhentsy*; 65% of the *vydvizhentsy* were either of working-class origin or had at some time been workers by occupation; 37% were Communists in 1928, and a further 23% entered the party during the First Five-Year Plan. All but one of the *vydvizhentsy* in the government sample and Central Committee were men (the exception was Kovrigina, Minister of Health in 1952).

Of those *vydvizhentsy* in the government sample whose occupation immediately before entering higher education is known, 50% were workers and 26% were employed in administrative jobs (Komsomol, soviet, trade union or party). But these proportions were almost exactly reversed for the Central Committee *vydvizhentsy*: 25% of them had been workers at the bench, and 53% had been employed in administrative jobs. Of the 57 *vydvizhentsy* in the government group, 42 went to enginering VTUZy and 33 worked as plant engineers immediately after graduation. In the years 1936–41, two-thirds of the *vydvizhentsy* received a major promotion – often, in fact, a series of major promotions from chief engineer to enterprise director to head of a trust or a senior position in an industrial commissariat of the All-Union government. By 1941 – ten years after the graduation of the first of the First Five-Year Plan *vydvizhentsy*, four years after the graduation of the last of them – 30 *vydvizhentsy* held the position of commissar, deputy commissar or head of a department within a commissariat, and 17 were directors or deputy directors of industrial enterprises and trusts.

In the 1952 leadership, we find *vydvizhentsy* of the NEP period as well as the First Five-Year Plan. In addition to the 42 ministers and deputy ministers who had entered VTUZy as *vydvizhentsy* during the First Five-Year Plan, 22 had entered VTUZy during NEP – many of them graduating during the First Five-Year Plan and having similar career patterns to the First Five-Year Plan *vydvizhentsy*. This brought the total contingent of VTUZ *vydvizhentsy* (excluding those who entered VTUZy after 1932) to 56% of the whole government group. Among the NEP contingent were such notable individuals as Tevosyan, Kabanov and S. Z. Ginzburg.

The 1952 Central Committee contained only a small number of NEP *vydvizhentsy* who had studied engineering. Two of them, however, subsequently achieved prominence in fields quite remote from their area of study. Alexander Fadeev, a Civil War veteran and party member from 1918, spent a few years as a student at the Moscow Mining Academy with Tevosyan and Emelyanov (all three of them signed a student letter condemning the Trotskyite Opposition in 1924[55]), and then devoted himself to writing, and became first a leader of the proletarian writers' association (RAPP) and later head of the Union of Soviet Writers. G. M. Malenkov, also a Civil War veteran, joined the party in 1920, was sent to the Moscow Higher Technical School in 1921, and entered the Central Committee apparat immediately after graduation.

During NEP, it was the social science students – those who were sent to the Sverdlov and Zinoviev Communist Universities, the Plekhanov Economics Institute, the Institute of Red Professors and (until the mid-1920s) the social science faculties of Moscow and Leningrad Universities – who were seen as the *smena*, or future political leadership. Clearly their place had been to a large extent usurped by the engineering *vydvizhentsy* trained during the First Five-Year Plan. But the NEP social science group was not unrepresented in the political leadership of 1952. Few of its members are to be found in our sample of ministers and deputy ministers of 1952, although this may be because the sample is biased in favour of the industrial ministries. But the group had a number of representatives in the 1952 Central Committee: Mekhlis and Poskrebyshev (who had signed the same anti-Trotsky letter as Tevosyan and Emelyanov in 1924); Yudin and Mitin, activists on the philosophical front of Cultural Revolution; M. Z. Saburov; M. G. Pervukhin; M. A. Suslov.

The general dominance of the enginering *vydvizhentsy* must also be qualified in another way. There were simply not enough engineering *vydvizhentsy* to fill all the top positions; and, if we look outside the central political and governmental leadership of 1952 to the leadership in the provinces and national republics, we find a different pattern of recruitment.

In a sample of 70 regional first secretaries in 1952 who were *not* members of the Central Committee, more than half were without any kind of higher or secondary specialized education;[56] 22 of the group who had such education had been sent to VUZ, technicum or rabfak during the First Five-Year Plan, but only 5 of these went to VTUZy. Although half of the whole group were of working-class origin or had at some time been workers by occupation, only 8 had prolonged experience in industry, either as workers or as specialists and managers. The basic experience of 24 members of the group was in agriculture (as agronomists, members of rural soviets, local agriculture departments, sovkhozy, MTS, etc.), while the basic experience of 15 was in educational work (as teachers, school inspectors and directors, education department officials and so on).

The long-term predominance of the First Five-Year Plan engineering *vydvizhentsy* in the highest positions is graphically illustrated by comparing the background of industrial and construction ministers from 1941 to 1965. In 1941, 15 out of 21 ministers on whom data is available had engineering education, and the average date of graduation was 1931. All the new ministers of the 1940s and 1950s had engineering education, and their average date of graduation was 1932/33. In 1965, the average graduation date of industrial and construction ministers was 1935 – still within the limits of First Five-Year Plan *vydvizhenie*.[57]

If we turn to the Soviet Politiburo of July 1977, we find perhaps the most striking confirmation of the long-term impact and political significance of the First Five-Year Plan *vydvizhenie*. Out of 14 Politburo members, Suslov is the sole representative of the social science *smena* sent to higher education during NEP. No less than half of the Politburo of June 1978 – Brezhnev, Kosygin, Kirilenko, Ustinov, Gromyko, Kunaev and Pelshe – are First Five-Year Plan *vydvizhentsy*. All but Kunaev (a Kazakh from a white-collar family) are of working-class or peasant background. All but Gromyko and Pelshe (who went respectively to the Minsk Agricultural Institute and the Institute of Red Professors) were sent to VTUZy and graduated as engineers.[58]

The 'New Class' and the 'Great Retreat'

The emergence of a new privileged class in the Soviet Union – the intelligentsia stratum, in Stalin's terminology; the 'bureaucracy', as Trotsky called it in *The Revolution Betrayed*[59] – has been much discussed in the West. From the early 1930s, the New Class[60] acquired privileges and marks of status which set it apart from the rest of the population: dachas, access to special stores and resorts, better apartments, high salaries and bonuses. Earlier symbols of egalitarianism was discarded. An obkom secretary, as Andreev told Chuyanov, should be dressed in a manner appropriate to his position. Authority should be respected, and it should be visibly identifiable. By the end of the decade, ranks and uniforms had been re-established in the armed forces; and, as in Tsarist times, the civilian service class followed the example of the military. Even the wives of industrial managers and military officers were encouraged to behave in a manner appropriate to their position in society: they should set an example of orderly household management, propriety and *kul'turnost'* (cultured behaviour) to the lower ranks.[61]

Timasheff linked the *embourgeoisement* of Soviet society with a 'Great Retreat' in ideology.[62] The Soviet regime, as he saw it, had abandoned the earlier goals of revolutionary transformation of society and culture, and was gradually reviving traditional norms and values. The *meshchanstvo* of the 1920s – observance of pre-revolutionary conventions of politeness and propriety, respect for hierarchical seniority, emphasis on family values, appreciation and care for material possessions – had become the *kul'turnost'* of the Stalin period. In effect, Vera Dunham argues, the party leadership had made a 'Big Deal' with the new elite: bourgeois life-style in exchange for political loyalty.[63]

In the educational sphere, there were many signs of a reassertion of traditional values in the 1930s and 1940s. Secondary-school pupils went back into uniform – pinafores for the girls, cadet-type uniforms for the boys – and were encouraged to look and behave like the gymnasium pupils of thirty years earlier. Labour Reserve schools also had a uniform, but it resembled that of the old apprentices,[64] underlining the social gulf between them and their contemporaries in the secondary school. The secondary-school curriculum came increasingly to resemble that of the old gymnasium. Schoolchildren learned patriotic history, as they had done in Tsarist times; and from the late 1930s they no longer took courses in 'labour'.[65] The school no longer claimed to be polytechnical, and educational methodology was discussed without any reference at all to social class.

At the beginning of the 1930s, workers and Communists had been sent to higher education to 'master technology', in other words, for avowedly instrumental purposes. The VTUZy continued to attract the brightest and most ambitious students. But by the late 1930s, it was highly unusual for any responsible spokesman to express a vulgarly utilitarian attitude to higher education. The purpose of higher education, as defined in a Central Committee resolution of 1936, was not simply to give professional, technical and political training. The country needed 'cultured cadres with an all-round education [*vsestoronne obrazovannykh i kul'turnykh kadrov*] who have mastered "the knowledge of all the riches which mankind has fashioned" (Lenin)'.[66]

Such a concept of higher education required the full restoration of the old universities, and by the beginning of the 1940s this had basically been accomplished.[67] The old philological faculties of the universities not only survived (though for most of the 1930s they existed in Moscow and Leningrad as independent institutes, separate from the parent universities, under the titles MIFLI and LIFLI), but attracted a highly elite group of students, many from professional families, and including sons of political leaders like Yuri Zhdanov and future politicians like Shelepin. When the young Solzhenitsyn dreamed of leaving Rostov for Moscow and studying literature at MIFLI,[68] he was not showing early signs of deviance but a very proper, officially endorsed, respect for culture – and, perhaps, sensitivity to and aspiration for elite status.

The regime's overt respect and generous financial support for the least utilitarian forms of culture is one of the paradoxes of the later Stalin period.[69] The material rewards available to the 'creative intelligentsia' were enormous; and, while this group suffered the

constraints of censorship and was required to conform to ortho-
doxies and established norms within the professions, it was also
permitted – even encouraged – to revive the traditions and sense of
professional identity which the Communist cultural revolutionaries
had earlier tried to destroy.

There were, of course, anomalies and contradictions. In educational
practice, for example, the Stalinist norms were very largely traditional, stressing formal procedures, respect for teachers and parents,
and academic standards. But in educational theory, Makarenko –
whose ideas became widely known in the late 1930s – represented
one stream of the labour-oriented, anti-academic progressive movement of the 1920s; and much of his support in fact came from
former activists of Cultural Revolution.[70]

Despite these contradictions, however, the Stalinist regime showed
an unmistakable preference for the 'real' culture of the Bolshoi
ballet, the Stanislavsky theatre and the classics of Russian nineteenth-century literature over the 'revolutionary' culture which
Communist intellectuals had tried to put in its place. This certainly
could be interpreted as capitulation to the superior culture of the
formerly privileged classes – a danger which Lenin himself had
pointed out in the early 1920s, though he was thinking of culture in
the anthropological sense rather than the narrow one – and hence as
a retreat from revolutionary ideals.

However, we have to ask ourselves at this point whose revolutionary ideals we are talking about. The aspirations of the intellectual
Communist avantgarde – the activists of Cultural Revolution, those
who combined Bohemian life-style with ideological militancy – were
firmly repudiated during the Stalin period. But their aspirations had
always been somewhat in conflict with the ideal of popular enlightenment put forward by Lenin and Lunacharsky in the first years
of Soviet power.

Lenin and Lunacharsky believed in the value of the inherited
cultural tradition. They did not advocate 'storming the fortresses'
of bourgeois culture, but instead wanted to bring workers and
peasants to the Bolshoi Theatre and teach them to appreciate the
classics of nineteenth-century literature. They rejected the idea that
kul'turnost' could be equated with *meshchanstvo*. They believed in
a broad general education and accepted the ideal of the all-round
cultured man. Their values, in short, had much in common with
those expressed by the Stalinist leadership in the second half of the
1930s.

The revolutionary ideals of the Communist avantgardists were also very different from those of the *vydvizhentsy* – and it was the *vydvizhentsy*, former workers and peasants, who formed the core of New Class of the 1930s and 1940s. As a group, the *vydvizhentsy* seem to have been highly motivated, hard-working and serious in their attitude to education. It is hard to believe that their feelings about traditional culture were iconoclastic, that they had any personal sympathy for the young Communist intellectuals from upper-class families, or that they ultimately differed from upwardly mobile groups in other societies in trying to acquire the culture and manners appropriate to their new position.

From the point of view of a *vydvizhenets*, 'studying' was enormously important;[71] and a school which emphasized discipline, grades, orderly instruction and examinations was surely a more desirable one than the progressive school of the 1920s, let alone the wildly experimental and disorganized school of the First Five-Year Plan. But the *vydvizhenets* wanted his children not only to study but to become cultured. As Vera Dunham points out, the theme 'Our children should have a better life than we did' is very prominent in the literature of the 1930s, and the better life included access to luxury goods in the cultural as well as consumer sphere. Thus for Pasha Angelina, a Stakhanovite tractor driver, her children's acquisition of culture is a matter of the greatest pride and satisfaction:

With astonishing ease my Svetlana recited one of Pushkin's fairy tales from beginning to end. I always very much enjoyed listening to Svetlana when she recited poetry and when later she sat down at the grand piano and played Chopin and Tchaikovsky. I would listen and see nothing except her face and her plump little hands flying like birds over the keyboard.

Stalinka, the younger daughter, asks if she too will learn to play the piano.

'Of course you will.' I listened to Stalinka with excitement and happiness. My childhood was different: I couldn't even think of music.[72]

The *vydvizhenets* was proud of his own promotion, and thought it appropriate that achievement should be visibly, if not ostentatiously, rewarded. Kochetov, a Soviet writer with a large 'New Class' readership, often touches on this theme, always simultaneously emphasizing the virtue of lower-class origins and the legitimate rewards available to those who rise above them. In one of his stories of an upwardly mobile working-class family, the father tells his son that 'a lord and master ought to dress like a lord and master', and they go out to buy 'the most expensive and the very best serge suit that could be found in the store'. The mistress of the house explains the family's prosperity to her prospective daughter-in-law:

We are workers, Zinocha, just as your papa and mama were, may they be in the kingdom of God. Our road is the same as the government's. When the government was poor, we too were poor; when the government became richer, we too took heart.[73]

In memoirs, as well as in fiction, the *vydvizhentsy* express identification with Soviet power, pride in its achievements, and the desire that these achievements should be celebrated in an appropriately cultural way. At the beginning of the 1930s, there was much discussion of the proposed Palace of Soviets (actually never built) which was to stand on the site of the old cathedral and the present Moscow swimming-pool near the Kremlin. Emelyanov – a *vydvizhenets* of the 1920s, student with Tevosyan at the Moscow Mining Academy, later a major figure in industry, government and scientific research – recalls the discussions that went on in his circle.

I remember that at one big social gathering a woman, whose living conditions were probably very difficult, expressed doubts about whether a Palace of Soviets ought to be built. [She said] it would be better to build more apartments. I remember the angry objections of the majority of those present.

'No, we need exactly this kind of monumental building. Everything that is ours, Soviet, ought to be the best and the most beautiful in the world. The best-quality goods, the best factories, the best subway.'[74]

These 'angry objections' are interesting not only for their content but as illustration of the very different preoccupations of the *vydvizhentsy* and the Communist intelligentsia formed in the 1920s. The debate among Communist intellectuals (and in the party leadership at that time) was on the questions of 'proletarian' versus 'modernist' style and 'proletarian' versus 'bourgeois' architects. The Communist intellectuals might or might not favour Le Corbusier's design for the Palace of Soviets; but they agreed that the 'monumental style' – mainly associated with some of the Grand Old Men of the Russian architectural profession – was out-dated and philistine.[75] To the *vydvizhentsy*, however, it was as natural to give 'monumental' expression to Soviet revolutionary achievements as to buy 'the most expensive and the very best serge suit in the store' to celebrate one's own promotion to a position of responsibility and social respect.

One of the conclusions that could be drawn is that Timasheff's

'Great Retreat' of the later Stalin period was really the secondary consequence of a successful social revolution: the mass promotion of former workers and peasants into the Soviet political and social elite. But it is not our purpose in these last paragraphs to do more than suggest that future research on a whole range of historical problems of the Stalin era – the 'New Class', the 'Great Retreat', the relations of the regime and the intelligentsia, the purges of the late 1930s – might profitably begin with the phenomenon of First Five-Year Plan *vydvizhenie* and its implications for later development.

In 1917/18, when the Bolsheviks were establishing themselves in power, they sometimes spoke as if a revolutionary government had an infinite variety of policy options, since revolution had liberated the society from the constraints of established tradition. (A similar assumption is often made by Western writers on the Soviet period, especially with regard to the Stalin era.) Yet, if we look back on the evolution of policy in the educational sphere from the beginning of the 1920s to the mid-1930s, we must be struck not only by the variety of policies considered and in different degrees implemented, but also by the existence of two overriding imperatives to which policy debate continually returned.

It was imperative that the Soviet Union should industrialize; and it was imperative that the new regime should create its own elite by promoting and educating workers, peasants and their children. Within the Communist Party, these were universally accepted truths. But they were also objectives which had substantial endorsement in the society as a whole, and this must surely be a factor in any explanation of Soviet achievement in these areas.

The First Five-Year Plan *shturmovshchina*, undertaken against the advice of the gradualists in the party leadership, had short-term consequences which were even worse than the gradualists had predicted. But it laid the foundations of Soviet industrialization and created the core of the new Soviet elite which was to continue the task. For the *vydvizhentsy*, industrialization was an heroic achievement – their own, Stalin's and that of Soviet power – and their promotion, linked with the industrialization drive, was a fulfilment of the promises of the revolution.

Notes

Chapter 1   Education and Soviet society

1. The class categories normally used by the Bolsheviks were 'workers'. 'peasants', 'employees' (white-collar workers and professionals) and 'others' (the lowest category, including entrepreneurs, merchants, artisans, priests, former Tsarist policemen, former nobles, etc.). There were a number of problems implicit in these categories. The peasant category included 'poor peasants', whom the Bolsheviks regarded as sympathetic to the regime, 'middle peasants', regarded as neutral, and 'kulaks', regarded as hostile; but these sub-groups – which were in any case extremely difficult to identify – were not distinguished in educational admissions. Agricultural labourers, as rural proletarians, were classified as workers. Artisans were clearly wrongly included in the category of 'others', since the regime did not really regard them as hostile 'social aliens' but as a more or less neutral group. There was considerable overlap between the categories of 'others' and 'employees' since even social aliens might and often did obtain salaried employment. Within the 'employee' category, *trudovaya intelligentsiya* (professionals) almost always had higher priority in educational admissions than ordinary office workers; and Communist administrators and their children obviously ranked as high as workers in principle, and higher in practice.
2. 'Principles of Communism' (1847), S. M. Kovalev (compiler) *O kommunisticheskom vospitanii*, 2nd ed. (Moscow, 1966), p. 26.
3. Marx, instruction to delegates to the First International (1866), in *ibid.*, p. 34.
4. *Ibid.*, p. 35.
5. Dewey, *School and Society*, as quoted in one of the most influential pedagogical works of the 1920s, A. P. Pinkevich's *The New Education in the Soviet Republic*, translated by Perlmutter and Counts (New York, 1929), p. 163.
6. 'Pearls of Narodnik hare-brained scheming' (on S. N. Yuzhakov), V. I. Lenin, *Polnoe sobranie sochinenii*, II, 5th ed. (Moscow, 1958), pp. 473–504.
7. See Lenin's sardonic comment of *circa* 1894, quoted N. K. Krupskaya, *Vospominaniya o Lenine*, 2nd ed. (Moscow, 1968), pp. 12–13.
8. See Leopold Haimson, 'The Problem of Social Stability in Urban Russia, 1905–1917', *Slavic Review*, December 1964 and March 1965.

9. See T. H. Rigby, *Communist Party Membership in the U.S.S.R. 1917–1967* (Princeton, 1968), ch. 2.

10. On Proletkult and Lenin's objections to it, see Sheila Fitzpatrick, *The Commissariat of Enlightenment* (London and New York, 1970), pp. 175–87 and *passim*.

11. See, for example, Lenin's speech to the First All-Russian Congress on Extramural Education (1919), *Polnoe sobranie sochinenii* XXXVIII, 5th ed., p. 330; and 'Better less, but better', *ibid.* LV, pp. 387ff.

12. See Jeremy R. Azrael, *Managerial Power and Soviet Politics* (Cambridge, Mass., 1966), pp. 30–2.

13. N. K. Krupskaya, *Narodnoe obrazovanie i demokratiya* (author's preface dated 1915) (St Petersburg: Zhizn' i znanie, 1917).

14. *Partiya i vospitanie smeny* (Leningrad, 1924), p. 37.

15. *Narodnoe prosveshchenie*, 1929 no. 3–4, p. 30.

16. A. Lunacharsky, 'The artistic policy of the Soviet state', *Zhizn' iskusstva*, 1924 no. 10 (Leningrad), p. 1.

17. See L. Trotsky, *The Revolution Betrayed* (New York, 1937), pp. 97–8.

18. I. N. Yudin, *Sotsial'naya baza rosta KPSS* (Moscow, 1973), p. 128.

19. *Industrializatsiya SSSR 1926–1928 gg. Dokumenty i materialy* (Moscow, 1969), p. 348.

20. O. I. Shkaratan, *Problemy sotsial'noi struktury rabochego klassa SSSR* (Moscow, 1970), p. 295.

Chapter 2   *The new Soviet school*

1. F. F. Korolev, T. D. Korneichik and Z. I. Ravkin, *Ocherki po istorii sovetskoi shkoly i pedagogiki 1921–1931* (Moscow, 1961), p. 447.

2. *Na putyakh k novoi shkole*, 1922 no. 3, pp. 3–5.

3. *Ibid.*, pp. 12–13.

4. The 1924 revised programmes for primary schools, quoted Korolev, Korneichik and Ravkin, *Ocherki*, p. 72.

5. For the debates of the Civil War period on this subject, see Fitzpatrick, *The Commissariat of Enlightenment*, ch. 3.

6. A. M. Bolshakov, *Derevnya 1917–1927* (Moscow, 1927), p. 234.

7. *Ibid.*, p. 233.

8. *Narodnoe prosveshchenie*, 1926 no. 4–5, p. 67, quoted *Russkaya shkola za rubezhom*, 1927–28 no. 32, p. 140.

9. A. Lunacharsky, *Prosveshchenie i revolyutsiya* (Moscow, 1926), p. 398.

10. P. P. Blonsky, *Moi vospominaniya* (Moscow, 1971), p. 172.

11. Korolev, Korneichik and Ravkin, *Ocherki*, pp. 72–3.

12. *Programmy GUSa V–IX klassov. Matematika* (1925), quoted Korolev, Korneichik and Ravkin, *Ocherki*, p. 73.

13. Quoted *ibid.*, p. 188.

14. See Krupskaya's defence of the Narkompros position in *Na putyakh*

k novoi shkole, 1928 no. 7–8, p. 7, and the attack by Oleshchuk, of the League of Militant Godless, in *Revolyutsiya i kul'tura*, 1928 no. 10, p. 21.

15. Lunacharsky's theory of 'Godbuilding' and his two-volume *Religiya i sotsializm* (1908, 1911) had been harshly criticized by Lenin in the pre-revolutionary years. However, Lunacharsky was never religious in any conventional sense.

16. On the atheism circles, see Korolev, Korneichik and Ravkin, *Ocherki*, pp. 292–6.

17. *Ibid.*, pp. 182–3.

18. *Na putyakh k novoi shkole*, 1926 no. 5–6, p. 63.

19. Korolev, Korneichik and Ravkin, *Ocherki*, p. 92.

20. *Russkii yazyk i literatura v trudovoi shkole*, 1928 no. 1, p. 81.

21. Quoted by Lunacharsky, *Literaturnoe nasledstvo*, vol. 82 (Moscow, 1970), p. 77.

22. *Ibid.*

23. For the views of Pokrovsky and other members of the Pedagogical Section of GUS on the teaching of history, see minutes of the debate of 24 March 1926 in *Na putyakh k novoi shkole*, 1926 no. 5–6, pp. 61ff.

24. See debates cited above, and discussion and resolutions on history teaching in *Na putyakh k novoi shkole*, 1926 nos. 10 and 11 and 1927 no. 3.

25. 'On the teaching of history in a Communist school', Lunacharsky, *Prosveshchenie i revolyutsiya* (1926), p. 106.

26. *Na putyakh k novoi shkole*, 1926 no. 5–6, pp. 61–2 and 76.

27. *Ibid.*, p. 67.

28. Quoted Korolev, Korneichik and Ravkin, *Ocherki*, p. 91, from M. N. Pokrovsky, *Istoricheskaya nauka i bor'ba klassov* (1933).

29. For categories of person deprived of the right to vote, see *Istoriya sovetskoi konstitutsii. Sbornik dokumentov, 1917–1957* (Moscow, 1957), p. 85, for 1918 Constitution of the RSFSR; and 1926 instructions on elections to urban and rural soviets in *Sobranie uzakonenii i rasporyazhenii rabochego i krest'yanskogo pravitel'stva RSFSR*, 1926 no. 75, art. 577.

30. N. Ognev, 'Dnevnik Kosti Ryabtseva', *Sobranie sochinenii*, III (Moscow, 1929), pp. 25–6.

31. See, for example, *ibid.* pp. 46–8; Yu. Libedinsky, *Rozhdenie geroya* Leningrad, 1930), pp. 145ff.

32. The School Soviet consisted of teachers and one representative of each grade between grade v and grade ix. Komsomol and trade union organizations also had the right to send representatives. 'Constitution of the United Labour School' (1923), *Direktivy VKP(b) i sovetskogo pravitel'stva o narodnom obrazovanii 1917–1947 gg.*, I (Moscow–Leningrad, 1947), pp. 129–32.

33. *Narodnoe prosveshchenie*, 1926 no. 9, p. 76. There is a similar report in *Prosveshchenie Sibiri* (Novosibirsk), 1926 no. 1, p. 35.
34. Krupskaya, B. Olkhovy, ed., *Zadachi agitatsii, propagandy i kul'-turnogo stroitel'stva* (Moscow–Leningrad, 1928), pp. 88–9.
35. *Ibid.*
36. See 'Laws of the Young Pioneers' (1922), *Tovarishch Komsomol. Dokumenty syezdov, konferentsii i TsK VLKSM 1918–1968* (Moscow, 1969), pp. 96–7.
37. *Narodnoe prosveshchenie*, 1928 no. 12, pp. 35 and 37.
38. Bukharin, report on youth, *XIII syezd RKP(b). Stenograficheskii otchet* (Moscow, 1963), pp. 515–19.
39. *Osnovnye uzakoneniya i rasporyazheniya po narodnomu prosvesh-cheniyu* (Moscow–Leningrad, 1929), p. 245.
40. For a Komsomol justification of this position, based on the experience of the European socialist movement in the First World War, see Chaplin, *VII syezd VLKSM. Stenograficheskii otchet* (Moscow–Leningrad, 1926), p. 53.
41. Bukharin, report on the Komsomol, *XIV syezd VKP(b). Steno-graficheskii otchet* (Moscow, 1926), p. 824.
42. *Itogi desyatiletiya sovetskoi vlasti v tsifrakh 1917–1927* (Moscow, 1927), p. 90.
43. *IV syezd RKSM. Stenograficheskii otchet* (Moscow–Leningrad, 1925), p. 350.
44. Ralph Fisher, *Pattern for Soviet Youth* (New York, 1959), p. 133.
45. *Vseobshchee obuchenie. Likvidatsiya negramotnosti. Podgotovka kadrov*, p. 79.
46. See *VII syezd VLKSM. Stenograficheskii otchet* (Moscow–Leningrad, 1926), p. 205.
47. Resolution of VI Komsomol Congress, *Tovarishch Komsomol*, pp. 158 and 162.
48. 'On the position and work of the RLKSM in the countryside', *Direktivy VKP(b) po voprosam prosveshcheniya* (Moscow–Leningrad, 1931), p. 194.
49. *Narodnoe prosveshchenie*, 1925 no. 2, p. 140.
50. The party leadership, however, issued numerous instructions to the Komsomol to establish friendly relations with the teachers. See, for example, the resolution on youth in *XIII syezd RKP(b)*, p. 674; the Central Committee resolution of 15 May 1925 on Komsomol work in the countryside, *Direktivy VKP(b) po voprosam prosveshcheniya*, p. 194; Zinoviev, *Partiya i vospitanie smeny* (Leningrad, 1924), p. 37.
51. *Narodnoe prosveshchenie*, 1926 no. 9, p. 77.
52. Narkompros–Komsomol Central Committee 'Statement on Pioneer outposts in the school', 8 January 1927, *Osnovnye uzakoneniya*, p. 240.
53. In 1927, 5% of teachers in the RSFSR were Communists and 6%

belonged to the Komsomol. *Rabotnik prosveshcheniya*, 1927 no. 17–18, p. 21.

54. In September 1924, 63.8% of Russian rural teachers were of peasant origin, 15.4% from the clergy, 13.7% from the intelligentsia and 7.1% from the working class. Of urban teachers, 40.8% were from the peasantry, 6.3% from the clergy, 34.8% from the intelligentsia and 18.1% from the working class. Oskar Anweiler, *Geschichte der Schule und Pädogogik in Russland vom Ende des Zarenreiches bis zum Beginn der Stalin-Ära* (Berlin, 1964), p. 293.

55. *XIII syezd RKP(b)*, p. 469.

56. *Direktivy VKP(b) po voprosam prosveshcheniya*, p. 180.

57. *Narodnoe prosveshchenie*, 1927 no. 4, p. 43; *ibid.*, 1926 no. 1, p. 34.

58. Krupskaya, co-report 'On work in the countryside' (with Kalinin), *XIII syezd RKP(b)*, pp. 454–7.

59. *Narodnoe prosveshchenie*, 1924 no. 8, pp. 10 and 130–31.

60. *Trud*, 25 December 1928, p. 2.

61. In 1927/28, only 8,000 out of 315,000 teachers were still outside the union. *Vseobshchee obuchenie. Likvidatsiya negramotnosti. Podgotovka kadrov*, p. 42.

62. Less than half the union's total membership in 1927 were schoolteachers. *Itogi desyatiletiya*, pp. 344–5.

63. For a biographical note on Aleksandr Alekseevich Korostelev, see *Rabotnik prosveshcheniya*, 1927 no. 19–20, p. 61.

64. *Narodnoe prosveshchenie*, 1926 no. 6, pp. 108–9.

65. *Ibid.*

66. *Direktivy VKP(b) i sovetskogo pravitel'stva o narodnom obrazovanii 1917–1947 gg.*, I, p. 130; *Narodnoe prosveshchenie*, 1928 no. 12, pp. 15–16.

67. P. S. (Dzhankoi), ' "Tricky passages" in the collective agreements', *Rabotnik prosveshcheniya*, 1928 no. 24, p. 19.

68. Zinoviev, 'Proletarian revolution and the teaching profession', *Pravda*, 24 April 1924, pp. 2–4.

69. *XIII syezd RKP(b)*, pp. 479–85 *passim*.

70. *Ibid.*, p. 477.

71. Decisions on the teachers are contained in the resolutions on Zinoviev's Central Committee report and the reports on the countryside, agitation and propaganda work, and youth. *XIII syezd RKP(b)*, pp. 60, 640, 659 and 674.

72. See Central Committee resolution and instruction of February 1925 on the procedure for enrolling teachers into the party in *Direktivy VKP(b) po voprosam prosveshcheniya*, p. 183.

73. *XIII syezd RKP(b)*, p. 601.

74. *Narodnoe prosveshchenie*, 1925 no. 2, p. 6.

75. *Ibid.*, p. 39.

76. *Ibid.*, pp. 72–3.

77. *Narodnoe prosveshchenie*, 1929 no. 8–9, pp. 103–4.
78. Kalinin, speech to VII All-Union Congress of Education Workers, *Pravda*, 7 March 1929.
79. *XIII syezd RKP(b)*, p. 470.
80. *Narodnoe prosveshchenie*, 1925 no. 2, p. 13.
81. Quoted Korolev, Korneichik and Ravkin, *Ocherki*, p. 121.
82. Lunacharsky, *Prosveshchenie i revolyutsiya* (1926), p. 398; Bolshakov, *Derevnya 1917–1927*, p. 426.
83. *Uchitel'skaya gazeta* (December 1924), quoted Korolev, Korneichik and Ravkin, *Ocherki*, p. 122.
84. Speech of peasant I. N. Glazkov at public meeting on education, Rostov on Don, June 1929, *Voprosy prosveshcheniya na Severnom Kavkaze* (Rostov), 1929 no. 11, p. 45.
85. *Narodnoe prosveshchenie*, 1926 no. 9, p. 82.
86. For reports on non-Marxist progressives in Soviet schools, see *Russkaya shkola za rubezhom*, 1925–26 no. 15–16, pp. 251–2.
87. It was reported that natural-science teachers (through the Society for the Spread of Natural–Historical Education and its journal *Zhivaya priroda*) took a leading part in the campaign of 1926/27 against the 'complex'. *Russkaya shkola za rubezhom*, 1927/28 no. 32, pp. 139–40.
88. *XIII syezd RKP(b)*, p. 512.
89. Speech to Fifth All-Russian Congress of Heads of Education Departments, *Narodnoe prosveshchenie*, 1926 no. 6, p. 7.
90. Krupskaya, *XIII syezd RKP(b)*, p. 457.
91. VTsIK XI sozyva, *Vtoraya sessiya* (Moscow, 1924), p. 151.
92. See Lunacharsky, 'Is there a new course in Narkompros?', *Narodnoe prosveshchenie*, 1926 no. 7, pp. 16ff.
93. The Dalton Plan, an American teaching method by which children worked individually on projects using teachers as consultants, was highly regarded by the Leningrad education department in the 1920s, though the central Narkompros methodologists thought it overemphasized the individual at the expense of the group.
94. N. Ognev, 'Dnevnik Kosti Ryabtseva. Tretii trimestr, 1923/24 g.', Ognev, *Sobranie sochinenii*, III, pp. 9 and 65–6.
95. For an endorsement (1923), see Lunacharsky, *Prosveshchenie i revolyutsiya* (1926), p. 229; for doubts (October 1925), see *ibid.*, pp. 397–9.
96. See below, p. 106.
97. Resolution 'On the condition of secondary schools', 23 July 1926, *Direktivy VKP(b) i postanovleniya sovetskogo pravitel'stva o narodnom obrazovanii*, I, p. 138.
98. *Izvestiya*, 3 November 1926, p. 7.
99. VTsIK instructed Narkompros 'to intensify its work on the simplification and clarification of programmes and methods of teaching in schools, and on the establishment and provision of a firm minimum of

knowledge and skills (ability to read, write and count) obligatory for primary schools'. *Narodnoe prosveshchenie*, 1926 no. 11, p. 5.

100. Korolev, Korneichik and Ravkin, *Ocherki*, p. 86. On the *profuklon*, see below, p. 56.

101. *Obshchestvovedenie v trudovoi shkole*, II–III (Moscow, 1927), pp. 7–8.

102. 'Social studies programme for senior secondary school', *ibid.*, pp. 109–25.

103. *Ibid.*, p. 118.

104. *Ibid.*, p. 97.

105. Quoted Korolev, Korneichik and Ravkin, *Ocherki*, pp. 172–3.

106. Korneichik (later co-author with Korolev and Ravkin of the best history of the Soviet school in the 1920s, cited above), *Obshchestvovedenie v trudovoi shkole*, II–III, p. 15.

107. *Ibid.*, pp. 10–11.

108. Lilina was almost constantly at odds with the Narkompros collegium; for her department's claims to be more progressive, see *Narodnoe prosveshchenie*, 1926 no. 3, pp. 83–92, and Lunacharsky, *Prosveshchenie i revolyutsiya* (1926), p. 398. However, when she died – expelled from the party as an Oppositionist and in disgrace – in 1929, this was not mentioned in the generous obituaries written by Lunacharsky (*Narodnoe prosveshchenie*, 1929 no. 6) and Krupskaya (*Na putyakh k novoi shkole*, 1929 no. 4–5).

109. The Siberian department was headed by N. V. Vikhirev, a Communist student activist in 1917 who worked in Narkompros' rabfak department at the beginning of the 1920s. For his hostile attitude to the old Narkompros leadership, see *Prosveshchenie Sibiri*, 1930 no. 6, pp. 3ff. On G. I. Broido, head of the Saratov department, see below, pp. 138 and 292 (note 15).

Chapter 3   The education system: problems of mobility and specialization

1. Narkompros RSFSR, 'Statute on the United Labour School' and 'Declaration on the United Labour School', *Izvestiya*, 16 October 1918, pp. 5–6.

2. *Protokoly VTsIK 5 sozyva* (Moscow, 1919), p. 231.

3. See Patrick L. Alston, *Education and the State in Tsarist Russia* (Stanford, 1969), chs. 6–7.

4. See Sheila Fitzpatrick, *The Commissariat of Enlightenment* (London and New York, 1970), pp. 59ff.

5. Paul N. Ignatiev, Dimitry M. Odinetz and Paul J. Novgorodtsev, *Russian Schools and Universities in the World War* (New Haven, 1929), pp. 146–7.

6. Only a few schools bore the name of 'technicum' before the Revolution, and the term seems to have come into widespread use during the Civil War (A. N. Veselov, *Professional'no-tekhnicheskoe obrazovanie*

v SSSR (Moscow, 1961), p. 149). In the 1920s, it was applied to all vocational secondary schools recruiting students with seven years general schooling, including teachers' training colleges (pedagogical technicums), agricultural and medical schools training semi-professionals, and schools training industrial technicians (*tekhniki*).

7. Veselov, *Professional'no-tekhnicheskoe obrazovanie*, pp. 191–2; Ryappo, *Kommunisticheskaya revolyutsiya*, 1928 no. 20, p. 38.

8. *Prilozhenie k byulletenyu VIII syezda sovetov, posvyashchaemoe partiinomu sobraniyu po voprosam narodnogo obrazovaniya* (Moscow, 10 January 1921), p. 9 and *passim*.

9. Kupidonov, *Izvestiya*, 24 April 1929, p. 3.

10. Preis, *Krasnoe studenchestvo*, 1927/28 no. 14, p. 54.

11. Ryappo, *Narodnoe prosveshchenie*, 1927 no. 4, p. 30.

12. *Ibid.*

13. The Party Meeting was first scheduled for November 1924 (TsGAOR 2306/1/3328, presidium of Narkompros RSFSR collegium, 14 August 1924). In the spring of 1925, Lunacharsky said that it was to be held in 'the near future' (*Narodnoe prosveshchenie*, 1925 no. 3, p. 7). In December 1927, the party Central Committee announced that it would be convened in March 1928 (*Pravda*, 3 December 1927, p. 3); and in May 1928 it was put off until the autumn (*Izvestiya TsK*, 1928 no. 16–17, p. 14); then rescheduled for 1929 and put off again until January 1930 (*Pravda*, 29 September 1929, p. 4). It was finally held in April 1930 – by that time, merely confirming the radical reorganization of both systems which had already been decided. As a broad generalization, the previous announcements that the Meeting was to be held coincide with defeats or unusual political weakness of Narkompros RSFSR, while the postponements represent Narkompros' recoveries.

14. Theses on 'Education of worker youth and reform of the school', *II vserossiiskii syezd RKSM* (Moscow–Leningrad, 1926), pp. 163–4.

15. *V vserossiiskii syezd RKSM* (Moscow–Leningrad, 1927), pp. 205–6.

16. Resolution on Shokhin's paper, *ibid.*, pp. 317–20.

17. The first FZU schools actually emerged in the early 1920s under trade union sponsorship, and were not very clearly distinguished from the existing trade schools. It was only after their transfer to Narkompros in 1924 that the Komsomol became an enthusiastic advocate of the FZU and the school assumed an identity quite distinct from that of the old trade schools.

18. E. N. Danilova, *Deistvuyushchee zakonodatel'stvo o trude SSSR i soyuznykh respublik*, 1 (Moscow, 1927), p. 584.

19. *Ibid.*, pp. 585 and 630.

20. *XIII syezd RKP(b). Stenograficheskii otchet* (Moscow, 1963), p. 464.

21. *Narodnoe prosveshchenie*, 1923 no. 2, p. 31.

22. N. K. Krupskaya, *Pedagogicheskie sochineniya*, II, p. 312.

23. *Narodnoe prosveshchenie* (monthly), 1920 no. 18–19–20, p. 7.
24. TsGAOR 2306/1/634: Narkompros collegium meeting of 18 August 1921 (report of V. P. Volgin on reduction of VUZy and resolution of collegium); I. I. Khodorovsky, ed., *Kakogo inzhenera dolzhny gotovit' nashi VTUZy?* (Moscow–Leningrad, 1928), p. 119.
25. See below, pp. 87–8.
26. *Ezhenedel'nik Narodnogo Komissariata po Prosveshcheniyu RSFSR*, 1924 no. 8(29), p. 10.
27. Khodorovsky, *ibid.*, 1924 no. 10(31), pp. 19–20.
28. *Narodnoe prosveshchenie*, 1924 no. 8, p. 6; *Ezhenedel'nik NKP*, 1924 no. 14(35), p. 26; *ibid.*, 1924 no. 8(29), p. 3.
29. *V vserossiiskii syezd RKSM. Stenograficheskii otchet* (1922), pp. 221–2.
30. A. Lunacharsky, *Prosveshchenie i revolyutsiya* (Moscow, 1926), p. 377 (article dated May 1924).
31. See V. Ukraintsev, *KPSS – organizator revolyutsionnogo preobrazovaniya vysshei shkoly* (Moscow, 1963), p. 83.
32. TsGAOR 2306/1/3328: resolution of presidium of Narkompros RSFSR collegium on motion of Khodorovsky, 11 June 1925.
33. 'Ten years of the rabfak', *Krasnoe studenchestvo*, 1928–29 no. 11, p. 2.
34. *Statisticheskii sbornik po narodnomu prosveshcheniyu RSFSR 1926 g.* (Moscow, 1927), pp. 174–5.
35. *Ibid.*
36. The social composition of urban primary schools in 1927/28 was given as 34.5% working-class, 25.3% employee, 12.2% peasant and 28% other in *Massovoe prosveshchenie v SSSR*, 1 (Moscow–Leningrad, 1932), p. 46. Excluding the immigrant peasant group, the working-class share goes up to 39% and the employee to 29% – both groups slightly over-represented, if we accept the calculation of TsSU for 1926/27 that workers and their families made up 33% of the urban population of the USSR and employees and their families 24% (*Statisticheskii spravochnik SSSR za 1928* (Moscow, 1929), pp. 42–3).
37. The breakdown for urban grades v–vii in 1926/27 was 26.3% working-class, 36.5% employee, 15% peasant and 22.2% other. *Massovoe prosveshchenie v SSSR*, 1, p. 46.
38. *K kharakteristike sotsial'nogo sostava uchashchikhsya sotsvosa i profobra* (Moscow–Leningrad, 1929), pp. 24–5.
39. The calculation – for the RSFSR only – is based on data in *Narodnoe prosveshchenie v RSFSR. Statisticheskii sbornik* (Moscow, 1928), pp. 46–7, 54–5, 70, 178–9; *Bor'ba za rabochie kadry* (Moscow, 1928), p. 9; and *Statisticheskii sbornik po narodnomu prosveshcheniyu RSFSR 1926 g.* (Moscow, 1927), p. 174.
40. *Narodnoe prosveshchenie*, 1929 no. 3–4, p. 45.
41. Data on Komsomol membership from TsGA RSFSR 1565/19/34: presidium of Narkompros RSFSR, 19 April 1929; *Vseobshchee*

obuchenie. Likvidatsiya negramotnosti. Podgotovka kadrov (Moscow, 1930), p. 79; *Narodnoe prosveshchenie*, 1927 no. 2, p. 77.

42. See Fitzpatrick, *The Commissariat of Enlightenment*, ch. 10.
43. *Narodnoe prosveshchenie*, 1923 no. 2, p. 31.
44. See the resolution of the Narkompros collegium on the undesirability of this practice in *Narodnoe prosveshchenie*, 1924 no. 8, p. 161.
45. These plans were drawn up following the rather half-hearted resolution of VTsIK and Sovnarkom RSFSR 'On the introduction of universal elementary education in the RSFSR' (31 August 1925), *Direktivy VKP(b) i postanovleniya sovetskogo pravitel'stva o narodnom obrazovanii*, II (Moscow–Leningrad, 1947), pp. 92–5.
46. *Narodnoe prosveshchenie*, 1926 no. 7, pp. 20–1.
47. *Osnovnye uzakoneniya i rasporyazheniya po narodnomu prosveshcheniyu* (Moscow–Leningrad, 1929), pp. 90–1.
48. *Ibid.*
49. *Ibid.*, p. 104. For members of the 'free professions' the maximum was 150 roubles; for persons living on unearned income, 300 roubles.
50. *Na putyakh k novoi shkole*, 1929 no. 1, p. 47.
51. The Moscow Soviet, after reportedly charging very high fees for grades VIII–IX, abolished secondary-school fees altogether for workers, peasants and employees (*Pravda*, 1 September 1927, p. 6).
52. *Na putyakh k novoi shkole*, 1929 no. 1, p. 94.
53. *Ibid.*, 1929 no. 2, p. 80.
54. L. S. Rogachevskaya, *Likvidatsiya bezrabotitsy v SSSR 1917–1930* (Moscow, 1973), pp. 175 and 251.
55. According to the 1926 census, there were 12 million men and women aged 25–29, 13.8 million aged 20–24, 17 million in both the 15–19 and 10–14 age groups, and 15.3 million aged 5–9. The 15–19 age group had been particularly affected by wartime dislocation of schools: male literacy in this group was 72% compared with 79–80% in the 20–29 age group (*Vsesoyuznaya perepis'*, VII, pp. 8–13).
56. In the population as a whole in 1926 there were 72 employees for every 100 workers. But among 20-year-olds in 1926 there were only 46 employees for every 100 workers, and among 16-year-olds in 1923, 22 for every 100. Data from *Statisticheskii sbornik SSSR za 1928*, p. 42, and B. Urlanis, *Istoriya odnogo pokoleniya* (Moscow, 1968), pp. 174–5 and 179.
57. Combining the data for 1923–27 in *Itogi desyatiletiya sovetskoi vlasti v tsifrakh 1917–1927* (Moscow, n.d., 1927), pp. 336–7, with those for 1925–29 in *Sotsialisticheskoe stroitel'stvo SSSR* (Moscow, 1934), pp. 344–5, we get the following pattern of employment of workers under 18 in census industry:

1 Jan. 1923	89,350	= 6.6% of the total labour force
1924	80,390	5.5%
1925	87,400 (92,600)	5.2% (5.2%)

1926 133,850 (130,000) 5.9% (5.7%)
1927 137,330 (136,100) 5.8% (5.7%)
1928 120,000 4.7%
1929 116,800 4.2%

58. Adolescents registered unemployed in the USSR for the month of October numbered 118,300 in 1924; 125,800 in 1925; 144,100 in 1926; 168,800 in 1927; 240,300 in 1928 (L. S. Rogachevskaya, *Likvidatsiya bezrabotitsy v SSSR 1917–1930* (Moscow, 1973), pp. 92, 133 and 147). From 1925, the adolescent share of total unemployment tended to rise.

59. A. Lunacharsky and A. Shokhin, *K edinoi sisteme narodnogo obrazovaniya* (Moscow–Leningrad, 1929), p. 55.

60. A. Lunacharsky, *Tretii front* (Moscow, 1925), p. 116.

61. *Narodnoe prosveshchenie*, 1924 no. 8, p. 51.

62. See below, pp. 98–100.

63. Khodorovsky, *Narodnoe prosveshchenie*, 1924 no. 8, p. 5.

64. *XIII syezd RKP(b). Stenograficheskii otchet* (Moscow, 1963), p. 672.

65. Chaplin, *VI syezd RLKSM. Stenograficheskii otchet* (Moscow, 1924), p. 131.

66. The minutes of the July 7 meeting are not filed with the others in TsGAOR 2306/1/2945: it took place between meetings no. 38/590 and 39/591. A report was published in *Narodnoe prosveshchenie*, 1924 no. 8, pp. 51-4, Epshtein, head of the Narkompros schools administration, hints at pressure, *ibid.*, 1927 no. 1, p. 11.

67. F. F. Korolev, T. D. Korneichik and Z. I. Ravkin, *Ocherki po istorii sovetskoi shkoly i pedagogiki 1921–1931* (Moscow, 1961), p. 39.

68. *Narodnoe prosveshchenie*, 1926 no. 7, pp. 131–2. Narkompros recommended 7–9 hours on the *uklon* in grade VIII and 11–13 hours in grade IX (Korolev, Korneichik and Ravkin, *Ocherki*, p. 80).

69. *Russkaya shkola za rubezhom*, 1927/28 no. 25, p. 18.

70. *Narodnoe prosveshchenie*, 1927 no. 2, p. 114.

71. *Komsomol'skaya pravda*, 12 May 1928, p. 3.

72. Narkompros endorsed the instruction of the Commissariat of Labour that 'graduates of schools with a pedagogical bias may be included in the lists of those seeking [teaching] work only after they have taken the labour exchange tests of expertise established for unemployed persons who have had a considerable time away from work' (*Narodnoe prosveshchenie*, 1929 no. 3–4, pp. 139–40).

73. *Narodnoe prosveshchenie*, 1927 no. 3, p. 25.

74. *Ibid.*, 1928 no. 4, p. 106.

75. Deev-Khomyakovsky of the Teachers' Union reported 'a massive block on the teaching market' caused by provincial teachers coming to seek work under better conditions in the capitals, and gave a figure of 62,680 unemployed union members (including *obsluzhivayushchii*

personal) for the RSFSR. *Rabotnik prosvesheniya*, 1928 no. 5, p. 14.

76. See below, pp. 106, 123.
77. See below, p. 106.
78. *Narodnoe prosveshchenie*, 1927 no. 11–12, p. 92.
79. *Ibid.*, p. 119. Of the remainder, 35% had graduated in 1926 and 36.9% in previous years.
80. Smolensk Archive, WKP 33: meeting of bureau of Smolensk gubkom, 22 December 1927 (appended document headed 'Results of recruitment to Smolensk State University and Smolensk Rabfak in 1927').
81. *Narodnoe prosveshchenie*, 1926 no. 7, pp. 131–2.
82. Peasants were divided into *bednyaki* (poor peasants), *batraki* (landless agricultural labourers), *serednyaki* (middle peasants), *zazhitochnye* (prosperous peasants) and kulaks. The first two categories belonged to the proletariat, the last to the exploiting classes.
83. Meeting in the Central House of Peasants, Moscow, 16 April 1927, reported in *Narodnoe prosveshchenie*, 1927 no. 6, p. 67.
84. *Ibid.*, p. 66.
85. Lunacharsky and Shokhin, *K edinoi sisteme*, pp. 28–9.
86. James C. McClelland, 'Proletarianizing the Student Body: The Soviet Experience during the New Economic Policy', *Past and Present*, August 1978, p. 135.
87. M. Ya. Sonin, *Vosproizvodstvo rabochei sily v SSSR i balans truda* (Moscow, 1959), p. 180.
88. O. I. Shkaratan, *Problemy sotsial'noi struktury rabochego klassa* (Moscow, 1970), p. 304.
89. See Narkompros circular of 27 December 1923, *Ezhenedel'nik NKP*, 1924 no. 1(22), pp. 36–8.
90. The Ukrainian ShKM experimented briefly with the teaching of large-scale farming techniques and inculcation of 'the necessary collective habits' during NEP, but in 1927 – on the instruction of the Ukrainian Central Committee – the Ukrainian Narkompros fell in line with the Russian Narkompros' emphasis on individual farming (*Narodnoe prosveshchenie*, 1927 no. 1, p. 56, note). On the ShKM during collectivization, see below, pp. 166–7.
91. Korolev, Korneichik and Ravkin, *Ocherki*, p. 27; Lunacharsky and Shokhin, *K edinoi sisteme*, p. 17.
92. See above, p. 8.
93. A. Lunacharsky, *Prosveshchenie i revolyutsiya* (1926), p. 357.
94. *Ibid.*
95. *Narodnoe prosveshchenie*, 1925 no. 5–6, pp. 189–99.
96. *Statisticheskii spravochnik SSSR za 1928*, p. 867.
97. In 1928, Epshtein of Narkompros reported that 14.5% of ShKM teachers were party members, as against 5% of all secondary-school teachers. *Pravda*, 20 December 1928, p. 5.
98. *Komsomol'skaya pravda*, 20 April 1928, p. 3.

99. *Izvestiya*, 7 April 1926, p. 5; TsGA RSFSR 1565/19/34: meeting of Narkompros RSFSR collegium, 19 April 1929.

100. *Plenum Sibirskogo Kraevogo Komiteta VKP(b), 3–7 marta 1928 goda. Stenograficheskii otchet*, part 1 (Novosibirsk, 1928), pp. 17–18. Similar data are cited in Yu. S. Borisov, *Podgotovka proizvodstvennykh kadrov sel'skogo khozyaistva SSSR v rekonstruktivnyi period* (Moscow, 1960), p. 159.

101. During the First Five-Year Plan period, the term ShKM was often used for the rural secondary school in general; and in 1927, Narkompros RSFSR had in fact instructed that all rural secondary education should be remodelled along ShKM lines (*Narodnoe prosveshchenie*, 1927, no. 5, pp. 33ff.). But the original ShKMs had only about one eighth of the total number of students in all rural secondary schools of the USSR in 1926/27 (see *Statisticheskii spravochnik SSSR za 1928*, p. 867; *Kul'turnoe stroitel'stvo SSSR* (1956), pp. 122–3.

102. Data from *Kul'turnoe stroitel'stvo SSSR* (1956), pp. 82–5.

103. *Ibid.*

Chapter 4 Professors and Soviet power

1. *Permskii Gosudarstvennyi Universitet* (Perm, 1966), pp. 22–3.

2. *Tomskii Gosudarstvennyi Universitet* (Tomsk, 1934), p. 16.

3. *Krasnoe studenchestvo*, 1927/28 no. 4–5, p. 118; *Tomskii Gosudarstvennyi Universitet*, p. 16.

4. S. E. Belozerov, *Ocherki istorii Rostovskogo Universiteta* (Rostov, 1959), p. 163.

5. On the early relations of the universities and the Soviet government, see Sheila Fitzpatrick, *The Commissariat of Enlightenment* (Cambridge, 1970), ch. 4.

6. P. Sorokin, *The Long Journey* (New Haven, 1963), p. 182; *Istoriya Leningradskogo Universiteta* (Leningrad, 1969), p. 196.

7. V. I. Prokofyev, *Moskovskoe Vysshee Tekhnicheskoe Uchilishche: 125 let* (Leningrad, 1955), p. 297; *Moskovskaya Sel'sko-Khozyaistvennaya Akademiya imeni K. A. Timiryazeva. K stoletiyu osnovaniya, 1865–1965* (Moscow, 1969), p. 112.

8. See Novikov's own account, M. M. Novikov, *Ot Moskvy do N'yu-Iorka* (New York, 1952).

9. N. V. Krylenko, *Sudebnye rechi* (Moscow, 1964), pp. 57–60.

10. *Sobranie uzakonenii*, 1921 no. 65, art. 486; 1922 no. 43, art. 518.

11. V. S. Emelyanov, *O vremeni, o tovarishchakh, o sebe*, 2nd ed. (Moscow, 1970), p. 55.

12. See *Permskii Gosudarstvennyi Universitet*, p. 31; *Istoriya Leningradskogo Universiteta*, p. 268; L. Milkh, *Pravda*, 3 April 1928, p. 4.

13. *Partiya i vospitanie smeny* (Leningrad, 1924), pp. 122–3.

14. Among such Communist officials was Evgeny Preobrazhensky, co-author with Bukharin of *Azbuka kommunizma*, economist, organizer of the Trotskyite Opposition campaign in 1923/24 – who was at this time head of Narkompros' administration of higher and technical education, though at loggerheads with others in the Narkompros collegium. He was blamed, probably rightly, for provocative handling of the professors both in 1921 and 1922. After the second strike he was reprimanded and removed from the job.

15. See V. I. Lenin, *Polnoe sobranie sochinenii*, LII, 5th ed. (Moscow, 1965), p. 388.

16. See *Istoriya Moskovskogo Universiteta*, II (Moscow, 1955), pp. 88–9, and V. Stratonov, 'Moscow University's loss of freedom', V. B. Elyashevich, A. A. Kizevetter and M. M. Novikov, ed., *Moskovskii Universitet 1755–1930* (Paris, 1930), pp. 226–35. Stratonov was then head of the physics and mathematics school of Moscow University.

17. Stratonov, 'Moscow University's loss of freedom', p. 218.

18. *Istoriya Leningradskogo Universiteta*, p. 211; Novikov, *Ot Moskvy do N'yu-Iorka*, pp. 122–3.

19. *Istoriya Leningradskogo Universiteta*, p. 211.

20. Novikov, *Moskovskii Universitet*, pp. 122–3.

21. *Istoriya Leningradskogo Universiteta*, pp. 211–12.

22. On the early history of party schools, see L. S. Leonova, *Iz istorii podgotovki partiinykh kadrov v sovetsko-partiinykh shkolakh i kommunisticheskikh universitetakh (1921–1925 gg.)* (Moscow, 1972).

23. M. N. Pokrovsky, 'What Lenin was for our higher school', *Pravda*, 27 January 1924, p. 2.

24. L. V. Ivanova, *U istokov sovetskoi istoricheskoi nauki. Podgotovka kadrov istorikov-marksistov 1917–1929* (Moscow, 1968), p. 13.

25. Early in 1921, Pokrovsky asked Lenin's opinion about the desirability of employing Mensheviks (naming Groman, Ermansky, Sukhanov, Cherevanin and Martov) in the Moscow University FON. Lenin's answer was: 'I am very doubtful, and think it had better be put before the Politburo of the Central Committee' (Ivanova, *U istokov*, p. 22, quoting *Leninskii sbornik* XXXV, p. 231). Whether or not there was a Politburo resolution, a number of Mensheviks were in fact employed.

26. Ivanova, *U istokov*, p. 14.

27. *Iz istorii Moskovskogo Universiteta* (Moscow, 1955), p. 118.

28. *Istoriya Moskovskogo Universiteta*, II, pp. 82–3.

29. Sovnarkom resolution of 4 March 1921 'On the plan of organization of schools of the social sciences in Russian universities', *Sobranie uzakonenii*, 1921 no. 19, art. 117.

30. *Iz istorii Moskovskogo Universiteta*, p. 113.

31. *Saratovskii Universitet 1909–1959*, p. 33.

32. For lists of Communists sent to the Moscow University School of

Social Sciences, see Ivanova, *U istokov*, pp. 23 and 25–6; Ukraintsev, *KPSS – organizator revolyutsionnogo preobrazovaniya vysshei shkoly* (Moscow, 1963), p. 115; *Istoriya Moskovskogo Universiteta*, II, pp. 250–1; *Moskovskii Universitet za 50 let* (Moscow, 1967), pp. 57 and 457; G. D. Alekseeva, *Oktyabr'skaya revolyutsiya i istoricheskie nauki v Rossii (1917–1923 gg.)* (Moscow, 1968), p. 260.

33. Detailed instructions on the subject were published in *Izvestiya TsK* in 1922 and 1923. The XII Party Congress resolved 'to draw all members of the old party guard completely into service both in the Communist VUZy and the VUZy in general. It is necessary to put an end to the casual attitude which a number of the most responsible comrades have to the business of teaching in the higher school.' Quoted *Izvestiya TsK*, 1923 no. 6(54), pp. 53–4.

34. *Iz istorii Moskovskogo Universiteta*, p. 134. In 1922, V. P. Volgin, N. M. Lukin, M. N. Reisner and I. D. Udaltsov were the most prominent Marxists on the faculty of the Moscow University School of Social Sciences. Reisner and Lukin may have been teaching full-time (though not only at Moscow University), but Udaltsov and Volgin (who was Rector of the University as well as holding a responsible position in Narkompros) were certainly not. The faculty included such notable non-Marxists as the jurist A. M. Vinaver and S. A. Kotlyarevsky, the medieval historian D. M. Petrushevsky, the philosopher P. F. Preobrazhensky, the linguist A. M. Selishchev and the formalist literary scholar M. D. Eikhengolts. See list of faculty in *Otchet o sostoyanii i deistviyakh I-go Moskovskogo Gosudarstvennogo Universiteta za 1922 g.* (Moscow, 1923), pp. 22–32.

35. M. K. Korbut, *Kazan'skii Gosudarstvennyi Universitet imeni V. I. Ul'yanova-Lenina za 125 let 1804/5–1929/30*, II (Kazan, 1930), p. 309.

36. Rabochii fakul'tet Kazan'skogo Gosudarstvennogo Universiteta imeni V. I. Lenina, *Na putyakh k vysshei shkole. Vosem' let raboty 1919–1927* (Kazan, 1927), pp. 156–7; Alekseeva, *Oktyabr'skaya revolyutsiya*, p. 260.

37. See, for example, *Izvestiya TsK*, 1923 no. 2(50), p. 20: in 1922 Ter-Vaganyan was sent as a lecturer to Kursk, Dvolaitsky to Voronezh, Skvortsov-Stepanov to Kharkov, Ekaterinoslav and Kiev and Felix Kon to Bryansk.

38. *Tomskii Gosudarstvennyi Universitet*, p. 17.

39. Ivanova, *U istokov*, pp. 23–4.

40. The Kazan school of social sciences reverted to a law school (Korbut, *Kazan'skii Gosudarstvennyi Universitet*, p. 311) and the Perm school of social sciences to teacher-training (*Permskii Gosudarstvennyi Universitet*, p. 35). Konstantin F. Shteppa, then an historian at Kiev University, says that the second course was more common (Shteppa, *Russian Historians and the Soviet State* (New Brunswick NJ, 1962), p. 11).

41. Quoted S. E. Belozerov, *Ocherki*, pp. 164–5.
42. See the comment by V. N. Yakovleva at a meeting of VUZ rectors, *Ezhenedel'nik NKP*, 1924 no. 1(22), p. 18.
43. Ivanova, *U istokov*, p. 35. Members of the commission included Pokrovsky, A. S. Bubnov and K. A. Popov.
44. *Moskovskii Universitet za 50 let*, pp. 60, 563, 564–5.
45. *Istoriya Leningradskogo Universiteta*, pp. 226–9.
46. For the first version, drafted by Lenin, see Sovnarkom resolution of 4 March 1921 'On the establishment of a general scientific minimum compulsory for teaching in all higher schools of the RSFSR', *Sobranie uzakonenii*, 1921 no. 19, art. 119.
47. Sovnarkom resolution of 1 November 1922, signed Kamenev, *Sobranie uzakonenii*, 1922 no. 75, art. 929.
48. *Partiya i vospitanie smeny*, p. 104.
49. *Pravda*, 19 January 1924, p. 5.
50. Quoted Leonova, *Iz istorii podgotovki partiinykh kadrov*, p. 115.
51. Robert C. Tucker, *Stalin as Revolutionary* (New York, 1973), pp. 316–19.
52. *Krasnaya molodezh'* (monthly journal of the Central Moscow Bureau of Proletarian Students), 1924 no. 1 (May), pp. 45–9.
53. *Iz istorii Moskovskogo Universiteta*, p. 141.
54. Ukraintsev, *KPSS – organizator*, p. 114.
55. *Krasnaya molodezh'*, 1924 no. 1, p. 103.
56. Ivanova, *U istokov*, p. 39; *Programmy po istorii klassovoi bor'by v Rossii, istorii klassovoi bor'by na zapade, istorii VKP(b). Na fakul'tete sovetskogo prava I-go MGU* (Moscow: MGU, 1928). The *programmy*, unlike those for secondary school, include bibliographies. Lenin's works predominate in the course on party history, though there is also some Marx, Engels, Pokrovsky and Stalin (*Voprosy leninizma* and speech to the XIV Party Congress).
57. See V. Astrov, *Krucha* (Moscow, 1969), pp. 173–4, 210–11, 288–9, 403–5 and *passim*.
58. *Istoriya Leningradskogo Universiteta*, p. 282.
59. Loboda, *Nauchnyi rabotnik*, 1927 no. 10, pp. 57–8.
60. *Izvestiya*, 18 May 1926, p. 3.
61. *Upadochnoe nastroenie sredi molodezhi* (Moscow, 1927), pp. 68–9.
62. Stratonov, 'Moscow University's loss of freedom', pp. 214–18; Loboda, *Nauchnyi rabotnik*, 1925 no. 1, pp. 160–1.
63. On the Committee and its dissolution, see Fitzpatrick, *The Commissariat of Enlightenment*, pp. 233–4, and Bertram D. Wolfe, *The Bridge and the Abyss* (London, 1967), pp. 109–18.
64. Stratonov, 'Moscow University's loss of freedom', pp. 214–16.
65. The memoir, as already cited, was published in Elyashevich, Kizevetter and Novikov, ed., *Moskovskii Universitet 1755–1930* (Paris: Sovremennyya zapiski, 1930).

66. *Izvestiya TsK*, 1922 no. 11–12, pp. 47–8.
67. For membership of the group expelled and information on their academic disciplines and institutional affiliations, see Sorokin, *The Long Journey*, p. 192; Stratonov, 'Moscow University's loss of freedom', pp. 241–2; *Istoriya Moskovskogo Universiteta*, II, p. 83; *Iz istorii Moskovskogo Universiteta*, p. 118; *Istoriya Leningradskogo Universiteta*, p. 244; Korbut, *Kazan'skii Gosudarstvennyi Universitet*, p. 318; A. Solzhenitsyn, *Arkhipelag Gulag*, I–II (Paris, 1973), p. 378.
68. *Izvestiya TsK*, 1923 no. 4(52), p. 25: Central Committee report to the XII Party Congress.
69. Speech to First Congress of Scientific Workers, November 1923, *Pravda*, 24 November 1923, p. 4.
70. Report to the Petrograd guberniya conference of scientific workers, *Pravda*, 9 November 1923, p. 4. This statement was greeted with great approval by the Petrograd intelligentsia, and Zinoviev was elected a member of the Scientific Workers' Section of the Teachers' Union.
71. On Shklovsky's return, see Victor Erlich, *Russian Formalism: History–Doctrine*, 2nd ed. (The Hague, 1965), p. 136.
72. *Nauchnyi rabotnik*, 1925 no. 2, pp. 185ff., and 1925 no. 3, pp. 16off.: 'Losses to Russian science'.
73. See below, note 83; and Loren R. Graham, *The Soviet Academy of Sciences and the Communist Party, 1927–1932* (Princeton, 1967), p. 88.
74. Resolution of First Congress of Workers in Education and Socialist Culture (1920), quoted *Nauchnyi rabotnik*, 1928 no. 2, p. 44.
75. *Nauchnyi rabotnik*, 1927 no. 1, p. 7.
76. *Ibid.*, p. 21.
77. *Ibid.*, pp. 4 and 7.
78. See above, pp. 30–31.
79. Earlier, the Commission had been on the Narkompros budget. When Narkompros decided in 1924 to liquidate the institution and transfer its assets to the Section of Scientific Workers, Sovnarkom RSFSR took it over. TsGAOR 2306/1/2101: meetings of presidium of Narkompros collegium, 3 and 10 September 1924; TsGAOR 2306/1/3328: meeting of Narkompros collegium, 1 September 1924; *Pyat' let raboty tsentral'noi komissii po uluchsheniyu byta uchenykh pri Sovete Narodnykh Komissarov RSFSR (TseKUBU)* (Moscow, 1927), p. 8.
80. *Pyat' let raboty*, pp. 19–25 and 28–35.
81. *Nauchnyi rabotnik*, 1930 no. 3, p. 61.
82. *Pyat' let raboty*, p. 11.
83. *Nauchnyi rabotnik*, 1930 no. 3, p. 58.
84. *Vechernyaya Moskva*, 5 February 1930, p. 2.
85. Khodorovsky, *Narodnoe prosveshchenie*, 1925 no. 5–6, p. 3; Lunacharsky, *Krasnaya molodezh'*, 1924 no. 1, p. 96.
86. *Pyat' let raboty*, p. 18.

87. *Narodnoe prosveshchenie*, 1925 no. 5–6, p. 3; *Krasnaya molodezh'*, 1925 no. 5(9), p. 118, quoted in Ukraintsev, *KPSS – organizator*, p. 134.

88. Salaries as expressed in *byudzhetnye* roubles were about 60% of what was actually paid in *chervonnye* roubles (see, for example, tables in *Itogi desyatiletiya sovetskoi vlasti*, pp. 342–3). Most writers do not differentiate, and there was an obvious temptation for Narkompros or professorial spokesmen asking for higher salaries to use the budgetary measure for pathetic effect.

89. An investigation of 268 Section members throughout the USSR showed that they held 466 academic jobs, an average of 1.66 per person. *Nauchnyi rabotnik*, 1925 no. 3, p. 113.

90. *Nauchnyi rabotnik*, 1925 no. 1, p. 176; 1925 no. 2, p. 145.

91. Professor Sergievsky in 1925 gave 200–250 roubles as an average professorial income (*Nauchnyi rabotnik*, 1925 no. 1, p. 177); 350 roubles was the level at which the Commission discontinued salary supplements (*Pyat' let raboty*, p. 18).

92. See above, p. 30.

93. *Itogi desyatiletiya sovetskoi vlasti*, pp. 342–3 and 347.

94. *Nauchnyi rabotnik*, 1925 no. 1, p. 177.

95. Resolution of VTsIK and Sovnarkom RSFSR of 31 July 1924, *Nauchnyi rabotnik*, 1925 no. 1, pp. 212–13.

96. *Pyat' let raboty*, p. 43.

97. *Nauchnyi rabotnik*, 1927 no. 1, p. 41.

98. See, for example, Seifullina's story 'Invasion', in Lidia Seifullina, *Izbrannye sochineniya*, 1 (Moscow, 1958), pp. 387ff.

99. Mitskevich, letter to the editor, *Izvestiya*, 31 August 1926, p. 4.

100. Decree of Sovnarkom RSFSR of 21 January 1924, *Sobranie uzakonenii*, 1924 no. 7, art. 44; and Narkompros instructions reminding VUZy of the Sovnarkom decree in *Nauchnyi rabotnik*, 1925 no. 3, p. 165.

101. Decree of VTsIK and Sovnarkom RSFSR of 15 December 1924, in *Nauchnyi rabotnik*, 1925 no. 1, p. 217.

102. In the 1924 enrolment for Russian VUZy, the Section was allocated 350 VUZ places. For the 1926 enrolment, it got 560 places, 164 of them in Moscow and 135 in Leningrad. *Nauchnyi rabotnik*, 1925 no. 2, pp. 172–3; 1926 no. 4, pp. 36 and 95.

103. Central Committee circular of 25 May 1923 'On the creation of new teaching cadres in the VUZy', *Izvestiya TsK*, 1923 no. 6(54), p. 83.

104. *Statisticheskii sbornik po narodnomu prosveshcheniyu RSFSR 1926 g.*, pp. 38–9.

105. Pokrovsky, *Izvestiya*, 11 April 1926, p. 3, and 19 May 1926, p. 3.

106. Pokrovsky, speech to Fifth Plenum of the Soviet of Scientific Workers, December 1928, *Nauchnyi rabotnik*, 1929 no. 1, p. 20.

107. There was, at least formally, a 'compulsory Marxist minimum' for

all graduate students between 1925 and 1927 (*Istoriya Leningradskogo Universiteta*, p. 252). For Pokrovsky's defensive comments on it to the Section of Scientific Workers, see *Nauchnyi rabotnik*, 1927 no. 3, pp. 41–3.

108. *Izvestiya*, 17 April 1927, p. 5. The speaker was Pozern.

109. *Izvestiya*, 17 April 1927, p. 6.

110. *Sud'by sovremennoi intelligentsii* (Moscow: Moskovskii komitet RKP(b), 1925), p. 17.

111. Bukharin, 'On the world revolution, our country, culture and other matters', *Krasnaya nov'*, 1924 no. 1 and 2. I. P. Pavlov's text, which Bukharin quotes extensively, was apparently not published.

112. Stephen F. Cohen, *Bukharin and the Bolshevik Revolution* (New York, 1973), p. 237.

113. *Sud'by sovremennoi intelligentsii*, p. 27.

114. *Trenirovka* was a word much used by the theatre director Vsevolod Meyerhold in connection with the 'bio-mechanical' preparation of actors. It was also used by the poet and theorist of the scientific organization of labour, A. K. Gastev (see below, pp. 126–7).

115. Sakulin, writing in *Nauchnyi rabotnik*, 1928 no. 5–6, p. 45, said that Bukharin had promised that concessions would be made 'kogda nam skazhet politicheskii razum, a razum skazhet verno'. This remark does not appear in the published stenogram of the debate, *Sud'by sovremennoi intelligentsii*.

116. See Oldenburg, 'The tasks of the Section of Scientific Workers in cultural revolution', *Nauchnyi rabotnik*, 1928 no. 5–6.

117. The idea of such a partnership, implicit in many of Oldenburg's statements, may also be found in the resolution of the First Congress of Scientific Workers calling for 'struggle for the creation of a free society built on the *union of science and labour*' (my emphasis added), *Pravda*, 24 November 1923, p. 4.

118. *Izvestiya*, 12 February 1927, p. 2.

119. *Ibid.*

120. *Ibid.*

121. At this time, the All-Union Vesenkha was pressing for transfer of various higher educational and scholarly institutions from the Russian Narkompros to Vesenkha (see below, ch. 6). The Academy of Sciences had recently passed out of Narkompros control into that of the Academic Committee (Uchenyi komitet) under TsIK. Thus the scientific workers' demand for organizational change in the Narkompros administration of higher education and scientific research, reported by Loboda in *Nauchnyi rabotnik*, 1927 no. 1, pp. 16–17, strongly suggested that the Section might look to Vesenkha or TsIK for support if Narkompros failed to satisfy them.

122. See below, pp. 113ff.

123. For the worsening situation of rural teachers, see above, ch. 2. Writers,

who were under pressure from the militant young Communists of RAPP, also had grounds for pessimism about the future. For a more detailed discussion of these questions, see Sheila Fitzpatrick, 'The "Soft" Line on Culture and Its Enemies: Soviet Cultural Policy 1922–1927', *Slavic Review*, June 1974.

124. Lunacharsky, 'The intelligentsia and its place in socialist construction', *Revolyutsiya i kul'tura*, 1927 no. 1 (15 November), pp. 32–3.

125. *Ibid.*, p. 29.

Chapter 5   Recruitment to higher education

1. Vikhirev, later head of Narkompros' rabfak department, joined a Bolshevik group of seven at the Shanyavsky People's University in August 1917 (*Krasnoe studenchestvo*, 1927–28 no. 4–5, p. 67). In the Moscow Commercial Institute, there was a small but active Bolshevik group whose members quickly went into full-time party work (K. V. Ostrovityanov, *Dumy o proshlom* (Moscow, 1967), *passim*); and the same was evidently true of the Petrograd Polytechnical Institute, whose Bolshevik cell a few years earlier had included Molotov, Syrtsov, Epshtein (later of Narkompros?), Stetsky and Andreev (*Krasnoe studenchestvo*, 1927–28 no. 4–5, p. 95). For further information, see L. M. Shalaginova, 'The student movement on the eve and during the February Revolution', *Voprosy istorii KPSS*, 1967 no. 2.

2. Ostrovityanov, *Dumy o proshlom*, p. 165; *Istoriya Leningradskogo Universiteta 1819–1969* (Leningrad, 1969), p. 194.

3. Ostrovityanov, *Dumy o proshlom*, pp. 260–2.

4. Sovnarkom decree of 2 August 1918 'On rules of enrolment in higher educational institutions', *Sobranie uzakonenii i rasporyazhenii rabochego i krest'yanskogo pravitel'stva RSFSR*, 1918 no. 57, art. 632.

5. For a view from each side, see V. Stratonov, 'Moscow University's loss of freedom', *Moskovskii Universitet 1755–1930* (Paris, 1930), and A. Ya. Vyshinsky, quoted in V. I. Bessonova, 'Creation and development of workers' faculties in 1919–1921', in *Iz istorii velikoi oktyabr'skoi sotsialisticheskoi revolyutsii* (Moscow, 1957), pp. 153–4.

6. Quoted V. V. Ukraintsev, *KPSS – organizator revolyutsionnogo preobrazovaniya vysshei shkoly* (Moscow, 1963), p. 74.

7. M. K. Korbut, *Kazan'skii Gosudarstvennyi Universitet imeni V. I. Ul'yanova-Lenina za 125 let 1804/5–1929/30*, II (Kazan, 1930), p. 307.

8. *Istoriya Leningradskogo Universiteta*, p. 264.

9. Quoted N. M. Katuntseva, *Rol' rabochikh fakul'tetov v formirovanii kadrov narodnoi intelligentsii v SSSR* (Moscow, 1966), p. 13. Essentially the same story is told in Bessonova, 'Creation and development of workers' faculties', pp. 153–4.

10. Rabfak figures from *Narodnoe prosveshchenie*, 1929 no. 3–4, pp. 164–5; VUZ figures from *Narodnoe prosveshchenie v RSFSR* (Moscow, 1928), pp. 46–7.

11. *Krasnoe studenchestvo*, 1927/28 no. 4–5, pp. 101 and 126.

12. Stratonov, 'Moscow University's loss of freedom', p. 201.

13. *Istoriya Leningradskogo Universiteta*, pp. 266–7. The Menshevik journal *Sotsialisticheskii vestnik*, publishing in Berlin in 1924, gave well-informed reports on the purge in nos. 10, 14 and 15 of that year, implying the continued existence of Menshevik groups among the students.

14. Quoted Ukraintsev, *KPSS – organizator*, pp. 72–3.

15. Sovnarkom resolution of 17 September 1920 'On workers' faculties', quoted Ukraintsev, *KPSS – organizator*, p. 73, and Katuntseva, *Rol' rabochikh fakul'tetov*, p. 27.

16. *Istoriya Moskovskogo Universiteta*, II (Moscow, 1955), p. 40.

17. *Izvestiya TsK*, 1922 no. 9(45), p. 9: report of the registration and allocation department of the Central Committee for the period 15 July–15 September.

18. See *Izvestiya TsK*, 1921 no. 34, pp. 12–14; 1921 no. 35, p. 4; 1922 no. 3(39), pp. 7 and 61; 1922 no. 9(45), pp. 5 and 9.

19. Narkompros instruction of 21 June 1921, quoted *Istoriya Leningradskogo Universiteta*, p. 259.

20. *Iz istorii Moskovskogo Universiteta (1917–1941)* (Moscow, 1955), p. 111.

21. *Istoriya Leningradskogo Universiteta*, p. 260.

22. Narkompros instruction of 27 February 1923, *Byulleten' ofitsial'nykh rasporyazhenii i soobshchenii Narodnogo Komissariata Prosveshcheniya*, 1923 no. 15, p. 10.

23. *Ezhenedel'nik Narodnogo Komissariata Prosveshcheniya RSFSR*, 1924 no. 14(35), p. 26.

24. 'On enrolment in higher educational institutions' (signed Molotov, Central Committee secretary, 15 June 1923), *Izvestiya TsK*, 1923 no. 6(54), p. 17.

25. *Istoriya Leningradskogo Universiteta*, p. 260.

26. Quoted Katuntseva, *Rol' rabochikh fakul'tetov*, p. 19.

27. *Molodaya gvardiya*, 1924 no. 5, pp. 206ff.

28. *Rukovodyashchie kadry R.K.P. (bol'shevikov) i ikh raspredelenie*, 2nd ed. (Moscow, n.d. (1924)), p. 159.

29. *Industrializatsiya SSSR 1926–1928* (Moscow, 1969), p. 370; *Narodnoe prosveshchenie v RSFSR* (Moscow, 1928), pp. 46–7.

30. *Pravda*, 14 December 1923, p. 1.

31. Chaplin, *VI syezd RLKSM. Stenograficheskii otchet* (Moscow, 1924), p. 132.

32. *Rukovodyashchie kadry*, p. 164.

33. Quoted Zinoviev, *Partiya i vospitanie smeny* (Leningrad, 1924), p. 14.

The students were from Sverdlovsk Communist University and the Moscow University social science school.

34. See *Izvestiya TsK*, 1924 no. 5(63), p. 16: Central Committee report 'Towards the XIII Congress of RKP(b)'.

35. See V. Astrov, *Krucha* (Moscow, 1969), pp. 53–4. This is an autobiographical novel of political life in Sverdlov Communist University in the 1920s; the author later worked with Bukharin on *Pravda* and supported the Right Opposition. I am indebted to Stephen F. Cohen for drawing my attention to this work.

36. *Izvestiya TsK*, 1923 no. 9–10, p. 14; *Pravda*, 30 December 1923, p. 3. All but four of those named as members of the 'Rabochaya pravda' group were students: four of them were associated with Sverdlov Communist University, two with Moscow Higher Technical School and its rabfak, and two with Moscow University.

37. E. Enchmen, *18 tezisov o 'teorii novoi biologii' (proekt organizatsii Revolyutsionno-nauchnogo Soveta Respubliki i vvedeniya fiziologicheskikh pasportov* (Pyatigorsk, 1920), discussed by David Joravsky, *Soviet Marxism and Natural Science, 1917–1932* (New York, 1961), p. 94.

38. See Sheila Fitzpatrick, 'Sex and Revolution. An Analysis of Statistical and Literary Data on the Sexual Mores of Soviet Students in the 1920s', *Journal of Modern History*, June 1978.

39. *Pravda*, 4 January 1924, p. 5. Bukharin's article ' "Enchmeniada" ' was published in *Krasnaya nov'*, 1923 no. 6.

40. *Pravda*, 15 January 1924, p. 5 (letter paraphrased by Bubnov, of Central Committee agitprop department).

41. *Pravda*, 14 December 1923, p. 1.

42. L. Trotsky, 'The New Course' (letter to party meetings preparing for the XIII Party Conference), *Pravda*, 11 December 1923, p. 4.

43. Quoted Zinoviev, *Pravda*, 21 December 1923, p. 4.

44. *Pravda*, 6 January 1924, p. 5.

45. *Ibid.*

46. *Pravda*, 21 December 1923, p. 5; 8 January 1924, p. 4. In December, the Sverdlov Communist University cell voted as follows: 554 for Preobrazhensky's resolution (i.e. for Trotsky); 421 for resolution supporting the Central Committee majority; 7 for resolution proposed by Shlyapnikov.

47. Zinoviev, *Pravda*, 3 February 1924, p. 4; Robert V. Daniels, *The Conscience of the Revolution* (New York, 1969), p. 227.

48. *Pravda*, 5 February 1924, p. 5.

49. *Pravda*, 12 February 1924, p. 5 (information from Ilya Vardin, a supporter of the Central Committee majority).

50. N. Akimov, *Krasnoe studenchestvo*, 1927/28 no. 6, p. 47.

51. V. S. Emelyanov, *O vremeni, o tovarishchakh, o sebe*, 2nd ed. (Moscow, 1970), p. 57.

52. *Pravda*, 19 January 1924, p. 6.
53. See, for example, *Pravda*, 27 February 1924, p. 3: 'Breakthrough in the VUZy', on the Second Moscow University.
54. *Pravda*, 9 and 11 January 1924, with additional signatures published 13 and 15 January. The initiative seems to have come from a group of working-class Communists in the engineering schools: see Emelyanov's account (Emelyanov, *O vremeni*, pp. 58–9) of his own participation and that of fellow Mining Academy student Tevosyan (who, like Emelyanov, later became a major industrial administrator) and Fadeev (who headed the Soviet Writers' Union in the 1930s and 1940s).
55. *Pravda*, 19 January 1924, p. 5: Resolution on the results of the discussion and on petty-bourgeois deviation in the party.
56. *Pravda*, 4 January 1924, p. 5.
57. *Pravda*, 5 February 1924, p. 5: speech to Communist fraction of Second Congress of Soviets of the USSR.
58. See list of expulsions, *Izvestiya TsK*, 1924 no. 4(9), appendix 2, pp. 3–8.
59. *Krasnoe studenenchestvo*, 1928/29 no. 14, p. 4.
60. L. S. Leonova, *Iz istorii podgotovki partiinykh kadrov v sovetsko-partiinykh shkolakh i kommunisticheskikh universitetakh (1921–1925 gg.)* (Moscow, 1972), p. 46.
61. *Industrializatsiya SSSR 1926–1928*, p. 370.
62. TsGAOR 2306/1/2945: Narkompros collegium meeting of 17 March 1924 (Zinoviev's request announced by Lunacharsky).
63. TsGAOR 2306/1/2945: Narkompros collegium meeting of 26 March 1924.
64. *Narodnoe prosveshchenie*, 1925 no. 3, p. 19.
65. See Sovnarkom resolution of 16 May 1924 'On the reduction of the number of pupils in the VUZy of the RSFSR', *Pravda*, 17 May 1924, p. 5; statements by Khodorovsky, *Pravda*, 30 April 1924, p. 1, and *Krasnaya molodezh'*, 1924 no. 1, p. 113.
66. *Pravda*, 20 May 1924, p. 8.
67. TsGAOR 2306/1/2945: Narkompros collegium meeting of 7 May 1924. K. A. Popov represented the agitprop department of the Central Committee on the Commission.
68. Smolensk Archive, WKP 518: report on work of the guberniya agitprop department for March–May 1924, p. 56.
69. V. Sh-rin, 'They are purging' (described as an account 'from life, and according to official documents'), *Krasnaya molodezh'*, 1924 no. 2, p. 126.
70. TsGAOR 2306/1/2903: Narkompros instruction no. 445, dated 21 August 1924 and endorsed by Rykov (president of Sovnarkom), on the liquidation of the Central Purge Commission.
71. A. V. Lunacharsky, *Na fronte prosveshcheniya* (report to Second Session of VTsIK, 9 October 1924) (Moscow, n.d.), p. 34.

72. *Istoriya Leningradskogo Universiteta*, p. 262.
73. *Sotsialisticheskii vestnik*, 1924 no. 15, p. 14.
74. TsGAOR 2306/1/3328: meeting of presidium of Narkompros collegium, 25 September 1924.
75. Smolensk Archive, WKP 518, p. 71: letter from agitprop department of Smolensk guberniya committee dated 27 September 1924.
76. TsGAOR 2306/1/3328: Narkompros collegium meeting of 23 September 1924 (resolution proposed by Lunacharsky).
77. *Ezhenedel'nik NKP*, 1924 no. 21(41), 15 October, p. 2.
78. *Narodnoe prosveshchenie*, 1925 no. 4, p. 118.
79. Data from *Narodnoe prosveshchenie v RSFSR* (Moscow, 1928), pp. 46–7 (total enrolments at beginning of year); *Narodnoe prosveshchenie*, 1925 no. 4, p. 118 (enrolment in May); *ibid.*, 1925 no. 3, p. 20 (admissions); *ibid.*, 1926 no. 11, p. 76 (graduations).
80. See above, note 79.
81. *Industrializatsiya SSSR 1926–1928 gg.*, p. 370.
82. See below, p. 183.
83. *Narodnoe prosveshchenie v SSSR za 1928–29 g.* (Moscow, 1930), p. 39; *Kul'turnoe stroitel'stvo SSSR* (Moscow, 1940), p. 113.
84. Bukharin, *Partiya i vospitanie smeny*, p. 108; Rykov, *Nauchnyi rabotnik*, 1925 no. 2, p. 95.
85. See *Sotsial'nyi i natsional'nyi sostav VKP(b). Itogi vsesoyuznoi partiinoi perepisi 1927 g.* (Moscow, 1928), p. 26, for a discussion of the inadequacy of social origin as a determinant of class.
86. *Krasnaya molodezh'*, 1924 no. 2, p. 126.
87. Using data cited above (notes 79 and 81), the following table can be compiled for VUZy of the RSFSR:

	Total	Workers	Peasants	Employees and Others	
Student enrolment 1923/24	150,893	23,087	35,460	36,818	55,529
Admitted 1924	15,280	5,424	4,508	5,348	
Student enrolment 1924/25	117,485	24,319	28,784	42,060	22,322
Loss through drop-out, purge and graduation	48,688	4,192	11,184	33,313	

Numbers in each class category are calculated from percentages, in a source which gives no aggregate figure for enrolment. With the total enrolment figures used in this table, 'employees' would show a loss only if fewer than 106 'others' were among the 5,348, 'employees and others' admitted in 1924. However, if the class percentages were applied to the student body as of May 1924 (135,000 students instead of 150,893), 'employee' numbers would actually appear to have *increased* during the purge year by 4,000–9,000.

88. *Partiya i vospitanie smeny*, p. 14.
89. On *Eseninshchina*, see Fitzpatrick, 'Sex and Revolution.' For contemporary discussions of the moral degeneracy of youth, see I. T. Bobryshev, *Melkoburzhuaznye vliyaniya sredi molodezhi* (Moscow, 1928); S. I. Gusev, ed., *Kakova zhe nasha molodezh'?* (Moscow–Leningrad, 1927); I. M. Razin (compiler), *Komsomol'skii byt* (Moscow, 1927); *Upadochnoe nastroenie sredi molodezhi. Eseninshchina* (Moscow: Kommunisticheskaya Akademiya, 1927).
90. The full title is *Luna s pravoi storony, ili neobyknovennaya lyubov'*. It was first published in *Molodaya gvardiya*, 1926 no. 9, and appeared in book form in 1927. Malashkin's suggestion – later repeated by Gusev and others – that Trotsky was in some way responsible for the degeneracy of youth was probably prompted by the emotional essay written by Trotsky on Esenin's death ('In memory of Sergei Esenin', *Pravda*, 19 January 1926, p. 3), often cited as an encouragement of 'Eseninist' tendencies.
91. *Upadochnoe nastroenie sredi molodezhi*, p. 112.
92. K. Radek, 'It is not the thermometer which is to blame', *Komsomol'skaya pravda*, 27 June 1926, p. 2. For other comments from Oppositionists on the degeneracy phenomenon, see speeches by Preobrazhensky and Radek, *Upadochnoe nastroenie sredi molodezhi*, and G. Lelevich, 'The crisis of Soviet culture and class war in ideology', *Kommunisticheskii put'* (Saratov), 1927 no. 21(84).
93. 'It is not the thermometer which is to blame', *Komsomol'skaya pravda*, 27 June 1926, p. 2.
94. E. Troshchenko, 'VUZ youth', *Molodaya gvardiya*, 1927 no. 4, p. 137.
95. A. Milchakov, *Pervoe desyatiletie. Zapiski veterana Komsomola*, 2nd ed. (Moscow, 1965), p. 148.
96. The Komsomol journal *Molodaya gvardiya* published several detailed and only minimally critical reports of the Opposition platform in 1926: see, for example, Milchakov, *Molodaya gvardiya*, 1926 no. 4, p. 83, and Khanin, *ibid.*, 1926 no. 9, p. 100. The recommendations on student life were made by Radek in 'It is not the thermometer which is to blame', *Komsomol'skaya pravda*, 27 June 1926, p. 2.
97. On Komsomol Oppositionism 1925–27, see V. Sulemov, *Soyuz molodykh bortsov* (Moscow, 1971), pp. 199–209.
98. Reports on VUZ discussions of the Opposition platform indicating very small overt support for the Opposition are to be found in *Izvestiya*, 8 October 1926, p. 2, and 10 October 1926, p. 3. Further discussions were held in November 1927, with a reported Opposition vote in the VUZy of Moscow, Leningrad, Nizhny Novgorod and Rostov on Don ranging from 2% to 4% of the more than 13,000 votes cast. In Moscow, the biggest Opposition vote was in the Plekhanov Institute (129 out of 1,850), with 93 Opposition votes out of a total of 1,805 in Moscow University and 43 out of a total of 976 in Moscow

Higher Technical School. The Opposition vote in the Leningrad Polytechnical Institute and Leningrad University was about 4%. *Pravda*, 10 November 1927, p. 7.

99. N. Akimov, in *Krasnoe studenchestvo*, 1927/28 no. 6, p. 47. The only firm report of an 'appearance' by an Opposition leader was that of Radek at a meeting held in an apartment and attended by 30 Leningrad VUZ students (*Molodaya gvardiya*, 1927 no. 12, p. 172). However, Trotsky and Zinoviev were described as having suddenly become 'accessible to the lower cells' at a meeting of Communist scholars in the autumn of 1926. *Izvestiya*, 8 October 1926, p. 2.

100. The figure which is for the RSFSR alone is calculated from data in *Narodnoe prosveshchenie*, 1925 no. 3, p. 20; 1925 no. 10–11, p. 167; 1926 no. 11, p. 76; 1927 no. 11–12, pp. 89, 91 and 92.

101. *Sotsial'nyi i natsional'nyi sostav VKP(b)* (Moscow, 1928), p. 41.

102. *Izvestiya TsK*, 1926 no. 49, p. 8. Although the author (L. Milkh) was writing specifically of the Urals, the statement quoted seems to have general application.

103. V. Strelnikova, 'Son of Professor Malkov', *Krasnoe studenchestvo*, 1927/28 no. 1, p. 14.

104. Potashnikov, in *Krasnoe studenchestvo*, 1927/28 no. 2, pp. 35ff.

105. L. Milkh, 'Party work in the VUZy', *Krasnoe studenchestvo*, 1927/28 no. 1, pp. 44–5. VUZ students were not the only Komsomol members unable to enter the party: Chaplin, of the Komsomol Central Committee, reported that in 1926 there were 123,000 *pererostki* (over-age Komsomols) unable to enter the party. 'On an average about 20,000 *pererostki* ought to leave every year. Most of them are from the countryside. Most of them, undoubtedly, cannot be accepted into the party' (*Molodaya gvardiya*, 1926 no. 2, p. 96).

106. Troshchenko, *Molodaya gvardiya*, 1927 no. 4, pp. 133–4.

107. Speech to XVI Moscow guberniya party conference in 1927, quoted Korbut, *Krasnoe studenchestvo*, 1927–28 no. 11, p. 32.

108. In the RSFSR, only 15,280 students were admitted in 1924, as against 34,815 in 1923. In 1925, admissions rose slightly to 19,257. *Narodnoe prosveshchenie*, 1924 no. 3(12), p. 81; 1925 no. 3, p. 20; 1925 no. 10–11, p. 167.

109. *Narodnoe prosveshchenie*, 1926 no. 11, p. 76.

110. TsGAOR 2306/1/3328, Narkompros collegium meeting of 26 June 1925: theses of a report to the Rykov commission of Sovnarkom. Vesenkha's intervention is further discussed in Chapter 6.

111. *Narodnoe prosveshchenie*, 1926 no. 4, pp. 36–8. The reserved places for children of specialists were distributed among the appropriate unions, the greatest number going to engineers, followed by professors, rural schoolteachers and doctors.

112. *Narodnoe prosveshchenie*, 1926 no. 11, p. 80. According to Khodorovsky, the introduction of rabfak finals produced a 30% drop-out in

transition from rabfak to VUZ. From 1926, rabfak graduates were also directed to technicums.

113. For the professorial endorsement, see Kancheev, of the Scientific Workers' Section of the Teachers' Union, in *Izvestiya*, 3 November 1926, p. 7. Concern for working-class percentages was expressed by L. Milkh, of the agitprop department of the Central Committee, in *Kommunisticheskaya revolyutsiya*, 1927 no. 8, p. 46.

114. Derived from the admission percentages for employees (33%) and intelligentsia (an additional 12.5%) given for 1926 in *Narodnoe prosveshchenie*, 1926 no. 11, pp. 124–5.

115. Working-class admissions were 35.5% of the total in 1924, 32.5% in 1925, 28.7% in 1926 and 34.7% in 1927. *Narodnoe prosveshchenie*, 1927 no. 11–12, p. 91.

116. See Table 2 and, for 1927–28 figures, O. Schmidt, 'Vysshie uchebnye zavedeniya', *Bol'shaya sovetskaya entsiklopediya*, XIV, 1st ed. (Moscow, 1929), p. 34.

117. Sources as above, note 100.

118. The 1924/25 figures from *Industrializatsiya SSSR 1924–1928*, p. 370; 1927/28 figures from Schmidt, 'Vysshie uchebnye zavedeniya', p. 34. To estimate total Communist–Komsomol numbers, allowance must be made for the 8–10% of Komsomol members who were also party members in the latter years of NEP. *Slavnyi put' Leninskogo Komsomola*, 1 (Moscow, 1974), p. 356.

119. Calculated from data in *Narodnoe prosveshchenie*, 1927 no. 11–12, p. 89. It should be noted that only 7% of the applications came from 'others' who, according to some population breakdowns, ought to constitute 15–20% of the population (see, for example, *Statisticheskii spravochnik SSSR za 1928* (Moscow, 1929), pp. 42–3; *Moskva i moskovskaya guberniya 1923/4–1927/8* (Moscow, 1929), pp. 68–9). 'Others' may, of course, have simply been too discouraged to apply. But it seems more likely that many in this category succeeded in obtaining a more desirable social classification for purposes of school entry. The statistics in *Moskva i moskovskaya guberniya* suggest that the 'others' category was highly unstable: one set of figures, for December 1926, classifies less than 10% of primary-school pupils as 'others', while the figures for December 1927 have 15–20% of primary-school pupils in this category (pp. 68–9).

120. *Narodnoe prosveshchenie*, 1927 no. 11–12, p. 109.

121. *Statisticheskii sbornik po narodnomu prosveshcheniyu RSFSR 1926 g.* (Moscow, 1927), p. 169.

122. *Sobranie uzakonenii*, 1922 no. 35, art. 413.

123. There are reports that many or most students worked at outside jobs in the early 1920s in *Saratovskii Universitet 1909–1959* (Saratov, 1959), p. 33, and in *Permskii Gosudarstvennyi Universitet imeni A. M. Gor'kogo. Istoricheskii ocherk, 1916–1966* (Perm, 1966), p. 32.

In 1924, Bukharin said that most students worked, as labourers, care-takers etc. (*Partiya i vospitanie smeny*, p. 104).

124. *Narodnoe prosveshchenie*, 1928 no. 5, p. 14.

125. *Upadochnoe nastroenie sredi molodezhi*, p. 121.

126. *Pravda*, 5 July 1928, p. 3.

127. Calculated from *Statisticheskii sbornik po narodnomu prosvesh-cheniyu RSFSR 1926 g.*, p. 169.

128. *Narodnoe prosveshchenie*, 1926 no. 9, p. 7; *Nauchnyi rabotnik*, 1926 no. 3, p. 47; *Krasnoe studenchestvo*, 1927/28 no. 3, p. 33.

129. *Narodnoe prosveshchenie*, 1926 no. 9, p. 7; *Krasnoe studenchestvo*, 1927/28 no. 3, p. 33; *Pravda*, 9 February 1928, p. 5 (survey of Moscow VUZy by Professor Zalkind).

130. In the RSFSR, white-collar students were strongly represented in the medical VUZy (40.1%) as well as in the pedagogical; but in the medical VUZy an unusually high percentage were adult employees rather than children of white-collar families (*Narodnoe prosvesh-chenie*, 1926 no. 11, p. 125). 8.4% of pedagogical students and 11.9% of medical students were rabfak graduates; and, for Communists, the corresponding figures were 9.2% and 7.4%. (Agricultural VUZy were somewhat better supplied both with rabfak graduates and Com-munists.) In all three types of VUZ, students tended to be young and the graduation rates higher than average. Data from *Statisticheskii sbornik po narodnomu prosveshcheniyu RSFSR 1926 g.*, pp. 162–3.

131. *Vseobshchee obuchenie. Likvidatsiya negramotnosti. Podgotovka kadrov* (Moscow, 1930), p. 128. In 1929/30, over 40% of medical and pedagogical students were under 23 – 10% higher than the average for all VUZy.

132. *Statisticheskii sbornik*, pp. 162–3; 58.7% of pedagogical students were women, compared with 31% in all types of VUZ.

133. Women constituted only 15% of Communists studying in all types of educational institution in January 1927. *Sotsial'nyi i natsional'nyi sostav VKP(b)*, pp. 42 and 50.

134. See, for example, the survey of Odessa students published by D. I. Lass, *Sovremennoe studenchestvo (byt, polovaya zhizn')* (Moscow–Leningrad, 1927). This survey is analysed by Fitzpatrick in 'Sex and Revolution'.

135. *Molodaya gvardiya*, 1927 no. 4, p. 139. The observer, E. Troshchenko, was evidently one of the rare Communist or Komsomol activists among the women students.

136. *Statisticheskii sbornik*, pp. 162–3; *Vseobshchee obuchenie*, p. 128. In 1926, the largest concentrations of Communists were in the Moscow socio-economic VUZy (3,274 students) and the Moscow industrial–technical VTUZy (3,455 students). Rabfak graduates, also concentrated in Moscow and Leningrad, made up 35.1% of all students in socio-economic VUZy and 29.7% in industrial–technical

VTUZy in 1926. In 1929/30, almost 70% of students in industrial and transport VTUZy were aged 25 years or over, as against less than 50% in all VUZy (this figure reflects the mobilizations of 1928 and 1929, and is therefore too high for the NEP period, but no earlier data on age is available).

137. The total working-class percentage in socio-economic VUZy was 27, and in industrial-technical VUZy 32.4. This compared with an average for all VUZy of 25.4%. But the crucial factor was the high representation of adult workers. The admissions data quoted here is from *Narodnoe prosveshchenie*, 1927 no. 11–12, p. 95.

138. *Statisticheskii sbornik po narodnomu prosveshcheniyu RSFSR 1926 g.*, p. 169.

139. *Ibid.*, p. 170. For all VUZy, 15.3% of students were Jewish.

140. In 1926, Jews constituted 0.56% of the population of the RSFSR and 15.3% of VUZ students (*Statisticheskii spravochnik SSSR za 1928*, pp. 32–5, and note 139 above). 4% of all party members in 1927 were Jewish (*Itogi desyatiletiya sovetskoi vlasti v tsifrakh 1917–1927*, p. 26). But it is likely that the Jewish percentage among Communist VUZ students was higher than that of the party as a whole.

141. A. V. Lunacharsky, *Ob antisemitizme* (Moscow–Leningrad, 1929), pp. 43–4 and 9–10.

142. *Statisticheskii sbornik po narodnomu prosveshcheniyu RSFSR 1926 g.*, p. 169.

143. See I. N. Yudin, *Sotsial'naya baza rosta KPSS* (Moscow, 1973), p. 181.

Chapter 6   The 'great turning-point' of 1928–1929

1. *Pravda*, 10 March 1928, p. 1: editorial and 'Information on the discovery of a counter-revolutionary economic conspiracy' from the Prosecutor of the Supreme Court of the Soviet Union.

2. *Ekonomicheskaya kontrrevolyutsiya v Donbasse. Itogi Shakhtinskogo dela. Stat'i i dokumenty* (Moscow, 1928), p. 120.

3. *Deyatel'nost' partiinoi organizatsii Tatarii po osushchestvleniyu leninskikh idei stroitel'stva sotsialisticheskogo obshchestva* (Kazan, 1971), pp. 188–9. For a history of the factory, see A. S. Klyuchevich, *Istoriya kazanskogo zhirovogo kombinata imeni M. N. Vakhitov (1855–1945)* (Kazan, 1950).

4. *3 sessiya Tsentral'nogo Ispolnitel'naya Komiteta Soyuza SSR 5 sozyva. Stenograficheskii otchet* (Moscow, 1931), Bulletin 10, p. 13.

5. See, for example, V. N. Ipatieff, *The Life of a Chemist* (Stanford and London, 1946); E. J. Larsons, *An Expert in the Service of the Soviet* (London, 1929).

6. S. A. Fedyukin, *Velikii oktyabr' i intelligentsiya* (Moscow, 1975),

pp. 303–4; A. Solzhenitsyn, *Arkhipelag Gulag*, I–II (Paris, 1973), pp. 340–45.

7. *Pravda*, 24 February 1924, p. 5.

8. For other NEP trials of engineers for wrecking and sabotage, see S. A. Fedyukin, *Sovetskaya vlast' i burzhuaznye spetsialisty* (Moscow, 1965), p. 105, note 1.

9. For local reports of intensified *spetseedstvo* resulting from the Shakhty trial, see Fedyukin, *Velikii oktyabr' i intelligentsiya*, pp. 386–7. The Smolensk archives contain a report of June 1928 that 'things are very bad with the specialists; 20 out of 40 persons in the industrial section have been put under suspicion. The mood of the engineers is panic-stricken. . .The engineering section requests, if it is possible, that specialists should not be pulled out in bunches but gradually, so as not to denude industry' (Smolensk Archive, WKP 33: bureau of Smolensk gubkom, 11 June 1928). In April 1929, the secretary of the engineering union reported that 'after the Shakhty affair the number of engineers in production jobs declined by 17%'. *Spetseedstvo* had increased, especially with the influx of inexperienced peasant workers, but the engineers were afraid to complain about it (Report of Congress of Engineers and Technicians of the USSR, *Rabochaya gazeta*, 17 April 1929, p. 8).

10. Klyuchevich, *Istoriya*, p. 206; *Ocherki istorii partiinoi organizatsii Tatarii*, 2nd ed. (Kazan, 1973), pp. 381–2.

11. A. I. Krinitsky, *Osnovnye zadachi agitatsii, propagandy i kul'turnogo stroitel'stva* (Moscow–Leningrad, 1928), p. 17.

12. See, for example, Lenin's 1923 article 'On cooperation', and, for a compilation of Lenin's writings on the subject, G. Karpov (compiler), *Lenin o kul'turnoi revolyutsii* (Moscow, 1967).

13. For a detailed discussion of this phenomenon, see Sheila Fitzpatrick, ed., *Cultural Revolution in Russia, 1928–1931* (Bloomington, Ind., 1978).

14. The quotation, from the Oppositionist Lelevich, was made by Krinitsky at the xv Party Congress in December 1927. *XV syezd VKP(b). Stenograficheskii otchet*, II (Moscow, 1962), p. 1,237.

15. See Alfred G. Meyer, 'The War Scare of 1927', *Soviet Union*, 1978 no. 1.

16. See Theodore Draper, 'The Strange Case of the Comintern', *Survey*, vol. 18, no. 3(84), Summer 1972, on the adoption of the Comintern's 'class against class' policy and the initial attitudes of Stalin and Bukharin.

17. A. Avtorkhanov, *Stalin and the Soviet Communist Party* (London, 1959), p. 29, says that Stalin, against the wishes of Yagoda (head of the GPU), decided to turn a 'conspiracy' unmasked by Evdokimov (head of the North-Caucasus regional GPU) into a national *cause célèbre*. Evdokimov's role is also mentioned by Ordzhonikidze, then

head of the Central Control Commission of the party, *XVI syezd Vsesoyuznoi Kommunisticheskoi Partii. Stenograficheskii otchet*, 1 (Moscow, 1931), p. 568.

18. I. Stalin, *Sochineniya*, XI, pp. 54–7, 63–4: 'On the work of the April joint plenum of the TsK and TsKK' (13 April 1928).

19. *Ibid.*, pp. 57–8.

20. Speech to the Eighth Congress of the Komsomol (16 May 1928), *ibid.*, pp. 76–7.

21. Stalin, *Sochineniya*, XIII, p. 41: 'On the tasks of the industrialists' (4 February 1931).

22. Speech to the Eighth Congress of the Komsomol, Stalin, *Sochineniya*, XI, p. 75.

23. Stalin, *Sochineniya*, XIII, pp. 66–7: 'A new situation – new tasks of economic construction' (23 June 1931).

24. Statement by Kaganovich, *XVI syezd VKP*, I, p. 77.

25. Stalin, 'On the work of the April joint plenum of the TsK and TsKK', *Sochineniya*, XI, p. 59.

26. A. I. Lutchenko, 'CPSU leadership in the formation of cadres of technical intelligentsia (1926–1933)', *Voprosy istorii KPSS*, 1966 no. 2, p. 31.

27. 'The Shakhty affair and practical tasks in the struggle with deficiencies of economic construction', *KPSS v rezolyutsiyakh i resheniyakh syezdov, konferentsii i plenumov TsK*, IV (Moscow, 1970), p. 90.

28. N. I. Skorutto and L. G. Rabinovich, together with engineer S. G. Imenitov, made up the 'Moscow centre' of the plot. *Ekonomicheskaya kontrrevolyutsiya v Donbasse*, pp. 154–8.

29. *Sotsialisticheskii vestnik*, 3 August 1928, p. 14.

30. *Pervaya moskovskaya oblastnaya konferentsiya Vsesoyuznoi Kommunisticheskoi Partii (bol'shevikov). Stenograficheskii otchet*, part I (Moscow, September 1929), p. 45. For a further discussion of Molotov's attitudes, especially on the link between internal and external enemies, see my article 'The Foreign Threat during the First Five-Year Plan', *Soviet Union*, 1978 no. 1.

31. Estimates of the numbers of engineers arrested after the Shakhty trial range from 2,000 to 7,000. See Kendall E. Bailes, 'The Politics of Technology: Stalin and Technocratic Thinking among Soviet Engineers', *American Historical Review*, April 1974, p. 446.

32. *Pravda*, 30 March 1928, p. 3 (Kuibyshev); *ibid.*, 28 March 1928, p. 1 (Ordzhonikidze).

33. Ordzhonikidze, speaking at *XVI syezd VKP* I, p. 568.

34. *Pravda*, 30 March 1928, p. 3. See also Kuibyshev's remarks quoted in Fedyukin, *Velikii oktyabr' i intelligentsia*, pp. 382–3, 389.

35. Lutchenko, 'CPSU leadership', p. 33.

36. *Vtoroi plenum MK VKP(b), 31 yanv.–2 fev. 1928. Doklady i rezolyutsii* (Moscow, 1928), p. 43.

37. Krinitsky, *Osnovnye zadachi*, p. 53. In February 1929, Lunacharsky referred to this pamphlet and its recent publication as 'directed against Narkompros and its local organs' (*Narodnoe prosveshchenie*, 1929 no. 3–4, p. 10).

38. See below, p. 128.

39. Quoted from *Narodnoe prosveshchenie*, 1928 no. 5, p. 7, and *Nauchnyi rabotnik*, 1928 no. 5–6, p. 25.

40. See Sheila Fitzpatrick, 'The Emergence of Glaviskusstvo. Class War on the Cultural Front, Moscow, 1928–29', *Soviet Studies*, October 1971.

41. See below, pp. 196–7.

42. *Narodnoe prosveshchenie*, 1928 no. 12, p. 3; *Vechernyaya Moskva*, 17 October 1928, p. 1; *Pravda*, 20 December 1928, p. 5.

43. *Pravda*, 16 August 1928, p. 2.

44. Krinitsky, *Osnovnye zadachi*, p. 53. Krinitsky accused Narkompros of 'passivity' in regulating the social composition of the schools.

45. Editorial 'Militant tasks of cultural revolution', *Pravda*, 5 February 1929, p. 1. This editorial recommended 'renewal [*osvezhenie*] of the class composition' and 'review of the student cadres' in the schools.

46. Instruction of 18 April 1929, published *Ezhenedel'nik NKP*, 1929 no. 20–1, pp. 20–3.

47. Krupskaya, 'Class war in educational institutions', *Pravda*, 8 June 1929, p. 2.

48. TsGAOR 5462/11/12: speech to Congress of Teachers' Union, March 1929, p. 45.

49. *Ibid.*, p. 12.

50. Information of Lunacharsky's former secretary, I. A. Sats.

51. TsGAOR 5462/11/12, pp. 38–40.

52. A. Kamensky, 'VUZy and industry', *Krasnoe studenchestvo*, 1928/29 no. 3–4, p. 59.

53. *Narodnoe prosveshchenie*, 1925 no. 7–8, pp. 30–1.

54. Kamensky, 'VUZy and industry', p. 58.

55. *Izvestiya*, 8 January 1927, p. 2. A. P. Smirnov, deputy chairman of Sovnarkom RSFSR, led the opposition to Vesenkha's proposal.

56. Reported by Khodorovsky in *Narodnoe prosveshchenie*, 1927 no. 6, p. 28.

57. TsGAOR 5574(186)/5/33: 'Themes for the report of A. V. Lunacharsky at the Vesenkha meeting', dated 19 September 1927.

58. *Izvestiya*, 28 September 1927, p. 3.

59. *Torgovo-promyshlennaya gazeta*, 4 October 1927, p. 2; *Komsomol'-skaya pravda*, 5 October 1927, p. 1; *Pravda*, 28 September 1927, p. 3. Such a resolution *was* passed at the meeting, since it was later confirmed by the presidium of Vesenkha USSR (*Komsomol'skaya pravda*, 25 January 1928, p. 2).

60. From the meeting's resolution on a paper by G. B. Ioffe (Vesenkha

RSFSR) on engineering profiles, *Torgovo-promyshlennaya gazeta*, 4 October 1927. p. 2. The issue had earlier been raised in the autumn of 1926, when Gosplan RSFSR had proposed a draft resolution evidently approved by Vesenkha on the training of specialists according to 'broad' and 'narrow' profiles. Sovnarkom RSFSR rejected the idea, which was accounted a victory for Narkompros, and the amended resolution ('On types of specialists produced by higher educational institutions', 23 February 1927) was published in *Izvestiya*, 13 April 1927, p. 7. For further information on the controversy, see articles by Khodorovsky and Osadchy, I. Khodorovsky, ed., *Kakogo inzhenera dolzhny gotovit' nashi VTUZy?* (Moscow, 1928).

61. See the contribution by GOMZA engineer Manuilov in Khodorovsky, ed., *Kakogo inzhenera*, pp. 119–20.

62. A. E. Beilin, *Kadry spetsialistov SSSR. Ikh formirovanie i rost* (Moscow, 1935), pp. 137 and 209.

63. See Kendall E. Bailes' discussion, *Technology and Society under Lenin and Stalin* (Princeton, 1978), pp. 176–7.

64. TsGAOR 5574/5/33: Theses of report by G. G. Ioffe, p. 13; *Izvestiya*, 29 September 1927, p. 3.

65. For Shabshai's views on the engineering profession, see his article 'The engineering intellectual and the engineer without diploma', *Krasnoe studenchestvo*, 1927/28 no. 2 and 3. A favourable comment on Shabshai's Institute by Molotov (himself a former student of the Petersburg Polytechnical Institute) is in *ibid.*, 1928/29 no. 1, p. 17. Critical views are expressed in Professor B. Bekker, 'Engineering "intellectual" or engineering "ignoramus"', *ibid.*, 1927/28 no. 8, and Lunacharsky, *Pravda*, 12 July 1928, p. 5.

66. *Torgovo-promyshlennaya gazeta*, 28 September 1927, p. 1 (editorial).

67. See *Komsomol'skaya pravda*, 22 September 1927, pp. 1 and 4; *ibid.*, 25 September 1927, p. 5; *ibid.*, 28 January 1928, p. 4; *ibid.*, 1 February 1928, p. 4; *Narodnoe prosveshchenie*, 1928 no. 1, p. 27; *ibid.*, 1928 no. 4, p. 114.

68. *Komsomol'skaya pravda*, 5 October 1927, p. 1; *Torgovo-promyshlennaya gazeta*, 4 October 1927, p. 2.

69. *Ustanovka rabochei sily*, 1928 no. 1–2 (20–21), p. 6.

70. See Lunacharsky in *Pravda*, 2 June 1928, p. 7.

71. *Bor'ba za rabochie kadry* (Moscow: Narkompros RSFSR, 1928), p. 38.

72. Lunacharsky, 'The problem of training worker cadres', *Narodnoe prosveshchenie*, 1928 no. 11, p. 52.

73. Dogadov (VTsSPS), *Ustanovka rabochei sily*, 1929 no. 1–2, p. 32.

74. Lunacharsky, *ibid.*, p. 20.

75. *Komsomol'skaya pravda*, 21 April 1928, p. 6.

76. *Ekonomicheskaya zhizn'*, 10 May 1928, p. 2.

77. *Nauchnyi rabotnik*, 1928 no. 7, p. 7.

78. *Komsomol'skaya pravda*, 22 April 1928, p. 4.

79. *Pravda*, 22 April 1928, p. 7.
80. V. Molotov, 'Training of new specialists', *Krasnoe studenchestvo*, 1928/29 no. 1 (1 October 1928), pp. 17–18.
81. 'On the results of the July plenum of the TsK VKP(b)' (13 July 1928), I. Stalin, *Sochineniya*, XI, p. 216.
82. A. I. Lutchenko, *Sozdanie inzhenerno-tekhnicheskikh kadrov v gody postroeniya sotsializma v SSSR 1926–1958 gg.* (Minsk, 1973), p. 47.
83. *Ibid.*
84. See Skrypnik's statement in March 1929, after the transfer of the Stalino Mining Institute from the Ukrainian Narkompros to Vesenkha USSR, that 'only an inveterate, dyed-in-the-wool chauvinist could demand that on the transfer of the Mining Institute in Stalino. . ., scientific disciplines and business in general would have to change from the Ukrainian language to Russian'. A. V. Lunacharsky and N. A. Skrypnik, *Narodnoe obrazovanie v SSSR v svyazi s rekonstruktsiei narodnogo khozyaistva* (Moscow, 1929), p. 36.
85. Stalin, *XVI syezd VKP*, I, p. 293.
86. Krupskaya's association with the Right was well known, and in 1929/30 she was frequently heckled on this attack at party meetings. In the midst of the last struggle of the Right Opposition (and of Narkompros' last struggle on educational policy), Krupskaya publicly supported the Rightist line on agriculture ('Lenin and kolkhoz construction', *Pravda*, 20 January 1929), and Bukharin, in return, published a glowing tribute to her on the occasion of her 60th birthday (*Pravda*, 27 February 1929).
87. Quoted E. H. Carr and R. W. Davies, *Foundations of a Planned Economy*, I (London, 1969), p. 594.
88. Stalin, *XVI syezd RKP*, I, p. 293.
89. Central Committee resolution 'On improving the training of new specialists' (12 July 1928), *KPSS v rezolyutsiyakh*, IV, p. 115. The VTUZy transferred were Moscow Higher Technical School (MVTU), Leningrad Technological Institute, Moscow Mining Academy, Mendeleev Chemical Institute, Stalino Mining Institute and Moscow Textile Institute (*Pravda*, 14 July 1928, p. 5).
90. There were 48 Central Committee votes needed for a two-thirds majority, but in a straightforward factional vote the Right would scarcely have mustered 20 votes, even if the whole trade union and Moscow party groups had voted as a bloc.
91. 'On improving the training of new specialists', *KPSS v rezolyutsiyakh*, IV, pp. 111ff.
92. Lunacharsky's temperament led him to prefer non-coercive solutions to problems, and he had good personal relations with Rightists like Rykov and A. P. Smirnov. However, his relations with Bukharin and Tomsky were always strained; and his unpublished diaries for 1930 (briefly shown to the present author by his daughter I. A. Lunachar-

skaya) seem to indicate an attitude of increasing impatience with the Right and respect for Stalin's leadership qualities.

93. Gastev, in *Pravda*, 7 June 1928, p. 6.

94. *Pravda*, 2 June 1928, p. 7.

95. For Tomsky's commitment to Gastev and his Institute, see *VIII syezd professional'nykh soyuzov. Stenograficheskii otchet* (Moscow, 1929), p. 192.

96. Lunacharsky, speech to the Dogadov commission on labour training, *Ustanovka rabochei sily*, 1929 no. 1–2, p. 18.

97. *Trud*, 10 November 1928, p. 3.

98. See his speech to the Eighth Congress of the Komsomol (May 1928) and greetings to *Komsomol'skaya Pravda* (May 1928), in Stalin *Sochineniya*, XI, pp. 72–4 and 78–9.

99. *VIII syezd professional'nykh soyuzov*, p. 116. A number of historians have confused I. P. Zhdanov, head of the labour and education department of the Komsomol Central Committee in 1928, with A. A. Zhdanov, then head of the Nizhny Novgorod kraikom but shortly to become one of Stalin's closest political associates.

100. *Ibid.*, p. 193.

101. *Komsomol'skaya pravda*, 12 March 1929, p. 2; *Torgovo-promyshlennaya gazeta*, 9 June 1929, p. 4; *Ezhenedel'nik NKP*, 1929 no. 26, pp. 10–11.

102. D. Petrovsky (head of Glavtuz), speaking in April 1929, in *XVI konferentsiya VKP(b). Stenograficheskii otchet* (Moscow, 1962), p. 253.

103. According to Vyshinsky's estimates, the budgets of Vesenkha VTUZy increased by 70%, with an 8% increase in student numbers, while the Narkompros budgets increased only 40–60%, with a 15% increase in student numbers (*Narodnoe prosveshchenie*, 1928 no. 8–9, p. 185). Slight variants of these figures are to be found in *Nauchnyi rabotnik*, 1929 no. 10, pp. 29 and 85.

104. *Voprosy istorii KPSS*, 1966 no. 2, pp. 33–4; *Krasnoe studenchestvo*, 1929/30 no. 1, p. 9.

105. *Pervaya moskovskaya oblastnaya konferentsiya VKP(b)*, p. 140.

106. *Ekonomicheskaya zhizn'*, 4 January 1930 (unnumbered page headed 'For the new school').

107. A. V. Lunacharsky and A. Shokhin, *K edinoi sisteme narodnogo obrazovaniya* (Moscow–Leningrad, 1929), p. 44.

108. *KPSS v rezolyutsiyakh*, IV, pp. 180–99.

109. See Sheila Fitzpatrick, 'Cultural Revolution as Class War', Fitzpatrick, ed., *Cultural Revolution in Russia 1928–1931*, p. 257, note 27.

110. 'On contradictions', *Pravda*, 7 March 1929, p. 2.

111. TsGAOR 5462/11/12, p. 48: Speech to Teachers' Union Congress, March 1929.

112. For Narkompros' attack, see above, pp. 12–13. Reports of the removal

of large numbers of 'anti-Soviet' and 'socially alien' persons from the electoral rolls (often including teachers and other members of the intelligentsia) are in *Izvestiya*, 26 March 1929, p. 2, and *Narodnoe prosveshchenie*, 1929 no. 3–4, p. 32. The ambiguous official stand on educational rights of children of *lishentsy* is in *Izvestiya*, 2 March 1929, p. 3; 5 March 1929, p. 3; 10 March 1929, p. 3; and 26 March 1929, p. 2.

113. This letter has not been published in full, but is preserved in the Central Party Archives in Moscow. The extract quoted appears in several Soviet sources including Fedyukin, *Sovetskaya vlast' i burzhuaznye spetsialisty*, p. 244.

114. This information is from a letter to the author, dated 27 December 1971, from I. A. Sats, Lunacharsky's former secretary. According to Sats' recollection, resignations were offered by Lunacharsky, Krupskaya, Pokrovsky, Yakovleva, Svidersky and M. S. Epshtein. 'Lunacharsky was released in April (or the beginning of May) but the decision was published in September...N. K. Krupskaya and Moisei Solomonovich Epshtein were not allowed to leave their posts.'

115. *Ibid.*

116. *Izvestiya*, 13 September 1929, p. 2 (Lunacharsky); *Pravda*, 24 September 1929, p. 2 (Yakovleva); *Izvestiya*, 11 September 1929, p. 5 (Svidersky). The departure of Lunacharsky and Yakovleva from Narkompros was described as 'by his (her) own request'.

117. See below, pp. 189–92.

118. See below, p. 199. In an interview shortly after Vesenkha's announcement on the FZU schools, Lunacharsky congratulated Kuibyshev and stated that Narkompros bore Vesenkha no ill-will over the transfer of the schools, as long as they were well looked after. *Zhizn' rabochei shkoly*, 1929 no. 6, pp. 12–13.

119. Quoted in *Kul'turnaya revolyutsia v SSSR. 1917–1965. gg.* (Moscow, 1967), p. 325.

120. 'On the creation of conditions of real accessibility of primary and secondary schools to children of workers, kolkhozniks, batraks and poor peasants', 31 January 1930, *Direktivy VKP(b) i postanovleniya sovetskogo pravitel'stva o narodnom obrazovanii*, 1 (Moscow–Leningrad, 1947), pp. 149–50; 'On removing abuses of electoral legislation of the USSR', 22 March 1930, *Istoriya sovetskoi konstitutsii. Sbornik dokumentov 1917–1957* (Moscow, 1957), p. 290. The issue is extensively discussed in the monthly TsIK journal *Sovetskoe stroitel'stvo* in 1930.

121. *Pravda*, 25 September 1928, p. 6 (interview with Vyshinsky, newly appointed to Narkompros).

122. I. Khodorovsky, ed., *Kakogo inzhenera dolzhny gotovit' nashi VTUZy?* (Moscow, 1928). Vyshinsky mistakenly rendered the title as *Kakoi inzhener nam nuzhen?*

123. A. Vyshinsky, 'The "Industrial Party" affair', *Nauchnyi rabotnik*, 1930 no. 11–12, pp. 24–5.
124. Vyshinsky recalled Lunacharsky's performance as a prosecutor in the 1922 show trial of the SRs. A. B. Khalatov, ed., *Pamyati A. V. Lunacharskogo* (Moscow, 1935), p. 41.
125. See below, pp. 217–20.
126. See Robert Conquest, *The Great Terror* (London, 1971), pp. 539–40 and 541, note. Khodorovsky's involvement was to a large extent determined by his last job as head of the Kremlin medical administration. Yakovleva had in fact been associated with Bukharin in his 'left Communist' phase, and she had also been a member of the Trotskyite–Zinovievite Opposition.

Chapter 7   Cultural Revolution and the schools

1. *Pravda*, 13 September 1929, p. 5.
2. For biographical details, see A. Binevich and Z. Serebryansky, *Andrei Bubnov* (Moscow, 1964).
3. *Narodnoe prosveshchenie*, 1929 no. 10–11, p. 144.
4. See resolution 'On results and immediate tasks in the struggle with bureaucratism' (April 1929), *XVI konferentsiya VKP(b). Stenograficheskii otchet* (Moscow, 1962), pp. 646–8.
5. *Molodaya gvardiya*, 1929 no. 3, p. 80; *Vechernyaya Moskva*, 7 February 1929, p. 2.
6. *Vechernyaya Moskva*, 8 April 1929, p. 1; *ibid.*, 19 April 1929, p. 2. A verbatim report of the collegium's meeting with workers of the Gosznak plant, in which a former Gosznak worker who had become a Narkompros *vydvizhenets* reported on his job and on the commissariat, is in TsGA RSFSR 2306/69/1879: collegium of Narkompros RSFSR, meeting of 28 September 1929.
7. *Vechernyaya Moskva*, 3 October 1929, p. 3.
8. *Ibid.*, 27 December 1929, p. 1.
9. *Narodnoe prosveshchenie*, 1930 no. 2, p. 3.
10. *Ibid.*, 1930 no. 6, p. 12; and *Izvestiya*, 14 May 1930, p. 3. Detailed reports on the Narkompros purge are in *Vechernyaya Moskva*, 24 February 1930, p. 1; 14 March 1930, p. 3; and 19 March 1930, p. 1. For all local and central branches of the government apparat subjected to the purge, the dismissal rate was around 11%. I. Trifonov, *Ocherki istorii klassovoi bor'by v gody NEPa, 1921–1937 gg.* (Moscow, 1960), p. 174.
11. *Ezhenedel'nik NKP*, 1929 no. 43, p. 3.
12. Central Committee resolution of 5 August 1929 'On leading educational cadres', *Partiinoe stroitel'stvo*, 1929 no. 1, p. 67. For further information on the Komsomol draftees, see *Vospominaniya o N. K.*

Krupskoi (Moscow, 1966), pp. 206–8; and Krupskaya, *Pedagogicheskie sochineniya*, XI, p. 358.

13. Glavpolitprosvet, Krupskaya's administration of political education, lost its separate identity during the reorganization of Narkompros in 1930. It became part of the new Sector for Mass Measures, mainly concerned with schools administration and headed by Shokhin.

14. The *kul'tpokhod* as a literacy campaign is discussed below, ch. 8.

15. Broido had been head of the State Publishing House and an *ex officio* member of the Narkompros RSFSR collegium from 1925 to 1927. TsGAOR 2306/1/3328: meeting of presidium of Narkompros collegium, 17 March 1925; *Izvestiya*, 2 June 1927, p. 2, and 23 June 1927, p. 3.

16. 'On the Saratov *kul'tpokhod*', cited from *Pravda*, 13 October 1929, V. A. Kumanev, *Sotsializm i vsenarodnaya gramotnost'* (Moscow, 1967), p. 191.

17. *Na putyakh k novoi shkole*, 1930 no. 1, p. 57.

18. Lunacharsky attended his last collegium meeting on 4 July 1929, Bubnov his first on 22 September. TsGA RSFSR 2306/69/1879.

19. The circular, dated 26 July 1929, was published in *Novye formy i metody prosvetitel'noi raboty* (Moscow: Narkompros RSFSR, 1929). The quotation is from p. 27.

20. 'On militant issues of public education' (editorial), *Pravda*, 30 August 1929, p. 1.

21. *Narodnoe prosveshchenie*, 1929 no. 12, p. 12.

22. M. A. Aleksinsky, *O reorganizatsii organov narodnogo obrazovaniya* (Moscow, 1930), pp. 18–19.

23. For a series of different versions of Narkompros' position on the relation of the new educational soviets to the old education departments, see *Nauchnyi rabotnik*, 1930 no. 5–6, pp. 102–3; *Byulleten' NKP*, 1930 no. 19, pp. 21ff.; and *Narodnoe prosveshchenie*, 1930 no. 19, pp. 21ff.; and *Narodnoe prosveshchenie*, 1930 no. 5, pp. 4–6.

24. 'On current tasks of cultural construction in connection with the results of the Second All-Union Meeting on Education', Central Committee resolution of 25 July 1930, *Byulleten' NKP*, 1930 no. 23, p. 5.

25. *XVI syezd VKP(b). Stenograficheskii otchet*, I (Moscow, 1935), p. 330.

26. V. N. Shulgin, *Pamyatnye vstrechi* (Moscow, 1958), pp. 3–9.

27. *Spornye voprosy marksistskoi pedagogiki* (Moscow, 1929), p. 71.

28. V. N. Osipova, 'V. N. Bekhterev's school and pedology', *Pedologiya*, 1928 book 1, pp. 11–13.

29. See, for example, articles 'On the social investigation of the rural schoolchild and statistical analysis of data obtained', 'The social and everyday environment of unruly schoolchildren' and 'Correlation between mental development and some data from social investigation of schoolchildren', P. P. Blonsky, ed., *Pedologiya i shkola*, II (Moscow, 1929); and articles, *Pedologiya*, 1929 no. 1–2, under headings 'The

methodology of pedological study of the environment', 'The environment and [physical] constitution' and 'The urban and rural child'.

30. For the focus of the Institute's work, see Shulgin, *Na putyakh k novoi shkole*, 1930 no. 1, pp. 63–4. The Institute's pedological department was headed by N. Rybnikov, whose article 'The ideology of the contemporary schoolchild' was published in *Pedologiya*, 1928 no. 1. Other Institute publications on similar themes are listed in *Pedologiya*, 1929 no. 4(6), pp. 595–612 *passim*.

31. Speech to the First Pedological Congress (1927), A. B. Zalkind, *Pedologiya v SSSR* (Moscow, 1929), p. 12.

32. The Kammerer story, including its Soviet ramifications, is related in A. Koestler, *The Case of the Midwife Toad* (New York, 1971). Lunacharsky's film scenario *Salamandra*, based on the Kammerer affair, is in *Lunacharskii o kino* (Moscow, 1965), pp. 299–309.

33. Speech to First Pedological Congress, reported *Na putyakh k novoi shkole*, 1928 no. 1, pp. 11–12.

34. See Loren R. Graham, 'Science and Values: The Eugenics Movement in Germany and Russia in the 1920s', *American Historical Review*, December 1977.

35. *Na putyakh k novoi shkole*, 1928 no. 4, p. 11.

36. Krupenina, *Za politekhnicheskuyu shkolu*, 1931 no. 1, p. 21.

37. For reports of anti-Communist, religious, pornographic and other illegal organizations in the schools, see E. Strogova, *Komsomol'-skaya pravda*, 1 April 1928, p. 2; I. Chernya, *Kommunisticheskaya revolyutsiya*, 1928 no. 17–18; *Narodnoe prosveshchenie*, 1928 no. 5, pp. 25, 32 and 39; and (a participant's account) M. Koryakov, '"Eseninshchina" and Soviet youth', *Vozrozhdenie*, xv (Paris, 1951). Communists were also concerned at the growth of religious youth organizations: in 1928 the Baptist 'Bapsomol' and Mennonite 'Mensomol' reportedly had more members than the Soviet Komsomol. M. Gorev, *Izvestiya*, 13 June 1929, p. 4; F. Oleshchuk, *Revolyutsiya i kul'tura*, 1928 no. 10, p. 21; *Kommunisticheskii put'* (Saratov), 1929 no. 19, p. 41.

38. *Spornye voprosy marksistskoi pedagogiki*, p. 44.

39. *Ibid.*, p. 18.

40. A. Lunacharsky, *O narodnom obrazovanii* (Moscow, 1958), pp. 464–5.

41. At the Narkompros meeting on pedagogical theory of December 1928, Shulgin objected to suggestions by Pistrak and Lunacharsky that he 'rejected the school'. *Spornye voprosy*, pp. 80 and 145.

42. Quotations from Shulgin's articles, *Narodnoe prosveshchenie*, 1925 no. 10–11, p. 126, and *Na putyakh k novoi shkole*, 1927 no. 9, p. 11, cited from F. F. Korolev, T. D. Korneichik and Z. I. Ravkin, *Ocherki po istorii sovetskoi shkoly i pedagogiki 1921–1931 gg.* (Moscow, 1961), pp. 437 and 414.

43. See Epshtein's comment in *Spornye voprosy*, p. 70.

44. Lunacharsky, *O narodnom obrazovanii*, pp. 459–60.

45. P. N. Gruzdev, *Spornye voprosy*, p. 37.

46. *Spornye voprosy marksistskoi pedagogiki* contained the stenogram of the meeting, which was held on 3 December, lasted seven hours, and was attended by 200 educationalists (*Na putyakh k novoi shkole*, 1928 no. 12, p. 139).

47. *Na putyakh k novoi shkole*, 1930 no. 7, p. 91.

48. *Kommunisticheskoe prosveshchenie*, 1931 no. 12, p. 18.

49. Quoted F. F. Korolev, *Sovetskaya shkola v period sotsialisticheskoi industrializatsii* (Moscow, 1959), pp. 26–7.

50. A. V. Lunacharsky and A. Shokhin, *K edinoi sisteme narodnogo obrazovaniya* (Moscow–Leningrad, 1929), pp. 55–62. See also Theses of the Komsomol Central Committee 'On labour and education of youth in connection with the Five-Year Plan of economic development', published *Komsomol'skaya pravda*, 25 March 1928, p. 2, and later endorsed by the VIII All-Union Congress of the Komsomol.

51. For Krupskaya's support of the Komsomol proposal to convert grades VIII–IX of general secondary school into technicums, see Korolev, *Sovetskaya shkola*, pp. 25–6. For her criticisms of the general secondary school in 1928, see Krupskaya, *Pedagogicheskie sochineniya*, X, pp. 268–9.

52. Theses on the education system, endorsed by the collegium of Narkompros RSFSR on 18 May 1929 and published in Lunacharsky and Shokhin, *K edinoi sisteme* (appendix).

53. The 'olive branch', in Pokrovsky's words, was extended by Ukrainian commissar Skrypnik in his article 'On the differences between the Ukrainian and Russian education systems', *Izvestiya*, 15 February 1929, p. 3. For reactions of Lunacharsky and Pokrovsky, see *Narodnoe prosveshchenie*, 1929 no. 3–4, pp. 6–7 and 41.

54. On the Ukrainian *profshkola*, see above, pp. 45–6.

55. Central Committee resolutions 'On improving the training of new specialists' (July 1928) and 'Cadres for the national economy' (November 1929), *KPSS v rezolyutsiyakh*, IV, pp. 117 and 341.

56. Korolev, Korneichik and Ravkin, *Ocherki po istorii sovetskoi shkoly i pedagogiki 1921–1931* (Moscow, 1961), p. 42.

57. On the creation of grade x, see resolution of Narkompros collegium of 20 December 1928, *Ezhenedel'nik NKP*, 1929 no. 2, p. 2; resolution of Sovnarkom RSFSR of 5 February 1929, quoted Korolev, *Sovetskaya shkola*, p. 27; and Narkompros instruction of 7 June 1929, *Ezhenedel'nik NKP*, 1929 no. 26(b), pp. 13–14. On admission of secondary-school graduates to VUZ without examination, see resolution of Narkompros collegium of 28 January 1929, confirmed by presidium of collegium on 2 April, TsGA RSFSR 2306/69/1877. This decision was strongly attacked, *Komsomol'skaya pravda*, 17 May 1929, p. 4, and defended by Epshtein, *ibid.*, p. 3.

58. *Vechernyaya Moskva*, 21 November 1928, p. 2.

59. *Narodnoe prosveshchenie*, 1929 no. 3–4, pp. 6–7.

60. Lunacharsky and Shokhin, *K edinoi sisteme*, pp. 4–5.

61. *Ibid.*, p. 142.

62. *Ibid.* This is no doubt a paraphrase rather than a direct quotation by Lunacharsky.

63. *Voprosy prosveshcheniya na Severnom Kavkaze* (Rostov), 1929 no. 8, pp. 56–8.

64. *Prosveshchenie Sibiri* (Novosibirsk), 1929 no. 6, p. 11.

65. Report from Smolensk education department, *Narodnoe prosveshchenie*, 1929 no. 3–4, pp. 20 and 45.

66. *Nizhnevolzhskii prosveshchenents* (Saratov), 1929 no. 3, p. 24; *ibid.*, 1929 no. 7–8; article by V. N. Markov.

67. *Izvestiya*, 17 February 1929, p. 4; N. K. Krupskaya, *Pedagogicheskie sochineniya*, II, p. 375.

68. *Prosveshchenie na Urale* (Sverdlovsk), 1929 no. 2, *passim*; *ibid.*, 1929 no. 4, p. 8.

69. *Ekonomicheskaya zhizn'*, 11 December 1929, p. 4; *Molodaya gvardiya*, 1930 no. 3, p. 66; *Voprosy truda*, 1930 no. 4, pp. 31–2.

70. This estimate is based on data from A. N. Veselov, *Professional'no-tekhnicheskoe obrazovanie v SSSR* (Mosow, 1961), p. 287, and *Podgotovka kadrov v SSSR 1927–1931* (Moscow, 1933), pp. 33, 64 and 74.

71. Totol numbers of pupils in grades VII–X in 1928/29 from *Kul'turnoe stroitel'stvo SSSR* (Moscow, 1956), pp. 122–3. Because of the 1930 reorganization of grades VIII–X into technicums, no exact estimate can be made of the secondary school's losses to the FZU during the 1929/30 school year.

72. *Narodnyi uchitel'*, 1930 no. 4–5, p. 24.

73. Shulgin, quoting his own *Pedagogika perekhodnoi epokhi* (1930), *Na putyakh k novoi shkole*, 1931 no. 3, p. 40.

74. Egorov (Vesenkha RSFSR), *Vtoroe vsesoyuznoe partiinoe soveshchanie po narodnomu obrazovaniyu. Stenograficheskii otchet* (Moscow, 1931), p. 69.

75. Statement of Bubnov, *Vtoroe vsesoyuznoe partiinoe soveshchanie*, p. 23.

76. Bubnov, *ibid.*, p. 188, rebuking Otto Schmidt of Narkompros, who had been advocating such a reorganization since 1920; Skrypnik, *Izvestiya*, 4 May 1930, p. 4, repudiating claims of a 'Ukrainian victory' made by his former deputy Ryappo.

77. *Izvestiya*, 4 May 1930, p. 4.

78. *Vtoroe vsesoyuznoe partiinoe soveshchanie*, pp. 80–1. The speaker was probably Mariya Orakhelashvili, sometime deputy commissar of education in Georgia and a Narkompros RSFSR worker in the mid-1930s. Her husband Mamiya was an Old Bolshevik member of the

Georgian Central Committee disciplined by Stalin and Ordzhonikidze in 1921/22.

79. Resolution of the party Central Committee, 25 July 1930, 'On current tasks of cultural construction in connection with the results of the Second All-Union Party Meeting on Education', *Byulleten' NKP*, 1930 no. 23, p. 4.

80. See below, pp. 217–20.

81. See, for example, remarks by Pozern, Krupskaya and Bubnov, *Vtoroe vsesoyuznoe partiinoe soveshchanie*, pp. 64, 86 and 187.

82. This expectation seems to have been quite accurate. Jurisdiction over buildings was predictably confused and contested by various authorities (*Byulleten' NKP*, 1930 no. 23, p. 13); but the end result, according to Bubnov in 1931, was that the 7-year schools which had formerly been 9- or 10-year schools lost their best teachers and many of their best buildings in the reorganization (*Kommunisticheskoe prosveshchenie*, 1931 no. 8, p. 85).

83. See *Novye formy i metody prosvetitel'noi raboty*, pp. 48–50; and Korolev, Korneichik and Ravkin, *Ocherki*, p. 270.

84. See above, p. 138.

85. F. Korolev, *Protiv antileninskoi teorii otmiraniya shkoly* (Moscow, 1932), p. 67. The slogan put forward by the Pioneer leaders was 'Ne shkola, a detskoe kommunisticheskoe dvizhenie'.

86. P. Blonsky, *Moi vospominaniya* (Moscow, 1971), p. 173.

87. *Na putyakh k novoi shkole*, 1932 no. 1, p. 7.

88. *Ezhenedel'nik NKP*, 1929 no. 50, p. 25.

89. *Byulleten' NKP*, 1930 no. 10, p. 49.

90. *Ibid.*, 1930 no. 5, pp. 15–16.

91. Korolev, Korneichik and Ravkin, *Ocherki*, p. 199.

92. Resolution of Sovnarkom RSFSR, 6 September 1930, 'On the results of the Congress on Polytechnical Education', *Sobranie uzakonenii*, 1930 no. 42, art. 519.

93. In 1924, the Komsomol had proposed that the normal primary school for working-class children should be an FZS, i.e. a primary school linked with an industrial enterprise and preparatory to the FZU school (TsGAOR 2306/1/3328: meeting of presidium of Narkompros collegium, 3 November 1924, discussing memorandum from Rudnev of the Komsomol Central Committee; *Narodnoe prosveshchenie*, 1924 no. 8, pp. 59–60). Narkompros agreed in principle with this suggestion, but its lack of enthusiasm is indicated by the fact that in 1929 Lunacharsky was still emphasizing the 'extraordinary complexity' of the task and the need for prolonged and careful consideration (Lunacharsky and Shokhin, *K edinoi sisteme*, pp. 16–17).

94. Narkompros collegium resolution 'On the factory 7-year school', 10 April 1930, *Politekhnicheskii trud v shkole*, 1930 no. 4–5, pp. 6off.

95. *Komsomol'skaya pravda*, 11 December 1928, p. 4; 12 December 1928, p. 1.

96. A. Ya. Shumsky, *Za shkolu Marksa-Lenina* (Moscow–Leningrad, 1931), p. 16.

97. *Na putyakh k novoi shkole*, 1930 no. 11–12, p. 66.

98. *Kommunisticheskoe prosveshchenie*, 1931 no. 5, p. 37.

99. *Na putyakh k novoi shkole*, 1932 no. 1, p. 36.

100. *Ibid.*, 1931 no. 3, pp. 66 and 69, note.

101. Shumsky, *Za shkolu*, p. 15.

102. Quoted *ibid.*, p. 13.

103. *Za politekhnicheskuyu shkolu*, 1931 no. 11–12, p. 27.

104. *Na putyakh k novoi shkole*, 1932 no. 1, p. 40.

105. *Byulleten' NKP*, 1930 no. 18, pp. 8–9.

106. *Byulleten' NKP*, 1930 no. 4, p. 14.

107. *Vtoroe vsesoyuznoe partiinoe soveshchanie*, p. 147. For reports of children's kolkhozy, see *Byulleten' NKP*, 1930 no. 19, p. 35; *Za kommunisticheskoe prosveshchenie*, 9 January 1931, p. 3; *Nizhnevolzhskii prosveshchenets*, 1929 no. 5–6, pp. 63ff.

108. Quoted Korolev, Korneichik and Ravkin, *Ocherki*, p. 99.

109. Kostyukevich, in *Bestuzhevki v ryadakh stroitelei sotsializma* (Moscow, 1969), p. 137.

110. *Za kommunisticheskoe prosveshchenie*, 15 April 1931, p. 3.

111. Korolev, Korneichik and Ravkin, *Ocherki*, p. 110.

112. *Byulleten' NKP*, 1930 no. 26, p. 38; *ibid.*, 1930 no. 28, p. 17.

113. Korolev, Korneichik and Ravkin, *Ocherki*, p. 110; M. E. Shilnikova, *Uchebno-vospitatel'naya rabota v shkoly v 1930–1934 gg.* (Moscow, 1959), p. 32.

114. See below, ch. 10.

115. Bubnov, *Statyi i rechi*, p. 198.

116. The trade unionists' outrage is described in TsGAOR 5451/15/715, pp. 24–5. The interdepartmental feud is expressed in a confidential letter from Petrovsky, head of Glavpromkadrov, to Mantsev, deputy chairman of Vesenkha (14 September 1930), bitterly complaining that the labour department was maliciously obstructing his methodological circulars – the main offender being Beilin, a statistician frequently quoted in these pages who had earlier been 'purged' from Petrovsky's department. TsGANKh 3429/79/63, p. 22: File of Glavpromkadrov, 1930.

117. Quoted Shumsky, *Za shkolu*, pp. 21–2.

118. *Pedologiya*, 1930 no. 3(9), pp. 408–19 *passim*; A. S. Zaluzhny, *Lzhenauka pedologiya v 'trudakh' Zalkinda* (Moscow, 1937), p. 31.

119. *Pedologiya*, 1930 no. 3(9), p. 335.

120. Cited by the head of the Urals agitprop department in *XI Ural'skaya oblastnaya konferentsiya VKP(b). Stenograficheskii otchet. 23–30. yanv. 1932 g.* (Sverdlovsk–Moscow, 1932), p. 112.

121. Bubnov, *Statyi i rechi*, p. 203.

122. See I. V. Stalin, *Sochineniya*, xii (Moscow, 1949), pp. 369–70.

123. *Za kommunisticheskoe prosveshchenie*, 20 May 1931, p. 3; *ibid.*, 1 June 1931, p. 2.

124. See David Joravsky, 'The Construction of the Stalinist Psyche', Fitzpatrick, ed., *Cultural Revolution in Russia, 1928–1931* (Bloomington, Ind., 1978), p. 122.

125. See below, pp. 229–30, and on the professional identity crisis, see *Na putyakh k novoi shkole*, 1932 no. 6, pp. 46–7, 51–2 and 54.

126. Narkompros RSFSR directive 'On the organization of pedological work under the education authorities', 6 May 1931, *Byulleten' NKP*, 1931 no. 14–15, pp. 21–3, and appendix 23–6; Sovnarkom RSFSR resolution 'On the organization of pedological work conducted by various government agencies in the Republic', 7 March 1931, *Byulleten' NKP*, 1931 no. 12, p. 3.

127. Narkompros directive 'On expanding the network of schools for physically defective and mentally retarded children and those suffering from speech handicaps in 1932', *Byulleten' NKP*, 1932 no. 17, pp. 2–3; Sovnarkom resolution 'On the procedure for enrolment of children in schools and recruitment of pupils to schools', 7 May 1933, *ibid.*, 1933 no. 11, p. 7; resolution of the Narkompros collegium 'On the conditions and task of pedological work', *ibid.*, 1933 no. 13, p. 6.

128. See Bubnov, *Statyi i rechi*, pp. 358–9. The collapse of pedology followed the Central Committee resolution 'On pedological distortions in the system of the education commissariats', 4 July 1936, *Direktivy i postanovleniya sovetskogo pravitel'stva o narodnom obrazovanii*, 1 (Moscow–Leningrad, 1947), pp. 190ff.

129. *Za kommunisticheskoe prosveshchenie* – the First Five-Year Plan title of *Uchitel'skaya gazeta* – was edited by Averbakh in April and May 1931. Until September 1931, he was also a member of the presidium of the Teachers' Union (*Za kommunisticheskoe prosveshchenie*, 22 September 1931, p. 1). His writings on education are to be found in L. Averbakh, *Kul'turnaya revolyutsia i voprosy sovremennoi literatury* (Moscow–Leningrad, 1928) and L. Averbakh, *Spornye voprosy kul'turnoi revolyutsii* (Moscow, 1929).

130. See *Za kommunisticheskoe prosveshchenie*, 10 April 1931, p. 2.

131. Shumsky, *Za shkolu*, p. 58.

Chapter 8   Mass education and mobility in the countryside

1. Y. V. Arutyunyan, 'The collectivization of agriculture and the freeing of labour force for industry', in *Formirovanie i razvitie sovetskogo rabochego klassa (1917–1961 gg.)* (Moscow, 1964), p. 111.

2. Frank Lorimer, *The Population of the Soviet Union: History and*

Prospects (Geneva, 1946), pp. 147–50, estimates that peasant migration to towns provided 23 million of the urban population growth in this period.

3. *XVI syezd VKP(b). Stenograficheskii otchet*, II (Moscow, 1935), p. 1,250.

4. For earlier goals, see *Pyatiletnii plan narodno-khozyaistvennogo stroitel'stva SSSR. Svodnyi obzor*, II, 2nd ed. (Moscow, 1929), pp. 218 and 263.

5. *Prosveshchenie Sibiri*, 1929 no. 4, p. 111.

6. *Prosveshchenie na Urale*, 1930 no. 1–2, p. 63.

7. *Izvestiya*, 17 April 1929, p. 3.

8. *Narodnoe prosveshchenie*, 1929 no. 12, pp. 41–3.

9. *Kommunisticheskaya revolyutsiya*, 1928 no. 20, p. 75.

10. Smolensk Archive, WKP 33: meeting of Smolensk gubkom and presidium of guberniya control commission, 30 June 1928.

11. *Pravda*, 11 July 1928, p. 1.

12. *Ezhenedel'nik NKP*, 1928 no. 42, pp. 12–13; *ibid.*, 1929 no. 7, p. 17; *ibid.*, 1929 no. 8–9, pp. 19–21; *Pravda*, 26 September 1928, p. 4.

13. See *Narodnoe prosveshchenie*, 1929 no. 3–4, pp. 25 and 39.

14. *Narodnoe prosveshchenie*, 1928 no. 6, p. 79.

15. *Ibid.*, 1929 no. 12, p. 52.

16. Smolensk Archive, WKP 215: letter of OGPU official to the oblast party committee, stamped 'absolutely secret', dated 8 August 1929.

17. See above, p. 137.

18. L. S. Frid, *Ocherki po istorii razvitiya politiko-prosvetitel'noi raboty v RSFSR ((1917–1929 gg)*. (Leningrad, 1941), p. 141.

19. See N. K. Krupskaya, *Pedagogicheskie sochineniya*, VII, p. 105, and X, p. 270.

20. *Izvestiya TsK*, 1925 no. 19–20, p. 7; *Izvestiya*, 16 March 1926, p. 2.

21. Krupskaya, *Pedagogicheskie sochineniya*, IX, pp. 390–91.

22. Rumour cited, V. A. Kumanev, *Sotsializm i vsenarodnaya gramotnost'* (Moscow, 1967), p. 221.

23. *Narodnoe prosveshchenie*, 1930 no. 7–8, p. 20.

24. Kumanev, *Sotsializm*, p. 226.

25. *Narodnoe prosveshchenie*, 1930 no. 2, pp. 30–1.

26. Kumanev, *Sotsializm*, p. 225. Other gruesome examples may be found in the Smolensk Archive, WKP 525: material of the criminal investigation department, p. 80; and *Prosveshchenie Sibiri*, 1929 no. 7–8, pp. 106–12.

27. *Narodnoe prosveshchenie*, 1930 no. 7–8, p. 8.

28. *Sbornik tsirkulyarov Narodnogo Komissariata Yustitsii RSFSR deistvuyushchikh na l iyunya 1931 g.* (Moscow, 1931), p. 210.

29. Oblastnoi Komitet VKP(b) Avtonomnoi Tatarskoi SSR, *Stenograficheskii otchet XV oblastnoi partiinoi konferentsii (5–15 iyunya 1930 g.)* (Kazan, 1930), p. 124.

30. I. Ya. Trifonov, *Likvidatsiya ekspluatatorskikh klassov v SSSR* (Moscow, 1975), p. 387.
31. Resolution of the Presidium of TsIK 'On the procedure for re-establishing the voting rights of children of kulaks', 17 March 1933, *Sbornik zakonov*, 1933 no. 21, art. 117.
32. Trifonov, *Likvidatsiya*, p. 389.
33. *Na putyakh k novoi shkole*, 1930 no. 4–5, p. 15.
34. *Narodnoe prosveshchenie*, 1930 no. 6, p. 16.
35. *Ibid.*, p. 17.
36. *Ibid.*, p. 16. For other similar examples, see *Sbornik tsirkulyarov Narodnogo Komissariata Yustitsii*, p. 111.
37. Smolensk Archive, WKP 525: material of the criminal investigation department, p. 199 (marked 'secret').
38. *Na putyakh k novoi shkole*, 1930 no. 2, p. 76.
39. *Iz istorii partiinykh organizatsii Urala*, ii (Sverdlovsk, 1973), p. 127.
40. *Za vseobshchee obuchenie*, 1930 no. 4, p. 19; *Byulleten' NKP*, 1930 no. 29, p. 4.
41. *Vechernyaya Moskva*, 1 April 1930, reporting instructions of Kolkhoztsentr; *Za vseobshchee obuchenie*, 1931 no. 7, p. 16 (directive of Kolkhoztsentr and Teachers' Union).
42. *Narodnoe prosveshchenie*, 1930 no. 7–8, p. 8. Even Kolkhoztsentr admitted that deductions of 10–25% of salary were common (*Za vseobshchee obuchenie*, 1931 no. 7, p. 16).
43. *Prosveshchenie Sibiri*, 1930 no. 11, p. 98; *Iz istorii partiinykh organizatsii Urala*, ii, p. 127.
44. Instruction of 11 November, signed by Narkompros, Kolkhoztsentr and other bodies, *Byulleten' NKP*, 1930 no. 34, p. 13.
45. In mid-1932, Narkompros tried to recover the school property which had earlier been transferred to kolkhozy and sovkhozy. See memorandum from Shokhin, dated 14 August 1932, *Byulleten' NKP*, 1932 no. 47, p. 11.
46. See above, p. 153.
47. *Za politekhnicheskuyu shkolu*, 1931 no. 9, p. 45.
48. See above, pp. 60–61.
49. *Na putyakh k novoi shkole*, 1929 no. 12, pp. 46–8.
50. Resolution of the collegium of Narkompros RSFSR, 5 February 1930, 'On the reconstruction of ShKMs in accordance with the tasks of total collectivization', *Byulleten' NKP*, 1930 no. 6, pp. 3–5.
51. *Kul'turnoe stroitel'stvo SSSR* (Moscow, 1956), pp. 122–3.
52. Compare data cited above (note 51) on numbers of pupils in all rural grades v–ix with data on numbers in ShKM schools in Yu. S. Borisov, *Podgotovka proizvodstvennykh kadrov sel'skogo khozyaistva v rekonstruktivnyi period* (Moscow, 1960), p. 161.
53. This is strongly suggested by the fact that at the beginning of the

Second Five-Year Plan the ShKM reverted to a purely general-educational function (Borisov, *Podgotovka*, p. 161).

54. *Na putyakh k novoi shkole*, 1930 no. 2, p. 75.
55. See report of Gosplan projections on training of cadres for kolkhozy and sovkhozy, in *Nauchnyi rabotnik*, 1929 no. 10, p. 86.
56. Borisov, *Podgotovka*, p. 97.
57. *Ibid.*, pp. 97–8; V. V. Melnikov, *Kul'turnaya revolyutsiya i Komsomol* (Rostov, 1973), p. 240.
58. 'On the kolkhoz movement and the progress of agriculture', *KPSS v rezolyutsiyakh*, IV, p. 457.
59. Borisov, *Podgotovka*, pp. 144–6.
60. In the last years of Tsarism, following a large expansion of primary education mainly sponsored by the zemstva, it had been planned to introduce universal primary education in European Russia by 1925. For more detail on pre-war projections and investment in primary education, see N. V. Chekhov, *Pedagogicheskaya entsiklopediya*, II (1928), pp. 122–4.
61. See data on literacy, broken down by age and sex, *Vsesoyuznaya perepis' naseleniya 17 dekabrya 1926 g. Kratkie svodki*, VII (Moscow, 1928), pp. 8–13.
62. For pre-war literacy, see A. G. Rashin, 'Literacy and education in Russia in the 19th and beginning of the 20th centuries', *Istoricheskie zapiski*, 1951 no. 37, p. 49.
63. *Narodnoe prosveshchenie v RSFSR v osnovnykh pokazatelyakh* (Moscow–Leningrad, 1932), p. 6 (data – for the USSR as a whole – is from the 1926 census).
64. For European Russia, literacy for the male age group 12–16 was 77–79% in 1926 – ten percentage points lower than the literacy of males in their 20s in 1926. *Vsesoyuznaya perepis'*, V, p. xvii.
65. Kumanev, *Sotsializm*, p. 167.
66. A drop in literacy was reported in Moscow guberniya in 1928, and literacy among the Orenburg Cossacks had fallen from a pre-war level of 98% to 90% (*Vechernyaya Moskva*, 21 August 1928, p. 2, and *ibid.*, 30 March 1929, p. 2).
67. *Kul'turnoe stroitel'stvo SSSR* (1956), pp. 122–3; *Rashin*, 'Literacy and education', p. 68.
68. *Pyatiletnii plan narodno-khozyaistvennogo stroitel'stva SSSR. Svodnyi obzor*, II (Moscow, 1930), part 2, pp. 217–18.
69. Lunacharsky said in 1926 that 60.5% of Russian children of primary-school age were in school (*Narodnoe prosveshchenie*, 1926 no. 11, p. 17); Krupskaya stated in 1928 that only 50% of these children were in school (*Pravda*, 1 May 1928, p. 7); and a year later Lezhava gave the figure of 55% (*XIV vserossiiskii syezd sovetov*, Bulletin 5, p. 18).
70. Resolution of the Central Committee 'On universal and compulsory

primary education', 25 July 1930, *KPSS v rezolyutsiyakh*, IV, p. 474.

71. For data on the social composition of Soviet primary schools, broken down by republics, see *Massovoe prosveshchenie v SSSR*, II, pp. 40–61.

72. Numbers of pupils in rural primary schools of the USSR rose from 7.3 million in 1927/28 to 8.8 million in 1929/30. Over the same period, urban numbers dropped by about 20,000. *Kul'turnoe stroitel'stvo SSSR* (1956), pp. 82–5.

73. *Za vseobshchee obuchenie*, 1931 no. 4, p. 11.

74. *Ibid.*, p. 10.

75. Resolution of TsIK and Sovnarkom USSR 'On the introduction of compulsory primary education', 14 August 1930, *Narodnoe obrazovanie v SSSR. Obshcheobrazovatel'naya shkola. Sbornik dokumentov 1917–1973 gg.* (Moscow, 1974), p. 113.

76. *Prosveshchenie Sibiri*, 1929 no. 10, p. 112.

77. *Za vseobshchee obuchenie*, 1931 no. 4, p. 10.

78. *Ibid.*, 1931 no. 2, p. 12; and *ibid.*, 1931 no. 4, p. 11.

79. The 1932 figure from K. Subbotina, *Narodnoe obrazovanie i byudzhet* (Moscow, 1965), p. 46. The TsIK and Sovnarkom USSR resolution of 14 August 1930 (see above, note 75) provided for central subsidy (1) through the school building fund and (2) through a special allocation on the All-Union budget at an amount to be determined. But Gosplan's projections for 1931 (for RSFSR without autonomous republics) indicate that no substantial contribution was forthcoming from either the All-Union or republican governments (*Za vseobshchee obuchenie*, 1931 no. 5, p. 32).

80. See editorial 'Self-taxation – the lever of cultural revolution', *Pravda*, 27 September 1929, p. 1, In 1931, for the RSFSR alone, self-taxation brought in 239 million roubles; in 1932, 327 million roubles. *Sotsialisticheskoe stroitel'stvo SSSR* (Moscow, 1934), pp. 458–9.

81. The decrees instituting the special tax are in *Sbornik zakonov*, 1931 no. 3, art. 34; 1931 no. 3, art. 35; 1932 no. 2, art. 9; and 1932 no. 2, art. 10. See also R. W. Davies, *The Development of the Soviet Budgetary System* (Cambridge, 1958), p. 225.

82. In 1929/30, only 3.7% of all pupils in literary schools in the USSR were in schools financed on the central budget; 39% were being taught by unpaid teachers, 19% were in schools maintained by various institutions, and the rest were in schools financed on the budget of the local soviets (*Massovoe prosveshchenie v SSSR*, II, p. 122).

83. See Central Committee resolution 'On universal and compulsory primary education', *KPSS v rezolyutsiyah*, p. 476.

84. *XVI syezd VKP(b). Stenograficheskii otchet*, I (Moscow, 1935), p. 330.

85. Kumanev, *Sotsializm*, pp. 187–9; Broido, *Narodnoe prosveshchenie*, 1928 no. 11, pp. 41–2.

86. On *kul'testafeta*, see Kumanev, *Sotsializm*, p. 249. The terms *start*,

finish, marshrut and *obshchestvennyi buksir* (referring to the 'towing' of a backward region by a more advanced one) came into use with the *kul'testafeta.*

87. *Pamyatnik uchastnika kul'testafeta (kul'tboitsa)* (Stalingrad, 1930), pp. 4–5, 7 and 11–12.

88. Kumanev, *Sotsializm,* p. 200; Bubnov, *XVI syezd VKP(b),* I, p. 331.

89. Kumanev, *Sotsializm,* p. 227. Other details on Baptist cultural activity – including the organization of a Day of Classless Solidarity with Brothers-in-Christ on May 1 and of a two-week Struggle against Biblical Illiteracy in Saratov, directly imitating the *kul'tpokhod* – will be found in *Kommunisticheskii put'* (Saratov), 1929, no. 19, p. 41.

90. Kumanev, *Sotsializm,* p. 232.

91. *Narodnoe prosveshchenie,* 1930 no. 2, p. 21.

92. Calculated from *Kul'turnoe stroitel'stvo SSSR* (1956), pp. 80–5.

93. Melnikov, *Kul'turnaya revolyutsiya,* p. 196.

94. *Trud v SSSR. Statisticheskii spravochnik* (Moscow, 1936), p. 321.

95. *Trud v SSSR (1934 god)* (Moscow, 1935), p. 265; Melnikov, *Kul'turnaya revolyutsiya,* p. 196.

96. *Kul'turnoe stroitel'stvo SSSR* (1956), pp. 122–3.

97. *Massovoe prosveshchenie v SSSR* I, p. 6. In 1931–2, there were 17.7 million children in grades I–IV (and preparatory grades) in the Soviet Union (source as above, note 96), and probably 13–14 million in the 8–11 age group (extrapolated from Lorimer, *Population,* p. 143). An age breakdown, for the RSFSR only and excluding preparatory grades, suggests that around 73% of children in grades I–IV in 1931/32 were aged 8 to 11 (*Narodnoe prosveshchenie v RSFSR v osnovnykh pokazatelyakh,* p. 76).

98. *Massovoe prosveshchenie v SSSR* I, pp. 27 and 29.

99. V. N. Panfilov, *Kul'turnye pyatiletki* (Moscow, 1930), p. 108.

100. TsGA RSFSR 2306/69/1879: meeting of Narkompros collegium, 11 July 1929.

101. *Kul'turnoe stroitel'stvo SSSR v tsifrakh 1930–1934* (Moscow, 1935), p. xvi.

102. *Kul'turnoe stroitel'stvo SSSR* (Moscow, 1940), p. 84.

103. *Itogi vypolneniya pervogo pyatiletnego plana razvitiya narodnogo khozyaistva SSSR* (Moscow, 1933), p. 222.

104. A later edition of *Itogi vypolneniya* reduced the figure, without explanation, to 30 million (*Summary of the Fulfilment of the First Five-Year Plan for the Development of the National Economy of the USSR,* 2nd revised ed. (New York, n.d., p. 246)); Bubnov gave the estimate of 29 million illiterates trained during the First Five-Year Plan, but, as a Soviet commentator adds, 'it has unfortunately not been possible to establish on what sources A. S. Bubnov based these figures' (Kumanev, *Sotsializm,* pp. 265–6); and, after the publication

of the 1939 census, it was officially estimated that 23 million illiterates had been trained in this period (*Kul'turnoe stroitel'stvo SSSR* (1940), p. 92).

105. Kumanev, *Sotsializm*, p. 168.

106. Lorimer, *Population*, pp. 198–9.

107. *Ibid.*

108. The 1926 data from *Vsesoyuznaya perepis' naseleniya 17 dekabrya 1926 g. Kratkie svodki*, VII, pp. 8–13; 1939 data calculated from Lorimer, *Population*, pp. 143–4 and 198.

109. The estimate of the total population on 1 January 1933 is from Lorimer, *Population*, p. 135, with a subtraction of 22.5% of total population to cover the 0–8 age group. (In 1926, 24% of the total population was aged 0–8; and in 1939, 21%.)

110. See *Kul'turnoe stroitel'stvo SSSR* (1940), p. 92; 23 million illiterates were taught in the First Five-Year Plan period, according to these figures, and 25 million in the Second.

111. Kumanev (*Sotsializm*, pp. 162–3) calculates that 10 million adults were taught to read and write in the period 1918–27.

112. On illiteracy among the new members of trade unions, see *Profsoyuznaya perepis' 1932–1933 g.*, I (Moscow, 1934), p. 44. Urban literacy schools taught 5.5 million illiterates and semi-literates in the period 1927–32 and 8.8 million in the period 1933–38 (*Kul'turnoe stroitel'stvo SSSR* (1940), p. 92).

113. *Itogi vsesoyuznoi perepisi naseleniya 1959 goda SSSR* (*Svodnyi tom*) (Moscow, 1962), p. 89.

114. A. I. Vdovin and V. Z. Drobizhev, *Rost rabochego klassa SSSR. 1917–1940 gg.* (Moscow, 1976), p. 127.

115. *Ibid.*, p. 133.

116. See above, p. 61.

117. Resolution of TsIK and Sovnarkom USSR 'On training of technical cadres for the economy of the Soviet Union', 13 January 1930, *Resheniya partii i pravitel'stva po khozyaistvennym voprosam (1917–1967 gg.)*, II (Moscow, 1967), p. 163.

118. *Narodnoe prosveshchenie*, 1929 no. 3–4, pp. 3 and 7.

119. Quoted by Lunacharsky, *Ustanovka rabochei sily*, 1929 no. 1–2, p. 20.

120. Vdovin and Drobizhev, *Rost rabochego klassa SSSR*, p. 119. In 1930, only 15% of FZU students were peasants according to this breakdown. But by the autumn of 1935, 50% of new admissions were peasants.

121. See M. T. Goltsman, 'Composition of construction workers of the USSR in the years of the First Five-Year Plan (on materials of the trade union censuses of 1929 and 1932)', in *Izmeneniya v chislennosti i sostave sovetskogo rabochego klassa* (Moscow, 1961), pp. 124ff.

122. TsGAOR 5451/15/715: VTsSPS, Sector of Industrial Cadres (1931), p. 57.

123. Trifonov, *Likvidatsiya*, pp. 379, 381–2.

124. John Scott, *Behind the Urals* (Bloomington, Ind., 1973), p. 85.
125. M. Ya. Sonin, *Vosproizvodstvo rabochei sily v SSSR i balans truda* (Moscow, 1959), p. 182 (Table 45).
126. Borisov, *Podgotovka*, pp. 273–4.
127. Melnikov, *Kul'turnaya revolyutsiya*, p. 240.
128. Borisov, *Podgotovka*, p. 275. See also Arutyunyan, 'Collectivization', p. 111.
129. TsGA RSFSR 2306/69/1877: presidium of Narkompros collegium, meeting of 11 June 1929.
130. Resolution of TsIK and Sovnarkom USSR 'On training of technical cadres for the economy of the Soviet Union', 13 January 1930, *Resheniya partii*, p. 163.
131. Data from TsGAOR 5451/15/715, p. 18.
132. *Trud v SSSR. Statisticheskii sbornik* (Moscow, 1968), pp. 268–9 and 286–7.
133. See below, pp. 237–8.

Chapter 9 *The making of a proletarian intelligentsia*

1. I. Stalin, *Sochineniya*, XIII, 1951, p. 41, and XI, p. 58.
2. Developments in higher military education are described in A. I. Iovlev, *Deyatel'nost' KPSS po podgotovke voennykh kadrov* (Moscow, 1976), ch. 2. On the need to strengthen the 'worker and party nucleus' in the Army command, see the Central Committee resolution 'On the command and political composition of the Red Army', 25 February 1929, *KPSS v rezolyutsiyakh*, IV, pp. 176–9; and on the need to improve the technical expertise and general educational level of the officers, see the Central Committee resolution 'On the command and political composition of the Red Army', 5 June 1931, *ibid.*, pp. 521–4.
3. The Industrial Academies (*Promakademii*) offered high-status training to a small number of mature students with administrative experience: although highly publicized and praised, their contribution to the First Five-Year Plan *vydvizhenie* was actually less significant than that of the VTUZy. In 1932, the 11 Industrial Academies had 3,507 students (*Voprosy istorii KPSS*, 1976 no. 10, p. 83).
4. See above, ch. 6; and V. Molotov, 'The training of new specialists', *Krasnoe studenchestvo*, 1928/29 no. 1, pp. 9–21.
5. *Sotsial'nyi i natsional'nyi sostav VKP(b). Itogi vsesoyuznoi perepisi 1927 goda* (Moscow, 1928), p. 42; *Kommunisty v sostave apparata gosuchrezhdenii i obshchestvennykh organizatsii. Itogi Vsesoyuznoi perepisi 1927 g.* (Moscow, 1929), p. 25 (data on *otvetrabotniki* is for 32 guberniyas of RSFSR).
6. M. Ryutin, 'Leading cadres of the VKP(b)', *Bol'shevik*, 1928 no. 15, p. 20 (data for 1927).

7. *Sotsial'nyi i natsional'nyi sostav*, p. 41; *Kommunisty v sostave apparata*, p. 14 (data for 32 guberniyas of RSFSR).

8. *Kommunisty v sostave apparata*, pp. 12 and 14; Ryutin, 'Leading cadres', p. 27.

9. See, for example, Stalin, *Sochineniya*, XI, pp. 57–9.

10. Yu. Borisov, *Podgotovka proizvodstvennykh kadrov sel'skogo khozyaistva v rekonstruktivnyi period* (Moscow, 1960), pp. 153–4.

11. *Komsomol'skaya pravda*, 9 September 1932, p. 3.

12. 'On the improvement of the training of new specialists', *KPSS v rezolyutsiyakh*, IV, pp. 114–17.

13. *Pravda*, 25 July 1928, p. 5.

14. *Izvestiya TsK*, 1928 no. 28; *Sovetskaya intelligentsia (Istoriya formirovaniya i rosta 1917–1965 gg)*. (Moscow, 1968), p. 176; *Krasnoe studenchestvo*, 1929/30 no. 30, p. 18.

15. In fact, the Thousanders did not like the social and academic atmosphere of Kagan-Shabshai's Institute: they organized a student protest movement there, and two-thirds of them left within a year. *Komsomol'skaya pravda*, 15 March 1929, p. 4; *Krasnoe studenchestvo*, 1929/30 no. 2, p. 8.

16. On the distribution of Party Thousanders, see *Pravda*, 24 July 1928, p. 4; *ibid.*, 26 July 1928, p.5; *Komsomol'skaya pravda*, 15 March 1929, p. 4; *Krasnoe studenchestvo*, 1929/30 no. 2, p. 8.

17. B. S. Telpukhovsky, 'The activity of the CPSU in strengthening the defence of the USSR in the years of socialist reconstruction of the economy (1929–1937)', *Voprosy istorii KPSS*, 1976 no. 8, p. 93; Colonel E. I. Soldatenko, *Ukreplenie oboronosposobnosti SSSR v pervoi pyatiletke (1929–1932 gg.)* (Kharkov, 1957), p. 49.

18. TsGAOR 5451/15/785: file on the Trade Union Thousanders (1931), p. 65; *Pervaya moskovskaya oblastnaya konferentsiya Vsesoyuznoi Kommunisticheskoi Partii (bol'shevikov). Stenograficheskii otchet*, part 1 (Moscow, 1929), pp. 139 and 157.

19. *Pervaya moskovskaya oblastnaya konferentsiya*, p. 157.

20. See, for example, interjections from the floor when Uglanov spoke disparagingly of working-class *vydvizhenie*, *Vtoroi plenum MK VKP(b), 31 yanv.–2 fev. 1928. Doklady i rezolyutsii* (Moscow, 1928), p. 43; *Pervaya moskovskaya oblastnaya konferentsiya*, p. 166.

21. *Pervaya moskovskaya oblastnaya konferentsiya*, p. 52.

22. TsGAOR 5451/15/785, p. 65: Table – Composition of Trade Union Thousanders (April 1931); TsGAOR 5451/15/715, p. 19: Report of Sector of Industrial Cadres, VTsSPS (1932).

23. Of the first trade union Thousand, 70% were classified as unprepared for immediate entry to VUZ, and there was a further 13% which the VTUZy tried (unsuccessfully) to reject outright. *Vechernyaya Moska*, 26 August 1929, p. 2.

24. TsGAOR 5451/15/715, p. 19.

25. *Krasnoe studenchestvo*, 1929/30 no. 17, p. 3.
26. TsGAOR 5451/15/715, p. 19; S. Fedyukin, *Sovetskaya vlast' i burzhuaznye spetsialisty* (Moscow, 1965), p. 243.
27. See, for example, Stalin, 'Speech to the VIII Congress of VLKSM' (16 May 1928), *Sochineniya*, XI, pp. 76–7; 'On the tasks of the industrialists' (4 February 1931), *Sochineniya*, XIII, pp. 41–2.
28. There were under 25,000 Communists in higher educational institutions of the USSR at the beginning of 1928 (*Podgotovka kadrov v SSSR, 1927–1931* (Moscow–Leningrad, 1933), pp. 13 and 19); over 30,000 Communists graduated in the period 1928–32 (I. N. Yudin, *Sotsial'naya baza rosta KPSS* (Moscow, 1973), p. 181); and in the 1932/33 school year there were 106,000 Communists in higher educational institutions (*Sotsialisticheskoe stroitel'stvo SSSR* (Moscow, 1934), p. 410, and N. de Witt, *Education and Professional Employment in the USSR* (Washington DC, 1961), pp. 638–9).
29. Calculated from *Sotsialististicheskoe stroitel'stvo SSSR*, p. 410, and de Witt, *Education and Professional Employment*, pp. 638–9.
30. Of all 89,000 party members with completed higher education in early 1937, 47.3% had entered the party as workers (Yudin, *Sotsial'naya baza*, p. 186). If the pre-1928 graduates are excluded (see data, *Sotsial'nyi i natsional'nyi sostav VKP(b)*, p. 41), the percentage of former workers is 51; and it must be still higher for the 1931–36 graduates who had entered the VUZy during the First Five-Year Plan. The working-class 50% which I have used in my calculations of the Communist *vydvizhenie* is almost certainly too low.
31. *Sostav rukovodyashchikh rabotnikov i spetsialistov Soyuza SSR* (Moscow, 1936), pp. 10–11. This survey (described in ch. 12, note 28) is not ideal for our purposes, since the bulk of First Five-Year Plan entrants to VUZ had yet to graduate, and probably a third to a half of the First Five-Year Plan graduates had entered VUZy before 1928. But no comparable data are available for later years.
32. *Kul'turnoe stroitel'stvo SSSR v tsifrakh (1930–1934 gg.)* (Moscow, 1935), p. 43.
33. *Vechernyaya Moskva*, 9 October 1929, p. 2; *Komsomol'skaya pravda*, 16 January 1929, p. 3.
34. *Krasnoe studenchestvo*, 1929/30 no. 4, p. 2.
35. TsGA RSFSR 2306/69/1879: Narkompros collegium meeting of 29 August 1929: report on uninterrupted practical work; *Nauchnyi rabotnik*, 1929 no. 7–8, p. 90; *ibid.*, 1929 no. 12, p. 100; *ibid.*, 1930 no. 8–9, pp. 34–8.
36. *Komsomol'skaya pravda*, 7 March 1929, p. 4.
37. *Pravda*, 13 April 1928, p. 4; *Krasnoe studenchestvo*, 1929/30 no. 24, p. 9; *Nauchnyi rabotnik*, 1930 no. 1, pp. 40–1.
38. *Krasnoe studenchestvo*, 1920/30 no. 20, p. 4; *Byulleten' NKP*, 1930 no. 31, p. 13.

39. For Gosplan statements, see *Pyatiletnii plan narodnokhozyaistvennogo stroitel'stva SSSR. Svodnyi obzor*, I, 2nd ed. (Moscow, 1929), pp. 78–9 and speech of Krzhizhanovsky, *XVI konferentsiya VKP(b). Stenograficheskii otchet* (Moscow, 1962), p. 264. On the German 'Technical Week', see *Vechernyaya Moskva*, 14 January 1929, p. 1, and Anthony C. Sutton, *Western Technology and Soviet Economic Development*, I (Stanford, 1968), p. 322.

40. *VARNITSO*, 1930 no. 2, p. 48.

41. Central Committee resolution 'On cadres for the national economy', November 1929, *KPSS v rezolyutsiyakh*, IV, p. 338.

42. I. P. Barmin, *Iz opyta raboty KPSS i sovetskogo gosudarstva po sozdaniyu kadrov sovetskoi intelligentsii (1928–1933 gg.)* (Moscow, 1965), pp. 38–9; *Za promyshlennye kadry*, 1931 no. 2, p. 119. Reversal of the trend began in late 1930: according to the VTsSPS Sector of Industrial Cadres, the credit belonged to Shvernik (VTsSPS head), who was the first to call for 'a struggle for quality of training against opportunistic whimperings about tempos and "leftist" attempts to reduce the length of training mechanically. After that, a number of party organizations directed the VUZ and VTUZ party committees to work in that direction (the disbanding of the Moscow Power Institute's party committee by the Bauman raikom, the analogous decision of the Stalino raikom, and so on)'. TsGAOR 5451/15/715, p. 24: Report prepared for IX Trade Union Congress (1932).

43. See above, ch. 7.

44. *Krasnoe studenchestvo*, 1930/31 no. 14–15, p. 11.

45. Moskovskii Institute Narodnogo Khozyaistva imeni G. B. Plekhanova, *50 let Instituta* (Moscow, 1957), p. 67. See also *Iz istorii Moskovskogo Universiteta 1917–1941* (Moscow, 1955), p. 248.

46. 'On cadres for the national economy', *KPSS v rezolyutsiyakh*, IV, p. 339.

47. A summary of the Schmidt commission's work, together with a collection of TsIK and Sovnarkom instructions, may be found in *Materialy po reorganizatsii VUZov, VTUZov, tekhnikumov i rabfakov SSSR* (Moscow, 1930). A complete list of Soviet VUZy and their administering institutions as of 1 January 1931 is in *Podgotovka kadrov v SSSR 1927–1931* (Moscow, 1933), pp. 198ff.

48. See, for example, Markov, 'Do we need universities?', *Krasnoe studenchestvo*, 1929/30 no. 3, pp. 10–11, and Laushtein, 'Do we need universities? (For discussion)', *Vechernyaya Moskva*, 19 February 1930, p. 2. Laushtein refers to a project for university reform, involving the splitting up of the universities into specialized institutes, which was presented to Narkompros RSFSR in November 1929 by Professor Pinkevich, educational theorist and Rector of the Second Moscow University.

49. *Kul'turnoe stroitel'stvo SSSR* (Moscow, 1940), p. 106.

50. E.g. the Commissariat of Health, which refused to accept the provincial medical schools, and the Commissariat of Justice, which refused all the law schools. *Krasnoe studenchestvo*, 1929/30 no. 29, p. 2.

51. Gorbunov, an Old Bolshevik, was a former Rector of Moscow Higher Technical School. His protest was occasioned by Sovnarkom USSR's resolution of 26 July 1930 'On programmatic–methodological direction of professional–technical educational institutions', and is filed in TsGANKh 3429/79/63, p. 56. The same file (Glavpromkadrov, Vesenkha USSR, 1930) contains a protest against the new law signed by Mantsev, deputy chairman of Vesenkha, and Petrovsky, head of Glavpromkadrov, addressed to the Central Committee and asking the Orgburo to review the decision.

52. Borisov, *Podgotovka proizvodstvennykh kadrov*, p. 191.

53. E. V. Mikhin, 'Class war and scientific workers', *Nauchnyi rabotnik*, 1930 no. 5–6, p. 16.

54. *Kommunisticheskaya revolyutsiya*, 1929 no. 1, pp. 19 and 21; Smolensk Archive, WKP 309: meeting of bureau of party cell of Smolensk Medical Institute, 25 February 1931.

55. See Vyshinsky, 'Re-election of professors and lecturers', *Pravda*, 9 June 1929, p. 2; and editorial, *Pravda*, 12 June 1929, p. 1.

56. Vyshinsky's original announcement was made in October 1928 (*Vechernyaya Moskva*, 30 October 1928, p. 2), but it took almost the full academic year to organize the first elections. When they were finally held, the Narkompros collegium concluded that it had been demonstrated 'that the majority of scientific workers in the VUZy are worthy of their appointments, difficult to replace, and will not even be opposed in the concourse' (*Nauchnyi rabotnik*, 1929 no. 9, p. 95) – seemingly a suggestion that further elections would not be necessary.

57. *Izvestiya*, 24 March 1929, p. 2.

58. *Vechernyaya Moskva*, 18 June 1929, p. 3; *Nauchnyi rabotnik*, 1929 no. 11, pp. 111–12.

59. *Vechernyaya Moskva*, 13 November 1929, p. 2.

60. *Nauchnyi rabotnik*, 1929 no. 9, p. 95; *Vechernyaya Moskva*, 28 May 1929, p. 3.

61. *Nauchnyi rabotnik*, 1929 no. 11, p. 103.

62. *Voprosy istorii KPSS*, 1966 no. 2, p. 34.

63. *Krasnoe studenchestvo*, 1929/30 no. 10, p. 5; Smolensk Archive, WKP 309: Communist fraction of Smolensk University administration, meeting of 3 October 1929.

64. *Podgotovka kadrov*, pp. 45–6; *Sovetskaya intelligentsiya*, p. 192.

65. *Vysshaya tekhnicheskaya shkola*, 1934 no. 1, p. 76.

66. By the beginning of 1934, the number of positions in scientific research institutes had grown to 96,000. *Kul'turnoe stroitel'stvo v tsifrakh (1930–1934 gg.)*, p. 148.

67. Data from *Podgotovka kadrov*, pp. 46–7 and 162–3.

68. *Ibid.*, p. 47.

69. *Ibid.*, and *Kul'turnoe stroitel'stvo SSSR 1935* (Moscow, 1936), p. 97.

70. Resolution of Narkompros RSFSR collegium, *Nauchnyi rabotnik*, 1929 no. 10, p. 97.

71. *Vysshaya tekhnicheskaya shkola*, 1934 no. 1, p. 84.

72. *Pravda*, 26 July 1928, p. 5, and *ibid.*, 4 August 1928, p. 8; 1,674 applications were received for the 43 places at Moscow Higher Technical School.

73. *Komsomol'skaya pravda*, 29 July 1928, p. 3; Lunacharsky and Skrypnik, *Narodnoe obrazovanie v SSSR*, p. 96.

74. See, for example, *Komsomol'skaya pravda*, 29 July 1928, p. 3.

75. See the resolution of a local party conference (August 1928) 'to carry out a ruthless purge of rabfaks and VUZy', Smolensk Archive, WKP 33; and purge recommendation from the party committee of Krasnaya Presnya raion (Moscow), V. Ukraintsev, *KPSS – organizator revol-yutsionnogo preobrazovaniya vysshei shkoly* (Moscow, 1963), p. 64.

76. Lominadze, who visited Smolensk as Central Committee rapporteur on the July (1928) plenum, evidently raised the question of excluding social aliens from the VUZy, since one of the questions put to him after his speech was: 'Comrade Lominadze, you say that sons of priests, kulaks and the like are studying in the VUZ; but why does [Narkompros] reinstate those that have been expelled, even if it is just in Smolensk University?' (Smolensk Archive, WKP 33: plenum of Smolensk gubkom, 16 July 1928). The Central Committee's only published recommendation on social purging came in November 1929, in the resolution 'On cadres for the national economy', which approved 'purging [*ochishchenie*] of hostile elements from the VTUZy – not as a campaign, but by systematically studying and improving the com-position of the student body' (*KPSS v rezolyutsiyakh*, IV, p. 340). But by this time, the mass purging of VUZy had died down, and the Central Committee may actually have been taking a moderate stand *against* purging by failing to approve local purge 'campaigns'.

77. *Kul'turnaya revolyutsiya v SSSR 1917–1965 gg.* (Moscow, 1967), p. 325.

78. Smolensk Archive, WKP 51: bureau of Western Oblast party com-mittee, 28 October 1929. See also *ibid.*, WKP 309: party fraction of Smolensk University administration, 4 July 1929, and bureau of party collective of the University, meetings of 2 and 20 March 1930; and *ibid.*, WKP 155: file of obkom agitprop department, letter from Rector of Smolensk University dated 9 January 1930.

79. *Kommunisticheskoe prosveshchenie*, 1936 no. 1, p. 21.

80. E.g. in the drop of 17,000 in the number of VUZ students classified as 'others' in 1928 (Robert A. Feldmesser, 'Aspects of Social Mobility in the Soviet Union', unpublished Ph.D. diss. (Harvard, 1955, p. 162);

and in the 11% drop-out of final-year students in Russian industrial VTUZy in the same year disclosed in *Vseobshchee obuchenie. Likvidatsiya negramotnosti. Podgotovka kadrov* (Moscow, 1930), p. 139.

81. *Sotsialisticheskoe stroitel'stvo SSSR*, pp. 406 and 410.
82. Data from *Podgotovka kadrov*, p. 19; *Sotsialisticheskoe stroitel'stvo*, p. 410; and de Witt, *Education and Professional Employment*, pp. 638–9.
83. *Krasnoe studenchestvo*, 1928/29 no. 13, p. 5.
84. *Komsomol'skaya pravda*, 2 August 1928, p. 3.
85. See, for example, the pseudonymous but apparently autobiographical account, M. Moskvin, *Khozhdenie po vuzam* (Paris, 1933).
86. John Dornberg, *Brezhnev, The Masks of Power* (New York, 1974), pp. 54–5; *Leonid I. Brezhnev. Pages From His Life* (New York, 1978), pp. 26–32.
87. Calculated from data in *Kul'turnoe stroitel'stvo SSSR* (Moscow, 1956), pp. 122–3, and *Podgotovka kadrov v SSSR*, pp. 14, 31, 36 and 64. For the 1928/29 calculation, general secondary schools with an industrial bias are not included in the industrial-training category.
88. de Witt, *Education and Professional Employment*, pp. 638–9.
89. *Itogi vypolneniya pervogo pyatiletnego plana razvitiya narodnogo khozyaistva SSSR* (Moscow, 1933), pp. 173 and 175.
90. See above, p. 126.
91. According to Gosplan's calculations, evidently made in the spring of 1929, even doubling the output of the FZU schools and tripling that of TsIT courses by 1932/33 would leave a deficit of approximately one million skilled and semi-skilled (*kvalifitsirovannye*) industrial workers. *Pyatiletnii plan*, I, p. 79. Note the misprints in the table, giving FZU figures to trade schools, TsIT figures to FZU, etc. The correct categories are quoted by speakers at the XVI Party Conference (April, 1929).
92. A general swing of opinion towards the FZU school in April and May of 1929 is noticeable in the discussion in *XVI konferentsiya VKP(b)*, especially pp. 210–14 (approving interjections during a Komsomol attack on TsIT principles and defence of the FZU), and the resolution on cultural construction of the XIV Congress of Soviets of the RSFSR, *XIV vserossiiskii syezd sovetov* (Moscow, 1929), Bulletin 19, p. 15.
93. Directive to all glavki, presidents of trusts and directors of enterprises, published *Komsomol'skaya pravda*, 9 June 1929, p. 1.
94. Accompanying order to all trusts and enterprises published *Torgovo-promyshlennaya gazeta*, 9 June 1929, p. 4; A. V. Koltsov, *Kul'turnoe stroitel'stvo v RSFSR v gody pervoi pyatiletki* (Moscow, 1960), p. 162.
95. TsGAOR 5451/15/715, p. 42: VTsSPS, Sector of Industrial Cadres.
96. *Itogi vypolneniya pervogo pyatiletnego plana*, p. 175.
97. *TsIT i ego metody NOT* (Moscow, 1970), p. 119.

98. *Ibid.*, p. 137; quotation from M. Anstett, *La Formation de la Main-d'Oeuvre qualifiée en Union sovietique de 1917 à 1954* (Paris, 1958), p. 115. Vesenkha, in a joint instruction with the Commissariat of Labour (21 March 1931), directed all construction organization 'immediately to begin short-term training of skilled construction workers by TsIT methods', but added the provision 'that the training should be undertaken directly on the construction sites', that is, not on the TsIT training bases. TsGANKh 3429/1/5254, p. 492: Orders of Vesenkha.

99. This was one of the main solutions to the critical shortage of labour at Krammashstroi reported by Serebryakov on 10 July 1931 (TsGANKh 3429/1/5242, p. 3: Minutes of Presidium of Vesenkha SSSR); and a similar case involving the Nizhny Novgorod auto plant was reported in *Ekonomicheskaya zhizn'*, 6 December 1929, p. 4.

100. TsGAOR 5451/15/715, p. 58: VTsSPS, Sector of Industrial Cadres, 1931; *Industrializatsiya SSSR 1929–1932* (Moscow, 1970), pp. 415–16.

101. Central Committee resolution 'On the work of the Central Institute of Labour', *Partiinoe stroitel'stvo*, 1931 no. 23, 63–4.

102. 'On cadres for the national economy', *KPSS v rezolyutsiyakh*, IV, pp. 344–5.

103. Vesenkha issued an order on the creation of higher and middle technical courses in enterprises on 24 May 1930. A memo from Petrovsky (Glavpromkadrov) to Dogadov (deputy chairman of Vesenkha) noted that such an order was long overdue, not because of the Central Committee's resolution (which was not mentioned) but because it 'is in fact only a formalization of the spontaneous movement to create such courses which exists at almost all the big enterprises'. TsGANKh 3429/1/5220, pp. 82–5.

104. It is unclear how common this practice was, but on 3 December 1932 the Commissar of Heavy Industry, Ordzhonikidze, signed an order awarding the title of engineer to the first graduating class (34 persons) of the Stalin Metallurgical *Zavod-VTUZ* in Leningrad. TsGANKh 7297/1/9: Orders of the Commissariat of Heavy Industry of the USSR.

105. See above, ch. 7.

106. TsGAOR 5451/15/715, pp. 227 and 230: VTsSPS, material of the VUZ and VTUZ group of the Sector of Industrial Cadres (1931).

107. *Nauchnyi rabotnik*, 1930 no. 2, p. 106; *ibid.*, 1930 no. 8–9, p. 99; *Krasnoe studenchestvo*, 1929/30 no. 30, p. 6; Barmin, *Iz opyta KPSS*, pp. 46–7.

108. A. N. Veselov, *Professional'no-tekhnicheskoe obrazovanie v SSSR* (Moscow, 1961), p. 296.

109. See reports in Iz. Kuzminov, 'Mastering the new factories and the new technology and the problem of cadres', *Problemy ekonomiki*, V (1935).

110. TsGAOR 5451/15/751, p. 65. According to this report, 100% of workers were in study programmes at the 'OGPU' mine, 45% at Rosselmash and 25% at 'Serp i molot' plant in Moscow.

111. See below, pp. 237–8.

112. Industrial, building and transport VTUZy graduated 62,700 students in the years 1931–34. About 11,000 of the graduates were in transport, but the great majority of the rest came from VTUZy under the Commissariat of Heavy Industry – approximately 50,000. The output of industrial technicums in the same period was around 110,000. But the number of persons holding engineers' and technicians' jobs in the enterprises of heavy industry increased by only 34,632 and 74,452 respectively in the years 1931–34. Many of the technicum graduates (40% of the graduating class of 1932!) went straight on to VTUZy. while a substantial proportion of VTUZ graduates went to work in the central apparats or proceeded on to graduate school. Data from *Kul'turnoe stroitel'stvo SSSR* (1940), p. 112; A. E. Beilin, *Kadry spetsialistov SSSR. Ikh formirovanie i rost* (Moscow, 1935), pp. 324–5; *Vysshaya tekhnicheskaya shkola*, 1934 no. 2, p. 97.

113. Beilin, *Kadry spetsialistov*, pp. 324–5.

114. TsGAOR 5451/15/734, pp. 96–7 and 171: VTsSPS, Sector of Industrial Cadres (1931): Stenogram of Leningrad meeting on part-time training of cadres; Memo to presidium of TsKK–RKI on training in industry.

115. Veselov, *Professional'no-tekhnicheskoe obrazovanie*, p. 297.

116. White-collar students constituted 17.3% of FZU pupils in 1930 and 15.4% in 1931, compared with 11.7% in 1928/29, when the total FZU numbers were very much smaller (Kuzminov, 'Mastering the new factories', p. 39; Veselov, *Professional'no-tekhnicheskoe obrazovanie*, p. 208). This was the immediate result of the influx following the collapse of the upper level of general secondary school. In the admissions of the autumn of 1931 (with the exception of Moscow and Leningrad schools), the white-collar percentage was much lower and the percentage of peasants rose (see above, ch. 8, note 120).

117. Although the large recruitment of peasants into industry had an impact on the composition of the apprenticeship school, there was a markedly lower percentage of peasants among the apprentices than among the adult workers in most major branches of industry: see data in M. Goltsman and L. Kogan, *Starye i novye kadry proletariata* (Moscow, 1934), p. 35. In the FZU schools of heavy industry, 68% of students in 1930 and 47% in 1932 were working-class (*Novye kadry tyazheloi promyshlennosti*, p. 106).

118. *Za promyshlennye kadry*, 1933 no. 5–6, p. 66; Veselov, *Professional'no-tekhnicheskoe obrazovanie*, p. 314.

119. *Za promyshlennye kadry*, 1933 no. 8–9, p. 72. This author was probably describing a situation more characteristic of Moscow and

Leningrad than, for example, Magnitogorsk. Whereas white-collar children constituted only 7% of those admitted to all Russian FZU schools in the autumn of 1931, they provided 15% and 13% of admissions in Moscow and Leningrad. TsGAOR 5451/15/715, pp. 45 and 179: VTsSPS, Sector of Industrial Cadres.

120. Veselov, *Professional'no-tekhnicheskoe obrazovanie*, p. 285.
121. Resolution of Sovnarkom USSR 'On speeding up the training of specialist–technicians from among the more qualified young workers', 21 June 1931, *Sobranie uzakonenii*, 1931 no. 42, art. 288.
122. *Za promyshlennye kadry*, 1933 no. 8–9, p. 76.
123. Data from Veselov, *Professional'no-tekhnicheskoe obrazovanie*, p. 285; Kuzminov, 'Mastering the new factories', p. 39; de Witt, *Education and Professional Employment*, pp. 604–5 and 636–7. For the purposes of this calculation, it is assumed that admissions to the VTUZy and technicums of heavy industry made up three-quarters of those in the general category of 'industry and construction'.
124. *Byulleten' vsesoyuznogo komiteta po vysshemu tekhnicheskomu obrazovaniyu pri TsIK SSSR*, 1933 no. 9–10, p. 7.

Chapter 10 The restoration of order: new policies in education, 1931–1934

1. See Kendall E. Bailes, *Technology and Society under Lenin and Stalin* (Princeton, 1978), ch. 7.
2. Bukharin was, of course, a former 'Right Oppositionist'. Krzhizhanovsky, though never an oppositionist, had had an acrimonious dispute with Stalin and Molotov over energy policy in 1930/31, as a as a result of which he was removed from the chairmanship of Gosplan and then from leadership of Vesenkha's energy authority: see Yu. N. Flakserman, *Gleb Maksimilianovich Krzhizhanovskii* (Moscow, 1964), ch. 6.
3. A list of such enterprises – including the Dnepr Hydroelectric Station, the metallurgical plants of Magnitogorsk and Makeevka, the Nizhny Novgorod Auto Plant, the Kramatorsk Machine-Building Plant and the chemical plants at Berezniki and Bobriki – is given in *Vtoraya sessiya TsIK Soyuza SSR 6 sozyva. Stenograficheskii otchet i postanovleniya 22–28 dek. 1931 g.* (Moscow, 1931), Bulletin 9, pp. 7–8.
4. Provision of worker cadres – for the new enterprises in general, for Magnitogorsk, Kuznetsk, Kramatorsk, Bobriki, the Nizhny Auto Plant etc. – was on the agenda of almost all meetings of the presidium of Vesenkha USSR (1931) in TsGANKh 3429/1/5239 and 3429/1/5242. It was a central preoccupation of the Sector of Industrial Cadres of VTsSPS (1931), as is indicated by the material in files TsGAOR 5451/15/715 and 5451/15/734. For the concern of the party leadership, see *Spravochnik partiinogo rabotnika*, vypusk 8 (Moscow, 1934), pp. 389–499.

5. Reference to this decision is in the resolution of Sovnarkom USSR and the Central Committee 'On the complete cessation of mobilization of workers from the bench for the needs of current campaigns by local party, soviet and other organizations', 25 March 1931, *Spravochnik partiinogo rabotnika*, vypusk 8, p. 386.

6. 'On the complete cessation of mobilization of workers...', *Spravochnik partiinogo rabotnika*, vypusk 8, pp. 385–6. In June, Vesenkha USSR cancelled its previous decrees (all dated 1929) giving students from the factories a 2-hour reduction of the working day, releasing engineers from the enterprises for the time necessary for teaching, and reducing the workload in the factory for workers enrolled in preparatory courses for VTUZ. TsGANKh 3429/1/5256, p. 293: Vesenkha instruction, signed Kosior, 25 June 1931.

7. Central Committee resolution 'On checking the implementation of the decision of the Central Committee of 25 March 1931...', 26 May 1931, *Spravochnik partiinogo rabotnika*, vypusk 8, pp. 386–7.

8. TsGAOR 5451/15/785, *passim* and p. 36: VTsSPS, Sector of Industrial Cadres (1931), file on the Trade Union Thousanders.

9. TsGAOR 5451/15/734, pp. 60 and 97: VTsSPS, Sector of Industrial Cadres (1931), file on the training of industrial cadres without taking them out of production.

10. See *Za industrializatsiyu*, 2 September 1931, p. 2, and *Vechernyaya Moskva*, 10 August 1932, p. 3.

11. Resolution 'On study programmes and regime in the elementary and middle school', 25 August 1932, *Narodnoe obrazovanie v SSSR. Obshcheobrazovatel'naya shkola. Sbornik dokumentov 1917–1973 gg.* (Moscow, 1974), p. 164.

12. *Vechernyaya Moskva*, 23 June 1932, p. 3.

13. *Ibid.*, 10 August 1932, p. 3.

14. *Ibid.*

15. I. Stalin, 'A new situation – new tasks of economic construction', 23 June 1931, *Sochineniya* xiii, p. 77.

16. On the industrialists' discussion of wages and salaries, see below, note 22, and articles by A. Yurisov, *Za industrializatsiyu*, 4 June 1931, p. 3, and 5 June 1931, p. 2. On *uravnilovka*, see *Za industrializatsiyu*, 12 March 1931, p. 2; on *obezlichka*, see *ibid.*, 26 April 1931, p. 2.

17. None of the newspapers published Stalin's speech of 23 June until 5 July, and the meeting of industrialists at which he spoke was not reported even in *Za industrializatsiyu*. *Pravda*'s editorial 'Work in a new way, lead in a new way' (25 June 1931), gave part of the content of Stalin's speech without attributing it to Stalin.

18. *Za industrializatsiyu*, 2 July 1931, p. 2; *ibid.*, 23 June 1931, p. 2.

19. Speech to the joint plenum of the Central Committee and Central Control Commission (December 1930), V. Molotov, *V bor'be za sotsializm. Rechi i statyi*, 2nd ed. (Moscow, 1935), pp. 63–4. Molotov

had made the same point at the Moscow party conference in September 1929, adding that the comrades he had in mind were 'especially...the Communist industrialists'. Ordzhonikidze, making a later appearance at the same meeting, expressed very lukewarm support for the attacks on the specialists: he said that he knew Groman, the Gosplan 'wrecker', to be 'a man who could not be bought', although his ideology made him dangerous. *Pervaya moskovskaya oblastnaya konferentsiya Vsesoyuznoi Kommunisticheskoi Partii (bol'shevikov). Stenograficheskii otchet*, part 1 (Moscow, 1929), pp. 42 and 181–2.

20. See his remarks to the Industrialists' Conference, *Za industrializatsiyu*, 2 February 1931, p. 2, and reproduced in the paper's editorial on 23 June 1931, p. 2.

21. *Za industrializatsiyu*, 27 June 1931, p. 2.

22. See speeches by Pavlunovsky (Vesenkha USSR), Veinberg (VTsSPS) and Ordzhonikidze and subsequent discussion, *Za industrializatsiyu*, 3 February 1931, pp. 1 and 3, and *ibid.*, 9 February 1931, p. 1.

23. In heavy industry, employees and engineering–technical personnel earned an average of 188% of an average worker's wage in 1925/26, 183% in 1926/27 and 174% in 1929. Data from *Sovetskoe stroitel'stvo SSSR* (Moscow, 1934), pp. 316–17.

24. See A. Putyatin, '*Uravnilovka* survives in the payment of engineering–technical personnel', *Za industrializatsiyu*, 15 December 1932, p. 3.

25. See tables in *Sovetskoe stroitel'stvo SSSR*, pp. 316–17, and M. Yanowitch, 'The Soviet Income Revolution', *Slavic Review*, December 1963, p. 688. In 1932, engineering–technical personnel earned an average of 263% and employees an average of 150% of an average worker's wage. This dropped to 236% and 126% (1935), 210% and 109% (1940) and 175% and 93% (1950).

26. *Pravda*, 8 August 1931, p. 1. Simultaneously, Vesenkha awarded prizes of 10,000 roubles to Professors Lebedev and Yushkevich, and 5,000 roubles to each of four engineers involved in the research projects. TsGANKh 3429/1/5259, p. 64: Order of Vesenkha, signed Ordzhonikidze, 7 August 1931.

27. See S. V. Krasikov, *S. M. Kirov v Leningrade* (Leningrad, 1966), pp. 96–109.

28. On the specialists' privileges during NEP, see above, ch. 4.

29. *Za industrializatsiyu*, 6 September 1931, p. 3.

30. *Pravda*, 3 August 1931, p. 2.

31. An eloquent and appropriate response to Stalin's speech of June 23 was the publication by the State Legal Publishing House of a 350-page collection of unrepealed laws guaranteeing various privileges to the specialists. See notice of publication of *Zakonodatel'stvo o spetsialistiakh v promyshlennosti, sel'skom khozyaistve, na transporte*, in *Za industrializatsiyu*, 14 July 1931, p. 4.

32. A. K. Grigoryants, *Formirovanie i razvitie tekhnicheskoi intelligentsii Armenii (1920–1965)* (Erevan, 1966), p. 169.

33. John Scott, *Behind the Urals* (Bloomington, Ind., 1973), pp. 231–5 and *passim*.

34. Resolution of Sovnarkom USSR and the Central Committee of the party 'On constructing houses for specialists', 25 March 1932, *Za industrializatsiyu*, 26 March 1932, p. 1.

35. *XVII konferentsiya VKP(b). Stenograficheskii otchet* (Moscow, 1932), p. 21.

36. *Za industrializatsiyu*, 27 January 1932, p. 3. Vesenkha's VTUZy alone graduated 12,026 new engineers in 1931.

37. *Ibid.*, 14 February 1932, p. 3; 8 March 1932, p. 3; 2 July 1932, p. 2.

38. *Ibid.*, 27 January 1932, p. 3; 1 February 1932, p. 3.

39. See Ordzhonikidze's comment, quoted above, p. 217, and Molotov, *XVII konferentsiya VKP(b)*, p. 154.

40. S. Koff, 'New tasks in the struggle for the higher school', *Za industrializatsiyu*, 2 July 1932, p. 2, and 4 July 1932, p. 2.

41. *Front nauki i tekhniki* was created in 1930 out of a merger of *Nauchnyi rabotnik*, the organ of the Section of Scientific Workers of the Teachers' Union, and *VARNITSO*, the organ of the Association of Scientific and Technical Workers for Support to Socialist Construction.

42. *Kommunisticheskoe prosveshchenie*, 1931 no. 2, p. 37.

43. *Front nauki i tekhniki*, 1932 no. 7–8, p. 104.

44. 'On study plans and regime in the higher school and technicums', 19 September 1932, *Narodnoe obrazovanie v SSSR*, pp. 420–26. Note that it was unusual for TsIK to issue such a decree: most of its major resolutions were issued together with Sovnarkom USSR; and in this period the main resolutions on educational questions normally came from the party Central Committee, or jointly from the Central Committee and Sovnarkom USSR.

45. At the end of 1933, the Committee had only 42 responsible workers listed in *Sostav rukovodyashchikh rabotnikov i spetsialistov Soyuza SSR* (Moscow, 1936), pp. 8–9, compared, for example, with 516 in the All-Union Radio Committee under Sovnarkom and 815 in the Supreme Council for Physical Culture of the USSR.

46. GUUZ, created in December 1932, took over responsibilities earlier held by the Commissariat's Sector of Cadres. TsGANKh 7297/1/9, p. 240: Orders of the Commissariat of Heavy Industry.

47. *Za industrializatsiyu*, 9 December 1932, p. 4; *Byulleten' vsesoyuznogo komiteta po vysshemu obrazovaniyu pri TsIK SSSR*, 1933 no. 9–10, p. 21; *Za promyshlennye kadry*, 1933 no. 1, p. 65.

48. In this capacity, he often acted as liaison between the scientific community and the commissariat. In January 1931, for example, he conveyed a request from the Academy of Sciences' Council for the Study

of Natural Productive Forces that Vesenkha finance its work. The request was approved by the presidium of Vesenkha. TsGANKh 3429/1/5239, p. 7: Minutes of the Presidium of Vesenkha, meeting of 13 January 1931.

49. See, for example, *Vysshaya tekhnicheskaya shkola*, 1934 no. 1, pp. 21–2.

50. Maltsev (deputy Commissar of Education of RSFSR), *Za industrializatsiyu*, 24 July 1932, p. 4.

51. TsGANKh 7297/1/8, pp. 98–9: Order of the Commissariat of Heavy Industry, signed Ordzhonikidze, 23 October 1932, on the creation of 'qualification commissions' for awarding academic titles. The commission scrutinizing professors, which included four Academicians, was headed by Professor Veger; the commission on *dotsenty* was headed by Professor Butyagin.

52. *Vysshaya tekhnicheskaya shkola*, 1934 no. 1, pp. 73–5.

53. TsGANKh 7297/1/8, p. 252: Order of the Commissariat of Heavy Industry, signed Kaganovich (Mikhail, not Lazar), 19 November 1932, on *aspirantura* in the VTUZy of heavy industry; *Za promyshlennye kadry*, 1933 no. 8–9, p. 174.

54. *Za promyshlennye kadry*, 1933 no. 7, p. 3.

55. The total number of VUZy and VTUZy dropped from 719 in 1932/33 to 594 in 1933/34. Among those downgraded was Kagan-Shabshai's Institute. *Kul'turnoe stroitel'stvo SSSR* (Moscow, 1940), p. 105; *Za promyshlennye kadry*, 1933 no. 5–6, p. 116.

56. Numbers of students in industrial and transport VTUZy dropped from 233,400 in 1932/33 to 188,300 in 1933/34. In 1933/34, 13% of all students in these VTUZy were part-timers, and 23% of students in industrial and transport technicums. N. de Witt, *Education and Professional Employment in the USSR* (Washington DC, 1961), pp. 638–9; *Kul'turnoe stroitel'stvo SSSR v tsifrakh 1930–34 gg.* (Moscow, 1935), p. 56.

57. In 1934, 14.6% of all those admitted to VUZ were secondary-school graduates, while 16.5% came from technicums and 40% from rabfaks. By 1938, the secondary schools provided 58.8% of VUZ entrants, while the share of technicums and rabfaks fell to 12.9% and 22.9%. *Kul'turnoe stroitel'stvo SSSR 1935* (Moscow, 1936), p. 96; *Kul'turnoe stroitel'stvo SSSR* (1940), p. 127.

58. Such articles appeared in *Krasnoe studenchestvo* from the October issue of 1932 (no. 23–4). For a student's lament that he had failed to learn basic work habits in four semesters at the VTUZ, see *Za promyshlennye kadry*, 1933 no. 4, pp. 72–9.

59. *Za promyshlennye kadry*, 1933 no. 1, pp. 40ff.

60. See above, p. 156.

61. *XVII syezd VKP. Stenograficheskii otchet* (Moscow, 1934), p. 564.

62. Bubnov reported that such suggestions were made at a meeting of

technicum representatives, probably held in July 1931 (*Kommunisti-cheskoe prosveshchenie*, 1931 no. 17, p. 5).

63. *Pravda*, 19 August 1931, p. 2.

64. See, for example, Bubnov's reflections on 'service relationships between people, the ordering of authority,...duties based on conscious proletarian discipline', *Kommunisticheskoe prosveshchenie*, 1933 no. 4, p. 26.

65. Epshtein's name appears with increasing frequency in Narkompros instructions published in the weekly bulletins. In April 1933, remaining deputy commissar, he was put in charge of the schools sector (the job he had held under Lunacharsky); and in June Bubnov signed an order celebrating his ten years of service to the commissariat and naming two schools in his honour. *Byulleten' NKP*, 1933 no. 9–10, p. 9; *ibid.*, 1933 no. 13, p. 9.

66. This backhanded tribute came from the young Korneichik, later an historian of Soviet education. It was published in *Kommunisticheskoe prosveshchenie*, 1933 no. 3, p. 23.

67. One account of the pre-history of the resolution states that 'Stetsky, then head of the *kul'tprop* department of the Central Committee... called a meeting of former directors and teachers of Tsarist gymnasia. The foundations of the new "reform" were laid here' (unpublished manuscript by I. A. Sats of Moscow, quoted with his permission). But Bubnov, at any rate, delivered the report (or one of the reports) to the Central Committee in July 1931 on the state of the schools. See A. S. Bubnov, *Shkola na povorote* (Moscow, 1931), p. 18.

68. The text of the decree is in *Narodnoe obrazovanie v SSSR*, pp. 156–61. The decree is often dated 5 September 1931, but this was actually the date of its publication in *Pravda*.

69. See below, pp. 227, for Krupskaya's comment of April 1931 on unidentified forces 'now organizing a campaign for the old school'.

70. *Za politekhnicheskuyu shkolu*, 1931 no. 11–12, p. 4.

71. Reports on local reactions from *Byulleten' NKP*, 1931 no. 52, p. 3; 1931 no. 55, p. 5; 1932 no. 1, p. 2; 1932 no. 2–3, p. 4; and *Kommunisticheskoe prosveshchenie*, 1933 no. 2, p. 107.

72. See *Kommunisticheskoe prosveshchenie*, 1933 no. 2, p. 107.

73. Bubnov, instruction of 29 January 1932 'On transfer of the schools to work on the new programmes', *Byulleten' NKP*, 1932 no. 10, p. 4.

74. Quoted M. E. Shilnikova, *Uchebno-vospitatel'naya rabota shkoly v 1930–1934 gg.* (Moscow, 1959), pp. 29–31. On the new programmes and methodological instructions, see *ibid.*, pp. 16–25, and *Krupskaya, Pedagogicheskie sochineniya*, x, pp. 428–37.

75. *Byulleten' NKP*, 1931 no. 48–9, p. 12; *Za politekhnicheskuyu shkolu*, 1931 no. 10, pp. 52ff. (model contract for the guidance of schools and enterprises).

76. *Za politekhnicheskuyu shkolu*, 1932 no. 4, pp. 3–4.

77. *XVII syezd VKP*, p. 565.

78. The Central Committee resolutions on the school 1931–35 were as follows: 'On the elementary and middle school' (25 August 1931); 'On the study programmes and regime in the elementary and middle school' (25 August 1932); 'On textbooks for the elementary and middle school' (12 February 1933); 'On the overloading of school-children and Pioneers with social and political tasks' (23 April 1934); 'On the teaching of civil history in the schools of the USSR' (with Sovnarkom USSR, 15 May 1934); 'On the teaching of geography in the elementary and middle schools of the USSR' (with Sovnarkom USSR, 15 May 1934); 'On the structure of the elementary and middle school in the USSR' (with Sovnarkom USSR, 15 May 1934); 'On the introduction of an elementary course of universal history and history of the USSR in the elementary and incomplete middle school' (9 June 1934); 'On the construction of schools in cities and on enrolment in higher pedagogical educational institutions' (with Sovnarkom USSR, 22 February 1935); 'On the publication and sale of textbooks for the elementary, incomplete middle and middle school' (with Sovnarkom USSR, 7 August 1935); 'On the organization of study and internal discipline in the elementary, incomplete middle and middle school' (with Sovnarkom USSR, 3 September 1935); and 'On school writing materials' (with Sovnarkom USSR, 14 September 1935).

79. B. M. Volin, formerly a RAPP activist, was head of the department in mid-1935 (*Kommunisticheskoe prosveshchenie*, 1936 no. 1, p. 21). The department was established in May 1935 by a Central Committee resolution on the reorganization of the former *kul'tprop* department quoted Malenko, *Voprosy istorii KPSS*, 1976 no. 2, p. 120.

80. 'On the study programmes and regime in the elementary and middle school', *Narodnoe obrazovanie v SSSR*, pp. 161–4.

81. 'On journal-textbooks', circular of 13 November 1931, signed by deputy commissar Maltsev, *Byulleten' NKP*, 1931 no. 53–4, p. 7.

82. *XVII syezd VKP*, pp. 564–5.

83. *Narodnoe obrazovanie v SSSR*, pp. 164–5.

84. 'On study programmes and regime in the elementary and middle school', *Narodnoe obrazovanie v SSSR*, p. 164.

85. See A. N. Veselov, *Professional'no-tekhnicheskoe obrazovanie v SSSR* (Moscow, 1961), pp. 297–9.

86. All-Union Commissariat of Heavy Industry, order on reconstruction of FZU schools dated 16 August 1933, *Organizatsiya truda*, 1933 no. 10(54) (no page number).

87. 'On factory apprenticeship schools', 15 September 1933, *Resheniya partii i pravitel'stva po khozyaistvennym voprosam*, II (Moscow, 1967), pp. 438–41.

88. Of 153,000 FZU drop-outs of 1933 on whom information was avail-

able, 53% left because of 'transfer to other study, change of work, change of profession and other reasons'. *Kul'turnoe stroitel'stvo SSSR v tsifrakh 1930–1934 gg.*, p. 74.

89. *Kul'turnoe stroitel'stvo SSSR* (1940), p. 107.
90. *Kul'turnoe stroitel'stvo SSSR 1935*, pp. 16–17; *Kul'turnoe stroitel'stvo SSSR* (1956), pp. 122–3.
91. *Kommunisticheskoe prosveshchenie*, 1931 no. 1, pp. 14–15. The announcement was followed by articles by A. Z. Ioanisiani 'On the theoretical front of pedagogy', *ibid.*, 1931 no. 2 and 4.
92. *Za kommunisticheskoe prosveshchenie*, 25 September 1931, p. 2.
93. *Kommunisticheskoe prosveshchenie*, 1931 no. 12, p. 14.
94. Quoted by Ravkin, *Narodnoe obrazovanie*, 1964 no. 2, p. 48.
95. Bubnov, *Kommunisticheskoe prosveshchenie*, 1931 no. 17, p. 18.
96. *Ibid.*, p. 9.
97. *Za politekhnicheskuyu shkolu*, 1931 no. 11–12, p. 11.
98. V. N. Shulgin, *Pamyatnye vstrechi* (Moscow, 1958), pp. 39–40.
99. Quoted Ravkin, *Narodnoe obrazovanie*, 1964, no. 2, p. 48.
100. A. Ya. Shumsky, *Za shkolu Marksa-Lenina* (Moscow–Leningrad, 1931), p. 58. This is the stenogram of Shumsky's speech to the joint meeting of the Central Committee of the Teachers' Union and the republican commissariats of education, 15 September 1931. Shumsky's role in the policy change is obscure, as is his career as a whole. He had been Ukrainian Commissar of Education between 1925 and 1927, but was purged from the Ukrainian government for nationalist deviations. He then appears to have spent some time in Leningrad before emerging on the Russian educational scene in the spring of 1931 (see above, p. 157) as an opponent of the pedagogical left. His tenure as head of the Teachers' Union was brief. In 1933, he was again branded a counter-revolutionary Ukrainian nationalist, and disappeared.
101. 'On some questions of the history of Bolshevism', *Proletarskaya revolyutsiya*, 1931 no. 6 (published late October or November); also, Stalin, *Sochineniya*, XIII, pp. 84–102.
102. *Sovetskaya pedagogika*, 1959 no. 3, p. 110.
103. Resolution of the Central Committee and Central Control Commission, 'On the fractional activity of Syrtsov, Lominadze and others', 1 December 1930, *VKP(b) v rezolyutsiyakh i resheniyakh syezdov, konferentsiyakh i plenumov TsK*, II (Moscow, 1941), p. 821.
104. *Vestnik Kommunisticheskoi Akademii*, 1931 no. 12, p. 41.
105. *Pedologiya*, 1931 no. 4(16), p. 11.
106. Krupskaya, *Pedagogicheskie sochineniya*, X, p. 450.
107. A. S. Zaluzhnyi, *Lzhenauka pedologiya v 'trudakh' Zalkinda* (Moscow, 1937), pp. 20–1.
108. *Na putyakh k novoi shkole*, 1932 no. 2–3, p. 72.
109. The phrase is from N. S. Timasheff, *The Great Retreat. The Growth*

and *Decline of Communism in Russia* (New York, 1946). For discussion of the concept, see below, p. 249.

110. See above, ch. 2.

111. The basic disciplines were twice listed in the decree, geography being included both times but history only once. *Narodnoe obrazovanie v SSSR*, pp. 157 and 158.

112. 'On the study programmes and regime in the elementary and middle school', *Narodnoe obrazovanie v SSSR*, pp. 161–2.

113. 'On the teaching of civil history in the schools of the USSR' and 'On the teaching of geography in the elementary and middle school of the USSR', 15 May 1934, *Narodnoe obrazovanie v SSSR*, pp. 166–7.

114. 'On the introduction of an elementary course of universal history and history of the USSR in the elementary and incomplete middle school', 9 June 1934, *Narodnoe obrazovanie v SSSR*, p. 168.

115. On 1 January 1935, only 22% of history teachers and 17% of social studies teachers had entered the teaching profession before 1925 (compared with 44% of mathematics teachers and 47% of language and literature teachers), 28% of the history teachers had entered the profession between 1931 and 1934. *Trud v SSSR. Statisticheskii spravochnik* (Moscow, 1936), p. 323.

116. S. Kh. Chanbarisov, *Formirovanie sovetskoi universitetskoi sistemy (1917–1938 gg.)* (Ufa, 1973), p. 287.

117. The scientists' letter is quoted, *ibid.*, p. 288, and the Central Committee's resolution 'On the functions [*tselevykh ustanovkakh*] of the universities' is paraphrased, *ibid.*, p. 292. The Central Committee resolution, which was not published, is referred to by other Soviet historians like Kim and Ukraintsev, but always without citation of source.

118. Chanbarisov, *Formirovanie*, pp. 294 and 299–30; E. V. Chutkerashvili, *Razvitie vysshego obrazovaniya v SSSR* (Moscow, 1961), p. 185.

119. M. A. Verchenko, 'The re-establishment of the historical faculty and its role in the struggle for training of cadres of Marxist historians', *Iz istorii Moskovskogo Universiteta 1917–1941* (Moscow, 1955), p. 262.

120. See George M. Enteen, 'Marxist Historians during the Cultural Revolution: A Case Study of Professional In-Fighting', Sheila Fitzpatrick, ed., *Cultural Revolution in Russia, 1928–1931* (Bloomington, Ind., 1977).

121. L. P. Bushchik, *Ocherki razvitiya shkol'nogo istoricheskogo obrazovaniya v SSSR* (Moscow, 1961), p. 262.

122. The outlines were prepared by Vanag, a former student of Pokrovsky; Mints, also a former Pokrovsky student but an adherent of the Yaroslavsky faction; and the Ukrainian Marxist Lozinsky. Resolution of Sovnarkom USSR and the Central Committee, 'On the front of

historical science', *Direktivy VKP(b) i postanovleniya sovetskogo pravitel'stva o narodnom obrazovanii 1917–1947 gg.*, II (Moscow–Leningrad, 1947), p. 183.

123. The perhaps impressionistic comment on Kirov's unwillingness is from Adam B. Ulam, *Stalin* (New York, 1973), p. 379.

124. 'Notes on the outline of a textbook on "History of the USSR"' and 'Notes on the outline of a textbook on "Modern History"', signed I. Stalin, A. Zhdanov and S. Kirov, dated 8 and 9 August 1934, I. V. Stalin, *Sochineniya*, I (XIV) (Stanford, 1967), pp. 37–45.

125. Bushchik, *Ocherki*, pp. 275 and 282.

126. Pokrovsky died in 1932. In 1936, Sovnarkom and the Central Committee noted the 'harmful tendencies and attempts to liquidate history as a science, linked in the first place with the mistaken historical views characteristic of the so-called "historical school of Pokrovsky" and widespread among some of our historians'. These views were described as 'anti-Marxist, essentially anti-Leninist, liquidationist [and] anti-scientific' ('On the front of historical science', *Direktivy VKP(b)*, II, p. 183). A number of Pokrovskyite historians were arrested. In 1939 and 1940, two volumes of denunciation of Pokrovsky appeared under the titles *Protiv istoricheskoi kontseptsii M. N. Pokrovskogo* and *Protiv antimarksistskoi kontseptsii M. N. Pokrovskogo*.

127. See Konstantin F. Shteppa, *Russian Historians and the Soviet State* (New Brunswick, NJ, 1962), p. 179 and *passim.*

128. 'Bourgeois' authors of basic historical texts published after the 1934 decree include V. I. Picheta, M. N. Tikhomirov, V. S. Sergeev, E. V. Tarle, E. A. Kosminsky, M. V. Bazilevich and S. V. Bakhrushin. Bakhrushin, Bazilevich, Picheta and V. Grekov (one of the most prominent of the 'bourgeois' historians) contributed to the two-volume attack on Pokrovsky published in 1939/40. *Moskovskii Universitet za 50 let* (Moscow, 1967), p. 570, note 1; Bushchik, *Ocherki, passim.*

129. The reference is to the *Kratkii kurs istorii VKP(b)* (Moscow, 1938), written by a collective of party historians under Stalin's close supervision or, according to contemporary rumour, by Stalin himself.

Chapter 11   The 'New Class': social mobility and education under Stalin

1. This statement is not to be found in any of Stalin's published speeches or articles. But there are at least two authoritative citations attributing it to Stalin. In 1938, S. Kaftanov, chairman of the All-Union Committee on the Higher School, warned against unjustified expulsion of students whose relatives had been arrested, since this was contrary to 'the instructions of comrade Stalin, the party's Leader, that "a son does not answer for his father"' (*Vysshaya shkola*, 1938 no. 3, p. 16).

At the XVIII Party Congress of 1939, Zhdanov referred to the premise 'more than once emphasized by Stalin' that 'a son is not answerable for his father [*syn za ottsa ne otvetchik*]' (*XVIII syezd VKP(b). Stenograficheskii otchet* (Moscow, 1939), p. 523).

2. *Izvestiya*, 24 February 1930, p. 5, carries two small personal announcements typical of the genre: 'I, as the son of a former priest, break all ties with the spiritual calling. [Signed] Yurii Mikhailovich, Teacher.' 'I, Evgeniya Afanasyevna Golubtsova, renounce my father, a psalm-reader.'

3. 'On admissions to higher educational institutions and technicums', resolution of TsIK and Sovnarkom USSR, 29 December 1935, *Narodnoe obrazovanie v SSSR. Obshcheobrazovatel'naya shkola. Sbornik dokumentov, 1917–1923 gg.* (Moscow, 1974), p. 426.

4. 'On the draft of the constitution of the USSR', 25 November 1936, Stalin, *Sochineniya* 1 (XIV), edited by Robert H. McNeal (Stanford, 1967), p. 169.

5. One must always be hesitant about drawing a negative conclusion, but this is strongly suggested by the absence of questions on social origin or parents' occupations in the forms filled out by schoolchildren, VUZ applicants, etc. in the late 1940s. The data are examined in my paper 'Social Mobility in the Late Stalin Period: Recruitment into the Intelligentsia and Access to Higher Education, 1945–1953', delivered at the Kennan Institute Conference 'The Soviet Union in the 1940s' (Washington DC, April 1977).

6. Social breakdown of VUZy from *Kul'turnoe stroitel'stvo SSSR* (Moscow, 1940), p. 114; population breakdown from N. de Witt, *Education and Professional Employment in the USSR* (Washington DC, 1961), p. 352.

7. *Pedagogicheskii slovar'*, II (Moscow, 1960), p. 246. There was apparently no decree abolishing the rabfaks: they were gradually phased out in Russia and elsewhere as the secondary schools gained strength. However, it should be noted that institutions similar to rabfaks were created in newly acquired Soviet territories and in post-war Eastern Europe. See, for example, the resolution of the Estonian Sovnarkom in 1941 'On the organization of preparatory courses for the entry of young people from the toiling masses into higher educational institutions', *Kul'turnaya zhizn' v SSSR 1928–1941* (Moscow, 1976), p. 769.

8. Resolution of Sovnarkom USSR 'On the establishment of tuition fees in the senior classes of middle schools and in higher educational institutions of the USSR and on change in the procedure of awarding stipends', 2 October 1940, *Sobranie postanovlenii pravitel'stva SSSR*, 1940 no. 27, art. 637.

9. See resolutions of Sovnarkom USSR 'On the formation of the Chief Administration of Labour Reserves under Sovnarkom USSR' and

'On the conscription of urban and kolkhoz youth into trade schools, railway schools and FZO schools' (October 1940), *Sobranie postanovlenii pravitel'stva SSSR*, 1940 no. 25, articles 602 and 603; and E. S. Kotlyar, *Gosudarstvennye trudovye rezervy SSSR v gody Velikoi Otechestvennoi voiny* (Moscow, 1975).

10. For a more detailed discussion, see Fitzpatrick, 'Social Mobility in the Late Stalin Period'.

11. *Statisticheskii spravochnik SSSR za 1928 g.* (Moscow, 1929), pp. 42–3; *Itogi vsesoyuznoi perepisi naseleniya 1959 goda* (Moscow, 1962), pp. 164–5.

12. See, for example, Solomon M. Schwarz, *Labor in the Soviet Union* (New York, 1951), pp. 77–8.

13. Kotlyar, *Gosudarstvennye trudovye rezervy*, p. 14.

14. A. G. Aganbegyan and V. F. Mayer, *Zarabotnaya plata v SSSR* (Moscow, 1959), p. 202.

15. Alex Inkeles and Raymond Bauer, *The Soviet Citizen* (New York, 1968), p. 145 and ch. 6, *passim*.

16. A. N. Veselov, *Professional'no-tekhnicheskoe obrazovanie v SSSR* (Moscow, 1961), p. 298.

17. For a teacher's account of the *fakul'tety osobogo naznacheniya* (FONy) raising the qualifications of managers, see Alexander Miropolsky, 'Faculties of Special Purpose: Odessa', George L. Kline, ed., *Soviet Education* (New York, 1957).

18. *Kul'turnoe stroitel'stvo SSSR* (1940), p. 137. Outside industry and transport, the biggest worker training programmes in 1937/38 were in agriculture and trade, and the biggest specialist training programmes were for economists, lawyers and teachers.

19. *Profsoyuzy Moskvy. Ocherki istorii* (Moscow, 1975), p. 228.

20. Resolution on 'The Third Five-Year Plan', *KPSS v rezolyutsiyakh*, v (Moscow, 1971), p. 367.

21. L. Trotsky, *The Revolution Betrayed* (New York, 1937), ch. 5.

22. Data from de Witt, *Educational and Professional Employment*, p. 781, and *Kul'turnoe stroitel'stvo v SSSR* (1940), p. 112.

23. Kendall Bailes, *Technology and Society under Lenin and Stalin* (Princeton, 1978), pp. 188–9, takes the absence of social data on graduations as an indication that Soviet policies of proletarian *vydvizhenie* may have been less effective than claimed; and, in further support of this argument, he cites de Witt's computation – based on figures for admissions and graduations during the First and Second Five-Year Plan – of a drop-out rate much higher than that shown in official VUZ statistics. There certainly *were* extravagant claims, especially those based on statistics for admissions in the early 1930s. But there is really no mystery about the publication of social data on admissions but not on graduations: the VUZy collected admissions data because they had to meet Central Committee require-

ments which were expressed in terms of admissions percentages. No central bureaucracy set targets for graduations, so such data were rarely collected.

In fact, both the social and aggregate data on admissions are almost worthless because of very high student mobility, especially during the reorganization of VUZy in the early 1930s, which resulted in more than one VUZ claiming the same student in the annual report on admissions. This makes de Witt's computation a rather academic exercise (and, as the present author discovered, it also makes it impossible to calculate purge-related drop-out for different social groups during the early years of the First Five-Year Plan: some groups register a statistically remarkable *negative* rate of drop-out). Almost all the social data cited in this study refer to total student population, not admissions. It is very unlikely that the official statistics conceal an excessively high rate of drop-out for *vydvizhentsy*, since the data on Communist VUZ students can be checked from other sources: of approximately 110,000 Communists entering higher education during the First Five-Year Plan, 70–80,000 had already graduated by January 1937, and the large entering class of 1932 was still in school (see above, pp. 187–8, and below, pp. 241–2).

24. *Sotsialisticheskoe stroitel'stvo SSSR* (Moscow, 1934), p. 410.
25. *The Second Five-Year Plan for the Development of the National Economy of the USSR* (London, 1937), pp. 632–3. The 1937 figures are estimates, but where they can be checked against de Witt's actual figures they appear to have been quite accurate.
26. *Sostav rukovodyashchikh rabotnikov i spetsialistov Soyuza SSR* (Moscow, 1936), pp. 18–19.
27. A. V. Iovlev, *Deyatel'nost' KPSS po podgotovke voennykh kadrov* (Moscow, 1976), p. 129.
28. M. N. Rutkevich, 'Social sources of recruitment of the Soviet intelligentsia', *Voprosy filosofii*, 1967 no. 6, pp. 22–3.
29. Yu. V. Arutyunyan, *Sotsial'noe i natsional'noe. Opyt etnograficheskikh issledovanii po materialam Tatarskoi ASSR* (Moscow, 1973), pp. 46–7.
30. I. N. Yudin, *Sotsial'naya baza rosta KPSS* (Moscow, 1973), p. 186.
31. *Ibid.*, p. 181.
32. *Kommunisticheskaya partiya – um, chest' i sovest' nashei epokhi* (Moscow, 1969), pp. 221–2.
33. *Sostav rukovodyashchikh rabotnikov i spetsialistov Soyuza SSR*, pp. 8–9. The group included responsible personnel in commissariats and other government agencies (down to the raion level), industrial administration and enterprises (down to the level of *mastera* and *desyatniki*), scientific research institutes and VUZy. Military officers and party officials were excluded, as were certain categories of trained specialists working in their professions, notably doctors and teachers.

34. *Ibid.*, pp. 8–11.
35. *Partiinoe stroitel'stvo*, 1937 no. 10 (May 15), p. 24. This figure, unlike that in Yudin (*Sotsial'naya baza*, p. 181), evidently included Communists in the armed forces with higher military education.
36. *Ibid.*, and *Partiinaya zhizn'*, 1977 no. 21, p. 30.
37. Yudin, *Sotsial'naya baza*, p. 186; *Vsesoyuznaya partiinaya perepis' 1927 goda. Osnovnye itogi perepisi* (Moscow, 1927), p. 58.
38. See his speeches to the February–March plenum of the Central Committee (1937), I. V. Stalin, *Sochineniya*, edited by Robert H. McNeal, vol. 1 (XIV) (Stanford, 1967), pp. 203 and 236. The question of Stalin's intentions and the link between the *vydvizhenie* and the Great Purge is discussed in my article (Stalin and the Making of a New Elite, 1928–1939', *Slavic Review*, forthcoming).
39. The Great Purge and the emergence of the 'Men of 1938' are illuminatingly discussed in Jerry F. Hough, *The Soviet Prefects* (Cambridge, Mass., 1969), pp. 38–47, and David Granick, *Management of the Industrial Firm in the USSR* (New York, 1954), ch. 3.
40. *Bol'shaya sovetskaya entsiklopediya*, XXXIV, 2nd ed. (Moscow, 1955), pp. 142–3.
41. A. Chuyanov, *Na stremnine veka. Zapiski sekretarya obkoma* (Moscow, 1976), pp. 1–41, *passim*.
42. *Ibid.*, pp. 41–2.
43. 'From the report of the Commissariat of Heavy Machinery of the USSR to the Central Committee of the Communist Party on work with leading cadres' (not earlier than 1 December 1939), *Industrializatsiya SSSR 1938–1941 gg. Dokumenty i materialy* (Moscow, 1973), pp. 228 and 230.
44. *Ibid.*, p. 230.
45. These examples come from David Granick's card files on industrial enterprises and managers in the 1930s. The data on Morozov is from *Mashinostroenie*, 27 July 1939, p. 4, and on Padalko from *Industriya*, 11 April 1938, p. 4.
46. On turnover of industrial managers 1936–41, see Granick, *Management*, ch. 3. Outside the industrial sphere, see P. A. Serebryakov's brief but poignant account of his promotion in 1938, as a 29-year-old Komsomol activist and junior faculty member, to be director of the Leningrad Conservatorium of Music: *Leningradskaya konservatoriya v vospominaniyakh* (Leningrad, 1962), p. 282.
47. 'Extract from a memorandum of TsSU USSR to the Presidium of Gosplan USSR on the results of the count of leading cadres and specialists on 1 January 1941', *Industrializatsiya SSSR 1938–1941 gg.*, pp. 269–79.
48. *Kul'turnoe stroitel'stvo SSSR* (1940), p. 112.
49. 'Extract from a memorandum of TsSU USSR', *Industrializatsiya SSSR 1938–1941 gg.*, p. 270.

50. These examples are taken from the Hough files (see below, note 51).
51. Based on Jerry Hough's card files on party and government personnel. For 104 of the 125 full members of the 1952 Central Committee, the biographies are complete enough to determine whether the subject did or did not have higher education, and when and where he received it. (There are, of course, possibilities of error, especially in those cases when date of graduation but not date of entrance to higher education is given.) Those who went to Communist VUZy, the Institute of Red Professors or Marxist–Leninist courses under the Central Committee are included as having higher education; those who went to Higher Party School or other types of Marxist–Leninist courses, or whose biographies attribute to them an unspecified type of 'incomplete higher education', are excluded.
52. Khrushchev's own account of his days at the Industrial Academy is in *Khrushchev Remembers* (Boston, 1970), pp. 34–44. The great battle with the 'right opportunists' is recalled in *Za industrializatsiyu*, 1 June 1932, p. 3.
53. For short outlines of Brezhnev's career, see *Ezhegodnik Bol'shoi Sovetskoi entsiklopedii 1971* (Moscow, 1971), p. 583, and *Deputaty verkhovnogo soveta SSSR. Sed'moi sozyv* (Moscow, 1966), p. 72.
54. The Hough files include biographical data, including data on education, for 115 ministers and deputy ministers in the All-Union government in 1952 – about 20% of the total; 15 of the ministers were also full members of the Central Committee, and are thus included in the analysis of Central Committee members offered above as well as the analysis of the government group.
55. See above, p. 96.
56. Hough files. Members of this group were neither full nor candidate members of the Central Committee in 1952. Their oblasts were the less important ones, and predominantly agricultural rather than industrial.
57. Hough, *The Soviet Prefects*, pp. 47 and 76.
58. For short biographies of these men, see *Ezhegodnik Bol'shoi entsiklopedii 1971* and *Deputaty verkhovnogo soveta SSSR* (1966).
59. L. Trotsky, *The Revolution Betrayed* (New York, 1937).
60. The phrase comes from M. Djilas, *The New Class. An Analysis of the Communist System* (London, 1966).
61. See *Vsesoyuznoe soveshchanie zhen khozyaistvennikov i inzhenerno-tekhnicheshkikh rabotnikov tyazheloi promyshlennosti. Stenograficheskii otchet 10–12 maya 1936 g.* (Moscow, 1936), and *Vsesoyuznoe soveshchanie zhen komandnogo i nachal'stvuyushchego sostava RKKA. Stenograficheskii otchet* (Moscow, 1937).
62. Nicholas S. Timasheff, *The Great Retreat. The Growth and Decline of Communism in Russia* (New York, 1946).
63. Vera S. Dunham, *In Stalin's Time. Middleclass Values in Soviet Fiction* (Cambridge, 1976), ch. 1.

64. Kotlyar, *Gosudarstvennye trudovye rezervy*, p. 220.

65. For Krupskaya's appeals and protests to Ordzhonikidze, Andreev and Zhdanov in 1936/37 against the removal of labour from the curriculum, see Dridzo, *Istoricheskii arkhiv*, 1960 no. 2, 184–5; Sharapov, *Voprosy istorii KPSS*, 1959 no. 1, pp. 149–50; and Krupskaya's letter to Zhdanov of 9 February 1937, *Sovetskaya pedagogika*, 1961 no. 11, pp. 142–3. According to his biographers, Bubnov also objected to the removal of labour from the curriculum and the abolition of school workshops. A. Binevich and Z. Serebryansky, *Andrei Bubnov* (Moscow, 1964), p. 65.

66. Resolution of Sovnarkom USSR and the Central Committee 'On the work of higher educational institutions and the leadership of the higher school', 23 June 1936, *Narodnoe obrazovanie v SSSR*, p. 428.

67. The universities of Erevan and Central Asia re-established philological faculties in 1933; and in the Ukraine, the universities of Kharkov and Kiev revived philosophy, literature and economics from around 1926. Leningrad University recovered its philological faculty (the former LIFLI) in 1937. The last to achieve full restoration was Moscow University, whose professors and administration agitated in vain for the return of the philological faculty (then existing independently as MIFLI, the Moscow Institute of Philosophy, Literature and Art) in 1933 and again in 1935. MIFLI was in fact merged with Moscow University in 1942. E. V. Chutkerashvili, *Razvitie vysshego obrazovaniya v SSSR* (Moscow, 1961), p. 89; Sh. Kh. Chanbarisov, *Formirovanie sovetskoi universitetskoi sistemy (1917–1938 gg.)* (Ufa, 1973), pp. 299 and 307–8; *Istoriya Leningradskogo Universiteta* (Leningrad, 1969), p. 336; *Moskovskii Universitet za 50 let sovetskoi vlasti* (Moscow, 1967), pp. 74, 459 and 628.

68. See N. Reshetovskaya, *Sanya. My Life with Aleksandr Solzhenitsyn* (Indianapolis and New York, 1974), pp. 15–17.

69. This is discussed at greater length in my 'Culture and Politics under Stalin: a Reappraisal', *Slavic Review*, June 1976.

70. See Fitzpatrick, 'Culture and Politics under Stalin', p. 226.

71. See Inkeles and Bauer, *The Soviet Citizen*, ch. 6; Dunham, *In Stalin's Time*, pp. 91–3, 107–8, 149–50.

72. Quoted Dunham, *In Stalin's Time*, p. 92, from P. Angelina, 'People of the kolkhoz fields', *Oktyabr'*, 1948 no. 6, p. 125.

73. Quoted Dunham, *In Stalin's Time*, p. 108, from V. Kochetov, 'The Zhurbin family', *Zvezda*, 1952 no. 1, pp. 25 and 55.

74. V. S. Emelyanov, *O vremeni, o tovarishchakh, o sebe*, 2nd ed. (Moscow, 1974), pp. 238–9.

75. The most controversial entries in the competition were those of Corbusier and I. V. Zholtovsky, a respected 'bourgeois' architect of pre-revolutionary reputation whose preference was for the style of the Italian Renaissance. The committee, headed by Molotov, awarded

no first prize, but gave second prize to the wedding-cake design submitted by B. Yofan, V. Gelfreith and V. Shchuko. Lunacharsky evidently clashed with Molotov on the committee; and after the result was announced in 1932 he received a passionate protest from Le Corbusier on the incongruity of the committee's choice and Soviet modernization objectives. See Anatole Kopp, *Town and Revolution. Soviet Architecture and City Planning 1917–1935* (London, 1970), pp. 214 and 222–3; A. V. Lunacharsky, *Ob izobrazitel'nom iskusstve*, I (Moscow, 1966), pp. 479–88 (Theses of Lunacharsky's paper on the tasks of proletarian architecture in connection with the construction of the Palace of Soviets), and 489–92 (letter of Le Corbusier to Lunacharsky, dated 13 May 1932).

Bibliography

I. Archival sources

Central State Archive of the National Economy of the USSR (TsGANKh), Moscow
Central State Archive of the October Revolution and Socialist Construction of the USSR (TsGAOR), Moscow
Central State Archive of the RSFSR (TsGA RSFSR), Moscow

Materials used from these three archives include:
(1) The Commissariat of Education of the RSFSR (Narkompros): protocols of meetings of the collegium and presidium of the collegium, June 1918 to September 1929 (1928 and some months of 1926 and 1927 are missing).
(2) The Central Council of Trade Unions of the USSR (VTsSPS), Sector of Industrial Cadres: stenograms, correspondence and other materials, 1931–33
(3) The Supreme Council of the National Economy of the USSR (Vesenkha): protocols of meetings of the presidium, 1931; orders and instructions of the commissar and his deputies, 1930/31; material of Glavpromkadrov, the department responsible for educational institutions under Vesenkha, 1930
(4) The Commissariat of Heavy Industry of the USSR (Narkomtiazhprom): orders and instructions, 1932/33
(Citations of Soviet archival material are by *fond/opis'/delo*.)

Smolensk Archive. This archive, now in the possession of the US government, is available on microfilm. It includes a large amount of material on Smolensk University, 1928–30. For a general survey of its contents, see Merle Fainsod, *Smolensk under Soviet Rule* (London, 1958)

II. Newspapers

Ekonomicheskaya zhizn'
Izvestiya
Komsomol'skaya pravda
Pravda

Rabochaya gazeta

Torgovo-promyshlennaya gazeta (renamed *Za industrializatsiyu* in January 1930)

Trud

Uchitel'skaya gazeta (renamed *Za kommunisticheskoe prosveshchenie* in 1930; reverted to original title in 1936)

Vechernyaya Moskva

III. Journals

Byulleten' komiteta po vysshemu tekhnicheskomu obrazovaniyu pri TsIK SSSR, from 1933

Byulleten' Oppozitsii (Bol'shevikov–Lenintsev), journal of Trotskyite emigration, published Paris etc. from 1929

Ezhenedel'nik Narodnogo Komissariata Prosveshcheniya RSFSR, house journal of Narkompros, publishing circulars, instructions, decrees etc.; from 1930, appeared under title *Byulleten' Narodnogo Komissariata po Prosveshcheniyu RSFSR*

Front nauki i tekhniki, published from 1931 as organ of VARNITSO and the Section of Scientific Workers of the Teachers' Union

Izvestiya TsK, organ of the agitprop department of the Central Committee; from November 1929, appeared as *Partiinoe stroitel'stvo*

Khozyaistvo i upravlenie, organ of TsKK and Rabkrin USSR, 1925–27

Kommunisticheskaya revolyutsiya, journal of agitprop (later, kultprop) department of the Central Committee, 1920–35

Kommunisticheskii put' (Saratov)

Kommunisticheskoe prosveshchenie, monthly journal of Narkompros RSFSR, from 1930

Krasnaya molodezh', journal of proletarian students, edited by V. M. Molotov, 1924/25

Krasnoe studenchestvo, organ of Central and Moscow Bureaux of Union of Proletarian Students from 1923/24

Molodaya gvardiya, organ of Komsomol Central Committee

Na putyakh k novoi shkole, organ of pedagogical section of GUS, Narkompros, and later of the Society of Marxist Pedagogues of the Communist Academy, 1922–33

Narodnoe prosveshchenie, Narkompros monthly, 1918–30

Narodnyi uchitel', monthly organ of the Central Committee of the Teachers' Union, 1924–35

Nauchnyi rabotnik, monthly organ of the Section of Scientific Workers of the Teachers' Union, 1925–30

Nizhnevolzhskii prosveshchenets (Saratov)

Organizatsiya truda, organ of Central Institute of Labour, 1921–40

Pedologiya, 1928–32

Planovoe khozyaistvo, organ of Gosplan USSR

Politekhnicheskii trud v shkole, organ of schools administration of Narkompros RSFSR 1929/30; subsequently appeared as *Za politekhnicheskuyu shkolu*, 1931–34

Proftekhnicheskoe obrazovanie, journal of Narkompros RSFSR, renamed *Za kachestvo kadrov* in 1931

Prosveshchenie na Urale (Sverdlovsk)

Prosveshchenie Sibiri (Novosibirsk)

Rabotnik prosveshcheniya, journal of the Teachers' Union

Revolyutsiya i kul'tura, published by *Pravda* from 1927

Rodnoi yazyk i literatura v trudovoi shkole

Russkaya shkola za rubezhom, published in Prague from 1923

Sotsialisticheskii vestnik, journal of Menshevik emigration

Sovetskoe stroitel'stvo, organ of TsIK from 1926

Statisticheskoe obozrenie, 1927–30

Ustanovka rabochei sily, organ of Central Institute of Labour, 1926–31

Vestnik Kommunisticheskoi Akademii, 1922–35

Vestnik truda, monthly journal of the Central Council of Trade Unions until 1929

Voprosy prosveshcheniya na Severnom Kavkaze (Rostov on Don)

Vysshaya tekhnicheskaya shkola, journal of the Committee on Higher Technical Education under TsIK, 1934–36

Za promyshlennye kadry, organ of Vesenkha, later of the Commissariat of Heavy Industry of the USSR, 1930–37

Za vseobshchee obuchenie, organ of the Committee for Universal Primary Education of Sovnarkom RSFSR and Narkompros RSFSR

Zhizn' rabochei shkoly, 1923–31

IV. *Laws, collections of documents and archival materials*

Danilova, E. N. *Deistvuyushchee zakonodatel'stvo o trude SSSR i soyuznykh respublik*, 2 vols., 2nd ed. (Moscow, 1927)

Direktivy VKP(b) i postanovleniya sovetskogo pravitel'stva o narodnom obrazovanii, 1917–1947 gg., 2 vols. (Moscow–Leningrad, 1947)

Direktivy VKP(b) po voprosam prosveshcheniya, 3rd ed. (Moscow–Leningrad: Narkompros RSFSR, 1931)

Industrializatsiya SSSR, 1926–1941. Dokumenty i materialy, 3 vols. (Moscow, 1969–1973)

Istoriya kolkhoznogo prava. Sbornik zakonodatel'nykh materialov SSSR i RSFSR, 1917–1958 gg., 2 vols. (Moscow, 1958–59)

Istoriya sovetskoi konstitutsii. Sbornik dokumentov, 1917–1957 (Moscow, 1957)

Karateev, V. F. (compiler). *Spravochnik dlya zaveduyushchego nachal'noi i srednei shkoly: ofitsial'nye materialy* (Moscow, 1933)

Komsomol i vysshaya shkola. Dokumenty i materialy syezdov, konferen-

tsii, TsK VLKSM po rabote vuzovskogo komsomola (1918–1968 gg.)
(Moscow, 1968)

KPSS v rezolyutsiyakh i resheniyakh syezdov, konferentsii i plenumov TsK, 10 vols., 8th ed. (Moscow, 1970–73)

Materialy po reorganizatsii VTUZov, VTUZov, i rabfakov SSSR. Sbornik postanovlenii i rasporyazhenii TsIK i SNK SSSR (Moscow: Komissiya po reforme vysshego i srednego obrazovaniya SNK SSSR, 1930)

Narodnoe obrazovanie v SSSR. Obshcheobrazovatel'naya shkola. Sbornik dokumentov, 1917–1973 gg. (Moscow, 1974)

Nauchno-issledovatel'skie instituty in vysshie uchebnye zavedeniya SSSR v 1932 godu (Titul'nye spiski i tablitsy) (Moscow: TsUNKhU, 1933) (distributed to delegates to the All-Union Conference on the Planning of Science during the Second Five-Year Plan; marked 'dlya sluzhebnogo pol'zovaniya')

Osnovnye uzakoneniya i rasporyazheniya po narodnomu prosveshcheniyu (Moscow–Leningrad, 1929)

Otchet o sostoyanii i deistviyakh Pervogo Moskovskogo Gosudarstvennogo Universiteta za 1922 g. (Moscow, 1923)

Programmy po istorii klassovoi bor'by v Rossii, istorii klassovoi bor'by na zapade, istorii VKP(b), statistike, na fakul'tete sovetskogo prava I-go MGU (Moscow, 1928)

Resheniya partii i pravitel'stva po khozyaistvennym voprosam (1917–1967 gg.), 11 vols. (Moscow, 1967–77)

Sbornik tsirkulyarov i razyasnenii Narodnogo Komissariata Iustitsii RSFSR (Moscow, 1934)

Sbornik tsirkulyarov Narodnogo Komissariata Yustitsii RSFSR deistvuyushchikh na 1 iyunya 1931 g. (Moscow, 1931)

Sbornik zakonov i rasporyazhenii raboche-krest'yanskogo pravitel'stva SSSR (Moscow, 1924–37); cited as *Sbornik zakonov*

Sobranie uzakonenii i rasporyazhenii rabochego i krest'yanskogo pravitel'stva RSFSR (Moscow, 1917–38); cited as *Sobranie uzakonenii*

Spravochnik partiinogo rabotnika, vypusk 8 (Moscow, 1934)

Tovarishch Komsomol. Dokumenty syezdov, konferentsii i plenumov TsK VLKSM 1918–1968, vol. 1 (1918–41) (Moscow, 1969)

VKP(b) v rezolyutsiyakh i resheniyakh syezdoz, konferentsii i plenumov TsK, vol. 2 (1925–39) (Moscow, 1941)

V. Stenographic reports of congresses, conferences, meetings, trials

XIII syezd RKP(b). Mai 1924 goda. Stenograficheskii otchet (Moscow, 1963)

XIV syezd VKP(b). 18–31 dek. 1925 g. Stenograficheskii otchet (Moscow–Leningrad, 1926)

XV syezd VKP(b). 2–19 dek. 1927 g. Stenograficheskii otchet (Moscow, 1927)

XVI syezd VKP(b). 26 iyunya–13 iyulya. Stenograficheskii otchet, 2 parts (Moscow, 1935)

XVII syezd VKP(b). 20 yanv.–10 fev. 1934 g. Stenograficheskii otchet (Moscow, 1934)

XVI konferentsiya VKP(b). 23–29 apr. 1929 g. Stenograficheskii otchet (Moscow, 1962)

XVII konferentsiya VKP(b). Yanv.–fev. 1932 g. Stenograficheskii otchet (Moscow, 1932)

IV syezd RKSM, 21–28 sent. 1921 g. Stenograficheskii otchet (Moscow–Leningrad, 1925)

V vserossiiskii syezd RKSM, 11–19 okt. 1922 g. Stenograficheskii otchet (Moscow–Leningrad, 1927)

VI syezd RLKSM. 12–18 iyulya 1924 g. Stenograficheskii otchet (Moscow–Leningrad, 1924)

VII syezd VLKSM. 11–22 marta 1926 g. Stenograficheskii otchet (Moscow–Leningrad, 1926)

VIII vsesoyuznyi syezd VLKSM. 5–10 maya 1928 g. Stenograficheskii otchet (Moscow, 1928)

IX vsesoyuznyi syezd VLKSM. Yanvar', 1931 g. Stenograficheskii otchet (Moscow, 1931)

VIII syezd professional'nykh soyuzov SSSR. 10–24 dek. 1928 g. Stenograficheskii otchet (Moscow, 1929)

XIV vserossiiskii syezd sovetov. 11–18 maya 1929 g. Stenograficheskii otchet (Moscow, 1929)

V vsesoyuznyi syezd sovetov. 20–28 maya 1929 g. Stenograficheskii otchet (Moscow, 1929)

VTsIK XI sozyva. Vtoraya sessiya, 7–16 okt. 1924 g. Stenograficheskii otchet (Moscow, 1924)

3-aya sessiya Tsentral'nogo Ispolnitel'nogo Komiteta Soyuza SSR 5-go sozyva. 4–12 yanv. 1931 g. Stenograficheskii otchet (Moscow, 1931)

2-aya sessiya TsIK Soyuza SSR 6-go sozyva. Stenograficheskii otchet i postanovleniya 22–28 dek. 1931 g. (Moscow, 1931)

3-aya sessiya TsIK Soyuza SSR 6-go sozyva. 23–30 yanv. 1933 g. Stenograficheskii otchet (Moscow, 1933)

Vtoroi plenum MK VKP(b), 31 yanv.–2 fev. 1928. Doklady i rezolyutsii (Moscow, 1928); numbered edition, marked 'Tol'ko dlya chlenov VKP(b)'

Pervaya moskovskaya oblastnaya konferentsiya Vsesoyuznoi Kommunisti-

cheskoi Partii (bol'shevikov). Stenograficheskii otchet, part 1
(Moscow, September 1929); marked 'Tol'ko dlya chlenov VKP(b)'

Yanvarskii obyedinennyi plenum MK i MKK, 6–10 yanvarya 1930 g.
(Moscow, 1930), numbered copy, marked 'sekretno'

XI Ural'skaya oblastnaya konferentsiya VKP(b). Stenograficheskii otchet, 23–30 yanv. 1932 g. (Sverdlovsk–Moscow, 1932)

Plenum Sibirskogo Kraevogo Kraevogo Komiteta VKP(b), 3–7 marta 1928 goda. Stenograficheskii otchet, part 1 (Novosibirsk, 1928); marked 'Khranit' na pravakh rukopisei'

Oblastnoi Komitet VKP(b) A[vtonomnoi] T[atarskoi] SSR, *Stenograficheskii otchet XV oblastnoi partiinoi konferentsii (5–15 iyunya 1930 g).* (Kazan, September 1930)

Ekonomicheskaya kontrrevolyutsiya v Donbasse. Itogi shaktinskogo dela. Statyi i dokumenty (Moscow, 1928)

Protsess 'Prompartii' (25 noyabrya–7 dekabrya 1930 g.). Stenogramma sudebnogo protsessa i materialy, priobshchennye k delu (Moscow, 1931)

Olkhovy, B., ed. *Zadachi agitatsii, propagandy i kul'turnogo stroitel'stva. Materialy Agitpropsoveshchaniya pri TsK VKP(b) (mai-iyun' 1928 g.).* (Moscow–Leningrad, 1928)

Pervaya vsesoyuznaya konferentsiya rabotnikov sotsialisticheskoi promyshlennosti. Stenograficheskii otchet (Moscow, 1931)

Sistema narodnogo obrazovaniya v rekonstruktivnyi period (meeting of Society of Marxist Pedagogues, March 1930) (Moscow: Kommunisticheskaya Akademiya, Obshchestvo Pedagogov–Marksistov, 1930)

Spornye voprosy marksistskoi pedagogiki. Stenogramma rasshirennogo zasedaniya kollegii Narkomprosa (Moscow, 1929)

Sud'by sovremennoi intelligentsii (speeches of Lunacharsky, Bukharin and others from debate on this theme) (Moscow, 1925)

Upadochnoe nastroenie sredi molodezhi. Eseninshchina (Moscow: Kommunisticheskaya Akademiya, Sektsiya literatury, iskusstva i yazyka, 1927)

Vtoroe vsesoyuznoe partiinoe soveshchanie po narodnomu prosveshcheniyu. Stenograficheskii otchet (Moscow, 1931)

VI. Statistical compilations, censuses

Beilin, A. E. *Kadry spetsialistov v SSSR. Ikh formirovanie i rost* (Moscow: TsUNKhU, 1935)

Bineman, Ya. and Kheinman, S. *Kadry gosudarstvennogo i kooperativnogo apparata* (Moscow, 1930)

Goltsman, M. T. and Kogan, L. M. *Starye i novye kadry proletariata. Po dannym perepisi 13 profsoyuzov 1932–1933* (Moscow, 1934)

Itogi desyatiletiya sovetskoi vlasti v tsifrakh 1917–1927 (Moscow: TsSU SSSR, 1927)

Itogi vsesoyuznoi perepisi naseleniya 1959 goda SSSR. Svodnyı tom (Moscow, 1962) (includes 1939 census material)

Itogi vypolneniya pyatiletnego plana razvitiya narodnogo khozyaistva SSSR (Moscow, 1933)

K kharakteristike sotsial'nogo sostava uchashchikhsya sotsvosa i profobra (Moscow–Leningrad: TsSU, Sektor sotsial'noi statistiki, 1929)

Kadry prosveshcheniya. Po materialam perepisi rabotnikov prosveshcheniya v 1944 g. (Moscow, 1936)

Kommunisty v sostave apparata gosuchrezhdenii i obshchestvennykh organizatsii. Itogi Vsesoyuznoi partiinoi perepisi 1927 g. (Moscow: Tsentral'nyi komitet VKP(b), Statisticheskii otdel, 1929)

Kontrol'nye tsifry pyatiletnego perspektivnogo plana 1928/29–1932/33 g. po narodnomu prosveshcheniyu RSFSR (bez avtonomnykh respublik) (Moscow–Leningrad: Narkompros RSFSR, 1929)

Kul'turnoe stroitel'stvo SSSR. Statisticheskii sbornik (Moscow–Leningrad, 1940)

Kul'turnoe stroitel'stvo SSSR. Statisticheskii sbornik (Moscow, 1956)

Kul'turnoe stroitel'stvo SSSR 1935 (Moscow: TsUNKhU, 1936)

Kul'turnoe stroitel'stvo SSSR v tsifrakh ot VI k VII syezdu sovetov (1930–1934 gg.) (Moscow, 1935)

Massovoe prosveshchenie v SSSR (k itogam pervoi pyatiletki), two parts (Moscow–Leningrad: TsUNKhU, 1932 and 1933)

Molodezh' SSSR. Statisticheskii sbornik, edited by A. V. Kosarev and I. A. Kraval (Moscow: TsUNKhU and TsK VLKSM, 1936)

Moskva i moskovskaya guberniya 1923/24–1927/28 (Moscow, 1929)

Narodnoe prosveshchenie v RSFSR. Statisticheskii sbornik (Moscow: Narkompros RSFSR, 1928)

Narodnoe prosveshchenie v RSFSR v osnovnykh pokazatelyakh. Statisticheskii sbornik, 1927/28–1930/31 g. (Moscow–Leningrad: Narkompros RSFSR, 1932)

Narodnoe prosveshchenie v RSFSR v tsifrakh za 15 let sovetskoi vlasti (Moscow–Leningrad, 1932)

Narodnoe prosveshchenie v SSSR za 1928/29 g. (Moscow–Leningrad: Narkompros RSFSR, 1930)

Narodnoe khozyaistvo SSSR. Statisticheskii spravochnik (Moscow–Leningrad, 1932)

Novye kadry tyazheloi promyshlennosti 1930–1933 (Moscow: Narodnyi komissariat tyazheloi promyshlennosti SSSR, 1934)

Podgotovka kadrov v SSSR 1927–1931 gg. (Moscow–Leningrad: TsUNKhU, Sektor kadrov, kul'tury i nauki, 1933)

Profsoyuznaya perepis' 1932–1933 g., vol. 1 (Moscow, 1934)

Pyatiletnii plan narodno-khozyaistvennogo stroitel'stva SSSR. Svodnyi obzor, 2nd ed. (Moscow, 1929)

Rukovodyashchie kadry R.K.P. (bol'shevikov) i ikh raspredelenie, 2nd ed. (Moscow: Tsentral'nyi komitet RKP, n.d. (1924))

The Second Five-Year Plan for the Development of the National Economy of the USSR (London, n.d. (1937))

Sostav novykh millionov chlenov profsoyuzov (Moscow: VTsSPS, Statisticheskii otdel, 1933)

Sostav rukovodyashchikh rabotnikov i spetsialistov Soyuza SSSR (Moscow: TsUNKhU, 1936)

Sotsialisticheskoe stroitel'stvo SSSR. Statisticheskii ezhegodnik (Moscow: TsUNKhU, 1934 and 1936)

Sotsial'nyi i natsional'nyi sostav VKP(b). Itogi vsesoyuznoi partiinoi perepisi 1927 g. (Moscow: Tsentral'nyi komitet VKP(b), Statisticheskii otdel, 1928)

Statisticheskii sbornik po narodnomu prosveshcheniyu RSFSR 1926 g. (Moscow: Narkompros RSFSR, 1927)

Statisticheskii spravochnik SSSR za 1928 (Moscow: TsSU SSSR, 1929)

Trud v SSSR. Spravochnik 1926–1930, edited by Ya. Bineman (Moscow, Gosplan SSSR, Ekonomiko–statisticheskii sektor, 1930)

Trud v SSSR. Ezhegodnik (1934 god) (Moscow: TsUNKhU, 1935)

Trud v SSSR. Statisticheskii spravochnik (Moscow: TsUNKhU, 1936)

Trud v SSSR (Moscow, 1968)

Vseobshchee obuchenie. Likvidatsiya negramotnosti. Podgotovka kadrov. Statististicheskii ocherk (Moscow: Gosplan SSSR, Ekonomiko-statisticheskii sektor, 1930)

Vsesoyuznaya partiinaya perepis' 1927 goda. Osnovnye itogi perepisi (Moscow: Tsentral'nyi komitet VKP(b), Statisticheskii otdel, 1927)

Vsesoyuznaya perepis' naseleniya 17 dekabrya 1926 g. Kratkie svodki, 10 vols. (Moscow: TsSU SSSR, Otdel perepisi, 1927–29)

VII. *Selected books and articles (in Russian)*

Alekseeva, G. D. *Oktyabr'skaya revolyutsiya i istoricheskie nauki v Rossii (1917–1923 gg.)* (Moscow, 1968)

Aleksinsky, M. A. *O reorganizatsii organov narodnogo obrazovaniya* (Moscow, 1930)

Anikst, A. M. *Kul'turnoe stroitel'stvo v pyatiletke* (Moscow–Leningrad, 1929)

Arutyunyan, Yu. V. 'Collectivization of agriculture and freeing of labour power for industry', in *Formirovanie i razvitie sovetskogo rabochego klassa (1917–1961 gg.)* (Moscow, 1964)

Astrov, V. N. *Krucha. Roman* (Moscow, 1969)

Barmin, I. P. *Iz opyta raboty KPSS i sovetskogo gosudarstva po sozdaniyu kadrov sovetskoi intelligentsii (1928–1933 gg.)* (Moscow, 1965)

Beilin, A. E. *Podgotovka kadrov v SSSR za 15 let* (Moscow–Leningrad, 1932)

Vosproizvodstvo kvalifitsirovannoi rabochei sily. Voprosy rabochego obrazovaniya (Moscow–Leningrad, 1926)

Belkovich, N. N. and Shavrin, V. A. *Mestnoe khozyaistvo i mestnye byudzhety SSSR* (Moscow, 1938)

Belozerov, S. E. *Ocherki istorii Rostovskogo Universiteta* (Rostov, 1959)

Binevich, A. and Serebryansky, Z. *Andrei Bubnov* (Moscow, 1964)

Blinchevsky, F. L. and Zelenko, G. I. *Professional'no-tekhnicheskoe obrazovanie v SSSR* (Moscow, 1957)

Blonsky, P. P. *Moi vospominaniya* (Moscow, 1971)

Pedologiya v massovoi shkole pervoi stupeni, 3rd ed. (Moscow, 1927)

Bogdanov, I. M. *Gramotnost' i obrazovanie v dorevolyutsionnoi Rossii i v SSSR* (Moscow, 1964)

Bolshakov, A. M. *Derevnya 1917–1927* (Moscow, 1927)

Bor'ba za rabochie kadry (Moscow–Leningrad: Narkompros RSFSR, 1928)

Borisov, Yu. S. *Podgotovka proizvodstvennykh kadrov sel'skogo khozyaistva SSSR v rekonstruktivnyi period* (Moscow, 1960)

Bubnov, A. S. *Stat'i i rechi o narodnom obrazovanii* (Moscow, 1959)

Bushchik, L. P. *Ocherki razvitiya shkol'nogo istoricheskogo obrazovaniya v SSSR* (Moscow, 1961)

Chanbarisov, Sh. Kh. *Formirovanie sovetskoi universitetskoi sistemy (1917–1938 gg.)* (Ufa, 1973)

Chizhova, L. M. '*Vydvizhenie* – the most important form of training of leading party cadres (1921–1937)', *Voprosy istorii KPSS*, 1973 no. 9

Chutkerashvili, E. V. *Razvitie vysshego obrazovaniya v SSSR* (Moscow, 1961)

Chuyanov, A. *Na stremnine veka. Zapiski sekretarya obkoma* (Moscow, 1976)

Drobizhev, V. Z. 'The role of the working class of the USSR in the formation of commanding cadres of socialist industry (1917–1936)', *Istoriya SSSR*, 1961 no. 4

Emelyanov, V. S. *O vremeni, o tovarishchakh, o sebe*, 2nd ed. (Moscow, 1974)

Fedyukin, S. *Sovetskaya vlast' i burzhuaznye spetsialisty* (Moscow, 1965)

Velikii Oktyabr' i intelligentsia. Iz istorii vovlecheniya staroi intelligensii v stroitel'stvo sotsializma (Moscow, 1972)

Fenomenov, M. Ya. *Izuchenie byta derevni v shkole (issledovatel'no-kraevedcheskaya rabota po obshchestvovedeniyu)*, 4th ed. (Moscow, 1926)

Flakserman, Yu. N. *Gleb Maksimilianovich Krzhizhanovskii* (Moscow, 1964)

Frid, L. S. *Ocherki po istorii razvitiya politiko-prosvetitel'noi raboty v RSFSR (1917–1929 gg.)* (Leningrad, 1941)

Gastev, A. K. *Kak nado rabotat'. Prakticheskoe vvedenie v nauku organizatsii truda* (Moscow, 1966)

Goltsman, A. et al. *Goroda sotsializma i sotsialisticheskaya rekonstruktsiya byta* (Moscow, 1930)

Grigoryants, A. K. *Formirovanie i razvitie tekhnicheskoi intelligentsii Armenii (1920–1965)* (Erevan, 1966)

Gusev, K. V. and Drobizhev, V. Z. eds. *Rabochii klass v upravlenii gosudarstvom (1926–1937 gg.)* (Moscow, 1968)

Gusev, S. I., ed. *Kakova zhe nasha molodezh'? Sbornik statei* (Moscow–Leningrad, 1927)

Institut kadrov Vesenkha SSSR. *Kuda idet fabzavuch (shkola-predpriyatie ili predpriyatie-shkola)?*, discussion of report by S. E. Gaisinovich (Moscow–Leningrad, 1930)

Iovlev, A. M. *Deyatel'nost' KPSS po podgotovke voennykh kadrov* (Moscow, 1976)

Istoriya Leningradskogo Universiteta 1819–1969. Ocherki (Leningrad, 1969)

Istoriya Moskovskogo Universiteta, vol. 2 (Moscow, 1955)

Ivanova, L. V. *U istokov sovetskoi istoricheskoi nauki. Podgotovka kadrov istorikov-marksistov 1917–1929* (Moscow, 1968)

Iz istorii sovetskoi intelligentsii, edited by M. P. Kim (Moscow, 1966)

Iz istorii Moskovskogo Universiteta (1917–1941). Sbornik statei (Moscow, 1955)

Izmeneniya v chislennosti i sostave sovetskogo rabochego klassa. Sbornik statei (Moscow, 1961)

Kaganovich, I. Z. *Ocherki razvitiya statistiki shkol'nogo obrazovaniya v SSSR* (Moscow, 1957)

Katuntseva, N. M. *Rol' rabochikh fakul'tetov v formirovanii kadrov narodnoi intelligentsii v SSSR* (Moscow, 1966)

Khavin, A. F. *U rulya industrii* (Moscow, 1968)

Khodorovsky, I. I., ed. *Kakogo inzhenera dolzhny gotovit' nashi VTUZy?* (Moscow–Leningrad: Narkompros RSFSR, 1928)

Klenova, R. A. 'From the history of the introduction of factory apprenticeship schools (1921–1925)', *Voprosy istorii*, no. 12 (1963)

Koltsov, A. V. *Kul'turnoe stroitel'stvo v RSFSR v gody pervoi pyatiletki* (Moscow, 1960)

Korbut, M. K. *Kazan'skii Gosudarstvennyi Universitet imeni V. I. Ul'yanova-Lenina za 125 let 1804/05–1929/30*, vol. 2 (Kazan, 1930)

Korolev, F. F. *Protiv antileninskoi teorii otmiraniya shkoly* (Moscow, 1932)

Sovetskaya shkola v period sotsialisticheskoi industrializatsii (Moscow, 1959)

Korolev, F. F. Korneichik, T. D. and Ravkin, Z. I. *Ocherki po istorii sovetskoi shkoly i pedagogiki 1921–1931* (Moscow, 1961)

Koryakov, M. ' "Eseninshchina" and Soviet youth', *Vozrozhdenie*, xv (Paris, 1951)

Koval, A. E. and Sandin, B. I. *Meropriyatiya kommunisticheskoi partii po podgotovke sovetskoi tekhnicheskoi intelligentsii vo vtuzakh i tekhnikumakh v gody pervoi pyatiletki* (Leningrad, 1957)

Krinitsky, A. I. *Osnovnye zadachi agitatsii, propagandy i kul'turnogo stroitel'stva* (Moscow–Leningrad, 1928)

Krupenina, M. and Shulgin, V. *V bor'be za marksistskuyu pedagogiku* (Moscow, 1929)

Krupskaya, N. K. *O metode proektov* (Moscow–Leningrad, 1931)
 Pedagogicheskie sochineniya v 10-i tomakh, 11 vols. (Moscow, 1957–63)

Kul'turnaya revolyutsiya v SSSR. 1917–1965 gg. (Moscow, 1967)

Kumanev, V. A. *Sotsializm i vsenarodnaya gramotnost'. Likvidatsiya massovoi negramotnosti v SSSR* (Moscow, 1967)

Kuzminov, I. 'Mastering the new factories and the new technology and the problem of cadres', *Problemy ekonomiki*, no. 5 (1935)

Lass, D. I. *Sovremennoe studenchestvo (byt, polovaya zhizn')* (Moscow, 1928)

Lenin, V. I. *Polnoe sobranie sochinenii*, 55 vols., 5th ed. (Moscow, 1958–65)

Leonova, L. S. *Iz istorii podgotovki partiinykh kadrov v sovetsko-partiinykh shkolakh i kommunisticheskikh universitetakh (1921–1925 gg.)* (Moscow, 1972)

Lepeshkin, A. I. *Mestnye organy vlasti Sovetskogo gosudarstvo 1921–1936 gg.* (Moscow, 1959)

Lunacharsky, A. V. *Kul'tpokhod komsomola* (Moscow–Leningrad, 1929)
 O narodnom obrazovanii (Moscow, 1958)
 O vospitanii i obrazovanii (Moscow, 1976)
 Ob antisemitizme (Moscow–Leningrad, 1929)
 Prosveshchenie i revolyutsiya (Moscow, 1924)
 Prosveshchenie i revolyutsiya. Sbornik statei (Moscow, 1926)
 Tretii front (Moscow, 1925)
 Vospitanie novogo cheloveka (Leningrad, 1928)

Lunacharsky, A. and Akhmatov, I. *Likvidatsiya negramotnosti sredi batrachestva* (Moscow, 1929)

Lunacharsky, A. and Khalatov, A. *Voprosy kul'turnogo stroitel'stva RSFSR* (Moscow, 1929)

Lunacharsky, A. and Shokhin, A. *K edinoi sisteme narodnogo obrazovaniya* (Moscow–Leningrad, 1929)

Lunacharsky, A. V. and Skrypnik, N. A. *Narodnoe obrazovanie v SSSR v svyazi s rekonstruktsiei narodnogo khozyaistva* (Moscow, 1929)

Lutchenko, A. I. 'The leadership of the CPSU in the formation of cadres of technical intelligentsia (1926–1933)', *Voprosy istorii KPSS*, no. 2 (1966)

Sozdanie inzhenerno-tekhicheskikh kadrov v gody postroeniya sotsializma v SSSR 1926–1958 gg. (Minsk, 1973)

Melnikov, V. V. *Kul'turnaya revolyutsiya i komsomol* (Rostov, 1973)

Mikhailov, P. M. 'From the history of the Communist Party in training leading industrial cadres in the period of socialist reconstruction of the national economy', *Voprosy istorii KPSS,* 1976 no. 10

Mikoyan, A. I. *V nachale dvadtsatykh.* . .(Moscow, 1975)

Milchakov A. *Pervoe desyatiletie. Zapiski veterana Komsomola,* 2nd ed. (Moscow, 1965)

Molotov, V. M. *V bor'be za sotsializm. Rechi i stat'i,* 2nd ed. (Moscow, 1935)

Moskvin, M. *Khozhdenie po vuzam. Vospominaniya komsomol'tsa* (Paris, 1933)

Moskovskaya Gornaya Akademiya. 10 let (Moscow, 1929)

Moskovskaya Sel'sko-Khozyaistvennaya Akademiya imeni K. A. Timiryazeva 1865–1965 (Moscow, 1969)

Moskovskii Institut Narodnogo Khozyaistva imeni G. V. Plekhanova *50 let Instituta* (Moscow, 1957)

Moskovskii Universitet za 50 let (Moscow, 1967)

Novye formy i metody prosvetitel'noi raboty (Moscow–Leningrad: Narkompros RSFSR, 1929)

Obshchestvovedenie v trudovoi shkole, vols. 1 and 2–3 (Moscow, 1927)

Ognev, N. 'Diary of Kostya Ryabtsev', *Sobranie Sochinenii,* vol. 3 (Moscow, 1929)

Ordzhonikidze, G. K. *Stat'i i rechi,* vol. 2 (Moscow, 1956)

Ozerov, L. S. 'From the experience of the party's work in organizing *zavody-VTUZy*', *Voprosy istorii KPSS,* 1961 no. 6

Pamyatka uchastnika kul'testafety (Stalingrad, 1930)

Panfilov, V. N. *Kul'turnye pyatiletki* (Moscow, 1930)

Panfilova, A. M. *Formirovanie rabochego klassa SSSR v gody pervoi pyatiletki (1928–1932)* (Moscow, 1964)

Partiya i vospitanie smeny. Stat'i i doklady, N. Bukharin, G. Zinoviev, N. Krupskaya (Leningrad, 1924)

Patolichev, N. S. *Ispytanie na zrelost'* (Moscow, 1977)

Permskii Gosudarstvennyi Universitet imeni A. M. Gor'kogo 1916–1966 (Perm, 1966)

Profsoyuzy Moskvy. Ocherki istorii (Moscow, 1975)

Prokofyev, V. I. *Moskovskoe Vysshee Tekhnicheskoe Uchilishche: 125 let* (Leningrad, 1955)

Pyat' let raboty TsK po uluchsheniyu byta sovetskikh uchenykh pri Sovete Narodnykh Komissarov (Moscow, 1927)

Pyat' let (1919–1924) rabochego fakul'teta Kazan'skogo Gosudarstvennogo Universiteta imeni V. I. Ul'yanova (Lenina) (Kazan, 1924)

Ravkin, Z. 'In the struggle for the Leninist style of work of Narkompros', *Narodnoe obrazovanie,* 1964 no. 2

Razin, I. M. (compiler). *Komsomol'skii byt* (Moscow, 1927)

Rogachevskaya, L. S. *Likvidatsiya bezrabotitsy v SSSR 1917–1930 gg.* (Moscow, 1973)

Ryadom s Leninym. Vospominaniya o N. K. Krupskoi (Moscow, 1969)

Ryutin, M. 'Leading cadres of the VKP(b)', *Bol'shevik*, 1928 no. 15

Sabsovich, L. *SSSR cherez 10 let* (Moscow, 1930)

Saratovskii Universitet 1909–1959 (Saratov, 1959)

Shilnikova, M. E. *Uchebno-vospitatel'naya rabota shkol v 1930–1934 gg.* (Moscow, 1959)

Shkaratan, O. I. *Problema sotsial'noi struktury rabochego klassa SSSR (istoriko–sotsiologicheskoe issledovanie)* (Moscow, 1970)

Shulgin, V. N. *Osnovnye voprosy sotsial'nogo vospitaniya* (Moscow, 1924)

   Pamyatnye vstrechi (Moscow, 1958)

Shulgin, V. N. ed. *Pedagogika perekhodnoi epokhi* (Moscow, 1930)

Shumsky, A. Ya. *Za shkolu Marksa-Lenina* (Moscow–Leningrad, 1931)

Sinetsky, A. Ya. *Professorsko-prepodavatel'skie kadry vysshei shkoly' SSSR* (Moscow, 1950)

Slavnyi put' Leninskogo Komsomola, vol. 1 (Moscow, 1974)

Sonin, M. Ya. *Vosproizvodstvo rabochei sily v SSSR i balans truda* (Moscow, 1959)

Sovetskaya intelligentsiya (Istoriya formirovaniya i rosta 1917–1965 gg.), edited by M. P. Kim (Moscow, 1968)

Stalin, I. *Sochineniya*, 13 vols. (Moscow, 1946–51), plus 3 vols. (vols. xiv–xvi), edited by Robert H. McNeal (Stanford, 1967)

Strumilin, S. G. *Khozyaistvennoe znachenie narodnogo prosveshcheniya* (Moscow, 1924)

Subbotina, K. *Narodnoe obrazovanie i byudzhet* (Moscow, 1965)

Sulemov, V. *Soyuz molodykh bortsov. Iz istorii komsomol'skogo stroitel'-stva* (Moscow, 1971)

Tomskii Gosudarstvennyi Universitet. 50 let so dnya osnovaniya (Tomsk, 1934)

Trifonov, I. Ya. *Likvidatsiya ekspluatatorskikh klassov v SSSR* (Moscow, 1975)

TsIT i ego metody NOT (Moscow, 1970)

Ukraintsev, V. V. *KPSS – organizator revolyutsionnogo preobrazovaniya vysshei shkoly* (Moscow, 1963)

Ulyanovskaya V. A. *Formirovanie nauchnoi intelligentsii v SSSR 1917–1937 gg.* (Moscow, 1966)

Universitety i nauchnye uchrezhdeniya, 2nd ed. (Moscow–Leningrad: Narkompros RSFSR, 1935)

Urlanis, B. Ts. *Istoriya odnogo pokoleniya* (Moscow, 1968)

Vdovin, A. I. and Drobizhev, V. Z. *Rost rabochego klassa SSSR 1917–1940 gg.* (Moscow, 1976)

Veselov, A. N. *Professional'no-tekhnicheskoe obrazovanie v SSSR* (Moscow, 1961)

Vospominaniya o N. K. Krupskoi (Moscow, 1966)

Yudin, I. N. *Sotsial'naya baza rosta KPSS* (Moscow, 1973)

Zalkind, A. B. *Osnovnye voprosy pedologii* (Moscow, 1927)
   Pedologiya v SSSR (Moscow, 1929)
   Voprosy sovetskoi pedagogiki (Moscow, 1930)

Zaluzhny, A. S. *Lzhenauka pedologiya v 'trudakh' Zalkinda* (Moscow, 1937)

VIII. Selected books and articles (Western)

Anderson, C. Arnold and Bowman, Mary Jean, eds., *Education and Economic Development* (Chicago, 1965); articles on Russia by Arcadius Kahan

Anstett, Marcel. *La Formation de la Main-d'Oeuvre Qualifiée en Union Sovietique de 1917 à 1954* (Paris 1958)

Anweiler, Oskar. *Geschichte der Schule und Pädogogik in Russland vom Ende des Zarenreiches bis zum Beginn der Stalin-Ara* (Berlin, 1964)

Azrael, Jeremy R. *Managerial Power and Soviet Politics* (Cambridge, Mass., 1966)

Bailes, Kendall E. 'The Politics of Technology: Stalin and Technocratic Thinking among Soviet Engineers', *American Historical Review* (April 1974)
   Technology and Society under Lenin and Stalin. Origins of the Soviet Technical Intelligentsia 1917–1941 (Princeton, 1978)

Bauer, Raymond A. *The New Man in Soviet Psychology* (Cambridge, Mass., 1952)

Carr, E. H. and Davies, R. W. *Foundations of a Planned Economy 1926–1929*, 2 vols. (London, 1969 and 1971)

Counts, George S. *The Challenge of Soviet Education* (New York, 1957)

Crowther, J. C. *Industry and Education in Soviet Russia* (London, 1932)

de Witt, N. *Education and Professional Employment in the USSR* (Washington DC, 1961)

Djilas, M. *The New Class: An Analysis of the Communist System* (London, 1966)

Dunham, Vera. *In Stalin's Time. Middleclass Values in Soviet Fiction* (Cambridge, 1976)

Feldmesser, Robert A. 'Aspects of Social Mobility in the Soviet Union', unpublished Ph.D diss. (Harvard, 1955)

Fisher, Ralph T. *Pattern for Soviet Youth: A Study of the Congresses of the Komsomol, 1918–1954* (New York, 1959)

Fitzpatrick, Sheila. *The Commissariat of Enlightenment. Soviet Organ-*

ization of Education and the Arts under Lunacharsky, October 1917–1921 (London and New York, 1970)

'Culture and Politics under Stalin: A Reappraisal', *Slavic Review*, June 1976

'The Foreign Threat during the First Five-Year Plan', *Soviet Union*, 1978 no. 1

'Sex and Revolution. An Analysis of Literary and Statistical Data on the Mores of Soviet Students in the 1920s', *Journal of Modern History*, June 1978

'The "Soft" Line on Culture and Its Enemies: Soviet Cultural Policy 1922–1927', *Slavic Review*, June 1974

'Stalin and the Making of a New Elite (1928–1939)', *Slavic Review*, forthcoming

Fitzpatrick, Sheila, ed. *Cultural Revolution in Russia, 1928–1931* (Bloomington, Ind., 1978)

Fülop-Miller, R. *The Mind and Face of Bolshevism. An Examination of Cultural Life in Soviet Russia* (London and New York, 1927)

Goode, W. T. *School Teachers and Scholars in Soviet Russia* (London, 1929)

Graham, Loren R. *The Soviet Academy of Sciences and the Communist Party, 1927–1932* (Princeton, NJ, 1967)

Granick, David. *Management of the Industrial Firm in the USSR* (New York, 1954)

Soviet Metalfabricating and Economic Development. Practice versus Policy (Madison, 1967)

Grant, Nigel. *Soviet Education*, revised ed. (London, 1968)

Hans, N. and Hessen, S. *Education Policy in Soviet Russia* (London, 1930)

Hayashida, R. H. 'Lenin and "The Third Front"', *Slavic Review*, June 1969

Hough, Jerry F. *The Soviet Prefects: The Local Party Organs in Industrial Decision Making* (Cambridge, Mass., 1969)

Hough, Jerry F. and Fainsod, Merle. *How the Soviet Union is Governed* (Cambridge, Mass., 1979)

Inkeles, A. *Social Change in Soviet Russia* (Cambridge, Mass., 1968)

Inkeles, A. and Bauer, R. *The Soviet Citizen. Daily Life in a Totalitarian Society* (Cambridge, Mass., 1959)

Ipatieff, V. N. *The Life of a Chemist* (Stanford and London, 1946)

John Dewey's Impressions of Soviet Russia and the Revolutionary World: Mexico–China–Turkey, edited by William W. Brickman (New York, 1964)

Joravsky, David. *Soviet Marxism and Natural Science 1917–1932* (New York, 1961)

Khrushchev Remembers, edited by Strobe Talbott (Boston, 1970)

Kline, George L. ed. *Soviet Education* (New York, 1957)

Lane, David. 'The Impact of Revolution: The Case of Selection of Students for Higher Education in Soviet Russia, 1917–1928', *Sociology*, May 1973

Lapidus, Gail Warshofsky. 'Social and Modernity: Education, Industrialization, and Social Change in the USSR', *The Dynamics of Soviet Politics* edited by Paul Cocks, Robert V. Daniels and Nancy Whittier Heer (Cambridge, Mass., 1976)

Lilge, F. 'Lenin and the Politics of Education', *Slavic Review*, 1968 no. 2

Lorimer, Frank. *The Population of the Soviet Union* (Geneva, 1946)

McClelland, James C. 'Proletarianizing the Student Body: The Soviet Experience during the New Economic Policy', *Past and Present*, August 1978

McNeal, Robert H. *Bride of the Revolution. Krupskaya and Lenin* (London, 1973)

Mehnert, Klaus. *Youth in Soviet Russia* (New York, 1933)

Meissner, Boris, ed. *Social Change in the Soviet Union* (Notre Dame, Ind., 1972)

Pennar, J., Bakalo, I. I. and Bereday, G. Z. F. *Modernization and Diversity in Soviet Education* (New York, 1971)

Pethybridge, R. *The Social Prelude to Stalinism* (New York, 1974)

Pinkevich, A. P. *The New Education in the Soviet Republic*, translated by Perlmutter and Counts (New York, 1929)

Rigby, T. H. *Communist Party Membership in the USSR 1917–1967* (Princeton, 1968)

Schwarz, Solomon. *Labor in the Soviet Union* (New York, 1952)

Scott, John. *Behind the Urals* (Bloomington, Ind., 1973)

Soviet Youth. Twelve Komsomol Histories, edited by N. K. Novak-Deker, (Munich: Institute for the Study of the USSR, Series 1 no. 51, 1959)

Tandler, Frederika M. 'The Workers' Faculty (Rabfak) System in the USSR', unpublished Ph.D. diss. (Columbia, Teachers College, 1965)

Timasheff, N. S. *The Great Retreat. The Growth and Decline of Communism in Russia* (New York, 1945)

Timoshenko, S. T. *Engineering Education in Russia* (New York, 1959)

Trotsky, L. *The Revolution Betrayed* (New York, 1937)

Widmayer, Ruth. 'The Evolution of Soviet Education Policy', *Harvard Education Review*, vol. 24 (Summer 1954)

Index